W9-BMO-137
CADOGANguides

MADRID

DANA FACAROS & MICHAEL PAULS

About the authors

Dana Facaros and **Michael Pauls** have written over 30 books for Cadogan Guides, including all of the Spain series. They have lived all over Europe but have recently hung up their castanets in a farmhouse surrounded by vineyards in the Lot valley.

About the contributors

Kristina Cordero is 29 and lives in Madrid. She has written for Let's Go, Frommer's and various magazines. She is also a translator of Spanish and Latin American fiction, including novels by Alberto Fuguet, Jorge Volpi, Ray Loriga and Benjamin Prado.

Mary-Ann Gallagher is a travel writer and editor. She has lived in New York, Japan, Spain and London, and has written and updated several titles for Cadogan Guides, as well as writing for other travel publications.

About the updater

Mary McLean is a freelance travel writer who has been based in Spain since 1990. She has travelled extensively around the country including frequent trips to Madrid "one of the most vibrant and fascinating capitals in Europe". She is a regular contributor to several in-flight magazines and has both edited and researched around 20 guide books, including several Cadogan titles.

Mary would like to thank the Madrid tourist office for their assistance and patience. Also the various public relations offices at the museums, in particular the Prado and Reina Sofia. She also thanks Miguel and Ana Romero for their invaluable insight into Madrid nightlife and Susy Chambers for providing a spare bed and doing more than her fair share of pounding the pavements. Gracias also to the editorial staff at Cadogan, including Christine Stroyan and Antonia Cunningham, who consistently provided invaluable support.

Cadogan Guides
Highlands House, 165 The Broadway, London SW19 1NE
info@cadoganguides.co.uk
www.cadoganguides.com

The Globe Pequot Press
246 Goose Lane, PO Box 480, Guilford, Connecticut
06437–0480

Copyright © Dana Facaros and Michael Pauls 2004
Updated by Mary McLean 2004

Series design: Andrew Barker
Series cover design: Sheridan Wall
Book design: Sarah Rianhard-Gardner
Photography: Beth Evans
Maps © Cadogan Guides, drawn by Map Creation Ltd
Map Coordinator: Angie Watts

Managing Editor: Antonia Cunnigham
Editor: Anna Amari-Parker
Proofreading: Catherine Bradley
Indexing: Isobel McLean
Typesetter: Dorchester Typesetting Ltd.
Production: Navigator Guides
Printed in Italy by Legoprint
A catalogue record for this book is available from the British Library
ISBN 186011-1599

The author and the publishers have made every effort to ensure the accuracy of the information in this book at the time of going to press. However they cannot accept any responsibility for any loss, injury or inconvenience resulting from the use of information contained in this guide.

Please help us to keep this guide up to date. We have done our best to ensure that the information in this guide is correct at the time of going to press. But places and facilities are constantly changing, and standards and prices in hotels and restaurants fluctuate. We would be delighted to recieve any comments concerning existing entries or omissions. Authors of the best letters will recieve a copy of the Cadogan Guide of their choice.

All rights reserved. No part of this publication may be reproduced, stored in a retrieval system, or transmitted, in any form or by any means, electronic or mechanical, including photocopying and recording, or by any information storage and retrieval system except as may be expressly permitted in the UK 1988 Copyright Design & Patents Act and the USA 1976 Copyright Act or in writing from the publisher. Requests for permission should be addressed to Cadogan Guides, Highlands House, 165 The Broadway, London SW19 1NE, in the UK, or The Globe Pequot Press, 246 Goose Lane, PO Box 480, Guilford, Connecticut 06437–0480, in the USA.

Contents

Maps

Introduction

Madrid was not a willing capital city. It wasn't until 1561 that Philip II decided to set up court here (because the hunting was good), but even then the *madrileños* were in no hurry to celebrate their new status with a lot of pompous monuments: they were too busy going to the theatre. The city's skyline suffered – few capitals are as architecturally impoverished – but by the 18th century they were making up for lost time and building lavish palaces, laying out parks and richly endowing their convents and monasteries. And the city of Velázquez, Goya and connoisseur Habsburg kings stores one of the planet's greatest hoards of paintings in the Prado, Thyssen-Bornemisza and Reina Sofía, and in a number of fine smaller museums lurking in the shadows of the Big Three.

Madrid is still built around people rather than ornamentation; even now, the regeneration projects which are progressively cleaning up the dingier quarters concentrate on simple improvements such as wider pavements or broad squares with plenty of benches. And because the city is built on a human scale, most of its major attractions can be found within the atmospheric maze of the old town. Tramping the streets, perhaps as part of the *tapeo*' (a tapas bar crawl), and discovering the distinct characters of the individual neighbourhoods or *barrios*, is one of the city's greatest pleasures. Madrid suffers from the usual 21st-century ailments – particularly excessive traffic and pollution – but this is still Europe's greenest city, flanked by a leafy ring of parks where *madrileños* escape the fumes or the fierce summer heat.

For many, Madrid's biggest asset is its ability to show you a good time. The non-stop party of the 1980s celebrated in the films of Almodóvar may have slowed down in the past decade or so, but Madrid can still take on all comers when it comes to a good night out. The city of 'the cats' (*los gatos*, an old nickname for *madrileños*) proudly claims to stay up later than any in Europe, and there's good reason to stay awake, with an infinite variety of bars, restaurants and clubs that may make you forget all about Velázquez and Goya.

The Neighbourhoods

6 The view from the Faro de Moncloa, p.171

4 Ermita de San Antonio de la Florida, p.168

To the West

8 The old streets of Habsburg Madrid, pp.71–82

Royal Madrid

Old Ma

La La

In this guide, the city is divided into the eight neighbourhoods outlined on the map above, each with its own sightseeing chapter. This map also shows our suggestions for the Top Ten activities and places to visit in Madrid. The following colour pages introduce the neighbourhoods in more detail, explaining the distinctive character and highlights of each.

7 Real Monasterio de las Descalzas Reales, p.91

10 Shopping along
the Gran Vía,
pp.157–8

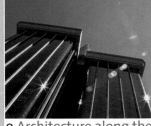

9 Architecture along the
Paseo de la Castellana,
pp.146–7

New Madrid

n Vía,
lasaña
Chueca

5 Tapas-tasting in
Santa Ana, p.226

anta Ana
nd Huertas

The Triángulo
de Arte

piés and
pajadores

1 The Golden Triangle:
Museo del Prado,
Colección Thyssen-
Bornemisza and
Centro de Arte Reina
Sofía, pp.98, 108
and 113

3 El Rastro fleamarket,
p.132

2 Parque del
Retiro, p.106

Old Madrid

Squeezed into a narrow mesh of streets between the Puerta del Sol and the Palacio Real is a solid, enduring Castilian town known as 'Los Austrias' because much of it was built during the reign of the Habsburg kings. Their greatest monument was the imposing Plaza Mayor, once the site of executions, bullfights and fairs, but now overflowing with cafés, bars and tourist kitsch. Once, all the town's gossip could be heard at the main gate to the city, the Puerta del Sol, which still teems with people night and day. Behind it, the city's oldest restaurants cluster along twisting streets lined with buildings that have barely changed since Goya first painted the delicate skyline of cupolas and spires.

Clockwise from top: Calle de Postas, Basílica de San Miguel, Plaza de la Paja, Plaza Mayor.

Old Madrid

Old Madrid chapter p.71
Hotels p.206 Restaurants p.218 Bars p.239
Bar and tapas crawl p.174

Royal Madrid

Madrid took a long time to settle into its role of capital city, but by the 18th century, when the opulent Palacio Real was constructed, convents, mansions and parks filled the city's west end. The re-opening of the graceful Teatro Real opera house on the Plaza de Oriente has restored a vital element of its leisurely, aristocratic atmosphere. The manicured gardens of the Campo del Moro offer the perfect antidote to the giddy, chandeliered excess of the Palacio Real. The convents have now opened their doors to visitors – whether simply for hand-baked cakes or for stunning collections of art in award-winning museums.

From top: Palacio Real, wrought-iron street lighting, Nuestra Señora de la Almudena.

Royal Madrid

The Triángulo de Arte

Madrid is rightly proud of its showcase 'Golden Triangle' – three superb museums all within strolling distance of each other, linked by the Paseo del Prado. The three collections complement each other neatly. The Museo del Prado is best known for its masterpieces of Spanish painting from the 12th to the early 19th centuries, as well as rich collections of Flemish and Italian art. The Museo Nacional Centro de Arte Reina Sofía picks up the thread with its permanent collection of 20th-century art, while the Museo Colección Thyssen-Bornemisza has a remarkable international collection spanning eight centuries. In case museum fatigue sets in, this quietly tasteful corner of Madrid also holds the refreshing Parque del Retiro and Real Jardín Botánico – and several lesser-known museums.

Anticlockwise from top: Parque del Retiro, Thyssen-Bornemisza, Centro de Arte Reina Sofía, near San Jerónimo el Real.

The Triángulo de Arte
The Triángulo de Arte chapter p.95
Hotels p.207 Restaurants p.224
Gardens walk p.181

Santa Ana and Huertas

The city's theatres, cafés, bars and brothels have always been concentrated in the higgledy-piggledy streets running off the Plaza Santa Ana. For better or worse, things have been cleaned up since Cervantes and Lope de Vega lived and squabbled here, and even since Hemingway mooched from bar to bar, but it's still one of the buzziest neighbourhoods in town, and everyone's first choice for a *tapeo* – a relaxed 'pub crawl' between tapas bars. There are still plenty of old-fashioned tiled bars, as well as flamenco joints, jazz clubs and grand theatres, attracting a cheerful mix of foreigners and locals.

All photos: streets around Plaza Santa Ana.

La Latina, Embajadores and Lavapiés

Madrid's *barrios bajos* ('low neighbourhoods'), clustered on the steep slopes running down to the river, come into their own for the Sunday-morning Rastro market and during the summer festivals. The traditional working-class atmosphere is changing – this may be the spiritual heartland of the *castizos* (dyed-in-the-wool *madrileños*), but it is fast becoming the most multicultural *barrio* in the city, with an influx of immigrants from China, Pakistan and Africa. The sounds of salsa or African rhythms drift across the rooftops as trendy *madrileños* flock to the Arabic teashops or the old-fashioned bars with zinc counters, bringing in their wake a new wave of hip cafés and clubs.

Top and middle: Plaza de Lavapiés; *bottom*: San Fernando.

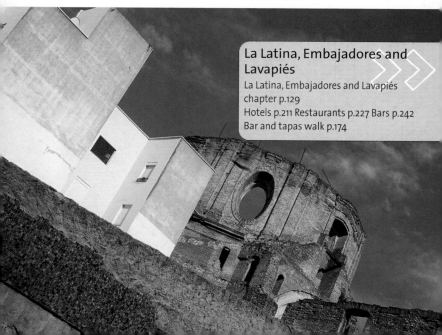

La Latina, Embajadores and Lavapiés

>>>

La Latina, Embajadores and Lavapiés
chapter p.129
Hotels p.211 Restaurants p.227 Bars p.242
Bar and tapas walk p.174

New Madrid

When Madrid, a walkable little city while stuck within its walls, began to expand in the late 19th century, it moved onto a different scale altogether. The rich built their sumptuous mansions in the airy grid of the Salamanca district, lining the Paseo de Recoletos with flamboyant palaces and institutions. Further north, broad Paseo de la Castellana has become Madrid's trophy boulevard, glittering with glassy towers and skyscrapers, home to big banks and businesses. This is still the city's smartest area, with chic shops and designer restaurants and bars, but you'll also find a couple of delightful museums – the Museo Lázaro Galdiano and the Museo Sorolla – peacefully tucked away.

Clockwise from top: Paseo de Recoletos, Plaza de Toros Monumental de las Ventas, Paseo de Recoletos, Puerta de Europa.

New Madrid

Gran Vía, Malasaña and Chueca

The Gran Vía hooks through the old city, linking east with west in a broad, busy boulevard crammed with crowds and honking traffic. It's Madrid's main shopping and business street, lined with an array of wildly eclectic buildings, including Madrid's first skyscraper, a string of opulent Art Deco cinemas with hand-painted billboards and several creamy Belle Epoque extravaganzas. Just north are the flavoursome neighbouring districts of Malasaña and Chueca, which offer the hippest nightlife in the city. Chueca is firmly established as the centre of Madrid's gay scene and is very popular with the fashion crowd.

Left-hand page from top: Metro sign, along the Gran Vía (middle and bottom); *right-hand page from top*: Plaza de Dos de Mayo, hand-painted billboard on the Gran Vía, Chueca (centre), Cine Callao, along the Gran Vía.

Gran Vía, Malasaña and Chueca

To the West

The west end of Madrid is its chief playground, with its largest parks and acre after acre of trees, and the realm of its university. It also has one of Goya's masterpieces in the Ermita de San Antonio de la Florida, an excellent museum of pre-Columbian art, and some surprises: a genuine Egyptian temple, a cable car up to a funfair where you'll find plenty of scary rides, a gloriously cluttered museum with the most delightful ballroom in Madrid, a lighthouse without a light, and yet another royal palace.

From top: Plaza de Moncloa, Casa de Campo, Faro de Moncloa.

Days Out in Madrid

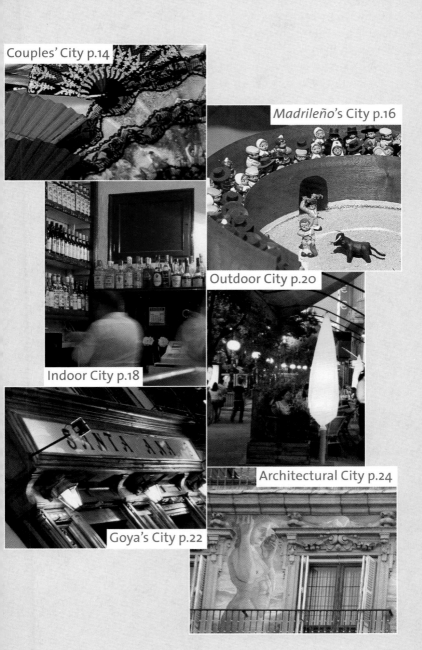

Couples' City p.14

Madrileño's City p.16

Outdoor City p.20

Indoor City p.18

Architectural City p.24

Goya's City p.22

COUPLES' CITY

Madrid is a city built on an intimate, human scale, making strolling the perfect way to discover it. Lovers sprawl in the parks and gardens or linger in the quiet museums on the fringes of the city. At sundown, make for a café with a view, dine at an elegant restaurant, catch some of the best flamenco in Spain or head for a sumptuous palace and tango till dawn.

One

Start: Metro Serrano or Colón.

Breakfast: A pastry at the **Embassy** café, a fashionable tearoom since 1931.

Morning: A stroll up the **Paseo de la Castellana**, past some striking modern architecture, to the delightful **Museo Sorolla**, with its Moorish gardens.

Lunch: At smart 19th-century **Gran Café Gijón**.

Afternoon: The fashionable **Salamanca** district for a spot of window-shopping, ending up at the **Parque del Retiro**. Hire a rowing boat on the grand lake or follow our **walking tour** of the gardens.

Dinner: **Casa Santa Cruz**, set in an exquisitely converted parish church near Sol.

Evening: Stamp your feet along with some of the finest flamenco in the city at **Casa Patas** in Lavapiés.

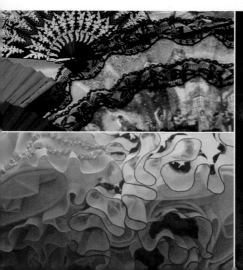

Two

Start: Metro Argüelles.

Breakfast: A pastry outdoors overlooking the Parque del Oeste at **Café Bruin**.

Morning: Wandering through the **Parque del Oeste**, stopping off at the rose gardens and the extraordinary Egyptian Templo de Debod. Then take in the rapturous Goya frescoes at the nearby **Ermita de San Antonio de la Florida**.

Lunch: **Casa Mingo**, an authentic Austrian *sidrería*, next to the Ermita.

Afternoon: Take the metro from Argüelles to Moncloa to get a bird's-eye view of the city from the **Faro de Moncloa**. Take the metro back to Opera to watch the sun set over the hills from the breezy terrace of **Terraza 'El Ventorillo'**.

Dinner: Eat in a 19th-century palace at **Cornucopia**, nearby.

Evening: A night at the opera at the opulent **Teatro Real**, or tango the night away at 19th-century **Palacio de Gaviria**.

MADRILEÑO'S CITY

Madrid must be the most down-to-earth capital city in Europe. Long famous for their ability to party non-stop, *madrileños* love to shop, eat, drink and make merry – whether in centuries-old tiled cafés and bars or in the new breed of elegant designer establishments. They love music and dance – from opera, zarzuela (home-grown operetta) and flamenco to some of the funkiest, wildest clubs in Spain.

Three (Sundays only)

Start: Metro Lavapiés.

Breakfast: **Pastelería Licorería El Madroño**, home of the *licore de madroño*, distilled from the city's trademark tree.

Morning: Pick up a bargain at one of the heaving stalls of the famous **Rastro fleamarket**. Then head for the bars around the **Plaza Humilladero**, where everyone congregates for the traditional post-Rastro *tapeo*.

Lunch: The best *cocido* in the city at **Malacatín**, but be sure to book at least a day in advance.

Afternoon: Wander up to the **Gran Vía**, the commercial, living heart of Madrid, and pop into the **Círculo de Bellas Artes**, an Art Deco cultural centre where *madrileños* go to find out what's new on the art scene.

Dinner: **Gula Gula** nearby, triumphantly camp and the place to see and be seen.

Evening: Sunday night is movie night in Madrid – catch a show at one of the Belle Epoque **cinemas** along the Gran Vía, or just admire their hand-painted billboards.

Four

Start: Metro Bilbao.

Breakfast: Settle into a leather arm-chair for a lazy breakfast at the **Café Comercial**, a Madrid institution.

Morning: The piquant neighbourhood of **Malasaña**, taking in the Plaza de Dos de Mayo and looking out for traditional shop signs. Check out some of the new galleries featuring up-and-coming Spanish artists in the neighbouring district of **Chueca** – Calle de San Lorenzo is a good place to start.

Lunch: **Tienda de Vinos** in Chueca, a famously scruffy restaurant renowned for selling every dish at the same low price.

Afternoon: Wander over to the **Santa Ana** district, home to Madrid's theatres and many of its playwrights and authors – follow our walking tour or just slouch from bar to bar.

Dinner: **Lombok**, a restaurant owned by disgraced game-show host Jesús Vasquez, very popular with ironic locals.

Evening: Follow our **bar and tapas crawl** through the old town, then finish up at **Joy Madrid**, the city's best-loved club.

Early morning: Grab some chocolate and *churros* at **Chocolatería San Ginés** – the traditional end to a big night out.

INDOOR CITY

Madrid has three of Europe's finest art museums within a few streets of each other, as well as some enjoyably eccentric lesser-known ones. The old town holds palaces, churches and monuments stuffed to the brim with treasures and curiosities. There's plenty to do in the evenings, from a night out at the opera to a dazzling flamenco show. Even the beautifully preserved old tiled bars and cafés around Plaza Santa Ana are conveniently squeezed up together, making the traditional *tapeo* an option whatever the weather.

Five

Start: Metro Serrano.

Breakfast: **Mallorca**, pastry shop extraordinaire.

Morning: Spend time with *La Dama de Elche* and other treasures of the **Museo Arqueológico Nacional**.

Lunch: **La Mazorca**, a homely vegetarian place with a chimney, near the Reina Sofía.

Afternoon: The luminous **Centro de Arte Reina Sofía** (*photo above*).

Dinner: **Pizzeria Cervantes**, a lively crêperie in a centuries-old *taberna*.

Evening: Follow the *tapeo* trail around the Plaza Santa Ana, perhaps beginning at **La Moderna**. Finally, take in some jazz at the elegant, mirrored **Café Central**, in nearby Plaza del Angel.

Six

Start: Metro Opera.

Breakfast: An elegant breakfast overlooking the Plaza de Oriente at the **Café de Oriente**.

Morning: Shiver at the extraordinary room full of relics at the **Real Monasterio de la Encarnación**, then twirl around the opulent ballroom at the little-visited **Museo Cerralbo**.

Lunch: Traditional, warming *cocido* stew at the old-fashioned **La Bola** *taberna*.

Afternoon: See how the other half lived in the **Palacio Real**.

Alternatively, catch a game of **basketball** at the Palacio de Deportes de Madrid in Salamanca (season runs from September to May).

Dinner: **La Cocina del Desierto** in Chueca, for warming North African food and exquisite décor.

Evening: Try some of the friendly bars in Chueca, perhaps starting at **Café Belén**.

Food and Drinks

La Bola, p.224
Café de Oriente, p.239
La Cocina del Desierto, p.232
Mallorca, p.231
La Mazorca, p.225
Pizzeria Cervantes, p.226

Sights and Activities

Basketball, p.261
Centro de Arte Reina Sofía, p.113

Museo Arqueológico Nacional, p.143
Museo Cerralbo, p.167
Palacio Real, p.86
Real Monasterio de la Encarnación, p.90

Nightlife

Café Belén, p.243
Café Central, p.249
La Moderna, p.227

OUTDOOR CITY

Madrid spills out onto the streets in summer, with bars and cafés opening up their pavement terraces. When it all gets too steamy, there are plenty of ways to cool off: the Casa de Campo has outdoor swimming pools as well as a funfair, boating lake and zoo; and the Parque del Retiro has deliciously cool fountains, lots of shady picnic spots and a very grand boating lake. And while you're just wandering, there's the architecture and atmosphere of the different *barrios* to soak up.

Seven

Start: Metro Argüelles.

Breakfast: Sit at one of the outdoor tables at **Café Rosales**, overlooking the Parque del Oeste.

Morning: Take the panoramic **teleférico** from the Parque del Oeste to the **Casa de Campo** and go for a swim at the outdoor pool at the **Piscinas Casa de Campo**.

Lunch: **Currito** in the Casa de Campo, serving some of the best open-air food around.

Afternoon: Hop on the metro for the pretty gardens at **Parque El Capricho**.

Early evening: Watch Real Madrid pound the opposition at the **Estadio Santiago Bernabéu**.

Dinner: At an outside table at **El Espejo**, overlooking the Paseo de Recoletos.

Night: **El Botánico** nearby, a relaxing outdoor bar near the Prado.

Eight

Start: Metro Banco de España.

Brunch: Splash out on a fancy brunch in the elegant gardens at the **Ritz** tearooms.

Morning: Take our **walking tour of the Parque del Retiro** (*photo above*) and hire a rowing boat on the lake. Then visit the nearby **Real Jardín Botánico**, bursting with plants from around the world.

Afternoon: Head for **Puerta del Sol** and meander through the lanes of **Old Madrid** (*photo bottom right*), built under the Habsburg kings.

Dinner: The rooftop terrace of **El Viajero** in La Latina.

Evening: Enter the smoky, late-night vibe at **Loba Loba**, perfect for watching the 'beautiful people'.

GOYA'S CITY

Francisco de Goya y Lucientes was born near Zaragoza and died in Bordeaux, but he spent most of his long life in Madrid. His remains were brought back to the city and buried in the magical Ermita de San Antonio de la Florida (*photo top left*). The old city is brought vividly to life in his works – from the fresh-faced carousers at the San Isidro pilgrimage and the cheeky *Majas* and *Majos* of Lavapiés to the patriotic uprising horrifically depicted in *Los Fusilamientos del Dos de Mayo*. He produced more than 60 tapestry designs for the Real Fábrica de Tapices; these now hang in the Prado, which also contains the malicious portraits he made while court painter to Charles IV, as well as the darker, hallucinatory paintings of his last years.

Nine

Start: Metro Atocha.

Morning: The **Real Fábrica de Tapices**, where Goya made his vivid cartoons for tapestry designs.

Lunch: Sample deliciously affordable *bocadillos* at **El Brillante**.

Afternoon: Admire Goya's original cartoons – along with a vast selection of his other works – at the **Prado**.

Dinner: A classic *madrileño* dinner at **Botín**, where Goya reputedly washed dishes in the evenings.

Evening: Sample some of the traditional bars in Lavapiés, Goya's old stamping ground – perhaps start off at **Café Barbieri**.

Ten

Start: Metro Sevilla.

Morning: The eccentric collection of Goya's works at the **Real Academia de Bellas Artes de San Fernando**.

Lunch: The elegant Art Deco arts centre, the **Círculo de Bellas Artes**.

Afternoon: Goya's burial place, the **Ermita de San Antonio de la Florida**, home of some angelic frescoes.

Dinner: Solid Castilian dishes at **Casa Ciriaco** on Calle Mayor, an historic tavern where the current king and queen sometimes eat.

Evening: Head for the Plaza de Dos de Mayo in **Malasaña**, depicted in one of Goya's most famous works and now filled with popular open-air bars.

ARCHITECTURAL CITY

Madrid has a very engaging hotch-potch of different styles. It didn't have the money to put on grand airs when it was made a capital in the 16th century (Philip II sucked it all up for El Escorial; see p.186), but Juan de Herrera left his stamp on the city nonetheless. The 17th century saw an explosion of ornate Baroque or Churrigueresque, followed the next century by cool Neoclassical works such as the Prado. Beautifully tiled cafés and bars date from the end of the 19th century. Skyscrapers began to sprout as early as the 1920s and, in the last few decades, extraordinary buildings have been popping up like surreal mushrooms along the Paseo de la Castellana.

Eleven

Start: Metro Opera.

Breakfast: A croissant at **Café Vergara** opposite the Teatro Real.

Morning: Madrid's oldest church, **San Nicolás de los Servitas**, the 16th-century **Plaza de la Villa** (*photo p.26 bottom left*) and the lovely **Capilla del Obispo**. Follow up with a stroll to the Río Manzanares for a view of Juan de Herrera's **Puente de Segovia** and Pedro de Ribera's **Ermita de la Virgen del Puerto**.

Lunch: Have an apéritif in arcaded **Plaza Mayor** (*photo top left*), then a hearty lunch round the corner surrounded by the sumptous décor of **Casa Santa Cruz**.

Afternoon: Wander along the Gran Vía, spotting Madrid's first skyscraper, **Telefónica**, and a host of Art Deco and French Belle Epoque delights, including the **Palacio de la Música** and **Grassy**. Head north for the **Museo Municipal** to see Pedro de Ribera's wildly ornate Baroque doorway, and then take in the lovely Art Nouveau **Sociedad General de Autores** nearby.

Dinner: In the mosaic-tiled dining room at **Paradis Madrid**.

Evening: Our **bar crawl** through the old town, taking in some ancient tiled bars.

Twelve

Start: Metro Atocha.

Morning: Start off with Juan de Villanueva's **Observatorio Astronómico** and then the **Palacio de Cristal** in the Parque del Retiro. Wander up the **Paseo del Prado**, taking in Ventura de Rodríguez' Neoclassical fountains. At Plaza de Cibeles, don't miss the fantastical **Palacio de Comunicaciones**.

Lunch: Sit out on the terrace of Art Nouveau **Gran Café Gijón** on the Paseo de Recoletos.

Afternoon: Take a bus up the Paseo de la Castellana, looking out for Rafael Moneo's **Bankinte**, and **Catalana Occidente** at Glorieta de Emilio Castelar. Get off the bus at

AZCA and seek out the sleek **Torre Picasso**, the tallest building in Madrid. Then hop on the bus yet again for the city's distinctive landmark, the **Puerta de Europa** (*photo previous page, top*).

Dinner and evening: Trendy **Teatríz** in Salamanca, a former theatre redesigned by Philippe Starck. It's a bar and disco in the evenings, too.

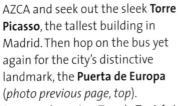

Roots of the City

860–1308: Arab Mayrit Becomes Madrid

Fui sobre agua edificada
mis muros de fuego son
esta es mi alcurnia y blasón
(I was built on water, my walls are of fire;
this is my lineage and emblem).
Madrid's motto

Settlements along the Manzanares have come and gone since the Palaeolithic era, but the first permanent town on its banks was built by the Arabs. After conquering most of Spain in the early 8th century, Córdoba's **Emir Mohammed I** constructed a fortress or Alcázar here sometime around 860. It stood on the cliff-top site of today's Palacio Real, along with a circuit of walls that extended only as far as the Plaza Mayor and the Plaza Isabel II. The Arabic name for the little settlement, Mayrit, 'place of many springs', describes one of the site's chief attractions. Another, and more important, one was Mayrit's wide-ranging views over the Sierra Guadarrama, which enabled it to guard the lines of communication between the important city of Toledo and Aragón from the increasing attacks by the Christian armies of the Reconquista.

Mayrit stood up to one of these attacks in 932, then, during the 970s it was used as the base for the campaigns of **Al-Mansur**, the chamberlain of the Caliph Hisham II, who reconquered many of the territories gained by the Christians. It was a time when the Moors were strong enough to erase the puny Christian kingdoms in the north had they

cared to. But upon Al-Mansur's death in 1002 the Caliphate entered a fatal period of factional struggles and civil war. The Christians regrouped and tried again in 1047, winning Mayrit in 1083, two years before Toledo; according to legend, **El Cid** may have been around to assist King **Alfonso VI** of Castile in its capture. The king's first task, at least according to the legends of the city, was to recover a statue of the Virgin of the Almudena, restoring the city's Christian credentials.

As elsewhere in Castile, the Reconquista brought in new Christian settlers from the north, who enclosed themselves in a new set of walls, made of adobe and flint. But for two centuries Mayrit would remain a little frontier outpost while the locals decided on a name (Maiorito, Magerito, Mayoritum, Majaeritum, Magerit, Madritum, Maidrit were among the score that were felicitously rejected). Many of the Moors remained, many now Christianized as Mudéjars, living side by side with Christians and a small Jewish community. The Mudéjars were responsible for channelling the many springs into kitchen gardens (some 60km of their irrigation tunnels are said to remain under the city). They were also in charge of much of the early building, although only a pair of minaret-like church towers survive, at San Pedro el Real and San Nicolás. The Arabs tried once more to take Madrid back in 1109, pitching their tents in the Campo del Moro, but failed. In 1202, this mostly agricultural settlement, or villa, of 3,000 people was given its Fueros, the **statutes** and rights of a free city, from **Alfonso VIII**.

860–1308

Museo Arqueológico Nacional, for an overview of Madrid's Upper Palaeolithic to Moorish history, p.143

Parque Emir Mohammed I, for the only surviving portion of Moorish Madrid and a copy of the statue of the Virgin of Almudena, p.88

San Pedro el Real and San Nicolás de los Servitas, for Mudéjar towers, p.82 and p.81

1309–1563: Madrid Becomes a Capital

The young and aggressive Christian kingdom of Castile managed for a long time without a capital. The **Cortes** (Parliament) traditionally alternated its meetings so that none of its cities would be offended, and the

Timeline

1898	Spanish–American War; Spain loses Cuba, the Philippines and Puerto Rico
1923	King Alfonso XIII recognizes General Miguel Primo de Rivera's coup d'état
1930	Primo de Rivera resigns with the Depression
1931	Alfonso XIII abdicates when municipal elections vote overwhelmingly for a Republic
1931–6	Republic tainted by political violence; José Antonio Primo de Rivera forms fascist Falange Español
1936	Left-wing Popular Front wins elections; military coup, which includes Francisco Franco, starts Civil War
1939	Madrid falls in final Nationalist victory; Franco keeps Spain out of Second World War
1953	Military co-operation treaty signed with the United States
1973	Resistance to Franco grows; Prime Minister Carrero Blanco blown up in Madrid bomb
1975	Death of Franco and coronation of Juan Carlos I
1978	Signing of a new social democratic constitution
1981	Officers' right-wing coup attempt defeated
1982	Spain joins NATO; Socialist Felipe González elected Prime Minister
1986	Spain and Portugal join the European Union
1992	500th anniversary of Columbus's voyage: Expo in Seville, Olympics in Barcelona; Madrid is the Cultural Capital of Europe
1996	Partido Popular (PP) under José María Aznar defeats González's Socialists in general elections
1999	The Basque separatist group ETA announces an end of its 14-month ceasefire
2000	José María Aznar wins a second term, with an absolute majority in Parliament

necessity of an occasional royal presence in all of Spain's diverse regions made all the earlier kings itinerate. In 1309 Madrid was chosen for the honour for the first time. If it made an impression, no one bothered to mention it. But like the rest of Castile the town was doing all right for itself: the kingdom's Crown-chartered cooperative of sheep farmers, the Mesta, supplied much of Europe's wool. Also, because of the experience of the Reconquista, when new hands were always needed to settle the newly conquered lands, economic feudalism ended in Castile long before anywhere else in western Europe. Still, the nobility flourished, exempt from tax and loaded with privilege.

Madrid first attracted serious royal notice in the 1360s, when **Pedro the Cruel** spent money turning the Alcázar into a residence, attracted by the good hunting in the surrounding forests. The next thing we hear is that the town managed to become something no one could have predicted: Armenian. In a strange interlude in the city's history, King Juan I gave Madrid in fief to the exiled last king of Little Armenia, Leon VI, in 1383, as a gesture of Christian solidarity and a consolation prize for losing his kingdom to the Turks. When Leon died four years later, Madrid returned to the Castilian fold. On a less generous note, the negative effects of the Reconquista were beginning to kick in: the bigotry that had been growing like a vicious weed saw the first pogrom of the Jews in 1391, instigated by the Church. Around the same time, **Henry III** gave Madrid its first Crown-appointed mayor, or *corregidor*, to preside over the local council.

Madrid was doing well enough to require a new wall in the 1430s, which incorporated a marketplace that would one day become the Plaza Mayor. More royal patronage came with **Henry IV** (1454–74), who gave the town the status of *muy noble y muy leal*. Henry tacked a Renaissance façade onto the Alcázar to make it a proper palace, and he married Juana of Portugal there in 1463.

dynastic dispute followed Henry's death, nd the victor was the king's sister Isabel I, vhose marriage to Ferdinand of Aragón nited Spain. In the unforgettable year of 492 the pair, known as **los Reyes Católicos** or their religious fervour, completed the econquista in Granada, sent **Columbus** to iscover the Americas and expelled those ews who refused to convert. Not long after, ney applied the same terms to the Moorish Mudéjars, and revitalized the **Inquisition** to errorize them. Then, with the army they had massed in Granada, they began to meddle European affairs, seizing Naples and narrying their daughter, known as **Juana the Mad**, to **Philip of Burgundy**, the son of absburg Holy Roman Emperor Maximilian.

Isabel and Ferdinand's role in Europe was rivial compared to that of their Habsburg randson, **Charles I**. His first act as the ruler f Spain was to bring in a whole troop of lemish and French outsiders to hold the nportant offices, and bleed Castile dry with axes so he could bribe the German Electors give him another title: Holy Roman mperor, as Charles V. These and other utrages occasioned the **Comunero Revolt** of 20–21, in which the cities of Old Castile rose defend their liberties – and their purses – nly to be crushed by Charles's foreign oops. Once it was bullied into submissive yalty, and could be counted on to supply he treasure from the Americas to finance ecades of futile wars, Charles became fond f Castile and especially of Madrid, giving the wn the fancy sobriquet of Imperial y oronada. He liked the climate because it ased his gout, and he went hunting at El ardo; when he captured his rival, King ancis I of France, at the Battle of Pavia, he nprisoned him in Madrid.

It was his son, **Philip II**, King of Spain and urgundy, who made the decision in 1561 nat changed the town's history. His travels Europe, and especially his long residency ith his court in Flanders, had convinced him at Spain needed to compete with other ates, which had permanent courts and

palaces that encouraged the arts and humanities. The fact that Spain was deeply in debt never stopped him for a second: the Habsburg monarchy needed a strong, central, specifically Castilian capital, and Madrid fitted the bill.

Still, the choice of a minor town without a navigable river seemed highly eccentric at the time, even if it was smack in the centre of Spain; until the invention of rail, most of Madrid was doomed to penury, owing to the high cost of transport. Philip's choice may have been influenced by the fact that the previous royal favourite, Valladolid, had an outbreak of heresy in 1559, followed by a devastating fire, and that the other leading contender, Toledo, the old capital of Spain, lacked the necessary space to house Philip's 4,000 courtiers and bureaucrats, much less their horses and carriages. Madrid, by contrast, had room to expand. But apparently the overwhelming factor in Philip's decision to make this town of 9,000 Spain's permanent capital was the fact that it was within easy distance of woodlands crammed with rabbits, boar, deer and even bears for the king to hunt (he was pretty good, by all accounts, with the bow). On his order, palatial hunting lodges went up around Madrid, at El Pardo, Aranjuez, Aceca, Vaciamadrid and elsewhere, all dwarfed by the monastery-cum-royal-pantheon extravaganza fit for a Pharaoh at El Escorial. While running Spain into the ground, the 'royal bureaucrat' spent a great deal of his time following every detail of their construction and landscaping.

1563–1700: Splendour and Dirt with the Horrible Habsburgs

Unfortunately, outside of refurbishing and enlarging the Alcázar, Philip didn't have any attention or money left over to lavish on his new capital. His star architect, **Juan de Herrera**, designed the great Plaza Mayor, although he didn't actually get around to building it. Nevertheless, thanks to the permanent presence of the court, Madrid's population boomed; by 1563, it had already risen to 16,000. A new wall went up in 1566; by 1600 the population was up to 84,000. Like other 'artificial' capitals, such as Washington DC, Madrid from the beginning was a city of people from other parts of Spain, giving rise to the paradox that survives to this day: it is the most Spanish city, although it is (by appearance) the least Spanish city. Nearly all who flocked here – from ambitious second sons of noble families to impoverished hidalgos – sought employment or patronage of some kind with the court, and from the start Madrid fitted directly into the hallowed European model of the parasitic capital, sucking in every luxury, talent and skill from the rest of the country to make the city the centre stage for Spain's Golden Age.

The neglect and overburdening of the Mudéjars' waterworks also made it 'the dirtiest and filthiest city in Spain', according to a Flemish visitor in 1570. Philip II tried, briefly, to clean it up, and admitted defeat; whenever an important guest arrived in the medieval squalor of Madrid, the king would whisk them away at once to his pristine El Escorial. Until the 18th century, Madrid would lag far behind other European capitals of the day in sanitation and other urban amenities.

But sanitation was far too much a thing of this world for kings who were busy placing their bets on the next; Philips II, III and IV founded a total of 48 monasteries and convents in Madrid, which took up much of the available space in a town growing at breakneck speed. The monasteries even accelerated the growth by acting as a magnet for the very poor who poured into Madrid, assured that they could always rely on monastic charity to eat. The pressure for lodging grew so acute that a law decreed that any house of more than one floor could be requisitioned for courtiers; the *madrileños* responded by building houses of only one floor, on streets of mud so thick even horsemen floundered. The law stayed on the books so long that a new kind of architecture developed, the *casas a la malicia* ('cunning houses'), that from the street appeared to have only one floor, but squeezed two storeys around the back; you can still spot them in the older parts of town. Another law promulgated by Philip II in 1585, banned profanity, gambling and other aspects of riotous living that had taken hold in Madrid from the start and led to the legend that, when Lucifer fell to earth, he fell on Madrid. Meanwhile, the many idle minds assembled in Madrid were spending the day at the show. The first purpose-built theatre, the Corral del Príncipe, was built in 1583, and it and others were packed every day.

Philip III (1598–1621), the product of an incestuous marriage (a Habsburg family tradition), was a shadow of his intelligent, duty-bound and wrong-headed father, and left most of the governing of Spain to his favourite, the **Duke of Lerma**. In 1601, Lerma shocked Madrid by declaring it a total mess and moving the Cortes to Valladolid. It just wasn't right; in a mere forty years Madrid, with its majority of people living off the Crown or Church, had already acquired the sparkle of a capital city that made workaday Valladolid seem provincial and backward, and back to Madrid the king and some 40,000 others traipsed after five years in exile. The fact that Madrid offered the king and Lerma 250,000 gold ducats and a percentage of the rents on all houses for a decade may have had something to do with

hanging their minds. 'Sólo Madrid es Corte,' declared Philip, and that was that.

Once it had been shown that the capital was indeed fixed and permanent, real efforts finally began to make it look like one. The superb Plaza Mayor, completed in 1620, gave Madrid a much needed focal point and central stage, as well as its first buildings of more than one storey. **Philip IV** (1621–65), product of another cousinly marriage, was little better than his father but a gallant with the ladies. He was happy to leave the running of the state to the energetic **Conde Duque de Olivares**, who in 1632 gave the king a proper home in Madrid: the magnificent Buen Retiro palace and park, on the eastern edge of the city. Other aristocrats (like the Church, the nobility was completely exempt from taxes) began to build palaces of their own. The city's population reached 170,000, and was enclosed in a new, rather shoddy wall in 1656, which was built not to protect Madrid but to ensure that the proper taxes and tolls were paid on goods coming in.

Most of all, the reign of Philip IV marked the Golden Age – the time of Velázquez, Cervantes, Calderón de la Barca, Tirso de Molina, Quevedo and Lope de Vega, of legendary pageants and fiestas, whose glittering dazzle hid the rot within. The Empire was collapsing. Spain's defeat at the hands of the Dutch, English and French in the **Thirty Years' War**, especially at Rocroy (1643), meant that Spain was no longer a respected power, and revolts in Catalunya and in Portugal (which had been annexed by Philip II) brought the trouble closer to home. The Conde Duque, who had spent his career

hiding unpleasant truths from the king, went mad and died shortly after.

In this twilight Philip IV managed at last to produce a living male heir, out of 13 legitimate daughters and countless illegitimate ones. This was the staring, drooling **Charles II** (1665–1700), whose mother was also his first cousin, and whose famous Habsburg jaw was so pronounced he couldn't eat solid food, part of the cause of his perpetual diarrhoea. With his mother as regent, he spent his reign playing in the crypt of El Escorial, while the police futilely searched the streets of Madrid for the sorceress whom the priests said had put a curse on him. Although married off twice, producing an heir was quite beyond him. Meanwhile, the royal families of Europe circled Spain like vultures, waiting for him to die. Madrid, a *muy leal* reflection of its monarch, seemed to be dying as well, dropping nearly half its population by the time of the **War of the Spanish Succession**.

1700–1808: Bourbons and More Palaces

The winner of the war, of course, was the grandson of Philip IV of Spain and Louis XIV of France, **Philip V** (1700–46), although it took 14 years to knock out the contenders, especially the Archduke Charles of Habsburg. A great centralizer like Louis XIV, Philip V also shared his grandfather's deep psychological need for more palaces. He started with La Granja, but this was only the warm-up for the 3,000-plus-room Palacio Real that replaced the Alcázar when it burnt down in 1734. The other accomplishment of the reign was also inspired by his grandfather: he founded academies of language and history, while his son, **Ferdinand VI** (1746–59), founded the Real Academia de Bellas Artes de San Fernando.

The one Bourbon who made a difference, especially in Madrid, was Ferdinand's brother the 'Mayor-King', **Charles III** (1759–88), a true son of the Enlightenment who, with his

ministers Floridablanca and Jovellanos, tried to reform everything. He expelled the dreadful Jesuits and cut the privileges of the other religious orders down to size. He commissioned sewers and streetlighting in Madrid, laid out the Paseo del Prado, founded worthy scientific bodies, built Madrid's first post office and, at the instigation of the dapper Italian minster the Marqués de Squillace, even tried to regulate fashion to put the *madrileños* in step with the rest of Europe, banning their long capes and wide-brimmed hats on the basis that the disguise made it easier to conceal weapons and go about incognito. This was going one step too far: the *madrileños* rioted and forced the government to back down.

Apart from the war over fashion, the mid to late 18th century was a happy time for Madrid. The population rose to 180,000 in 1800 and, unlike in the previous century, the citizens weren't entirely living off the court, but worked in various small manufactures – one that was just taking off, and would soon employ an entire quarter of the city's workforce, was the tobacco factory.

Unfortunately for Madrid and Spain, the son of Charles III, **Charles IV** (1788–1808), was as useless and stupid as any Habsburg, and perhaps best remembered for the indignities he and his horrible wife, Maria Luisa, suffered at the hand of their court painter, Goya. Their Rococo daydream was disrupted by the French Revolution. **Napoleon** first threatened Spain, then enticed Charles IV's corrupt minister (and Maria Luisa's lover) **Manuel Godoy** into cooperating in his campaigns, leading to the destruction of the Spanish fleet at Trafalgar.

Support of the godless French didn't sit well with the majority of the Spaniards, however, and in 1808 an anti-French riot shook Madrid. Godoy's house was attacked and the people proclaimed Ferdinand, son of Charles IV, the new king of Spain. Emboldened by the confusion, Napoleon sent down an army to take Madrid in March 1808, while the whole Spanish royal family fled into exile in France.

1808–1900: A Big Revolution and its Disappointing Results

Politically the city learned to speak for itself on 2 May 1808, in the famous revolt of the **Dos de Mayo**. Although the government was ready to cave in at once before the troops of General Murat, a spontaneous patriotic uprising occurred among the *madrileños*, who fought the French and their Egyptian Mamaluke mercenaries hand to hand in the streets. Although soon brutally suppressed by the French (as immortalized by Goya), it has been a golden memory for Madrid ever since.

The new king, **Joseph Bonaparte**, had no illusions about his popularity and the durability of his reign over what he himself described to his brother Napoleon as a 'nation of twelve million souls, exasperated beyond endurance'. In his six years in power, however, he did Madrid two big favours: he suppressed both the liquor tax and the city's excess convents and monasteries, demolishing them and turning them into squares – his nicknames, accordingly, were 'Joe Bottles' and *El rey de plazuelas*, 'the King of Squares'.

Meanwhile, the **Peninsular War**, led by the Duke of Wellington, led to privations that became extreme in 1812, when he took Madrid from the French, a battle that gravely damaged the Palacio del Buen Retiro. In the subsequent famine, some 30,000 died in the city alone. Politically, however, there was a ray of hope in the **Constitution**, Spain's first,

written by the Cortes while in exile in Cádiz. The ink was barely dry before it was declared invalid by the new king arrived from France, Charles IV's son **Ferdinand VII** (1808–33), as backward and absolutist as his 'Bourbons never forget and never learn' ancestors; he not only invited back the Jesuits, but the Inquisition as well, beginning the *desfrase* (out-of-synchness) that would characterize Spain's politics and its social realities for the next 150 years. With the reactionary Ferdinand at the helm there was no hope for change, but plenty for more humiliation as nearly all of Spain's colonies in Latin America rebelled and won their wars of independence. In 1820, the frustrated army rebelled under the leadership of General Rafael de Riego and forced the king to re-instate the constitution for three years. This breath of fresh air, known as the **Trienio Liberal**, saw the founding of Madrid's first real newspapers and the setting up of its first *tertulias* (cultural-political coffeehouse discussions), before it was suppressed with help from the French army in 1823. Riego was hanged.

Following the so-called 'ominous decade', Ferdinand's death in 1833 occasioned the **First Carlist War**, pitting the Liberal supporters of Ferdinand's elder daughter, the Infanta **Isabel II**, against Ferdinand's reactionary brother **Don Carlos** (the war, too, was Ferdinand's fault; one of the archaisms he reinstated was the Salic Law, which only allowed males to succeed to the throne; but this was before the last of his four wives finally gave him a daughter, who he insisted on succeeding him). The Liberals won, and under their first minister, **Mendizábal**, accomplished more than all the succeeding dictatorships of Isabel's generals and lovers, when in the *desamortización* of 1836 he expropriated the monasteries of Spain – in Madrid they had owned half of the town. The new secularized space offered the capital an unparalleled chance to put some order into its medieval warren of lanes, but Madrid declined the opportunity and used the land to throw up jerry-built housing for its growing popula-

tion. Also thanks to Mendizábal, there was a new intellectual element in the mix: that same year he moved the university from Alcalá de Henares to Madrid.

Even more important for Madrid was the completion of the first railways in the 1850s. The new communications finally made up for the lack of a navigable river and offered the city its first real chance to make its own way in the world. The opening of a new water supply from the Sierra de Guadarrama, the Canal Isabel II in 1858, was another major step for Madrid, which had been muddling through on wells and the dregs of the Manzanares.

By this time Madrid was bursting at the seams, with a population of over 300,000 inside its 200-year-old walls. In 1860, the suffocating city planned its first expansion or *ensanche*, designed by Carlos María de Castro. However, his waffle-iron grid of streets tempted few developers and for the next couple of decades it was all but politely ignored. Meanwhile, dissatisfaction with the corrupt court of Isabel II led to Spain's becoming a banana-monarchy, in which any ambitious general could deliver a *pronunciamiento* and strive for power. The First Republic was declared in 1868, but it soon succumbed to a **Second Carlist War** as futile as the first. A *pronunciamiento* by General Campos in 1876 restored the Bourbons in the form of Isabel's son **Alfonso XII**, who presided over a government kept stable only through a cynical deal under which the Liberals and Conservatives would alternate in power.

The average *madrileño* was fairly unaffected by all the *pronunciamientos*. In fact the city boomed in the 1880s. Country folk were pouring in at the rate of 10,000 a year, some finding jobs in the expanding number of workshops and small factories, others just getting by in the shanty towns that encircled the city. No longer able to squeeze into her girdle, Madrid decided to let herself spread with abandon in an orgy of new building in the *ensanche*, especially in the upper-class **Salamanca** district, named after the most

1808–1900

La Corrala, an example of a typical 19th-century tenement block, p.135

Museo del Prado, for Goya's paintings *Los Fusilamientos del Dos de Mayo* and *Los Fusilamientos de Moncloa*, p.98

Museo Romántico, for paintings and furnishings from the Romantic period, p.161

Salamanca, a slice of the ensanche from the 1880s, p.144

flamboyant of Madrid's speculators. In the 1890s, in response to the city's rapid growth, an engineer named Arturo Soria came up with one of the most innovative designs for new housing, the Ciudad Lineal (*see* p.45).

The century ended on a sour note, in the embarrassing defeat in the 1898 Spanish–American War that resulted in the loss of Spain's fleet as well as Cuba and the Philippines, her last important colonies. The country became introspective, and in Madrid's *tertulias* – frequented by leading figures of the 'Generation of '98' such as Antonio Machado, Miguel de Unamuno and José Ortego y Gasset – the main subject was Spain's curious destiny and how the country seemed incapable of modernity. People grew disenchanted with the inane political arrangement, and with the unpopular king, **Alfonso XIII** (1885–1931), who just barely missed being blown to smithereens on Calle Mayor in a bomb attempt on his wedding day.

1900–39: Republic and Civil War

The new century found Madrid with a population of half a million, and things not quite as gloomy as they might have seemed at the time. New factories and working-class districts were filling up the planned streets of the *ensanche*, and the loss of the colonies was actually good for the economy, as the money that once would have been sent abroad was reinvested at home. Banks and other financial institutions spread east along

the Calle de Alcalá, and mansions to house their bosses went up along the Paseos de Recoletos and Castellana. In 1910 the Gran Vía, a cross between a French boulevard and New York's Broadway, was bulldozed through the medieval centre as a showcase for the city's new love affair with modernity. In 1919 the metro made its inaugural run.

Spain's neutrality in the **First World War** made Madrid a nest of spies and intrigue, but was a boon to Spanish farmers and manufacturers, who sold goods to the Allies and positioned the country to reap a whirlwind of investment in the 1920s. Much of the action was in Madrid; the city's population doubled in 30 years. It was a time of cultural ferment, especially in the Residencia de Estudiantes, founded in 1910 as an open university of the liberal arts by Alberto Jiménez Fraud. Here leading writers and thinkers from around the world lectured and classes were attended by Unamuno, Alberti, the Machados, Buñuel, Dalí and Lorca.

Meanwhile, the rise of Anarchism in more industrialized Barcelona led to a new genera taking power, **Miguel Primo de Rivera**, who declared himself dictator under the king. Primo de Rivera was repressive and closed a number of Liberal establishments in Madrid, but he was rather genial and well-meaning as dictators go, and during his brief regime it began to occur to people that they didn't really need a shabby monarchy. The Depression brought about the resignation of Primo de Rivera and the decision by the government in 1931 to hold local elections. The results were an unexpected victory for Republican candidates all across Spain. In Madrid the exuberant population gathered at the Puerta del Sol to celebrate, and danced in the streets when it was announced that the king had abdicated.

The Second Republic saw the new moderate-left government of **Manuel Azaña** try to make the reforms the country's rural and industrial regions were crying out for. With the Depression and spiralling unemployment, the cards were stacked against

No Pasarán

Madrid is fond of remembering 2 May 1808, when its citizens spontaneously rose up against the Napoleonic invader, but you won't find any monuments to its equally heroic stand in the Civil War. A dispassionate observer might say that, on both occasions, Madrid's spirited citizen defence was in fact counterproductive, and that if they had just given in to the superior force, the *madrileños* would have been much better off at the end of the day. But the fact that on two occasions Madrid proved 'to have more balls than the horse of Espartero', as they say in the capital referring to General Baldomero Espartero's well-endowed equestrian monument on Calle de Alcalá), has given this city, a some-what artificial creation of kings and their court, a distinction and pride independent of its government. Franco did all he could to crush it for four decades, but didn't succeed. Madrid has a soul of its own, and it's very much alive.

The 1936 coup led by Generals Franco and Mola had thrown Madrid into revolutionary high gear. Everyone was addressed infor-mally as tú, the grand hotels were commandeered by trade unionists, the schools were radicalized, and as the four Nationalist columns massed in the Casa de Campo and besieged the city in late October, the cars of the wealthy were commandeered to transport troops to the front. It was a time of extremes: members of the armed forces and the police either supported the Nationalists or were suspected of doing so, and order and discipline went by the wayside. Churches were burnt and priests and nuns killed, as Spanish Catholicism openly supported the rebels.

The situation worsened when the Republican government, giving up the capital for lost, fled to Valencia (6 November 1936), leaving panic and disarray behind, increased by tales of atrocities committed by Franco's Moorish troops and General Mola's boasting of a 'Fifth Column' of sympathizers supposedly hidden within the city. It was all lies, but a new phrase was born, and the city's prisons were evacuated of potentially dangerous right-wing sympathizers, some 2,000 of whom were shot. Even the man left behind by the Republic to defend Madrid, General José Miaja, was certain that he had been chosen as a sacrificial lamb in a hope-less cause.

Franco's relief of the defenders of the Alcázar in Toledo, while a bonanza for Nationalist propaganda (another word that became known worldwide in the Civil War), allowed Madrid to prepare its defence. Most importantly, it allowed time for the arrival of arms from the Soviet Union (paid for with half of Spain's gold reserves) and the first units of the International Brigades, many of them German and Italian exiles who knew Fascism only too well. They would comprise about a fifth of Madrid's defenders, and their presence was a tremendous morale booster for the besieged city. They also gave the citizen militias quick lessons in the street tactics they had learnt battling the Fascists back home.

The Republican government's absence allowed the Communists to play a leading role in the capital's defence, and eventually

ny government, but in Spain, where desper-tion led people to take extreme positions, he situation was impossible: any change was regarded as 'Bolshevik' by the reac-onary upper classes and Church, while the Marxists and Anarchists saw the new government only as a prelude to a real revo-ution. Their abstention from the elections in 933 brought the radical right to power under **Gil Robles and Lerroux**, which was sufficiently alarming for the left to regroup as a **Popular Front** and win the election in 1936.

The situation immediately deteriorated. Street fighting and assassinations became an almost daily occurrence, much of it caused by extreme right-wing provocateurs, most notably a violent new fascist party, the

in the entire war. The most flamboyant of them all, Dolores Ibárruri, better known as 'La Pasionara', rallied the *madrileños* with her speeches: 'Madrid will be the tomb of Fascism!' and 'They shall not pass!' and 'It is better to die on your feet than live on your knees.' Their untrained citizen fighters, many women among them, wore street clothes and held meetings to discuss tactics with the officers; some actually commuted daily to the front on the metro. By mid-November, Madrid's southern suburbs and the Ciudad Universitaria at Moncloa were the scenes of savage hand-to-hand fighting. Bombardments from the Nationalists hit the poorer barrios hard, but avoided the wealthy homes of the Salamanca neighbourhood, where Mola's 'Fifth Columnists' presumably lived.

Franco's Moorish army came very close to capturing the centre of Madrid in late November 1936, only to be repulsed by the people in a stirring defence. Franco ordered an end to the attack, and General Miaja was declared a popular hero. But the result was a stalemate. In the Casa de Campo, Franco's army settled in for an intermittent siege; signs of the trenches remain, as well as the occasional unexploded shell (one was found during the recent expansion of the zoo). Republican attempts to push them back failed.

As the siege dragged on for three years, the lawlessness in Madrid that had prevailed in the previous months was replaced by an almost surreal normality; the papers went back to reporting social occasions and theatre reviews, while Franco's artillery aimed its fusillades along the Gran Vía, otherwise known as 'Avenida de los Obuses' (Howitzer Avenue). Despite the danger, nearly all the Gran Vía's shops remained open behind walls of bricks and sandbags. The *madrileños* became used to living in metro stations, just as Londoners would a few years later during the Blitz. Food and fuel were difficult to find; thousands of trees were chopped down in the severe winter of 1937–8, and furniture and even doors were burnt for heat. Most people survived on a daily ration of lentils, 'Dr Negrín's victory pills'. By late 1938, when the Republic's money was almost worthless, a barter economy took over. One telling story of the time concerns a gentleman going up to a market stall with a painting by Velázquez under his arm, which he offered to exchange for two tins of condensed milk. 'Is it a real Velázquez?' asked the seller. 'Yes indeed, signed and catalogued,' replied the gentleman. The seller was convinced. 'Then it's a deal,' he said. 'But you'll have to make up the difference in price with cash.'

As everyone knows, it ended badly. When the rest of Spain fell, fighting broke out between Madrid's defenders in a civil war within a Civil War – the Communists, wanting to fight to the bitter end, against the commander of the Army of the Centre and others who wanted to stop the killing and negotiate a settlement with Franco. But Franco was in no mood to compromise and, seeing resistance was at an end, his army entered the eerily silent streets of Madrid on 28 March 1939.

Falange Español, founded and led by **José Antonio Primo de Rivera**, son of the old dictator. The Left responded in kind, expropriating the property of aristocrats, burning churches and forming militias. On 13 July 1936 tension reached its height with the assassination of right-wing politician José Calvo Sotelo by revenge-seeking Republicans. At this point the army stepped in.

Spain's creaking military, with one officer for every six soldiers, had a long tradition of meddling in politics. Orchestrated by Generals **Francisco Franco** and **Emiliano Mola**, simultaneous uprisings took place across Spain on 17 July. The government was panicked into inaction, but the workers' militias took control of the situation in many areas and a substantial part of the army

emained loyal to the Republic. Instead of the
uick coup they had planned, the Generals
ot a Spain divided into two armed camps,
nd the **Civil War** was under way. Almost at
nce it became an international affair. Fascist
aly and Germany sent hundreds of aero-
lanes and some 200,000 troops. The only
overnment that helped the Republic was
ussia's, and then only in return for gold; the
ommunists organized the famous
ternational Brigades, but they were only a
andful. The overwhelming imbalance of
oreign help aiding Franco decided the war.
 In the early days of the conflict, most of
ranco's Army of Africa advanced to positions
vithin sight of the Palacio Real. The
epublican government, certain that the
apital would fall in a week, fled to Valencia –
n act seen as abandonment in Madrid –
eaving the defence of the city almost
ntirely in the hands of the newly formed
ocialist, Communist and Anarchist militias.
 the nick of time, morale was given an
normous boost by the arrival of the
ternational Brigades and the first
quadrons of Soviet aeroplanes and, as the
orld watched in suspense, Madrid held. '*No
asarán*' – 'they shall not pass' – was the
amous slogan coined by La Pasionara, and
ne city became a symbol that caught the
nagination of Europe, the first community
 that dark time to make a successful stand
gainst Fascism. Madrid spent the rest of the
ar under siege, bombarded from the Casa
e Campo and undergoing terrible priva-
ons. After Catalunya fell in January 1939
 was the only city still holding out and,
ompletely isolated, was forced to surrender
 March 1939.

1939–75: Four Miserable Decades with Francisco Franco

Before the Civil War, Madrid had grown into
a bright and cosmopolitan cultural capital;
most of the glitter, as well as the substance,
disappeared under 40 years of Franco. Badly
damaged, both physically and spiritually, by
the war, the first decade was especially dire.
There were massive reprisals against any and
all Leftists or their sympathizers – some 200
to 250 people a day were shot in Madrid
alone; altogether two million Republicans
were sent to prison or labour camps, forced
to build, among other things, Franco's chief
monument, the Valle de los Caídos. Any
Republicans who escaped death or prison
were just as likely to find their name on a
blacklist, limiting their possibilities of travel
or finding a decent job. The economy was in a
shambles and, while the rest of Europe was
engaged in the Second World War, Spain
suffered the 'years of hunger'.

Franco considered punishing Madrid even
further by moving the capital to Seville, only
to be foiled by the huge expense involved.
Plans were then made to convert the city
into an Imperial Fascist capital in the
Hitlerian kitsch mode, but luckily there was
no money in the pot for that either. Instead,
the defeat of Franco's old allies in the Second
World War saw the Caudillo scrambling to
present Spain afresh as a bulwark against
Communism and a safe haven for international capital. His efforts paid off in 1953,
when Spain signed a **treaty with the United
States**, exchanging military base sites for
international respectability and a huge infu-
sion of cash. To please his new friends, Franco
dismantled the cumbersome Fascist
economy and left it in the hands of a new
generation of technocrats (many of them
members of the secret Catholic society Opus
Dei). Their reforms and the American loans
began to pay off in the 1960s, when Spain
experienced an industrial take-off that gave
it the highest economic growth in the world,

1939–75

Palacio Real de El Pardo, with Franco's office left as it was when he died, p.172

Valle de los Caídos, built for Franco in the 1950s, p.190

although it was really just making up for lost time.

The Franco government, determined to see their Castilian capital outstrip Catalan, radical Barcelona, encouraged new industry and migration from all corners of Spain. Madrid's population in the 1960s rocketed to three million. But the costs were high; once-lovely tree-lined boulevards were flattened into urban motorways, and the outskirts of the city were disfigured by wastelands of industry and shanty towns. Strikes and protests by students and staff in the university led to frequent closings.

Confronted with inevitable social change, Franco (whose nicknames in Spain were 'the Sphinx' and 'Paco the Frog') remained stubbornly entrenched. A monarchist at heart, he declared in 1969 that his successor would be **Juan Carlos I**, grandson of Alfonso XIII and an unknown quantity, skipping over Juan Carlos' democratically minded father Don Juan. Meanwhile, clandestine political groups began to emerge, most of them just waiting for the old Caudillo to die. An exception was the Basques, who evolved the terrorist group ETA. They first rose to prominence in 1973, when their bombers assassinated Admiral Carrero Blanco, who had been the ageing dictator's strong man and his best hope for the continuity of the regime. Franco found no one hard enough to replace him.

1975 Onwards: Madrid of the Movida and Now

After Franco's death in 1975, Madrid's civic pride was allowed to resurface. First King Juan Carlos made his Bourbon ancestors spin in their graves and surprised everyone else by adroitly moving Spain back to a democracy.

His choice for Prime Minister, **Adolfo Suárez**, an ex-Falange bureaucrat, proved to be another surprise when he set about reforming the government and preparing it for elections. The transition, though it had its hiccups, was smoother than anyone could have imagined; Suárez's centre-right UCD party won the first general election in 1977, with the recently legalized Socialist Workers' Party coming in as the main opposition. Spain was given one of the most liberal constitutions in Europe in 1978, and the long heritage of Castilian centralism was undone, making Spain a **federal state** of 17 autonomous communities, like Germany and the United States (Madrid is the centre of the Comunidad de Madrid). The new democracy easily survived the old guards' last hurrah, when the Guardia Civil under **Colonel Tejero** attempted a coup by occupying the Cortes in February 1981. Elements in the army were behind it, but they backed down when ordered to do so by the king. Spain breathed a sigh of relief; the vast majority of Spaniards believed that too much blood had been shed and too much vengeance had been wreaked over the past 40 years for them to want to do anything that might conceivably restart the cycles of violence. When they refer to it, they call it the *pacto del olvido*, the pact of forgetfulness.

In 1982, real transition came, when general elections were won overwhelmingly by the Socialists under the suave Sevillian with the chipmunk cheeks, **Felipe González**, under whom Spain joined the **European Union**. As the 1980s progressed, the traditionally puritanical and austere Spaniards woke up to the attractions and pleasures of economic success, and Madrid found itself at the cutting edge of a social revolution. Earning (or otherwise acquiring) vast sums became a fashionable compulsion, and the popular press hispanicized the term *'los beautiful people'* for the new, money-flaunting jetset that filled Madrid's restaurants and terrazas The 1980s was the decade of the **movida madrileña**, when bars sprang up throughout

he city, legalized drug consumption flourished and under a Socialist government's patronage the arts underwent not so much a renaissance as a resurrection.

Former university professor **Enrique Tierno Galván**, who was elected Socialist mayor of Madrid in 1979, was seen by many as the sponsor and orchestrator of the city's great cultural revival. A remarkable mayor, he dedicated himself to improving the city's quality of life; he planted thousands of trees, created new parks in the outlying districts, poured money into the arts, repaired some of the damage done by the traffic planners, and even found some water to direct through the dusty stream bed of the city's oldest joke, the so-called Manzanares river. *Madrileños* nicknamed Tierno 'The Old Professor' for his habit of lecturing them on the importance of trees and greenery, and all of them, regardless of politics, mourned his death in 1986.

In the first five years after Spain joined the European Union, its economy grew faster than that of any other member country and, as property prices soared, Madrid benefited from much needed investment. Art fever gripped the city with the success of ARCO, Madrid's annual contemporary art fair, the opening of the Reina Sofía modern art museum and the acquisition of the famous Thyssen-Bornemisza collection. In 1991, the right-wing Partido Popular gained control of Madrid's regional parliament, and, under Mayor **José María Alvarez del Manzano**, one of their first priorities was to set about making final preparations for Spain's **golden year of celebrations**, 1992. Barcelona had won the Olympics, Seville was hosting the World Fair and Madrid came in a rather poor third as European Cultural Capital.

As it turned out, Madrid's contribution to the 1992 celebrations was not particularly remarkable; many of the projects planned to mark the event, such as the reopening of the Teatro Real, were still unfinished. But it was at the end of the year that the real blow came. For three years Felipe González's government had been artificially warding

off an economic slump by pouring money into construction projects to furnish the nation for the celebrations. Even before the fiesta was over, **recession** hit hard, with all the usual trappings—high unemployment, high interest rates and currency devaluation. Nobody appreciated this sudden downturn, and, in the 1993 general election, the Socialist party PSOE, its name already blackened by corruption scandals, lost control of the greater Madrid area to the new conservative Partido Popular. In 1996, the PP's **José María Aznar** won the general elections, and in March 2000 he won a second term, gaining an absolute majority in Parliament and lost in 2004.

In November 1999 the Basque separatist group **ETA** announced an end of its 14-month ceasefire, starting a campaign of car bombs and assassinations that have killed and injured dozens of people across Spain and the Basque region. At the time of writing, the government continued to take a security-first approach to the violence rather than looking for a political solution.

Madrid has now come to terms with the fact that the boom years are over; although city life has lost the hedonistic, opportunistic sparkle and easy glamour that distinguished it in the swinging 1980s, the *madrileñan* spirit is not dampened easily, and there's as

much optimism as caution built into their image of the future. This has manifested itself most vividly with the city's current *Plan Especial* (master plan) designed by Portuguese architect Álvaro Siza who won the Pritzker Prize in 1992 (architecture's nearest thing to an Oscar) for his restoration of the El Chiado neighbourhood in Lisbon. Siza's brief from Madrid's *Gerencia de Urbanismo* is to 'recuperate the environmental and landscape value of the historic centre, eliminating the negative impact of excessive traffic circulation and giving the area back to its original pedestrian users.' Construction is due to start in 2005 and includes a vast new underground car park near the Prado (in part for the coaches that currently block both traffic and views around the Neptuno fountain). There will also be an increase of pedestrian areas by 62 per cent, more open spaces and some buildings, such as the one that currently hides the Jardín Botánico from the Retiro side, will be made more visible. More controversial are the plans for some of the city's best-loved historical buildings, which include lowering the fountains of Cibeles and Neptuno to their original ground level, while the grand waterfall at the entrance of the cultural centre will be replaced by a modern sculpture which looks suspiciously like a giant-sized egg. There will also be modern extensions to the three major art museums. The plan is estimated to cost in the region of 633 million euros and the first phase is scheduled for completion in 2007, which also happens to be the year when, coincidentally, the current PP mayor, Ruiz-Gallardón, is up for re-election.

Architecture and Art

ARCHITECTURE

Madrid may have some of the most fabulous art collections of any city in the world, but most cities in Spain have grander, older and more beautiful buildings. Like Bonn or Washington, it is an artificial capital, perhaps less extraordinary for what it has (a central location) than for what it lacks – a beautiful setting, a navigable river or port, or even a tolerable climate ('three months of winter, nine months of hell' is the old saying). It was a quiet place in 1561 when Philip II made it the capital; the biggest show in town was the annual transhumance thundering of sheep herds down what is now Calle de Alcalá.

Even after 1561, the Habsburg and Bourbon obsession with constructing royal palaces left the city (with a few notable exceptions) to its own devices. Until the late 18th century, most of what was built was of cheap brick or rubble and mortar; with the high transport costs in a city without a port it could hardly be otherwise, especially when Spain's kings were squandering all their megatons of gold and silver from the New World on wars. Like Dublin, Madrid grew up as a city of theatre and literature rather than architecture, and like Dubliners the *madrileños* in the past two centuries have knocked down rather a lot of historic buildings. The surrounding cities of Castile have been less hasty, however; if you need a fix of Old Spain, Toledo and Segovia are among its most beautiful exemplars, both easy day trips from the capital.

Very little survives of Madrid prior to the mid-16th century. The oldest buildings are a pair of simple brick towers (San Nicolás de los Servitas and San Pedro el Real) built by the **Mudéjars**, or Christianized Moors, after the Reconquista; to see their masterpieces of decorative, geometric brickwork and azulejo tiles, you only have to go to Toledo. Toledo, in its cathedral, also has the best example of the succeeding **Gothic** style, inspired by the French; in Madrid there's the Torre de los Lujanes tower, but nearly everything else from the era was destroyed.

By the late 15th century, Castilian Gothic had evolved into a style similar to English Perpendicular known as **Isabelline Gothic** (San Juan de los Reyes, in Toledo). This in turn led to the uniquely Spanish Renaissance style called the **Plateresque** (from the *plateros* or 'silversmiths'), characterized by lavish sculptural decoration and façades that provide a striking contrast with the simpler lines of the rest of the building. Madrid has examples, in the Capilla del Obispo and the façade of the Casa de Cisneros.

Philip II's obsession with the construction of El Escorial may have spared his capital some frigid symmetry of its own; as it is, the death palace was far enough away to avoid infecting Madrid's organic squalor. The king did, however, begin the custom of appointing municipal architects to develop Madrid, beginning with **Juan Gómez de Mora**. Mora was a follower of El Escorial's chief architect, **Juan de Herrera**, whose austere *estilo desornamentado*, with its characteristic Flemish slate-topped towers and decorative motif of obelisks and balls (a favourite conceit of Philip's, derived from his days in Flanders), may be seen in the Habsburg-era buildings in Madrid proper. Herrera himself designed the stately Puente de Segovia over the Manzanares to provide Philip II with a quick escape from Madrid to the surrounding hunting grounds.

All of these are marked by an understated reserve, almost as if there was a tacit agreement to keep the canvas blank for the actors – the citizens – to write their own stories. This restraint also characterizes the surviving convents and churches from the reigns of Philips III and IV. Unfortunately the one Habsburg building that might have balanced the record, Philip IV's lavish Palacio del Buen Retiro, was damaged in the Peninsular War and later demolished.

The Bourbons of the early 18th century wanted to make Madrid look more like a proper European capital, and brought in Italians to do the job, beginning with Philip V's Palacio Real, designed by **Filippo Juvarra**

nd **Sachetti**. These were only the first of the ate Baroque Italian architects and artists vho would wash up in Madrid – **Giambattista Tiepolo**, **Luca Cambiaso** and **uca Giordano** were others.

Meanwhile, Madrid was blessed with a *orregidor*, the Marqués de Vadillo, who nade the home-grown **Pedro de Ribera** municipal architect. Pedro de Ribera intro- luced Baroque to Madrid, Spanish-style, ombining austere Herreran symmetry with avish, oozing surface decoration known as hurrigueresque after the Churriguera amily that made it famous, and with whom ibera sometimes worked. Ribera left Madrid

a number of fine structures, including the Puente de Toledo and the delightful Ermita de la Virgen del Puerto.

Charles III and his Enlightenment philos- ophy put him firmly into the Neoclassical camp of the late 18th century, and his favourite architect-engineer was another Italian, **Francesco Sabatini**, author of the Puerta de Alcalá and hospital that now holds the Reina Sofía museum. Towards the end of his reign, in Charles III's pet Paseo del Prado project, two Spanish architects left a greater imprint on Madrid: **Juan de Villanueva**, who built the Prado, an exceptionally elegant Neoclassical palace and one of the first in

The Ciudad Lineal

Arturo Soria y Mata was a *madrileño* who ot his fingers into everything that moved in is native town. Born in 1844, he made a areer as a journalist and a pro-Republican olitician, while finding time to invent an mproved telegraph and working unsuccess- ully to bring telephones and subways to the ity when such things were still new toys. In he 1880s he helped build Madrid's first treetcar line, and it was this interest in ransportation that led Soria to become nterested in the design of cities.

Madrid, booming, dirty and overcrowded ke all the capitals of Europe a century ago, vas full of discontents, and Soria, writing in he newspaper *El Progreso*, came up with a tartlingly original remedy – the Ciudad neal, the 'Linear City'.

It was a truly remarkable concept, and a mple one: a broad central street with sepa- te tracks for long-distance trains and local olleys in the middle, along with a single nnel for telephone and electric cables and as mains. On either side of this, a block or vo of houses, and no more. Everyone who ved in the Ciudad Lineal would be a inute's walk from shops and efficient ublic transport, and a minute's walk from pen countryside. Soria promoted his idea as e perfect form for the adaptation of the ty to modern technology, and he imagined

his linear cities one day running from Cadiz to St Petersburg, and from Peking to Brussels.

Madrid is one of the few places in the world where a utopian plan like this could not only be imagined, but actually attempted. Even then, however, the project didn't turn out to be exactly what Soria had in mind. He started a development firm, the Compañía Madrileña de Urbanización, but the only land he was able to acquire for a linear city was not between two existing towns, but on the periphery of the Madrid suburbs between Chamartín station and the eastern reaches of Calle de Alcalá. The plan is still visible on any city map (outside the area covered by maps in this guide) – two neatly parallel rows of blocks on either side of a broad boulevard, still just as Soria designed them. Only instead of passing through open country, the Ciudad Lineal now is part of one of the busiest neighbourhoods of Madrid – unfortunately, Soria was not able to stop other developers from building up all the land on either side. Visiting the site today, you will hardly see a hint of the original intention. But the world's planners still honour Soria as one of the most original urban designers ever, and the city of Madrid has commemorated him with the Ciudad Lineal metro stop, and with the central street of the original development, now named Calle de Arturo Soria.

Finding Madrid's Architecture

Europe specially designed to hold a museum (of natural history), and the more decorative and fanciful **Ventura Rodríguez**, who became the city's master fountain builder. In the 1880s **Ricardo Velázquez Bosco** designed the lovely Neoclassical Palacio de Velázquez and Palacio de Cristal in the Parque del Retiro.

The reign of Isabel II saw the culmination of Madrid's characteristically eclectic 19th-century architecture, dominated by a taste for the French Second Empire, especially in the fancy houses of the Salamanca district and the big banks that sprouted up along Calle de Alcalá. A late 19th-century reaction to this foreign fashion was the fancy brick-work and playful geometry of Neo-Mudéjar, a revival of 'Spain's national style' led by **Rodríguez Ayuso**. It found its greatest expression in Madrid over the next few decades, especially in Las Ventas bullring. On a more intimate scale, the Neo-Mudéjar love of colourful tiles extended to the city's shops

nd bars; few cities in Europe have so many
riginal interiors.

A cosmopolitan eclecticism with references
o Spain's past would continue to dominate
rchitecture well into the 20th century, most
trikingly along the Gran Vía, a street opened
p in 1910 to provide a setting for Madrid's
rst skyscrapers. The magnificent Art
Jouveau style or Modernismo of Barcelona
ever caught on in Madrid (although it has
ne celebrated example, the Socieded
ieneral de Autores), but Art Deco fared
etter. One of Madrid's chief architects into
he 1920s was **Antonio Palacios**, capable of
uch varied buildings as the Hollywoodesque
alacio de Comunicaciones and the cooler
írculo de Bellas Artes. On the domestic side,
he El Viso residential area north of
alamanca is one of the most interesting Art
eco projects in Europe.

The dictatorship of Primo de Rivera in the
920s initiated some of Madrid's heaviest
rojects: the Nuevos Ministerios and the
iudad Universitaria, both of which would be
ompleted under Franco. Perhaps Primo's
ost appreciated legacy was the founding of
he parador hotels in Spain's historic build-
gs. Franco's ingrained atavism and imperial
retensions are reflected in the grandiose
nd flaccid architecture he gave Madrid –
odernist plainness embellished with
erreran doodads, in the Edificio España
953) or the nearby Ministerio del Aire, a
isney-like replica of El Escorial. Like Philip II,
owever, Franco concentrated his attention
n constructing an extraordinary Pantheon
or his dead – in this case for the Nationalists
f the Civil War, in the Valle de los Caídos.

The desperate state of Spain's economy
onstricted building until the take-off in the
60s, although much of this was in the form
f anonymous *urbanizaciones* in the dreary
utskirts, thrown up to house the swelling
opulation drawn by Franco's industrializa-
on of Madrid. As Spain opened up to the
est, so Madrid's architects opened up to
e Rationalism, Functionalism and
odernism of the International style,

beginning with **Luis Gutiérrez Soto**, who
introduced all of the above to Madrid in the
1950s, after a trip to the USA. His more imaginative colleagues, **Alejandro de la Sota** and
Francisco Saénz de Oíza, are considered the
'fathers' of Madrid's current crop of architects, who have filled the Paseo de la
Castellana with enormous bank, insurance
and corporate headquarter towers, gleaming
like trophies over the busy street. Among the
most audacious are Europe's first leaning
towers since the Middle Ages – the Puerta de
Europa, completed in 1996.

Under the previous Socialist administration, Madrid also became the theatre for a
slew of new schools, community and neighbourhood cultural centres, and public
housing. The conservative Partido Popular
has since put the brakes on, and focuses its
attention on the restoration of old Madrid
and more commercial enterprises. Many of
the recent media-grabbing projects in Madrid
since the 1990s have been conversions of
historic buildings, in which Saénz de Oíza's
student, **Rafael Moneo**, has proved himself to
be the master (the Museo Thyssen-
Bornemisza and Estación de Atocha). At the
time of writing he was designing a new wing
for the Prado, next door to the Claustro de los
Jerónimos, with an underground tunnel to
connect it to the main building.

A WHIRLWIND ART TOUR

Madrid is one of Europe's great art cities; it
has been a magnet for artists from across
Spain and Europe off and on for 450 years.
But there's another art, in assembling and
keeping and enticing in new collections, and
at that Madrid is a pro: although the Prado,
Thyssen and Reina Sofía grab the headlines,
great paintings and sculpture await in the
Academia de Bellas Artes de San Fernando,
the Convento de las Descalzas Reales, the
Museo Lázaro Galdiano and, if you write

ahead long enough in advance to get on a tour, in the Duke of Alba's fabulous Palacio de Liria.

The country's top archaeological museum is the place to start for a chronological overview of Spanish art, beginning with its replica of the **Upper Palaeolithic** (12,000 BC) cave paintings at Altamira, although this is nearly as hard to get into as the original near Santander. On any given day, however, you can see the *Dama de Elche*, the masterpiece of **Iberian** sculpture, **Roman era** works (copies of Greek sculpture, statues of emperors and mosaics), dashing and intricate **Visigothic** jewellery in the Treasure of Gurrazar and Madrid's few bits and bobs from Spain's great **Moorish** civilization. Likewise, Spanish **Romanesque** and **Gothic** painting and sculpture are better represented elsewhere (in Barcelona in particular), but the fine *retablos* and triptychs in the Prado and Museo Lázaro Galdiano make a nice appetizer.

Madrid and art only really became insepar- able with the advent of the kingly collectors, who sent over crates of 16th-century Venetian and Flemish masterpieces. One Spanish painter whom Philip II patronized, **Alonso Sánchez Coello** (d.1588), founded the great Spanish tradition of portrait painting; one whom he didn't care for much was **El Greco** (d.1614), whose extraordinary Mannerist style properly begins the history of a distinctively Spanish school of painting and one of its principal currents, ecstatic mysticism. **Francisco Ribalta** (d.1628) and **José de Ribera** (d.1652) followed the same path, but not the great Cretan's style, preferring to wrap gloomily dramatic Caravaggiesque shadows around their Counter-reformation- approved holy pictures. Ribera is particularly noted for the human dignity he gave to his portraits and his keenness for using scruffy urchins and beggars as models in order to inject warts-and-all realism into his work. Others preferred saccharine mariolatry with floating angels: **Bartolomé Murillo**'s (d.1682) light, delicate style was considered the next best thing in the Counter-reformation, but can be too cloying for modern tastes. The

uneven **Alonso Cano** (d.1667) has a lower- calorie and more serene style.

The other great current of the Spanish school, flowing side by side with the river of saints eyeballing heaven, was realism; as Renaissance humanism was something of a non-starter in Spain, this, too, was derived ultimately from the Gothic tradition. The clarity, virtuosity and naturalistic perfection of the school's greatest master, **Diego Velázquez** (d.1660), stand out head and shoulders above the others. By the end of his career, in his masterpiece *Las Meninas*, he achieved a miraculous subtlety and shim- mering vividness, more real than real; examined close up, however, the forms magi- cally dissolve into blurs, as if Velázquez were making a statement on the nature of matter itself. Following on his heels is the restrained, direct, monumental spirituality of **Francisco de Zurbarán** (d.1664), whose remarkable portraits of saints and monks are among the highlights of the Prado and the Academia de Bellas Artes.

Good Spanish painting died suddenly after the 1660s. In the next century, to decorate the Palacio Real, Charles III had to look abroad, hiring the two most reputed painters in Europe, Venetian Rococo genius **Giambattista Tiepolo** (d.1770) and the German Neoclassical upstart **Antón Raphael Mengs** (d.1779). They didn't get along: Mengs the much younger man, once hid in a tree to pounce on the elderly Tiepolo, but missed and crashed to the ground instead; Tiepolo, a true gentleman, had him taken to hospital. Although artistically Mengs triumphed over Tiepolo at the time, Mengs' work today seems merely bland and sterile, while Tiepolo's last paintings, especially in the Prado, have a rare psychological depth. **Francisco Bayeu** (d.1795) of Zaragoza succeeded Mengs as court painter to Charles III; influenced by Tiepolo and Mengs, he ended up painting decorative slush (although his drawings are vivid and beautiful).

A real revival of Spanish art would have to wait for Bayeu's brother-in-law, **Francisco**

Finding Madrid's Art

Goya (d.1828), who started out painting cartoons for the Real Fábrica de Tapices tapestry factory), charming Rococo scenes of Madrid and *madrileños*. After a mysterious illness in 1792 that left him deaf, he would go on to become the most original artist of his time. Besides his unsparing court portraits, his scandalous Majas and the angelic Ermita de San Antonio de la Florida (which he executed with sponges), he painted and etched the brutality of war and corruption as no artist had ever done before. His most fero-cious work, the *Los Desastres de la Guerra* series (1810–14) and the 'Black Paintings', remained unknown to the public long after his death.

Goya, like Velázquez, looked forward to Impressionism, but had no worthy followers in Spain, although his influence lingered on in 19th-century Romantic realists such as **Mariano Fortuny** (d.1874), famous for his exotic subjects; **Joaquín Sorolla** (d.1923), who specialized in sun-filled outdoor scenes in the country or by the beach; and **Federico de Madrazo** (d.1894) – all of whose paintings are gathered in the Prado's Casón del Buen Retiro and Museo Sorolla.

Madrid's greatest 20th-century painter, the reclusive **José Gutiérrez Solana** (d.1947), made urban low life and horror the subject of his books and sombre paintings of dark, thickly applied colour; there's a whole roomful at the Centro de Arte Reina Sofía. But it was rival Barcelona that proved to be a hothouse for art in the 20th century, with **Miró**, **Dalí**, **Julio González**, **Juan Gris** and **Antoni Tàpies** all either born or working there – all of whom are well represented in

the Reina Sofía. **Picasso** (d.1973), who spent his early manhood in Barcelona before moving to France, left his greatest master-piece, *Guernica*, to Madrid.

Later *madrileño* artists include **Antonio López García** (1936–), a leading member of the Madrid Realism movement which was instrumental in the renewal of Madrid's art scene in the 1960s and 1970s; some of his urban portraits of Madrid are in the Reina Sofía. Madrid-born **Eduardo Arroyo** (1936–) was a member of the Pop Art movement.

Travel

GETTING THERE

By Air

Flights to Madrid are plentiful; the question is finding one that meets your needs – whether it's flexible travel dates or cheap prices. Prices vary wildly, depending on how far in advance you book and what kind of flight you are willing to settle for. But the offers are there.

From the UK

From the UK to Madrid, return tickets range from around £100 on a discount airline to £400 plus for a high-season, full-fare ticket.

Scheduled Flights

British Airways, t 0870 850 9850, **w** www.ba.com. Direct flights from London Heathrow and Gatwick, Manchester, Birmingham and Edinburgh. Tickets and other travel products available at BA Travelshops, **t** 0845 606 0747, located throughout the country (*open daily 6–6*).

British Midland, t 0870 607 0555, **t** (01332) 854000, **w** www.flybmi.com. Direct flights only from London Heathrow, but there are up to four daily, with connections to other cities in the UK, including Manchester, Leeds, Bradford, East Midlands, Edinburgh and many others.

Iberia, t 0845 601 2854, **t** (0180) 3000613, **w** www.iberia.com. Check the website for special offers (around £66 one-way) with daily flights from London Heathrow and Birmingham; services to and from other UK cities connect through Heathrow.

Lufthansa, t 0845 773 7747, **w** www.lufthansa.com. Has four direct flights daily from London Heathrow via Germany.

Low-Cost Airlines

The cheap no-frills low-cost carriers can offer astonishingly low prices if you book well in advance (usually two months at peak travel times). You can book directly over the Internet and a discount is usually offered if you do. Prices go up the closer you get to your leaving date; fares booked last minute

Flights on the Internet

The best place to start looking for flights is the Web – just about everyone has a site where you can compare prices (see the airlines listed below) and booking online usually confers a 10–20% discount.

In the UK and Ireland

w www.cheapflights.co.uk
w www.flightcentre.co.uk
w www.lastminute.com
w www.skydeals.co.uk
w www.sky-tours.co.uk
w www.thomascook.co.uk
w www.trailfinder.com
w www.travelselect.com
w www.cheapflights.com
w www.expedia.co.uk

In the USA

w www.air-fare.com
w www.airhitch.org
w www.expedia.com
w www.flights.com
w www.orbitz.com
w www.priceline.com
w www.travelocity.com
w www.smarterliving.com

In Canada

w www.flightcentre.ca
w www.lastminuteclub.com
w www.newfrontiers.com

are, in fact, not much cheaper than those of the major carriers. Each ticket has various conditions attached, for example whether you can get a refund or whether the date of the flight can be changed. All services may be less frequent in the winter.

EasyJet, t 0870 600 0000, **w** www.easy jet.com. Offers a bevy of supercheap flights to Madrid from London Luton, Gatwick and Liverpool (one way excluding taxes £21–172)

Virgin Express, t (020) 7744 0004, **w** www.virgin-express.com. Six flights a week between London Heathrow and Madrid, changing planes in Brussels. Returns start at around £95, excluding taxes.

Charter Flights

These can be incredibly cheap and offer the added advantage of departing from local airports. Companies such as Thomson, Airtours and Unijet can offer return flights from as little as £100. This can sometimes include basic accommodation. Check out your local travel agency, the Sunday papers and TV Teletext. In London, look in the *Evening Standard* and *Time Out*. Remember that there are no refunds for missed flights.

Airtours, *t* (01706) 240033, *w* www.airtours.co.uk.

Thomson, *t* 08705 502 554, *w* www.thomson-holidays.com.

Unijet, *t* 08706 008 009, *w* www.unijet.com.

From the Republic of Ireland

Aer Lingus, *t* (01) 886 8844, *w* www.fly erlingus.com. Four nonstop flights per day from Dublin to Madrid.

British Airways, *t* 1800 626 747, *w* www.ba.com. Daily flights from Dublin to Madrid, all connecting either through Heathrow or Gatwick.

British Midland, *t* (01) 407 3036, *w* www.flybmi.com. From Dublin to Madrid, with two or three flights daily.

Iberia, *t* 0845 601 2854, *w* www.iberia.com. One daily direct flight from Dublin; there are flights from other cities connecting through London Heathrow.

From the USA and Canada
Scheduled Flights

Direct flights in economy tend to range from US$600 to US$900, but non-direct flights tend to be much more competitive, especially with European carriers – you can get deals as low as US$500–600 in the summer and as low as $300 in the winter if you book well in advance.

Airlines with direct routes to Madrid:
Air Europa, *t* 1-888 238 7672, *w* www.aireuropa.com. One flight daily from New York JFK, and their prices tend to be lower than the rest.

Continental Airlines, *t* 800 231 0856, *w* www.continental.com. From Newark Airport (one daily), and connections can be made with Boston, Los Angeles and many other major US and Canadian cities.

Delta Airlines, *t* 800 221 1212 (in Montreal dial 3375520), *w* www.delta.com. From New York JFK and Atlanta, with connections to many of their US destinations.

Iberia, *t* 800 772 4642, *w* www.iberia.com. From New York, Miami and Chicago, but covers nearly all other major US and Canadian cities via a partnership with American Airlines, *t* 1800 433 7300, *w* www.aa.com.

US Airways, *t* 800 622 1015, *w* www.us airways.com. One daily flight from their hub in Philadelphia, but connections can be made to countless other US and Canadian cities.

Airlines with routes to Madrid via Europe:
Air Canada, *t* 888 247 2262, *t* 800 268 0024, *w* www.aircanada.com. Flies via Paris and London from Montreal, Toronto, Vancouver, Calgary, Winnipeg, Halifax and others.

British Airways, *t* 800 403 0882, *w* www.ba.com. Flights through Heathrow and Gatwick from a host of US cities.

KLM, *t* 800 225 2525, *w* www.klm.com. Flights via Amsterdam from many major US cities, including New York (Newark), Atlanta, Boston, Houston, Minneapolis, San Francisco, Los Angeles and Seattle.

Airline Offices in Madrid

Air Europa: *t* 91 393 7031.
American Airlines: *t* 91 453 1400.
British Airways: *t* 902 111 333.
Continental Airlines: *t* 91 559 27 10, *t* 91 305 46 26.
Delta Airlines: *t* 91 305 82 72.
EasyJet: *t* 902 29 99 92.
Iberia: *t* 902 40 05 00.
KLM: *t* 902 22 27 47, *t* 91 305 43 47.
Lufthansa: *t* 902 22 01 01, *t* 91 305 42 42.
TAP Air Portugal: *t* 91 305 58 68, *t* 91 305 42 37.
US Airways: *t* 91 393 71 46.
Virgin Express: *t* 91 662 5261.

Lufthansa, t *800 399 LUFT,*
w *www.lufthansa-usa.com.* Flies via Frankfurt from countless US and Canadian cities.

TAP Air Portugal, t *800 221 7370.* Flies from New York and Boston via Lisbon, and often has decent deals.

Virgin Atlantic, t *800 862 8621,*
w *www.virginatlantic.com.* Flights from most major US cities, via London Heathrow.

Charter Flights

Currently a charter from New York to Madrid varies between around US$300 and US$600, depending on the season. You may want to weigh this against the current price of transatlantic fares to London, from where in most cases you can get a low-cost flight to Madrid departing within a day or two of your arrival. The Sunday *New York Times* has the most listings. Major charter companies and consolidators include:

Council Travel, *205 East 42nd St, New York, NY 10017,* **t** *1 8888COUNCIL,* **w** *www.council travel.com.*

Spanish Heritage Tours, *120 Sylvan Avenue, Englewood Cliffs, NJ 076322,* **t** *800 456 5050,* **t** *(718) 793 4278,* **w** *www.shtours.com.* Uses Air Europa.

STA Travel, *48E 42nd St, New York, NY 10017,* **t** *800 777 0112,* **w** *www.statravel.com.*

Courier Flights

Global Courier Travel, w *www.courier travel.org.* A search engine that finds courier flights departing from New York.

Now Voyager, t *212 459 1616, 315 West 49th St Plaza Arcade, New York, NY 10019,* **w** *www.nowvoyagertravel.com.* Courier flights from the USA for 8–9-day stays in Madrid range from US$300 to US$450.

By Train

London to Madrid is a full-day trip, changing trains in Paris. The **Eurostar** through the Channel Tunnel from London Waterloo to Paris Gare du Nord is the quickest and easiest way to make the first leg of the journey (just under 3hrs). You must then change to the Gare d'Austerlitz to pick up the once-daily 13½-hour train to Madrid's Estación de Chamartín (*information office open daily 6.35am–11.55pm*). Prices vary depending on class and time, but the London–Paris leg can cost anywhere from £59 for a youth return up to £500 for a first-class ticket. From Paris to Madrid, it costs around €270 for a private berth, €190 for a two-person berth and €100 for a bed in a four-person couchette. Services are frequent on the London–Paris route, but book in advance to be sure. Contact:

Eurostar, *UK* **t** *(020) 7928 5163, UK* **t** *0870 6000 0796, US* **t** *800 EUROSTAR, Madrid* **t** *91 547 84 42,* **w** *www.eurostar.com.*

Rail Europe, *179 Piccadilly, London W1,* **t** *08705 848 848,* **w** *www.raileurope.co.uk; in North America, US* **t** *800 438 7245, Canada* **t** *800 361 RAIL,* **w** *www.raileurope.com.* For rail tickets to Spain from England, or vice versa. Take your passport when you book. Tickets for local Spanish services can be obtained from some UK travel agencies.

RENFE, *44 C/ de Alcalá (***metro** *Sevilla; K11).* **Open** *Mon–Fri 9.30–8.* You can buy rail tickets at this central RENFE office or from any travel agency that advertises *billetes de tren.* For more information, call **t** 902 240 202 or check the website (available in English) at **w** www.renfe.es.

By Coach

Eurolines (now part of National Express) offers departures several times a week in the summer (once a week out of season) from London Victoria to Spain. The journey to Madrid's Estación Sur de Autobuses takes 26–34hrs, with some buses stopping in Paris. Single fares are about £90; return fares around £75–150. Peak-season fares between 22 July and 4 September are slightly higher. There are discounts for anyone under 26, senior citizens and children under 12. In the summer, the coach can be the best bargain for anyone over 26; off-season you'll probably find a cheaper charter flight.

Information and booking:
UK: *Eurolines (National Express), Ensign*

ourt, 4 Vicarage Rd, Edgbaston, Birmingham
15 3ES, **t** 08705 808 080,
w www.eurolines.com.

Republic of Ireland: Bus Eireann, **t** (01) 836
111.

Spain: Enatcar-SAIA, 478 C/ de Alcalá, 28027
Madrid, **t** 91 327 13 81, **f** 91 327 1329.

Most, but not all, inter-urban and inter-
ational buses use the big new Estación Sur
e Autobuses, at C/ de Méndez Alvaro, **t** 91 468
2 00 (metro Méndez Alvaro; off maps). For
etails of bus services to destinations close
o Madrid, check the 'Getting There' sections
or those towns in the 'Day Trips' chapter.

By Car

From the UK via France you have a choice
f routes. Ferries from Portsmouth cross to
herbourg, Caen, Le Havre and St Malo. From
ny of these ports the most direct road route
akes you to Bordeaux, down the western
oast of France to the border at Irún. You may
nd it more convenient and less tiring to
ake the ferry from Plymouth to Santander
perated by **Brittany Ferries**, **t** 08705 561 600,
0870 901 2400, **w** www.brittany
rries.co.uk (high-season tickets for a car
nd four people cost from £700 to £1,350),
hich cuts out driving through France and
ves expensive autoroute tolls. There's also
e **P&O Ferries**, **t** 0870 242 4999, **t** 0990
80 555, **w** www.ponsf.com, route from
ortsmouth to Bilbao, departing twice
eekly and costing from £172 to £525 for a
r, plus £95–150 per adult.

To drive in Spain, you'll need a pink EU
riving licence or an International Driver's
cence. Although it's not compulsory, you
ay want to consider extending your motor
surance to include a bail bond: should you
ave an accident without one, your car will
e be impounded and you may find yourself
jail for the night. Carry your Green Card
d other vehicle documents with you at
l times.

Motoring in Madrid can drive you round
e bend in more ways than one, whether
u're stuck in endless traffic or sailing along

with the flow, for, once they get into third
gear, madrileños don't like to stop – a yellow
light means accelerate, not slow down. While
a car is certainly nice to have to get around
on day trips out of the city, it is fairly useless
for getting around Madrid because there's no
place to put your machine once you get
there. Some hotels have car parks; otherwise
you may as well put your car in the nearest
24-hour underground car park (rates are
approximately €15 for 24 hours, or €1 an
hour). Cars with foreign plates are especially
vulnerable to thieves. Parking is regulated by
ORA (Operación de Regulación del
Aparcamiento) and rules are in force Mon–Fri
9am–8pm and Sat 9am–2pm. Illegally
parked cars may well be towed; call **t** 91 345
00 50 to find out if they've nabbed yours.

SPECIALIST TOUR OPERATORS

There are lots of independent outfits that
offer everything from museum-oriented trips
to immersion courses and wine-tasting
tours. A good place to start is the official
Spanish Tourist Office nearest you (see
'Tourist Offices' in the 'Practical A–Z' chapter,
p.69). The following offer city breaks to
Madrid, most catering to a special interest.

In the UK

Abercrombie & Kent, St George's House,
Ambrose St, Cheltenham, Gloucs. GL50 3LG,
t 0845 070 0610, **w** www.abercrombie
kent.co.uk. Quality city breaks.

British Museum Traveller, 46 Bloomsbury
St, London WC1B 3QQ, **t** (020) 7436 7575,
f 7580 8677, **w** www.britishmuseum
traveller.co.uk. Guest lectures, art and architecture tours.

Cox and Kings, 4th Floor, Gordon House,
10 Greencoat Place, London SW1P 1PH,
t (020) 7873 5000, **w** www.coxandkings.co.uk.
Short breaks, gourmet and escorted cultural
tours with guest lecturers.

Euro Academy, *67–71 Lewisham High St, London SE13 5JX*, **t** *(020) 8297 5050*, **f** *8297 0984*, **w** *www.euroacademy.co.uk*. Art, cookery and language courses.

Magic of Spain, *Kings Place, 12–42 Wood Place, Kingston-upon-Thames KT1 1JF*, **t** *08700 270 480*, **w** *www.magictravelgroup.co.uk*. Cultural tours.

Martin Randall Travel, *10 Barley Mow Passage, Chiswick, London W4 4PH*, **t** *(020) 8742 3355*, **f** *8742 7766*, **w** *www.martin randall.com*. Cultural tours accompanied by a lecturer.

Page & Moy, *135–40 London Rd, Leicester LE2 1EN*, **t** *08700 106 212*, **w** *www.page-moy.com*.

Plantagenet Tours, *85 The Grove, Moordown, Bournemouth, Dorset BH9 2TY*, **t** *(01202) 521895*, **w** *www.plantagenet tours.com*. Historical tours.

Prospect Music and Art Tours, *36 Manchester St, London W1M 5PE*, **t** *(020) 7486 5704*, **f** *7486 5868*, **w** *www.prospecttours.com*. Tours of the big museums.

Saga Holidays, *The Saga Building, Enbrook Park, Sandgate High St, Sandgate, Kent*, **t** *0800 415 525*, **f** *01303 771 010*, **w** *www.saga.co.uk*. Holidays for the over-50s.

Seasons In Style, *Telegraph House, 246 Telegraph Rd, Heswall, Wirral, Merseyside CH60 7SG*, **t** *(0151) 342 0505*, **f** *0151 342 0516*, **w** *www.seasonsinstyle.co.uk*. Luxury tailor-made breaks.

Spanish Study Holidays, *67 Ashby Rd, Loughborough, Leics LE11 3AA*, **t** *(01509) 211612*, **f** *260037*, **w** *www.spanishstudy.co.uk*. Language courses in Madrid, with local accommodation arranged.

Travelsphere, *Compass House, Rockingham Rd, Market Harborough, Leics LE16 7QD*, **t** *(01858) 410 818*, **f** *434 323*, **w** *www.travel sphere.co.uk*. Single travellers, speciality trips and city breaks.

In Ireland

Abbey Travel, *44–45 Middle Abbey St, Dublin 1*, **t** *(01) 804 7100*, **f** *(01) 873 3163*, **w** *www.abbeytravel.ie*.

Go Holidays, *28 North Great Georges St, Dublin 1*, **t** *(01) 874 4126*, **f** *872 7958*, **w** *www.goholidays.ie*.

In the USA

Abercrombie and Kent, *152 Kensington Rd, Oak Brook, IL 60523*, **t** *800 323 7308*, **w** *www .abercrombiekent.com*. Quality city breaks.

Abreu Tours Inc., *350 Fifth Av, Suite 2414, New York, NY 10118-2414*, **t** *(212) 760 3301*, **t** *1800 223 1580*, **w** *www.abreu-tours.com*. Independent and escorted tours.

EC Tours, *12500 Riverside Dr, Suite 210, Valley Village, CA 91607*, **t** *800 388 0877*, **w** *www.ectours.com*. Tours and city packages.

Heritage Tours, *121 West 27 St, Suite 1201, NY 10011*, **t** *800 378 4555*, **t** *(212) 206 8400*, **f** *206 9101*, **w** *www.heritagetoursonline.com*. Custom-designed cultural tours.

Jet Vacations, *880 Apollo St, Suite 243, El Segundo, CA 90245*, **t** *800 JET 0999*, **f** *(310) 640 1700*, **w** *www.jetvacations.com*. Independent packages and customized group packages.

Kesher Tours, *347 Fifth Av, Suite 706, New York, NY 10016*, **t** *(212) 481 3721*, **f** *481 4212*, **w** *www.keshertours.com*. Kosher tours.

Marketing Ahead Inc., *381 Park Avenue South, Suite 718, New York, NY 10016*, **t** *800 223 1356*, **f** *(212) 686 0271*, **w** *www.marketingahead.com*. The leading hotel and parador agents in the USA.

Petrabax, *97 Queens Bd, Suite 600, Rego Park, NY 11374*, **t** *800 634 1188*, **w** *www.petra bax.com*. Escorted tours and hotels.

ENTRY FORMALITIES

Passports and Visas

Citizens of any European Union country or Switzerland can travel to Spain with their national identity card. If your country of residence does not issue cards (e.g. the UK), then a passport is the necessary document. For visitors to Spain from the USA, Canada, Australia and New Zealand, a visa is not necessary for stays of 90 days or less. For

onger stays, you will need a residence card (*tarjeta de residencia*), which can be applied for in advance (way in advance) at local consulates. Citizens of South Africa do need to apply for a visa, at their local consulate.

Thanks to the Schengen Agreement, Spain, Austria, Belgium, France, Germany, Italy, Luxembourg, the Netherlands and Portugal have effectively eliminated passport control at their common borders. They do, however, have the right to make random checks and as a general rule it is always wise to carry a certified copy of your passport or residence card. Don't carry the original as it may get lost or stolen.

Customs

Duty-free goods have been abolished on journeys within the European Union, but this does not necessarily mean that prices have gone up, as shops at ports, airports and the Channel Tunnel do not always choose to pass on the cost of the duty. It does mean that there is no limit on how much you can buy, as long as it is for your own use. Guidelines are issued (e.g. 10 litres of spirits, 100 cigarettes, 90 litres of wine, 110 litres of beer) and, if they are exceeded, you may be asked to prove that it is all for your own use. Non-EU citizens flying from an EU country to a non-EU country (e.g. flying home from Spain) can still buy duty-free. Americans can take home 1 litre of alcohol, 200 cigarettes and 100 cigars, etc. Canadians can take some 200 cigarettes and 1.5 litres of wine or 1.14 litres of spirits or 8.5 litres of beer. For more information, US citizens can consult www.customs.gov.

ARRIVAL

Aeropuerto de Barajas

The Aeropuerto de Barajas is 15km northeast of the city centre, off the A2 highway to Barcelona and also off the M40 and A10, the highways that come in from the northern tip

of the city. The airport is undergoing an expansion programme. There are now three terminals – T1 (international flights), T2 (national and regional flights) and T3 (Iberia shuttle to Barcelona and Air Nostrum flights) with a fourth terminal planned to open in 2004. If you have to connect, expect a slight hike (5–10mins between terminals).

In T1 there are both BBVA and American Express currency exchange offices (rates are usually exactly the same), as well as a BBVA cash machine covering Servired, Visa, Plus, Cirrus, Eurocheque and Telebanco banking networks. Terminal 1 also has a post office (*open Mon–Fri 8.30am–8.30pm, Sat 8am–1pm*); a RENFE office (*open daily 8am–9pm*); a pharmacy; a free accommodation service (*open daily 8am–midnight*) for three-, four- and five-star hotels as well as two-star *hostal-residencias*; all major car-rental agencies; and various green tourist information stands with unusually helpful attendants (*each terminal has one stand open 24 hours*). T2 has a convenient message-board service. There are two left luggage (*consigna*) locations, one in T1 next to Sala 2, the other in T2 near the entrance to the metro, and they are open round the clock. Prices are €2.60 for the first 24 hours; €3.25 per day thereafter. Long-term parking at the airport, run by Parking Express, t 91 418 58 96, costs about €12 a day.

Useful airport telephone numbers:
Airport / flight information: *t 91 393 60 00.*
Flight information: *t 902 35 35 70.*
Left luggage: *t 91 393 60 00, ext. 32180.*
Lost and found: *t 91 393 60 00, ext. 36119.*
RENFE office: *t 902 24 02 02.*

Getting to and from Aeropuerto de Barajas

By Bus

Fast, air-conditioned buses (no.89 white with yellow and green stripes) run between Barajas's national and international terminals and the underground bus terminal at Plaza de Colón every 15mins daily from

4.45am to 2am, taking around 25mins when the traffic is reasonable, and about an hour when not. The buses make stops along the way at Avenida de América, C/ de María de Molina, C/ de Velázquez and C/ de Serrano. The fare is €2.40 one way.

Airport bus information: t *91 406 88 43.*

By Metro

The metro to the airport is now up and running: fast, efficient and the cheapest way to Barajas, costing €1.10 for a one-shot (*sencillo*) ticket and €5.20 for a 10-trip Metrobús ticket. It takes about 45mins to get to the city centre, involving a relatively easy series of changes: take Line 8 (pink) to Mar de Cristal and then switch to Line 4 (brown), which takes you to the Alonso Martínez station. Here you can switch to Line 10 (dark blue) to get to Plaza de España and Line 5 (light green) to head for Gran Vía and Sol further into the centre. The metro runs from 6am to 1.30am daily.

Metro information: t *902 44 403,* **w** *www.metromadrid.es. (in English)*

By Taxi

A taxi from the airport to the centre will cost anything from €15 to €20, depending on where you are headed in the city centre.

GETTING AROUND

Madrid goes on and on – today it is home to 4 or 5 million people, depending how you add them up – but almost everything of major interest will be found within one mile of the Puerta del Sol between the Parque del Retiro in the east and Plaza de Oriente in the west, home of the opera house and the Palacio Real. Near the Retiro and the broad boulevard called the Paseo del Prado, you'll find the '*triángulo de arte*', Madrid's triple crown of art museums, the Prado, Thyssen and Reina Sofía. The Puerta del Sol sits squarely in the centre, and the oldest quarter of the city, around the Plaza Mayor, is just to the west of it. Keep these landmarks in mind,

Buying Bus and Metro Tickets

Bus and metro operate on the same ticket, with a single price for all journeys, costing €1.10. A Metrobús for 10 trips, which can be used on the bus and metro, costs €5.20 and is a good investment if you're going to be in the city for a few days. Each metro station has a manned ticket booth, though some stations now sport automated ticket machines that are relatively easy to use. There are information kiosks which sell Metrobus tickets in Plaza de Cibeles, Puerta del Sol and Plaza del Callao. *Estancos* (tobacconists) and news-stands also sell them.

and learn a few of the main streets, and you'll not get too lost – Madrid isn't nearly as complicated as it looks on the map.

Because the centre, where most of the interest lies, is so compact, Madrid is easy to get about on foot, however, if you've got sore feet, taxis are relatively cheap. That said, Madrid's buses and metro do come in handy to reach some of the more outlying sights.

By Metro

Opened in 1919, Madrid's metro is the third oldest system in Europe (after London and Paris). It is safe, clean and well used, even late at night: trains run from 6am to 1.30am. The metro's main fault is that its connections are often inconvenient.

Study the metro map carefully before setting out. There are so many stops and lines in the centre of the city that it's easy to be tricked into taking a half-hour ride (with a change or two) for a distance that could be covered in 10 minutes on foot. Stations are distinguished by a red diamond over the entrance. You may experience some disruption as an ongoing expansion programme is being carried out. For information, call **t** 902 44 403.

By Bus

Only a few EMT bus lines will be of use to the visitor (*see* 'Useful Bus Lines') – but buses

...an be preferable to the metro if you want to ...ee Madrid (remember, they both take the ...ame tickets). Many buses go through the ...laza de Cibeles, Puerta del Sol and Plaza del ...allao. You enter the bus at the front, pay the ...river or validate your ticket, and leave by the ...oors in the middle. Some drivers may object ...' you try to bring large suitcases on board. ...he sequence of places served from each ...top is usually clearly marked. Buses run ...rom 6am to midnight, after which there is a ...keleton night service through the city, ...aving from Plaza de Cibeles and Puerta del ...ol every half-hour until 3am, and every hour ...rom 3am to 6am.

EMT information: *t 91 406 88 10.*

By *Cercanías* (Local Trains)

Run by RENFE, Spain's national railway, this ...etwork is primarily useful for commuters, ...ut also comes in handy for day trips to El ...scorial or Aranjuez (*see* the 'Day Trips' ...hapter). Most local trains leave from the ...ain line stations, Charmartín and Atocha, ...lthough some stop between them at ...ecoletos and Nuevos Ministerias stations.

Cercanías **information:** *t 902 24 02 02.*

By Taxi

Madrid has 15,500 taxis, more than any city ...n the world except Cairo, so finding one is ...arely a problem. Local government-...egulated taxis are white with a red diagonal ...tripe on each front door. A lit-up green light ...long with a sign saying '*Libre*' means they're ...ree, '*Ocupado*' that they're not. All city taxis ...ave meters and they're expected to use ...hem, but don't be surprised if the fare ...omes out a little higher: there are ...urcharges for luggage, for the airports and ...us and railway stations, for journeys at ...ight (11pm–6am) and for leaving the city ...mits. As elsewhere in Spain, taxis are cheap ...nough: the average ride across the city ...entre costs well under €6. If you call a radio

Useful Bus Lines

Line 1: Moncloa–Plaza de España–Gran Vía–Plaza de Cibeles–Puerta de Alcalá–C/ de Velázquez–C/ de Ortega y Gasset (Salamanca district).

Line 3: Puerta de Toledo–Gran Via–C/ de Hortaleza–C/ Bravo Murillo–Estadio Bernabéu.

Line 14: Plaza del Conde de Casal–Atocha–Paseo del Prado–Paseo de Recoletos–Paseo de la Castellana–Chamartín.

Line 19: C/ de Serrano–C/ de Alfonso XII (Parque del Retiro)–Atocha–Méndez Alvaro (Estación Sur bus terminus).

Line 27: Atocha–Plaza Canovas del Castillo–Plaza de Cibeles–Plaza de Colón–Nuevos Ministerios–Plaza de Castilla.

Line 33: Príncipe Pío–Casa de Campo (for Parque de Atracciones and Zoo-Acuario).

taxi, the meter will be set from the spot where the driver receives the call.

Radio Taxi: *t 91 447 51 80.*

Radio Taxi Independiente: *t 91 405 5500, t 91 405 12 13.*

Radio Telefono Taxi: *t 91 547 82 00, t 91 547 85 00.*

Tele-Taxi: *t 91 371 21 31, t 91 371 37 11.*

Hiring a Car

This is moderately cheaper than elsewhere in Europe, especially if you hire from a local Spanish-owned company. You may find some interesting discounts with the big international firms if you book a car along with your flight or from your home country. To hire a car, you need to be at least 21 (though some agencies require you to be 23 or 25) and have held a licence for at least a year; you'll also need to have a credit card or be prepared to pay an enormous cash advance. You can save on parking fees by having the car delivered to your hotel when you're ready to use it. *See* 'By Car' under 'Getting There', above, for the trials of driving and parking in Madrid.

Rental companies include:

Atesa/National, *at the airport, t 91 393 72 32; 80 Gran Vía, 1A planta (**metro** Plaza de*

España; H9), ***t*** *91 542 50 15,* ***f*** *91 541 80 89 (general information* ***t*** *902 10 01 01 (national),* ***t*** *902 10 05 15 (international),* ***w*** *www.atesa.es).*

Avis, *at the airport,* ***t*** *91 393 72 22; 60 Gran Vía (**metro** Plaza de España; H9),* ***t*** *91 547 20 48 (general information* ***t*** *902 18 08 54,* ***w*** *www.avis.es).*

EasyCar, *at the airport. Book online at* ***w*** *www.easycar.com.*

Europcar, *at the airport,* ***t*** *91 393 72 35; 8 C/ de San Leonardo (**metro** Plaza de España; H9),* ***t*** *91 541 88 92; Estación de Atocha,* ***t*** *91 393 7235; Estación de Chamartín,* ***t*** *91 323 17 21 (general information* ***t*** *902 10 50 30,* ***w*** *www.europcar.es).*

Hertz, *at the airport,* ***t*** *91 393 82 65; Estación de Atocha,* ***t*** *91 468 07 53 (general information* ***t*** *902 40 24 05,* ***w*** *www.hertz.com).*

Guided Tours

By Bus

Madrid Vision buses offer a hop-on, hop-off circuit tour which covers the Plaza Mayor, Puerta del Sol, Plaza de Neptuno, Thyssen-Bornemisza, Atocha and the Reina Sofía, the Real Jardín Botánico, Prado, Puerta de Alcalá, Parque del Retiro, Plaza de Colón, Plaza de Cibeles, Gran Vía, Plaza de España, Palacio Real and the Teatro Real. You can start your journey at any of the stops, and buses pull in and out about every 10mins.

Madrid Vision, ***t*** *91 302 03 68.* Runs daily 9am–7pm, and in summertime night tours are also offered. Tickets are good for 24hrs and cost €10 (adults) or €5 (children over 6).

Night tours costs the same. Two day tours cost €12 (adults) or €6 (children).

The tourist office (*see* 'By Foot', below) offers bus tours outside Madrid, costing €6 for adults and €4.50 for under-25s and senior citizens.

On Foot

The city tourist office (Patronato Municipal de Turismo) runs an extensive series of walking tours for every possible desire – from basic historical tours (Madrid of the Austrias, Literary Madrid, Medieval Madrid, 19th-century Madrid) to neighbourhood-specific walks, art tours, museum tours, park tours. The best thing to do is get a copy of the *Descubre Madrid* brochure from the tourist office, which lists all the possibilities in exhaustive detail. Contact:

Patronato Municipal de Turismo, *69 C/ Mayor,* ***t*** *91 588 29 06,* ***f*** *91 588 29 30,* ***w*** *www.munimadrid.es.* ***Open*** *Mon, Tues, Thurs and Fri 8.30am–2.30pm, Wed 8.30–2.30 and 4–6.* Walking tours cost around €3 for adults and €2.50 for under-25s and senior citizens.

Practical A–Z

Climate

Located on the plateau of Castile at 2,165ft, Madrid is the highest capital in Europe, which contributes to its famous rarefied air. It also has the most godawful climate of any European capital – blistering in the summer under a sun like a giant X-ray machine and bone-freezing cold in the winter. It builds character.

Spring and autumn are the most comfortable times to visit, but, as in any great city, you can have a good time in Madrid year round. Even summer, traditionally touted as the season to avoid, isn't all that infernal, especially if you can manage to keep *madrileño* hours: do the cultural sights in the cooler morning hours, have a long boozy lunch and take a siesta from 4pm to 10pm. Although the city is at its emptiest in August, various organizations put on plenty of events to keep it from being dull.

Average daily temperatures in °C/°F

Jan	Mar	May	July	Sept	Nov
6 (41)	10 (51)	16 (60)	25 (75)	20 (67)	9 (48)

Crime and the Police

Crime is not a big problem in Spain, but you should take the same sorts of **precautions** as you do at home. In Madrid, pickpocketing and robbing parked cars are the specialities in crowded areas, and most notoriously at the Rastro fleamarket, but violent crime is rare. Walking around at night is safe – primarily because everybody does it – although you may want to avoid Calle de la Montera (running northeast off Puerta del Sol), the base for central Madrid's prostitutes; the Gran Vía, crowded during the day, can also be not so pleasant at night, especially on the streets heading north between Fuencarral and San Bernardo. And you probably shouldn't dawdle in the parks after dark. The Casa de Campo, on the other hand, is a cruiser's paradise at night, with its line-up of hookers strutting their stuff up and down the main thoroughfares. The Plaza Santa Ana, while lined with cheery bars and cafés,

is known for being the hunting ground of hungry charlatans who occasionally work in groups to relieve tourists of their bum bags.

There are several species of **police**. The Policía Nacional are dressed in black and white uniforms; their duties largely consist of driving around in cars and drinking coffee, although they are also chiefly responsible for crime control in the city. If you have to report a crime in Madrid, you'll have to make a statement (*denuncia*) at their headquarters for your insurance claim if nothing else (*Jefatura Superior de Policia, 19 C/ Leganitas, t 91 548 7986; metro Gran Via; H10*). Or just call **t** 091. Most traffic violations are payable on the spot; the traffic cops have a reputation for upright honesty.

Disabled Travellers

Although many of the big museums (especially the Prado, Reina Sofía and Thyssen) are wheelchair-friendly, facilities for disabled travellers are limited in Madrid. In our **museum** entries throughout this book, we use the term 'wheelchair accessible' for those places that are most accessible for disabled travellers. Note that most museums are only partially accessible: bathrooms and cafeterias are often located in inconvenient spots, so calling ahead to get the full picture is the safest bet. In our 'Eating Out' chapter we list those **restaurants** with wheelchair access and/or equipped with a wheelchair-accessible toilet, though they are few and far between (*madrileño* bar and restaurant managers usually do their best to accommodate with good cheer, though). In the 'Where to Stay' and 'Entertainment' chapters, we also list those hotels, cinemas, theatres, etc, that are wholly or partly accessible – but, as before, there's no substitute for calling ahead.

Public transport can be difficult. Although the new **metro** stations are being built with lifts, most of the old ones (that is, in the city centre) have lots of stairs. The Atocha train station has lifts, while the others are less user-friendly. The metro map (available at

ny metro station) clearly identifies, with a
ttle wheelchair symbol, which stations
ffer disabled access, whether via ramp or
ft, and this information can also be
ccessed by calling **t** 902 44 403 or on
w *www.metromadrid.es*. Nearly 100 of
Madrid's 179 **bus** lines are outfitted with
uses accessible to disabled travellers, with
tairs that fold into a ramp and special
eating for wheelchairs. These buses are
dentified by a sign that says '*piso bajo*'. For
nore detailed information about specific
nes, call **t** 91 406 88 10.

One **radio taxi** company has vehicles
dapted for wheelchairs. You can book on:
91 547 86 00, **t** 91 547 82 00.

Thanks to ONCE, the organization for the
lind financed by its own lottery, **pedestrian
rossings** in Madrid are specially textured
nd crossing lights are accompanied by a
hirping bird sound that slows down as time
uns out.

Organizations in Madrid

ALPE Turismo para Todos, *5 C/ de
asarrubuelos, **t** 91 448 08 64, **f** 91 594 23 38,
w www.alpe.com (**metro** Quevedo; H5).* An
rganization dedicated to travel for the phys-
ally disabled, it publishes an incredibly
seful guide to disabled-access hotels.

**Federación de Minusválidos Físicos de la
omunidad de Madrid (Association for the
hysically Disabled)**, *69 C/ de Galileo, **t** 91 593
5 50, information service **t** 91 447 54 99, **f** 91
93 29 43, **w** www.servicom.es/famma (**metro**
rgüelles or Moncloa; H5).* Publishes a *Guía de
ccesibilidad de Madrid* which is slightly hard
o come by but is really the bible of the
isabled traveller, with detailed information
n accessibility of airports, train stations, bus
tations, museums, malls, cinemas, theatres
nd sports facilities.

nternational Organizations

Accessible Europe, *Promotur-Mondo
ossibile, Piazza Pitagora 9, 10137 Turin, **t** (39)
11 309 6363, **f** 011 309 1201, **w** www.accessible
rope.com.* A network of specialist European
ravel agencies who can provide detailed

information on major sites and transport,
as well as organizing assistance for
disabled travellers.

Organizations in the UK

Holiday Care Service, *7th Floor,
Sunley House, 4 Bedford Park, Croydon,
Surrey CR0 2AP, **t** (0845) 124 9971,
w www.holidaycare.org.uk.* Up-to-date information on destinations, transportation and
suitable tour operators.

**RADAR (Royal Association for Disability
and Rehabilitation)**, *Unit 12, City Forum, 250
City Rd, London EC1V 8AF, **t** (020) 7250 3222,
f 7250 0212, **w** www.radar.org.uk.* Publishes
several books with information on everything travellers with disabilities need
to know.

Tripscope, *The Vassall Centre, Gill Avenue,
Bristol B516 2QG, **t** (0845) 758 5641, **f** (020)
8580 7022, **w** www.tripscope.org.uk.* Practical
advice and information on travel and transport for elderly and disabled travellers.
Information can be provided by letter or tape.

Organizations in the USA

**SATH (Society for the Advancement of
Travel for the Handicapped)**, *Suite 610, 347
5th Av, New York, NY 10016, **t** (212) 447 7284,
w www.sath.org.*

Organizations in Ireland

Irish Wheelchair Association, *Blackheath
Drive, Clontarf, Dublin 3, **t** (01) 833 8241,
w www.iwa.ie.* They publish guides with
advice for disabled holidaymakers.

Electricity, Weights and Measures

The electrical current is 225 AC or 220 V, the
same as most of Europe. Americans will need
converters, and the British will need two-pin
adapters for the different plugs. If you plan
to stay in the less expensive *hostales*, where
the current is often 125 V, it may be better to
leave your gadgets at home. Note that the
Spanish use commas and not full stops
(periods) to indicate decimal points.

Spain uses the metric system; below is a conversion chart for quick reference.

1 cm = 0.3937 inches
1 metre = 3.094 feet
1 kilometre = 0.6214 miles
1 kilogramme = 2.2 pounds
1 litre = 0.264 gallons
1 inch = 2.54 centimetres
1 foot = 0.3048 metres
1 mile = 1.6 kilometres
1 pound = 0.4536 kilogrammes
1 liquid pint = 0.4732 litres
1 gallon = 3.7853 litres

Embassies and Consulates

In Madrid

Canada: *35 C/ de Núñez de Balboa, t 91 423 32 50, f 91 423 32 51, w www.canada-es.org (metro Núñez de Balboa; 08).*

Ireland: *Paseo de la Castellana 4, t 91 436 40 95 (metro Rubén Darío; M5).*

UK: *16 C/ de Fernando el Santo, t 91 700 82 00, f 91 700 82 72, w www.ukinspain.com (metro Alonso Martínez; L7–8).*

USA: *75 C/ de Serrano, t 91 577 40 00, w www.embusa.es (metro Rubén Darío; M–N5).*

Abroad

Canada: *74 Stanley Av, Ottawa, Ontario K1M 1P4, t (613) 747 2252, f 744 1224, e spain@ docuweb.ca.*

Ireland: *17A Merlyn Park, Ballsbridge, Dublin 4, t (01) 269 1640, f 269 1854.*

UK: *20 Draycott Place, London SW3 2RZ, t (020) 7235 5555, w www.conspalon.org.*

USA: *2375 Pennsylvania Av NW, Washington DC 20037, t (202) 728 2332; San Francisco, t (212) 355 4080.*

Etiquette

Madrileños and the Spanish on the whole are as gracious a people as you'll find, but first-time visitors are often surprised by one habit: in bars, all the rubbish – napkins, olive stones, toothpicks, nut shells, cigarette butts and fish bones – goes straight on the floor.

Usually this is swept every hour, but at busy times you may find yourself ankle deep in litter by the counter; on weekend nights when everyone takes their drinks outside, whole streets end up looking like the bar-room floor in the wee hours, before the street sweepers attack the mess.

Spanish speakers accustomed to the more formal speech in the Americas will be amazed at how *madrileños* tend to address even perfect strangers familiarly as '*tu*' rather than '*usted*', and shouldn't take offence. As always, it is helpful to know a handful of Spanish words and phrases – even the most minimal efforts to speak in Spanish are usually rewarded with appreciation on the part of waiters, shopkeepers and other locals.

Health, Emergencies and Insurance

Madrid has a single number for all emergency services (fire, police, ambulance): **t** 112.

There is a standard agreement for citizens of EU countries, entitling you to a certain amount of free **medical care**. Ask for a leaflet called 'Before You Go' from the Department of Health and fill out form E111. Non-EU travellers should check with their policies at home to see if they are covered in Spain, and judge whether it's advisable to take out additional insurance.

You should always make sure you have **travel insurance**, covering you for delays, lost baggage, etc. Ring around for the best deal. Be sure to save all doctors' receipts (you'll have to pay cash on the spot), pharmacy receipts and police documents (if you're reporting a theft).

English-speaking **doctors** are on duty at the privately run British-American Unidad Médica Anglo-Americana, 1 C/ del Conde de Aranda, **t** 91 435 18 23 (metro Retiro; *open Mon–Fri 9am–8pm, Sat 10am–1pm*). They will also make house or hotel calls. Before resorting to a *médico* (doctor) and his £60 fee, go to a **pharmacy** and tell them your woes. Spanish *farmacéuticos* are highly skilled and, if there's a medicine that you

now will cure you, they'll often supply it without a doctor's note. *El País* and the other ational newspapers list *farmacías* that stay pen all night; alternatively, outside the door f every pharmacy you'll find the rota listing he nearest ones on duty.

In an **emergency**, ask to be taken to the earest hospital of the '*seguridad social*', all f which have 24-hour casualty (*urgencias*) epartments. Closest to the centre are: Hos-ital Gregorio Marañón, 45 C/ Ibiza, **t** 91 586 o oo (metro O'Donnell; off maps); El Clínico an Carlos, Plaza de Cristo Rey, **t** 91 330 30 00 metro Moncloa; F4); and Ciudad Sanitaria La az, 261 Paseo de la Castellana, **t** 91 727 73 39 metro Begoña; off maps).

nternet

Internet access is available at the following ybercafés:

Euronet, *1 C/ de Mayor, 4th floor,* **t** *91 523 20 9 (metro Sol; I11).* **Open** *daily 10–10.* A real heapie at just €1 an hour with free coffee.

Cibercafé Alamo, *7 C/ del Alamo,* **t** *91 542 82 2 (metro Plaza de España or Noviciado; H9).* **pen** *Mon–Fri 8.30–1am, Sat–Sun noon–1am.* Morning tostadas and croissants, plus aciones, sandwiches and snacks all day long. ccess costs around €1.80 per hour. If they're ull, try the larger, less homely Nevada 2000 cross the street.

Easy Everything, *10 C/ de la Montera,* **t** *91 23 29 44 (metro Sol; J11).* **Open** *24 hours.* rices fluctuate, but are a mere €0.60–2 per o minutes of Internet access.

Navegaweb, *30 Gran Vía,* **t** *91 522 39 14 metro Gran Vía; J10).* **Open** *daily 10–10.* art of massive Telefónica centre with an ourly online osting €1.70. You can also check ut phone books for the whole of Spain here nd make phone calls in relative peace.

Nexusone, *10 C/ Hileras,* **t** *91 559 48 73 metro Opera; H11).* **Open** *daily 10–1am.* here's a good atmosphere here and €2 will uy you an hour online including a drink.

Work Center, *1 C/ de Alberto Aguilera,* *91 448 78 77,* **w** *www.workcenter.es (metro rgüelles; I7).* **Open** *24 hours.* With photo-copying, Internet access, data storage, DHL dropoff, photo developing and more. It's pricey but reliable, and their computers can handle Word, Quark, Photoshop and lots of other programmes. Internet access €6 per hour. There's another branch at 9 C/ Reina Mercedes.

Lost Property

For general lost and found, call **t** 91 588 43 46. Objetos Perdidos, 7 Plaza de Legazpi, **t** 91 588 43 44 (metro Legazpi), is primarily for objects found on the metro or in taxis. If you've lost something on an EMT bus, go to 24 C/ de Alcántara, **t** 91 406 88 10 (metro Lista).

Media

The Socialist *El País* is Spain's biggest and best national **newspaper**. The other big papers are *El Mundo* (the middle-of-the-road challenger that revealed many of the Socialist scandals that *El País* daintily over-looked), *Diario 16* (centrist and good for coverage of the *toros*) and *ABC* (conserva-tive). Two free monthly magazines in English, the *Broadsheet* and the less glossy, free *In Madrid*, offer insights into the city, listings and ads, and are generally available in tourist offices, some kiosks, pubs and language schools. Major British newspapers are widely available, often on the day of publication, along with the American *International Herald Tribune*, the *Wall Street Journal* and the awful *USA Today*.

As for Spanish **TV**, the soaps and dopes and adverts that challenge the USA for sheer excess are great for honing your Spanish if nothing else. Canal Plus is the only hope for anyone looking for decent movies (European and American), as Spanish television is domi-nated, generally, by shameless rip-offs of American and British television programmes that may or may not be so great to begin with.

There are hundreds of **radio** stations in Spain. For Spanish and international pop

music, there is 40 Principales (top 40) at 93.9, Hit Radio at 107 and Cadena Cien at 99.5. Radio Nacional de España is the state-run public radio and has four stations: RNE 1 at 88.2 with current affairs; Radio Clásica at 96.5 with classical music; Radio 3 at 93.2 with rock and pop music; and RNE 5 with sports and entertainment news. Frequencies vary; charts can be found in the back of the Cartelera section of *El País* and in the back of the Madrid sections of most newspapers.

Money, Banks and Taxes

Spain is one of the 12 European Union countries to use a single **currency**, the euro (€). Notes are issued in denominations of 5, 10, 20, 50, 100, 200 and 500 euros.

One euro is divisible by 100 cents, and céntimo coins are issued in denominations of 1, 2, 5, 10, 20 and 50. Euro coins are issued in denominations of 1 and 2 euros, and in Spain you get to admire King Juan Carlos's smile on the flip side of both.

Madrid seems to have a bank on every street corner and most of them will exchange money; look for the '*cambio*' or '*exchange*' signs and the little flags. Most international banks have major branches around the Calle de Alcalá or in the Salamanca district. **Banking hours** in Madrid are Mon–Fri 8.30am–2pm and from October to April the same hours on Saturday. Most will change foreign currency and travellers' cheques from one of the major companies, even if they don't have a sign saying '*cambio*'.

Beware of **exchange offices**, which are conveniently open when banks are not, but often charge a hefty commission on all trans-actions. You can sometimes change money at travel agencies, fancy hotels, restaurants and big department stores. A Eurocheque card will be needed to support your Eurocheques, and even then they may not be welcome.

Credit cards will always be helpful and are accepted in most hotels, shops and restaur-ants (just look for the little signs in the windows). You will usually be asked to show some ID. The handiest way to keep yourself in

cash (and the best exchange rate) is by using the **automatic bank tellers** (*telebancos*) that are on most street corners – check with your bank before leaving to ensure your card can be used in Spain. But don't rely totally on hole-in-the-wall machines as your only source of cash: if, for whatever reason, the machine swallows your card, it can take up to 10 days to retrieve it. If this or some other mishap occurs, there are helplines: American Express, **t** 91 572 03 20 (24-hour); Diner's Club **t** 91 709 59 00; MasterCard/Eurocard, **t** 91 519 21 00; Visa, **t** 900 974 445.

American Express is at 2 Plaza de las Cortes **t** 91 743 77 40 (metro Banco de España; K11; *open Mon–Fri 9–7.30, Sat 9–2*). Besides offering travellers' cheque services, post restante for card-holders and other travel services, Amex is a reliable way to have cash sent from home. A couple of doors down is **Ria Envía**, 4 Plaza de las Cortes, **t** 91 760 13 70, **www.**ecastro@riafinancial.com (metro Banco de España; K11). Open Mon–Sat 10–9pm, Sun 11–7pm. You can wire or receive money to/from 70 different countries. The company has 400 branches throughout Spain and Western Europe.

Value-added tax is known in Spain as the *impuesto sobre el valor añadido*, or IVA, and is levied at 7 per cent on restaurant and hotel bills and 16 per cent on retail goods and car hire. Whenever buying anything, ask if the price includes the IVA – sometimes it does, sometimes it doesn't. Tourists from non-EU countries can claim a refund on any goods purchased in any one store (provided the shop takes part in the scheme, which is voluntary) whose total price exceeds €90, as long as they plan to take them out of the country within three months. Request a VAT (IVA) form, have it stamped by a customs official when you leave Spain or the EU and then mail the stamped document back to the store. Items excluded from the scheme are motor vehicles, boats you intend to sail to a destination outside the EU, goods for busi-ness purposes, bullion, unmounted gemstones, goods requiring an export licence and goods bought by mail order.

Opening Hours and Public Holidays

For bank and post office hours, *see* 'Money, Banks and Taxes' or 'Post and Fax'. **Shops and offices** in Madrid usually open Mon–Fri from 9am to 1 or 2pm, then reopen from 5 or 5.30 until 8 or 8.30pm. Most shops also open on Saturday mornings, while some, like book and record shops, may open on Sundays. More and more larger chain stores are open during the daytime siesta hours, and Corte Inglés, for example, is open on the first Sunday of the month, while its record shop open every Sunday.

The larger **churches** roughly keep shop hours, while the smaller ones are often only open for an hour or two a day. Some may close down altogether in August.

Museums and historical sites tend to follow shop opening hours too, though abbreviated in the winter months; nearly all close on Mondays (except for the Reina Sofía). Seldom-visited ones have a raffish disregard for their official hours, or open only when the mood strikes them. Don't be discouraged: bang on doors and ask around.

The Spanish sensibly try to have as many **public holidays** as possible. On public holidays, banks, offices, shops and many restaurants close, while most museums and public transport go onto Sunday schedules. However, on Christmas Day, Boxing Day and New Year's Day you will find most restaurants and nearly all museums closed. The tourist offices publish a leaflet listing those establishments that remain open – it's best to plan ahead at this time of year and book all meals several days in advance. If you want to eat out on New Year's Eve or Christmas Eve, make sure you book in advance and double-check the reservation on the day.

Packing

For summertime in Madrid, pack light and airy. In winter, the weather can be unpredictable: snow is unlikely, but rain isn't, so

1 Jan	Año Nuevo (New Year's Day)
6 Jan	Epifanía (Epiphany, also known as Reyes for the three kings)
March	Viernes Santo (Good Friday)
1 May	Fiesta del Trabajo (Labour Day)
2 May	Fiesta de la Comunidad de Madrid (Madrid Day)
May/June	Corpus Christi
25 July	Santiago Apóstol (St James's Day)
15 Aug	Asunción (Assumption, also known as Día de la Virgen de la Paloma)
12 Oct	Día de la Hispanidad (Columbus Day)
1 Nov	Día de Todos los Santos (All Saints' Day)
6 Dec	Día de la Constitución (Constitution Day)
8 Dec	Inmaculada Concepción (Immaculate Conception)
25 Dec	Navidad (Christmas Day)

stick some urban foul-weather gear in your bag. Gloves and scarves are a must.

Madrileños are a stylish crowd. It's a great place for dressing up – daring dressers definitely get vocal votes of approval by passersby, though in the more elegant neighborhoods (Retiro, Salamanca, Chamberí) Anglomania reigns – the casual uniform of pressed jeans and Barbour jackets, Lacoste sweater casually slung over the shoulder or tied round the waist. When it is bone-chillingly cold, fur coats and jackets are commonly worn without (it would appear) as much as a peep from animal rights activists. Dark shades are ubiquitous.

Photography

The big-name brands of film are available in Madrid. Disposable cameras are also easily available, but if you buy it in Spain you're best off getting it developed here. The city is filled with photo shops offering fast turn-around and decent-quality service (especially around Sol and Callao), but FNAC, the Corte Inglés and the Work Center (*see* 'Internet', above) are three highly reliable spots.

Post and Fax

The main post office is the Palacio de Comunicaciones on the Plaza de Cibeles (metro Banco de España; L10; *open Mon–Sat 8.30am–9.30pm, Sun 8.30am–2pm*). In central Madrid there are also post offices at a huge number of locations. The standard charge for sending a letter is €0.51 (European Union) and €0.75 (USA). Postboxes, marked '*Correos y Telégrafos*', are yellow; collections are generally Monday to Friday only. Most tobacconists sell stamps (*sellos*) and they'll usually know the correct postage for whatever you're sending. Stationery shops are the best places from which to send faxes.

Smoking

Old habits die hard, and Spain is still a place where you regularly see teenage girls and just about everyone else happily puffing away. Bars are smoke dens, as are restaurants (most of which do not have smoking sections) and public buildings, but things are changing. More often than not, you should ask your taxi driver if you can light up (he is allowed to refuse), and, at last glance, RENFE non-smoking cars were actually free of smoke, a minor miracle considering the nicotine-clogged cars of ten years ago. Vegetarian restaurants are, in general, nonsmoking, though some have smoking and nonsmoking sections. Museums are smoke-free, and lighting up is strictly prohibited. Officially it is prohibited on the subway, but butts abound in and around the tracks.

Students

The Universidad Complutense de Madrid and its Ciudad Universitaria lies in Moncloa, which makes Moncloa and Argüelles fun and lively. The art schools in and around Noviciado make the entire region from Plaza de España up to Moncloa and San Bernardo to the east a student's hunting ground. The neighbourhood is booming with Internet cafés, cheap restaurants and general student life. Two travel agencies are legendary in Madrid for all types of student travel needs, from ISIC Cards to Eurail passes and more:

TIVE, *88 C/ de Fernando el Católico*, **t** *91 543 74 12*, **f** *91 544 00 62*, **e** *tive.juventud@ comadrid.es* (*metro* Argüelles; H6). **Open** *Mon–Fri 9am–2pm*.

Viajes Zeppelin, *2 Plaza Santo Domingo*, **t** *91 542 51 54*, **w** *www.viajeszeppelin.com* (*metro* Santo Domingo or Callao; H10).

Telephones

Spain has a wide network of public phone booths, despite the cellphone craze that has taken over the nation. Local calls are relatively cheap, and it's easy to place international calls from any booth. Many of the old coin-operated phones now only accept **phonecards** (sold in *estancos* and post offices in denominations of €6 and €12). You can also call from metered booths at the Telefónica offices at 28 Gran Vía (J10; *open Mon–Sat 9am–midnight, Sun noon– midnight*), or at the Palacio de Comunicaciones Plaza de Cibeles (L10), during regular post office hours; they are indispensable for reversed charge or collect calls (*cobro revertido*).

Overseas calls from Spain are expensive: calls to the UK cost about €1–2 a minute, to the USA substantially more. Expect to pay a big surcharge if you do any telephoning from your hotel. Cheap rate is Mon–Sat 10pm– 8am and all day Sunday and public holidays.

For calls to Spain from the UK, dial 00 followed by the country code (34), the area code and the number. For international calls from Spain, dial 00, wait for the higher tone and then dial the country code (e.g. 00 44 for the UK, 001 for the USA). All local calls in Madrid require the 91 before them. Telephone numbers in Spain beginning with 900 are free, but those beginning with 901, 902 and 903 carry higher rates; rate information is available by calling **t** 1004 (a free call). For national directory enquiries, call **t** 1003; international directory enquiries, **t** 025.

Time

Spain is an hour ahead of Greenwich Mean Time and six hours ahead of Eastern Standard Time in the USA.

Tipping

Tips in Madrid are welcome, but not really expected. For taxis no tip is necessary, unless large pieces of luggage have been helpfully dealt with. In bars and restaurants, leave between 5 per cent and 10 per cent, and in hotels €1.50–2 a night for the chambermaid.

Toilets

Apart from in bus and train stations, public facilities are rare in Madrid. A few pay toilets are tucked in the Columnas Informativas – those brown plastic imitation Morriss columns covered with advertising. On the other hand, every bar on every corner has a toilet; don't feel uncomfortable using it without purchasing something – the Spaniards do it all the time. Just ask for '*los servicios*'. Disabled toilets, except in a few hotels and museums, don't really exist.

Tourist Offices

Abroad

Before you go, pick up more information from a Spanish National Tourist Office:

Canada: *Suite 3402, 2 Bloor St West, Toronto, Ontario, M4W 3E2, t (416) 961 3131, f 961 1992.*
UK/Ireland: *22–3 Manchester Square, London W1V 3PX, t (020) 7486 8077, f 7486 8034.*
USA: *Suite 956, 8383 Wilshire Bd, Beverly Hills, California, 90211, t (323) 658 7188, f 658 1061; 666 Fifth Av, 35th Floor, New York, NY 10103, t (212) 265 8822, f 265 8865; Water Tower Place, Suite 915 East, 845 N. Michigan Ave, Chicago, Illinois 60611, t (312) 642 1992, f 642 9817; Suite 1850, 1221 Brickell Av, Miami, Florida, 33131, t (305) 358 1992, f 358 8223. General Web site: w www.okspain.org.*

In Madrid

The tourist offices in Madrid are pretty basic. They offer maps and some brochures on typical sightseeing, and give out a free booklet called *En Madrid*, though it's worth the extra €1.50 to buy the *Guía del Ocio*, which is much more complete. They will make phone calls to help with accommodation, but when the offices are busy they will direct you to the accommodation services located in the train stations and airports. There's a general number for the tourist office: **t** 915 40 40 40.

Main tourist office: *2 C/ del Duque de Medinaceli, **t** 91 429 37 05 (**metro** Banco de España; K12). **Open** Mon–Fri 9–7, Sat 9–1.*

Aeropuerto de Barajas: t *91 305 86 56. **Open** Mon–Fri 8–8, Sat 9–1.*

Estación de Chamartín: *Gate 16, **t** 91 315 99 76. **Open** Mon–Fri 8–8, Sat 9–1.*

Mercado Puerta de Toledo: *1 Ronda de Toledo, Stand 3134, **t** 91 364 18 76 (**metro** Puerta de Toledo; H14; let us know if you find it!). **Open** Mon–Fri 9–7, Sat 9.30–1.30.*

City of Madrid office: *3 Plaza Mayor, **t** 91 366 54 77, **t** 91 588 16 36 (**metro** Sol; H12). **Open** Mon–Fri 10–8, Sat 10–3.*

Women Travellers

Women travelling alone in Madrid don't have it so tough. Spanish men, in general, are exceedingly polite and helpful to women. Women alone might think twice about walking at night through neighbourhoods like the area around and north of Gran Vía (especially between Fuencarral and San Bernardo), Tirso de Molina, Lavapiés (especially west of the plaza) and La Latina (especially the area stretching down and radiating off Calle de Toledo). At night-time, it's worth remembering that elegant residential areas such as Salamanca and Retiro become quite lonely as there is virtually no street life. As of summer 2003, the tourist office knew of no women-only residences, but there is such an abundance of good places to stay that this really isn't a problem.

Women's Services Information Line (Instituto de la Mujer): t *91 363 80 00.*

Women's Rape Hotline (Asociación de Asistencia a Mujeres Violadas): t *91 574 01 10.*

Emergency Hotline for Women Victims of Sexual Abuse: t *900 10 02 22.*

Working and Long Stays

Madrid poses fewer problems than most other European cities when it comes to finding work and somewhere to live. Indeed, in a country with more than 20 per cent unemployment, English-speaking foreigners will often find it easier to get started here than Spaniards arriving from the provinces. The capital boasts a substantial ex-pat community, many of whom were lured here in the middle and late 1980s by the *movida*. English-teaching and translating work are not difficult to find, and in a city where eating and drinking is a way of life, there is plenty of work to be found in bars and restaurants. However, Spanish bureaucracy can be tiresome. Anybody thinking seriously about setting up here, even if just for a year or so, should hire the services of a *gestor* – a combination of a solicitor and a public notary – who will deal with all the paperwork involved in registering, your tax return, VAT, driving licence, and even your flat rental. Look in the *Yellow Pages* or ask anybody already living here to recommend somebody.

For visits of under three months, EU, American, Canadian and New Zealand citizens do not require a **visa**. Those intending to stay longer are required by law to register with the police within 15 days of arrival to begin the process of obtaining a *permiso de residencia*, or residency permit. The police office dealing with foreigners' registration is located at the Comisaria de Extranjería at 9 C/ de los Madrazo (K11), **t** 91 521 93 50. To work legally, you must have a residency permit.

If you do not have a firm offer of work, or better still, a contract, then you must either show proof of being able to support yourself during your stay, or register as an *autonomo*, or self-employed. Again, the first step is the *permiso de residencia*. You then head for the tax office, where you will have to declare the nature of your profession.

American citizens be warned. It is best to consult the Spanish consulate in your home town or state. Otherwise you may have to make a return trip for such documents as a statement from the local police vouching for your good conduct.

Flat shares can be found on notice boards in the city's numerous Irish pubs, vegetarian restaurants, alternative theatres and student travel agencies (*see* 'Students', p.68), as well as in *Segundamano* – a thrice-weekly publication offering all types of rented accommodation, jobs and secondhand goods, also located at **w** *www.segundamano.es*

Increasingly, landlords ask either for a *nomina* (work contract) or an *aval bancario*, proof from your bank that you can pay the rent; one month in advance and a month's deposit is the norm. Contracts are legally valid for a five-year stay, renewable on a yearly basis at your discretion. Anybody stipulating a shorter period than five years is liable to offer a discount. Rents can only legally be increased on a yearly basis, in accordance with inflation. Again, if you are thinking about a long stay, a *gestor* will check the contract for you.

Old Madrid

Old Madrid

Squeezed into a tight half-kilometre between the Puerta del Sol and the Palacio Real is a solid, enduring Castilian town known as 'El Madrid de los Austrias', because most of it was built under the reign of those most prodigious of Austrian expats, the Habsburgs. Many of the streets and squares follow the town plan of the original Moorish settlement, and the buildings have changed little since Goya painted the city's delicate skyline of cupolas and spires in the 18th century.

Neither menaced by modern office blocks nor done up picture-pretty for the tourists, the quarter has enjoyed the best of possible fates – to remain as it was. Traditionally home to the Spanish nobility (look out for the plaques on the buildings), the area has profited from the economic boom in recent decades and has seen major refurbishment

1 Lunch

Botín, *17 C/ de Cuchilleros*, **t** *91 366 42 17*, **t** *91 366 30 26*; **metro** *Sol*. **Open** *daily 1–4 and 8–midnight*. **Expensive**. According to the *Guinness Book of Records*, it's the oldest restaurant in the world, founded in 1725; 19-year-old Goya worked in the evening washing dishes here. Justly renowned for its beautiful original interior and roasts.

2 Tea and Cakes

El Riojano, *10 C/ Mayor*, **t** *91 366 44 82*; **metro** *Sol*. Just a few steps from Sol, this charming shrine to cream puffery is nothing less than the purveyor of fine traditional pastries to Spain's senators since 1885.

3 Drinks

Casa Labra, *12 C/ de Tetuán*, **t** *91 531 00 81*; **metro** *Sol*; *wheelchair accessible*. **Open** *Mon–Sat 11–3.30 and 5.30–11*. One of the oldest surviving bar-tabernas in this area, founded in 1860, Casa Labra gets a mention in Spanish history books as the spot where the Spanish Socialist Party was founded in 1879.

of grand old *palacetes*. The neighbourhood is now home to Madrid's young, beautiful-people set – those who can afford the outrageous prices. The place is still a living neighbourhood, loud, busy and a bit unkempt, perhaps, but still Madrid's best and cosiest refuge from the cosmopolitan noise of the rest of the city. As you wander, don't miss the ceramic street signs, many of which illustrate the often quaint names of the lanes.

For a walk through this area, taking in some of the more, and less, traditional bars, see 'A Bar and Tapas Walk', p.174.

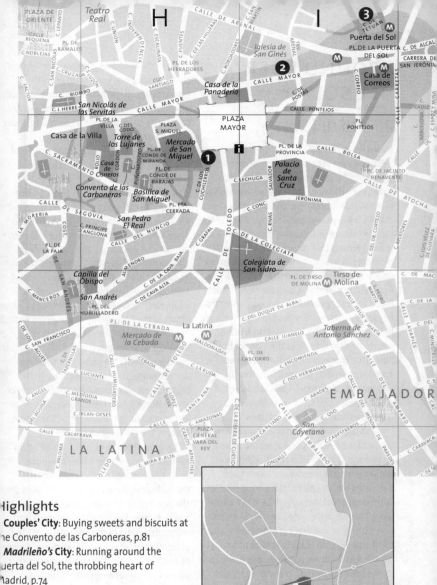

Highlights

Couples' City: Buying sweets and biscuits at the Convento de las Carboneras, p.81

Madrileño's City: Running around the Puerta del Sol, the throbbing heart of Madrid, p.74

Indoor City: The Capilla del Obispo, the city's Renaissance jewel, p.82

Outdoor City: A coffee in elegant Plaza Mayor, the prototype for all the other courtly squares in Spain, pp.76–7

Goya's City: Botín, the restaurant where Goya once did the washing-up, p.78

Architectural City: The lovely Baroque Basílica de San Miguel, p.80

All grid references in this chapter refer to the map above

AROUND PUERTA DEL SOL

Puerta del Sol I–J11

Metro Puerta del Sol.

Everyone agrees that Sol remains the centre of all things in Madrid if not in all Spain, even if it now holds the position in the same slightly obsolete manner as the sun does in the centre of the universe. Ten streets radiate from here, including some of the grand avenues that have witnessed crucial moments in the city's life: Alcalá and Carrera de San Jerónimo to the east, Mayor and Arenal to the west. It is also the nerve-centre for all forms of public transport: three metro lines and dozens of bus lines rumble through here; however you're travelling in Madrid, you're soon likely to cross the 'Gate of the Sun'. Little that is *auténtico* in Madrid ever strays far from Sol; jammed into this tight-knit district of narrow streets are scores of curious shops and family businesses that have been running for generations.

To the uninitiated the name conjures up a vision of the Great Inca or at least a clever ploy of the Spanish Tourist Office, but no: in the walls of 1478 there was a tower gate decorated with a relief of the sun, and hence Sol, though local lore affirms that the name is a reflection of the gate's eastward orienta-tion. Both gate and walls are long gone, and the great elliptical plaza is as chaotic and crowded as it always has been, but it endears itself to the *madrileños* in a way no formal plaza with a postcard view ever could.

When the gate and walls went down in 1539, new streets uncoiled like springs to the east, making Sol the centre of an intricate cat's cradle – old Madrid was never blessed nor cursed by planning, and its webs are organic and on a very human scale. You can walk to many of the old city gates, perhaps Puerta de Toledo to the south or Puerta de Alcalá to the east, in 10 to 15 minutes. And, until 1860, all of Madrid fitted inside.

When the medieval gate was demolished, this big space was soon filled up with monasteries, market stalls and taverns, none of which has survived. The plaza began to take on its current appearance in 1810 under Joseph Bonaparte, who demolished the monasteries, chased out market stalls and began the plans that doubled the size of the square.

Most of the new buildings featured large fashionable cafés on their ground floors, which made the Puerta del Sol the liveliest place in Madrid in the 19th century – a centre not only for gossip, but also for the revolts and demonstrations that convulsed the city. The most famous (thanks to Goya's remark-able painting) took place on 2 May 1808, when Napoleon's Egyptian Mameluke cavalry attacked the rioting mob that had gravitated here. A happier impromptu gathering occurred on 14 April 1931 when the municipal elections swept in Republican candidates across Spain – the expectant crowds that massed here were enough to make Alfonso XIII abdicate. When the Republic was announced from the balcony of the Casa de Correos, the cheering rocked the city.

The most recent modifications of Sol, in 1986, saw a new pedestrian area in the centre illuminated by the 'suppositories' – the nickname the *madrileños* bestowed on the new lighting fixtures, until the city cracked under the weight of mockery and reinstalled some of the originals – and the placement of an equestrian **statue of Charles III**. Madrid's greatest royal benefactor is set up on a plinth between two fountains, smiling at his Casa de Correos with his hand outstretched, as if to feed the pigeons. His presence dwarfs the sculpture of the **Oso y Madroño** ('bear and strawberry tree'; *see* 'Bear Necessities') at the mouth of Calle de Carmen. This small, unshowy bronze, a low-key symbol of community identity, is now a favourite spot for petition signings, buskers and a few prostitutes, spilling over from the red light district along Calle de la Montera. If you happen to be in Madrid on New Year's Eve, this is *the* place to be at midnight.

Bear Necessities

Madrid's emblem is the bear and strawberry tree, a totem that you'll see everywhere, from weathervanes down to the old sewer lids. Where the city found such a peculiar emblem, however, is a rather sticky subject. Most sources explain the bear, the older symbol (it appeared on a wax seal for the first time in 1381, although with a tower instead of a tree), by saying there were once plenty of them around Madrid. One bear in particular, an enormous specimen killed by King Alfonso XI in the late 13th century, made such an impression that it is recorded in his biography, or *Crónica*. There is some doubt, however, that the king's bear is precisely *the* bear, which, according to a petition from the city to Emperor Charles V in 1548, is not an *oso* but an *osa*, a she bear, a heraldic symbol of fertility – in particular ursine fertility, meaning more big game, which was Madrid's big attraction for the kings of Castile in the first place.

As for the strawberry tree or *Arbutus unedo*, the fact that *madroño* (its name in Spanish) has the same first syllable as Madrid more likely than not explains it all; all the other cities of Castile had castles or towers on their arms, so Madrid adopted a tree just to be different. This is a pretty boring story so over the years better ones have arisen. Some say that Madrid once had forests of these little evergreen bushes (it now has three bushes, to be precise, two in front of the building at 4 Calle del Madroño, near the bullring, and one in the Real Jardín Botánico), and that bears, when their eyes hurt, seek out strawberry trees to rub them against the prickly exterior of the tree's fruit. Others say that in the Middle Ages the leaves of the strawberry tree were considered a remedy for the plague, which is why the bear seems to be licking the tree as if it were a giant lollipop. Or that in the 13th century, when Madrid was being divided into parishes, the town and the clergy went to court over ownership of some land, and it was parcelled out in a curious fashion: the Church got the meadows and the town got all the land under the trees. The Madrid clergy, they say, had a bear grazing in a field for its emblem, while the city bear loves its trees.

The seven stars from the constellation of the Big Dipper or Plough or Great Bear, Ursa Major, were added much later, under Charles V in 1544. According to the document that made the symbol official, the stars merely symbolized the beautiful clear sky over the city, but others will have it that the stars of the constellation were rearranged to form a crown, hence the city's fancy title Coronado Villa de Madrid.

Paris Hotel J11

As the showcase of the nation, the Puerta del Sol saw Spain's first gas lights (1830), the first tramline (1871, pulled by mules), its first electric street lamps (1906), the first line of the city's metro (1919) and its most famous Tio Pepe sign, still in situ on top of the city's first luxury hotel, the Paris, which still has a faded, if shabby, air of grandeur. A plaque commemorates La Nueva Montaña, a famous literary café that once occupied the hotel's ground floor, where Galician playwright Ramón del Valle-Inclán lost his arm in an opera-buff duel.

Casa de Correos I11

Filling up the south end of the big square, Madrid's first post office, the Casa de Correos, is the oldest surviving building in Sol, built in 1768 by the 'mayor-king' Charles III. Ancient Rome had a Golden Milestone, from where all distances in the empire were determined; likewise Madrid has its Kilometro Cero in front of the door of the Casa de Correos, from where all distances in the nation are measured, a custom established by Philip V (although the current marker dates from 1950). Plaques on the Casa de Correos itself commemorate the victims of the Mameluke sabres, and the fact that you are 650.7m above sea level.

Just don't try to buy a stamp here: the building lost its postal purpose in 1847, when it became the Ministry of the Interior. Under Franco, the shadowy presence of the goons within led to the eclipse of Sol's lively cafés. Much of what occurred inside these walls under the dictatorship will remain unknown until Judgement Day, although the whole world knew of an event that happened just outside them in 1963, when Communist-agitator Julián Grimau was tossed from an upper window. He survived, only to be kept alive to meet a firing squad, in spite of inter-national protests. The building now houses the Comunidad de Madrid, Madrid's regional government.

The **clock** on top of the Casa de Correos was added as an afterthought in 1866 and has come to be regarded as Spain's official timepiece. On New Year's Eve, crowds come here to watch the clock for the countdown to midnight. They come bearing fireworks and grapes, one grape to be gobbled per stroke of the bell, to ensure luck throughout the year. Although architectural purists have always found fault with the little clock tower, it was rebuilt from scratch just as it was when it was at the point of collapse in 1996.

Palacio de Santa Cruz I12

1 Plaza de la Privincia; metro Sol.

Just to the southwest of Puerta del Sol stands another major Habsburg monument. Commissioned by Philip IV, the Palacio de Santa Cruz (1629) was designed by Juan Gómez de Mora in the El Escorial-inspired *estilo desornamentado*, with the de rigueur Herrera slate towers and pinnacles, although with a decorative frontispiece that softens its Herreran austerities. It's now the Foreign Ministry, but it may come as a surprise to know that it was built originally as a prison. Noble inmates were treated to cells with gilded bars, while those without a pedigree rotted in the oblivion of its lightless dungeons.

AROUND PLAZA MAYOR

Plaza Mayor H–I12

Metro Sol or Opera.

Like many a front parlour, the Plaza Mayor these days is mainly used for receiving visi-tors, while the family prefers the more lived-in streets around its sides. These are lined with funny old shops that leave you wondering just how many Spaniards collect miniature soldiers and old medals: their numbers must be legion.

This plaza was a scruffy market square in the time of Philip II, who seems to have been the first to come up with the idea that it might be something that better fitted the dignity of his new capital city. In 1532, he offi-cially baptised it as Madrid's Plaza Mayor and wasted little time in celebrating the event by holding the city's first bullfights within its walls. He got his favourite architect, Juan de Herrera, to make a few preliminary sketches, but the project went into abeyance until Philip III hired Juan Gómez de Mora to build newer, bigger plaza. Work began in 1617, and in 1620 the unveiling was held to coincide with the beatification of San Isidro, patron saint of the city. After several fires, the plaza achieved its present form in 1811 under the hand of Herrera's great disciple, Juan de Villanueva, who made his designs accommo-date the Casa de la Panadería, which survive the blazes.

Madrid's Plaza Mayor went on to become the great prototype for many *plaza mayores* across Spain: an enclosed, rectangular space surrounded by arcaded walks under build-ings, all more or less the same height, that resemble walls of a single structure and give the impression of a building turned inside out. Such a square counts for much more than just a knot in a tangle of streets: it is like a stage in the theatre, where public life can be acted out with proper Spanish dignity. The analogy to a stage is no accident, for

heatres of the Golden Age were perfect little *laza mayores*, with balconies all around and the proscenium at the narrow end.

The equestrian king in the centre is **Philip** **III**, a statue designed by Juan de Bolonia and Pietro Tacca. Much of the time His Majesty looks at sea amid the white plastic market stalls selling stamps and coins in spring and Christmas trees and trinkets in winter. Only when the plaza is blessedly empty of tents does he seem in command of his kingdom. Subsequent kings of Spain were crowned here, before a capacity audience of 50,000, and they would often return here to preside over fiestas, bullfights, carnivals, anachronistic but much loved knightly tournaments and the Inquisition's autos-da-fé, colourful public spectacles preceded by much pageantry and preaching, before the unlucky ones were led off to the stake.

In 1680, the last and biggest auto-da-fé in Spain's history was staged in the Plaza Mayor by the insane Charles II, a 14-hour affair that tried 120 backsliders and fried 21 alive. The bullfights that took place here lasted nearly as long and were almost as dangerous; one that took place in 1619 resulted in five fatalities, which evoked the comment in the chronicles of the time that the bulls that day were very well behaved.

Casa de la Panadería H–I11

Whenever a major spectacle took place in the Plaza Mayor, the city council would rent the balconies around the square from their owners to seat the distinguished visitors. Kings traditionally took their places in the elegant building with twin spires on the north side of the plaza, the Casa de la Panadería (1590), so called after the bakery that preceded it on the site. Its façade was decorated with murals in the late 17th century, and was decorated again in 1992 by Carlos Franco in a colourful baroque groovy neo-hippie celebration of Madrid, leaving the city's few historic preservationists gnashing their teeth in impotent rage.

Calle de Toledo H12–14

***Metro** La Latina.*

Calle de Toledo runs south from the Plaza Mayor and offers up several quirky old shops – one, the always crowded **Casa Hernanz**, at No.18, sells every conceivable kind of rope and espadrilles; another peddles teeny tiny gold flamenco shoes for babies. On the opposite end of the scale, the **Corsetería** (No.49) claims to offer the largest underwear in Spain, and, when inspiration strikes, they put on window displays that could be your most memorable vision in Madrid. Then there's **Caramelos Paco** (No.55), with a window display that is nothing less than the Sistine Chapel of boiled sweets.

Colegiata de San Isidro H–I12

*37–39 C/ de Toledo, **t** 91 369 20 37; **metro** La Latina. **Open** Mon–Sat 7.30–1 and 6.30–8, Sun and hols 8.30–2.30 and 5.30–8. No visitors during morning Mass (varying times); **adm** free.*

The biggest building on Calle de Toledo is the twin-towered church of San Isidro, which served as the city's stand-in cathedral until 1992, when the Almudena took over. Founded by a special bequest from Philip IV's wife, Mariana of Austria, this gloomy pile was begun in 1620 as the church of the Colegio Imperial. For a century it served as the Jesuit central headquarters in Spain, where the subtle doctors schooled the brightest stars of Spain's Golden Age: Calderón de la Barca, Lope de Vega and Francisco de Quevedo. The elaborate Churrigueresque façade was added later.

When Charles III sent the Jesuits packing in 1767, the church was rededicated to Madrid's humble but much beloved patron saint, Isidro, a 12th-century ploughman of exceptional piety. He was famous for his ability to find water, but is usually depicted in art lost in prayer, while two angels pop down from heaven to do the ploughing for him. His wife, María de la Cabeza, and their son, the hermit Millán (or Illán), have also been canonized, a record matched only by the

The Inquisition

Besides bullfighting and flamenco, the Inquisition is one of the things Spain is most famous for, an essential part of the 'Black Legend' of the dark days of Philip II. There's nothing to debunk and no need for a historical re-examination: the Inquisition was just as bloody and stupid and horrible as the Protestant propagandists of the day said it was. But what made them do it? Not surprisingly, the original motives were largely political. Ferdinand and Isabel re-introduced the Inquisition in 1480 as an institution entirely under the control of the Crown, and they used it as a means to suppress dissent; with their powers strictly limited under the secular laws, they turned to the Church courts as a way to get at their enemies. Originally, under the direction of a passionate ascetic, the famous Torquemada, the Inquisition's victims were nearly all *conversos*, baptized Jews with wealth or important positions in government or Church. Any of them found guilty of backsliding in the faith would have their property confiscated – if they weren't burnt at the stake. Much of this booty went to finance the wars against the Moors of Granada.

In the decades that followed, though, the Inquisition took on a life of its own. From the 1530s on, with the Catholic powers in a panic over the onset of the Reformation, a succession of Inquisitors much worse than Torquemada expanded the Holy Office to every city, with a corps of secret agents and investigators estimated at 20,000. Though terror of it spread to every household, application was crazily inconsistent; the Inquisition saw nothing wrong with the opinions of Copernicus, but sent hundreds of poor souls to the stake for reading the Bible in Spanish instead of Latin. Neither did the

original Holy Family. Isidro and María's remains are still over the high altar, imprisoned in the basilican gloom, although in memory of Isidro's skill as a dowser they are taken out on a tour of Madrid whenever it suffers from drought.

Plaza de la Puerta Cerrada and Calle de los Cuchilleros H12

Metro *La Latina.*

The Plaza Nueva crossroads just up from San Isidro merge to the west into the **Plaza de la Puerta Cerrada**, 'the closed gate'. When the old walls were still standing, this was officially known as 'the dragon gate', although it was rarely open because its design allowed robbers easily to ambush passers-by. The cross in the plaza is one of the last of hundreds that once stood in the streets of Madrid. They were removed in the 19th century because of the profane things people did to them; this one survived because it stops up a water pipe, even though many tourists mistakenly think it's a monument to the Civil War.

Plaza de la Puerta Cerrada is an essential crossroads on Madrid's gastronomic map. Here you'll find traditional *mesones* (some slightly touristy) serving up hearty Castilian fare, especially down along picturesque **Calle de la Cava Baja** and up **Calle de los Cuchilleros**, amid beautifully restored flats from the 19th century. At 17 C/ de Cuchilleros **Botín**, founded in 1725, is the oldest restaurant in the world, according to the *Guinness Book of Records*. Nineteen-year-old Goya worked in the evening washing dishes here when he first arrived in Madrid from his native Zaragoza, and it features, as the plaque reads, in a scene in the classic 19th-century novel about Madrid, *Fortunata y Jacinta*, by Benito Pérez Galdós.

Part way along Calle de los Cuchilleros is the **Arco de los Cuchilleros**, with its great stone staircase cascading operatically down from the Plaza Mayor. The *cuchilleros*, or knife-makers, for whom the street and arch are named, traditionally sold their sharp-tooled wares on this corner, between the butchers and the blacksmiths. At the top of

earned inquisitors care much for witch-unting after the late 1500s. The following entury saw an estimated 30,000 unfortu-ates burned for witchcraft in Britain, against almost none in Spain. Still, there vere victims enough to be found among the hristians. The first decade of the renewed nquisition (after 1478) was thorough – 5,200 ictims in Toledo alone in a single year, 1486. fter the Jews and freethinkers were dealt vith, the Inquisition began to look for new argets just to keep itself in business. lasphemy went under their jurisdiction in he 1490s, and some secular crimes in 1517. At s height, the Holy Office became a state vithin the state, answerable to no one and ependent on continuous terror to keep its nembers in jobs.

Despite its cumbersome bureaucracy and a reat pretence of legalism, the Inquisition vas little better than a kangaroo court.

Anyone denounced (even if it were by playful children) had a good chance of spending several years in solitary confinement while the Holy Office decided his or her case. Few were ever cleared, and even if they were they and their families were tainted forever. Torture was almost universal – as every-where else in Europe in that grim age – and after it the accused would be lucky to get let off with a public recantation, a flogging and the loss of all his property. Autos-da-fé ('works of faith') were colourful public spec-tacles, preceded by much pageantry and preaching, where sentences were given out, before the unlucky ones, dressed in capes decorated with flames and devils and bearing signboards explaining their crimes, were led off to the stake. The last, and biggest, was a 14-hour affair with 120 victims, personally staged in Madrid's Plaza Mayor in 1680 by the insane Charles II.

---

he street on the corner of Calle Mayor cands the charmingly rickety glass-and-iron-vork **Mercado de San Miguel**, painted a retty acqua. All of the city's markets origi-ally looked like this one, built in 1835 and ompleted in 1916, but have since been eplaced by more solid, if less aesthetically leasing, structures.

Calle Mayor G12–I11

Metro Sol.

For centuries, Calle Mayor was the main treet of Madrid, linking the Puerta del Sol to he original fortress, or Alcázar. At No.59, here's a rare Art Nouveau building (the style eally never caught on in Madrid) dating back o 1914. It houses one of the city's oldest oncerns, the **Real Farmacia de la Reina Madre**, founded as an alchemist's in 1578 and lled with blue and white apothecary jars om the 17th century and later. Its name omes from the highly strung Isabel Farnese, econd queen of Philip V, who always btained her potions here rather than in the oyal pharmacies for fear of being poisoned y her stepson. To the right, the very narrow

house at **No.61** has a plaque commemorating the playwright Pedro Calderón de la Barca, who died here in 1681, while the modern building opposite replaces the house that was the first home of his rival, Lope de Vega, who was born there in 1562, after his deter-mined mother tracked down his scalliwag father all the way from Valladolid.

At **84 C/ Mayor**, an upper balcony (above Casa Ciriaco) witnessed one of Madrid's most sensational assassination attempts, in 1906. A certain Mateo Morral tossed a bouquet down on the wedding procession of King Alfonso XIII and his bride Victoria Eugenia. The flowers hid a bomb, which killed some 26 bystanders but left its royal targets unscathed. Eyewitness accounts give the blood-spattered king credit for taking control of the situation and calming spirits. A bronze angel by the church of the Sacramento oppo-site commemorates the victims.

Plaza de la Villa H12

Metro Opera.

Plaza de la Villa started out as the Moorish souk and the first main square of Madrid.

It is dignified by some of the city's oldest buildings, as well as a statue of Philip II's most successful admiral, Alvaro de Bazán, who helped to win Spain glory at the Battle of Lepanto against the Turks in 1571, and who was spared from going down with the Invincible Armada by dying before his fleet left Portugal.

Casa de la Villa H12

Guided tours (in Spanish, for English call ahead) Mon at 5pm – meet at 5 Plaza de la Villa, t 91 588 10 00; adm free.

Now that the cars have been exiled from the plaza, you can fearlessly enjoy Madrid's distinguished city hall, the Casa de la Villa, designed by Gómez de Mora in his old age, although his original 1599 design of Herreran simplicity was corrupted by Baroque flourishes over the doors and on the tower by the architects who completed it in 1696.

The Monday guided tour (reports are that it's not the most interesting tour ever) is your one chance to visit the **Salón de Sesiones** (council chambers), where the elected officials of Madrid deliberate in a setting of unmatched parliamentary splendour, under a *trompe l'oeil* Baroque ceiling by Antonio Palomino. Another attraction is the enormous painting of *The Third of May* (1872) by Parmorli, a panorama of the city at dawn; in the foreground the women lamenting the dead from the famous uprising and soon-to-be-executed offer a hint that all is not well. There's also a copy of Goya's famous *Allegory of Madrid*, the original now in the Museo Municipal (*see* p.160).

Torre de los Lujanes H12

Opposite the Casa de la Villa, the Torre de los Lujanes, with its tri-lobed Gothic portal, Mudéjar arch and neighbouring palace, is the only secular complex to survive from 15th-century Madrid, although one that was very, very restored in 1910. Its plaque tells us that it was the birthplace of Federico Chueca, the '*castizo* prodigy of Madrid music', and, according to legend, it once served as a prison for no less a personage than King François I of France. This monarch, bitterest enemy of Charles V and Habsburg ambition, was captured at the Battle of Pavia in Italy in 1525. He spent a few months as Charles's unwilling guest in Madrid, and won his release by signing a treaty and agreeing to marry Charles' sister; once safely over the border, he said it was all a joke, and he and Charles were at war for most of the next 20 years.

Casa Cisneros H12

Guided tours (in Spanish only) Mon at 5pm; adm free.

The Casa Cisneros (1537) occupies the south end of the plaza, and is linked by a 'Venetian bridge' of 1915 to the Casa de la Villa. It was built for the nephew of the famous cardinal and now houses José María Alvarez del Manzano, the Partido Popular mayor of Madrid, who boasts that he keeps a crucifix in his office and otherwise spends much of his time worrying that his fellow citizens might be having too much fun. He is also famous for peppering the city with ugly outdoor statues. The Calle del Sacramento side of Casa Cisneros is a fine example of yet another Spanish national style, the Plateresque; note the intricate filigree detail and splendid doorway. Much of what you now see is the result of the 1909 Neo-Plateresque restoration; only the façades on Calle del Cordón and Calle del Sacramento are original.

Basílica de San Miguel H1

4 C/ de San Justo, t 91 548 40 11; metro Sol or La Latina. Open Mon–Sat 10–2 and 6–9, Sun 10–2.30 and 6–9.

Just round the corner stands the late 17th-century Basílica de San Miguel, a Baroque jewel by Italian Giacomo Bonavía, designed for the Archbishop of Toledo, Don Luis, who probably would have preferred a toy: he was only five at the time. While most Spanish churches of the period are only cosmetically Baroque, this basilica has Baroque bones, with its convex façade and undulating

terior. The busiest chapel in the basilica is
dedicated to José María Escrivá de Balaguer,
the founder of Opus Dei in 1928, who, amid
some controversy, was recently beatified by
John Paul II.

The basilica, run by Opus Dei priests, is not
a parish church and doesn't pertain to the
bishopric of Madrid, but rather to the
nunciatura, which answers directly to the
Pope. On spring and summer weekends, the
church steps tend to be strewn with flower
petals and extravagantly dressed *madrileños*
attending weddings of the city's smart set.

Convento de las Carboneras H12

*del Codo; **metro** Sol or La Latina. **Open** daily
30–1 and 4–6.30; press 'Monjas' on the
intercom.*

The early 17th-century Convento de las
Carboneras ('convent of the coal bins', so called
for a painting of the Virgin discovered in one,
leading to the building of the church) has a
nondescript brick façade facing the sadly
modernized Plaza del Conde de Miranda, at
the end of the Calle del Codo. Once buzzed in,
you'll walk through a series of stone patios
until reaching the cloistered nuns, who sell
their biscuits and sweets on a revolving drum
that preserves their privacy. This is one of only
two convents in Madrid that still supports
itself in this centuries-old fashion; the cloistered nuns at the Monasterio de la Natividad,
for instance, have traded in their rolling pins
for computers, and do the accounts for the
Corte Inglés department stores.

San Nicolás de los Servitas G11

*Plaza de San Nicolás, **t** 91 559 40 64; **metro**
Ópera. **Open** Mon 8–1.30 and 5.30–8.30,
Tues–Sat 8–9.30 and 6.30–8.30, Sun 9.30–2
and 6.30–9; **guided tours** can be arranged by
calling in advance.*

To the west along Calle Mayor from Plaza
de la Villa, Calle de San Nicolás leads shortly

to San Nicolás de los Servitas, the oldest
surviving church in Madrid, with its minaret-
like Mudéjar tower from the 12th century. The
church is believed to sit upon the site of an
old mosque and, according to some, its
minaret is actually preserved inside the
tower. If you come when it's open, inside you
will find a fine example of intricate
Mudéjar carving.

AROUND PLAZA DE LA PAJA

Plaza de la Paja G12

***Metro** La Latina.*

Attractive, irregular Plaza de la Paja (Straw
Square) was once, in spite of its name, the
most aristocratic square in medieval Madrid,
lined with proud palaces, nearly all of which
were torn down in the 19th century. Only the
large **Palacio de los Vargas** survives, after a
fashion, with a pseudo-medieval façade
trying to disguise the fact that it was rebuilt
in the 1920s and is now home to a school
rather than to the powerful family who once
hosted Isabel la Católica. The seated bronze
man in front reads the slogan that you may
have already noticed elsewhere, '*Entre Todos
Rehabilitamos Madrid*'; the city's rehabilitation squads have already led to a rebirth of
interest in this quiet, genteel corner of town.

Parroquia de San Andrés G13

*1 Plaza de San Andrés, **t** 91 365 48 71; **metro**
La Latina. **Open** Mon–Sat 8–1 and 5.30–8.*

Plaza de la Paja's church, San Andrés, typical
of the blank, severe style of Madrid's older
parishes, was burnt during the Civil War, and
recently restored: only the bell tower survives
from the original. The church's most significant claim to fame is its connection to
Madrid's patron saint, San Isidro Labrador,
who is said to have prayed here frequently
and was buried in its cemetery. His powers of

healing were known throughout the land:
legend has it that when King Philip III was on
his deathbed he ordered the saint's undeteri-
orated body to be delivered to his bedside.
After being placed between the sheets with
the saint, the King apparently was cured.

Capilla del Obispo H13

*9 Plaza de la Paja, with the entrance round
the back; metro La Latina.*

Behind San Andrés, on Costanilla San
Andrés, the splendid Capilla del Obispo
(Bishop's Chapel) luckily escaped the flames
of the Civil War and survives remarkably
intact. Designed in the 1540s as a pantheon
for the family of Don Francisco de Vargas,
Councillor to Ferdinand and Isabel and their
grandson Charles V, it is the finest
Renaissance work in Madrid, although even
at that late date the chapel's vaulting is
flamboyant Gothic. The intricate Plateresque
carvings, chapel furnishings, family tombs
(especially the alabaster monument of the
Bishop of Plasencia, covered with delightful
musical angels) and the stupendous gilded
high altar soaring to the ceiling, attributed to
Francisco Giralte, a pupil of Alonso
Berruguete, are the finest in Madrid.

Next door, restoration continues on the
façade of the lavish Baroque **Capilla de San
Isidro**, with its heavy ornate cornice; originally it held the relics of Madrid's patron, San
Isidro, which were long privately owned by
the Vargas family. Its Baroque dome was
added after Isidro's canonization in 1620. The
chapel was badly damaged in 1936, but the
sumptuous interior of polychrome marbles
and gilding has been recently restored. In
1769, Charles III had San Isidro's remains
moved to the Jesuit church on Calle de
Toledo and, as compensation, offered to
bump the San Andrés parish up a notch to
the category of royal parish, but the outraged
parish priest refused on principle.

San Pedro el Real H12

Costanilla de San Pedro; metro La Latina.

Here you'll find one of Madrid's two
surviving Mudéjar towers (the other is on
San Nicolás de los Servitas; *see* p.81); this one
is from the 14th century and attached to the
little church of San Pedro el Real, which was
built on the site of a mosque. The dirty beige
interior, jammed with a hodge-podge of
shrines, electric candles and old inscriptions
embedded in its pillars, is one of the most
frequented in Madrid. A statue of Jesus
wearing the crown of thorns, with a wooden
toe protruding through the glass case for
kissing, is the big draw, but don't miss the
processional float in the chapel on the left,
with its tractor steering wheel peeking out
from under the drapery.

Basílica de San Francisco el Grande G13

*Plaza de San Francisco, t 91 365 38 00; metro
Puerta de Toledo or La Latina. Open summer
Tues–Sat 11–1 and 5–8, winter Tues–Sat 11–1
and 4–6.30; adm €3 with guided tour.*

Madrid's largest church lives up to its big
name, topped with a dome measuring 108ft
in diameter and radiating chapels similar to
the Pantheon. It's built on the site of a
modest hermitage founded in the late 1200s,
perhaps by St Francis himself. In the 18th
century the order became wealthy enough to
build this oppressive gloomy pile, but there's
little more to say for it, except that it has an
early Goya, *San Bernardino of Siena*, in the
chapel of the same saint.

A separate entrance to the right leads into
the **Capilla del Cristo de los Dolores**, a fine
work of the 1660s, while a plaque on the left
is one of the last in Madrid referring to
Franco, who inaugurated the ungracious
busy street in front. Note the handsome
apartment building in coloured brick, opposite, at the beginning of Calle de la Calatrava.

Royal Madrid

Royal Madrid

Madrid was founded, in part, because of the strategic value of this easily defensible ridge over the Río Manzanares. The Moors built their castle, or *alcázar*, here in the 9th century. Under the Christian kings, this *alcázar* would go through countless alterations and refurbishments, until much to Philip V's delight it caught on fire and could be replaced by an elephantine royal palace. Throughout the ages, the royal presence here was a magnet for other prestigious institutions, including two remarkable convents, the Senate, opera house and most recently Madrid's cathedral.

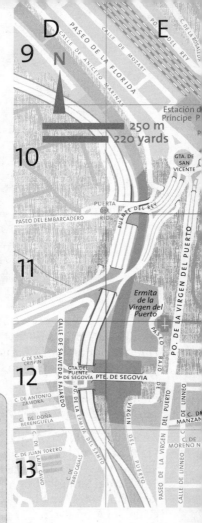

1 Lunch

La Bola, *5 C/ de la Bola,* **t** *91 547 69 30;* **metro** *Opera or Santo Domingo; wheelchair accessible.* **Open** *Mon–Sat 1–4 and 8.30–11, Sun 1–4. Cash only.* **Inexpensive**. Known for its peculiar version of *cocido madrileño* – served in a clay urn – La Bola's old-world interior is very much the place for a hearty meal on a cold winter's evening.

2 Tea and Cakes

Café Vergara, *1 C/ de Vergara,* **t** *91 559 11 72;* **metro** *Opera.* **Open** *Sun–Thurs 8am–midnight, Fri–Sat 8am–2am.* Welcoming, cushiony banquettes, mirrors and pretty portraits on the walls make this worthy of basking in the shadow of the Teatro Real across the street.

3 Drinks

El Anciano, *19 C/ de Bailén;* **metro** *Opera.* **Open** *Thurs–Tues 11–4 and 6–midnight.* With vermouth on tap and, as expected, a dizzying array of wines. An old-world atmosphere on a shady corner across the street from the Palacio Real.

Highlights

Couples' City: Attending a performance at
the Teatro Real, p.89

Madrileño's City: Lounging on a café terrace
in Plaza de Oriente, p.89

Indoor City: The museum of the Real
Monasterio de las Descalzas Reales, the
wealthiest convent in Christendom, p.91

Outdoor City: Watching the changing of
the guard in Plaza de la Armería, p.86

Goya's City: The royal portraits in the
Palacio Real, p.87

Architectural City: The church of the Real
Monasterio de la Encarnación, p.90

All grid references in this chapter refer
to the map above

AROUND THE PALACIO REAL

Palacio Real (Palacio de Oriente) G10–11

*C/ de Bailén, t 91 454 88 00; **metro** Opera; wheelchair accessible. **Open** April–Sept Mon–Sat 9–6, Sun and hols 9–3; Oct–Mar Mon–Sat 9.30–5, Sun and hols 9–12; closed frequently for official functions; **adm** €8 (includes the Farmacia), free to EU passport-holders on Wed. Optional **tours** are given in English and other languages for an extra €2.*

Any self-respecting Bourbon had to have one. Philip V, who commissioned the royal palace in 1738, chose the most celebrated architect of the day, Sicilian maestro Filippo Juvarra, who came up with a model four times larger than the monster that was actually built, then abruptly died. The project was inherited by his pupil, Giovanni Battista Sacchetti, who reduced the scale when Philip's wife Isabel Farnese convinced him that a modest 2,800 rooms would probably meet her needs. As it was, the first king to live in the finished structure was Charles III, while Alfonso XIII was the last king to use the palace as a residence. Juan Carlos' tastes are much more modest: he lives quite comfortably at the suburban Palacio de la Zarzuela (*see* p.172), without any semblance of an old-style court.

Originally this was the site of the Moorish *alcázar*, converted by Henry IV into Madrid's first royal palace. It was here that Velázquez lived and painted for Philip IV, and many of his works, including the celebrated *Las Meninas* in the Prado, are infused with the atmosphere of its old, shadowy chambers. A great fire at Christmas 1734 destroyed the *alcázar* and its great paintings, including some by Velázquez, and occasioned the 18th-century replacement, very much in the style of Versailles and other contemporary palaces.

Plaza de la Armería

Changing of the guard first Wed of each month, except July, Aug and Sept, at noon.

The entrance to the palace is by way of the Plaza de la Armería, a courtyard big enough to hold the entire Plaza Mayor, buildings and all. If you're around for the changing of the guard, it comes complete with a military band and some impressive horsemanship, all done in early 1900s style.

The Interior

Fortunately, not all 2,800 rooms are open, but even so expect a mild delirium after the first three dozen or so – each room with its tapestry from the Real Fábrica, portraits of bewigged sycophants, a nice inlaid table, a half-ton chandelier and indolent mythological deities painted on the ceiling by the likes of Francisco Bayeu, best remembered these days as Goya's master, and the German painter Anton Rafael Mengs.

Some rooms do stand out in the miasma of pomp: the **Grand Stair**, frescoed by Corrado Giaquinto of Naples, and the **Salón del Trono** (Throne Room), with ceilings on the subject of Venus commanding Vulcan to forge arms for Aeneas, by the last Italian master of fresco painting, Giambattista Tiepolo. His greatest work here, however, is his enormous *Apotheosis of Spain*, frescoed over a period of eight years. This was the last major project of Tiepolo's life, painted at the invitation of Charles III in 1762, although it is hardly his best work: some say the subject matter was too much of an oxymoron at the time for even the affable Tiepolo to swallow. The old man, aged 66 when he arrived in Madrid, also had to put up with the jealous rivalry of Mengs, who in 1770 connived to have Tiepolo's last paintings for the royal chapel of Aranjuez replaced with his own work. (Tiepolo died shortly thereafter, probably of chagrin. In his native Venice he would have got a fancy tomb, but in Madrid his remains shared the fate of all the city's famous men – they've been lost.)

Another room, the **Antecámara de Gasparini**, has copies of the two famous

airs of paintings of Charles IV and his wife
Maria Luisa by Goya, who succeeded Tiepolo
as court painter (the originals are in the
Prado). The next room, the **Salón de
Gasparini**, is a Rococo masterpiece of chinois-
erie, designed by Charles III's court painter.
One room is full of gold clocks collected by
Charles IV and, if you happen to be there at
noon, you can hear them all go off, a delicate
symphony of bells and chimes. Also to be
seen are violins by Stradivarius and other
fabulous musical instruments, and a
Comedor de Gala (State Dining Room)
wrapped in frescoes by Bayeu and Antonio
González Velázquez, with a table capable of
seating 145.

Farmacia Real and Armería Real

The **Farmacia**, the first set of rooms you
pass, near the ticket office, contains many
pottings and jars of the original, founded by
Philip II in 1594. Bar codes with the royal
crest, wrapped around the necks of the
flasks, add a quaint supermarket touch.

After a lengthy period of restoration, the
Armería Real reopened to the public in 2000,
with a stunning collection of pieces from
medieval days, as well as those of Charles V
and Philip II. Charles V, who lived in an age
when the medieval knightly manner of
warfare was rapidly becoming obsolete, had
a truly Quixotic fascination with armour. His
collection makes up most of what you see
today, and includes his favourite suit, the one
he wore at the Battle of Mühlberg and when
he posed for Titian. Even the royal dog could
be suited up in a full metal jacket in a chival-
rous version of Dr Who's K9. One sword in
the collection got a real workout – it
belonged to El Cid.

Nuestra Señora de la Almudena G11–12

C/ de Bailén, **t** *91 542 22 00;* **metro** *Opera;
wheelchair accessible.* **Open** *Mon–Sat 10–1.30
and 6–8, Sun 10–2 and 6–8.45; Mass Mon–Sat
at 10am and noon, Sun at 10.30am, noon,
6pm and 7pm.*

Amazingly, despite its four centuries as
capital of Catholic Spain, Madrid hardly
has a single church worth going out of
your way to visit (the Capilla del Obispo is
the great exception to the rule; *see* p.82).
For centuries part of the diocese of Toledo,
Madrid didn't even have a proper cathedral
until the official opening of this cathedral
in 1992.

It was Emperor Charles V who had the idea
of making the old parish church here into a
cathedral, back in 1518. But it was not until
22 December 1878 that the parishioners of
the then Iglesia de la Almudena turned to
the cardinal-archbishop of Toledo requesting
permission and funds to build a cathedral.
Architects Sachetti, Ventura Rodríguez and
Francesco Sabatini sketched plans for a
potential cathedral though it was the
Marqués de Cubas who made the final push,
and it was under his guidance that the first
brick was laid, on 4 April 1883. Inspired by
Viollet-le-Duc's Gothic architecture writings,
he wanted to build a cathedral like the one in
Reims, but his designs fell apart at the
seams. Various political and bureaucratic
delays got in the way, and for about a
hundred years the stones just sat there.
The result can only be described as architecturally eclectic, with a heavy neo-Baroque
dreamed up by Carlos Sidro and Francisco
Chueca Goitea, who retook the reins of the
project in the 1980s. The cathedral is not
quite the stunning culmination of *madrileño*
religious passion its builders had hoped for.
Nevertheless, its dedication in June 1993 was
marked with some ceremony, with the Pope
on hand to bless the new cathedral, fêted by
enthusiastic *madrileños* who showered him
with yellow and white confetti, made, true to
Madrid's public commitment to recycling,
from chopped-up phone directories.

Founded on the site of the old Almudena
Mosque, the most beautiful part of this
bulky, ungainly building is its high ceiling of
triangular panels painted with Moorish-
inspired patterns in muted earthy reds,
browns and greens. Overall, the cathedral
feels light and airy, but empty, in spite of all

the chapels; the abstract stained glass adds much needed splashes of colour.

Parque Emir Mohammed I G12

Metro Opera.

South of the cathedral is the only surviving bit of Moorish Madrid, a winsome fragment of wall in Parque Emir Mohammed I, named after the founder of Mayrit, and now surrounded by the detritus of Madrid's current restoration fervour. Facing it and overlooking a small and shabby square, a copy of the statue of the Virgin of the Almudena (from *almud*, or granary) stands in a niche, the *raison d'etre* for the cathedral and subject of a *muy loco* pious story that claims the image was brought to Spain by St James the Greater and hidden on this spot by a blacksmith in 712 when Madrid was taken over by the Moors. After the Reconquista, in 1085, Alfonso VI led the faithful here in search of the statue, unforgotten after all these years, and, when all requests for divine assistance failed, a woman claiming to be a descendant of the original 8th-century statue-hiders declared she would give her life to find the Virgin. At once part of the town wall fell on top of her, killing her instantly while revealing the statue hidden inside. The statue enshrined in the cathedral, however, is not the miraculous one, but a copy of the original, which went missing again in the 16th century and has yet to reappear.

Calle de Bailén south of here gives on to a handsome concrete viaduct over the Calle de Segovia, built in the 1930s and once Madrid's favourite suicide leap (to such an extent that the sides have been glassed in).

Ermita de la Virgen del Puerto and the Puente de Segovia E11–12

Metro Opera.

If you walk down from the cathedral through a slightly seedy park you'll come to the Paseo de la Virgen del Puerto, where you'll find one of the city's prettiest churches. The brick **Ermita de la Virgen del Puerto** was built by Pedro de Ribera in 1718 and wears a striking octagonal slate hat. Blown to smithereens in the Civil War, it was rebuilt exactly as it was in 1951.

On the way you can also admire the **Puente de Segovia**, a majestic bridge designed by Juan de Herrera in 1584 for Philip II, to allow him to make a quick escape from Madrid to his beloved Escorial. It dwarfs the puny Manzanares in the way that parents buy their children clothes a size or two too large, knowing that they will someday grow into them. But the river never grew, and in fact used to dry up completely in the summer. Over the centuries bridge and river have been cherished by local wits: Quevedo called the Manzanares 'a ditch learning to become a river', while Lope de Vega advised Madrid to either sell the bridge or buy a river; a German ambassador, Rhebinor, declared that the Manzanares was the best river in Europe, because one could navigate it in a horse and carriage. A polluted trail of spittle in the 1970s, the Manzanares became the pet project of Mayor Tierno Galván, who cleaned it and gave it some respect (and some water borrowed from the Sierra).

The home Goya purchased in 1819, La Quinta del Sordo ('the villa of the deaf man') once stood very near here, and in spite of suggestions at the time to preserve it as a Goya museum it was demolished, although the murals, the famous 'Black Paintings', were transferred to canvas and hence to the Prado.

Jardines del Campo del Moro F10–12

Paseo de la Virgen del Puerto; metro Príncipe Pío. Open winter Mon–Sat 10–6, Sun and hols 9–6; summer Mon–Sat 10–8, Sun and hols 9–8.

At the north end of the Paseo de la Virgen del Puerto is the entrance to the largest of the formal parks that make up the grounds

the Palacio Real, the quiet Campo del
oro, a miniature version of the Versailles
ardens. Its name recalls the Moorish
ncampment of 1109, when the Muslims
ade their last unsuccessful attempt to
capture Madrid. Planted like an English
ark in 1842, the Campo del Moro was
pened to the public in 1931, but was closed
on after by Franco and only reopened in
83. It has lovely views up to the palace.

AST OF THE
ALACIO REAL

laza de Oriente G11

etro Opera.

The Plaza de Oriente was the largest space
eared by 'the king of squares' Joseph
onaparte, although it wasn't laid out prop-
ly until 1844. Its name, confusingly, refers to
e fact that it is on the east side of the
alacio Real, even if it's on the west side of
adrid. Now pedestrianized and Frenchified
ith outdoor cafés, it makes a dignified
ont lawn for the Palacio Real. Statues of
spanic Roman emperors, Visigothic and
anish kings and queens, guard its alleys,
oking rather put out that they aren't lined
p on the palace roof as their makers
tended. Some say they were grounded
ter Philip V's wife, Isabel Farnese, had a
ream that there was an earthquake and
ey fell on her head; others say they were
moved by Charles III, who thought they
ere silly and pretentious, but said that they
ere too heavy. Perhaps the most inter-
sting statue is the equestrian statue of
hilip IV, a gift from Cosimo de' Medicis (*see
Horsing Around'*).

eatro Real H11

*aza de Oriente, **t** 91 516 06 60, for tours **t** 91
6 06 96; **metro** Opera; wheelchair acces-
ble. **Guided tours** (45mins) Tues–Fri every
alf-hour from 10.30am to 1.30pm, Sat–Sun
–1.30pm; closed Aug; **adm** €4.*

The centrepiece of the Plaza de Oriente, the
Teatro Real, reopened in 1997 after a 72-year
intermission. Begun in 1818 but completed
only in 1850, in time for Isabel II's 20th-
birthday gala, the theatre closed in 1925,
supposedly for refurbishment. Civil war
followed by 40 years of Franco (who couldn't
even be bothered to finish the nearby cathedral) kept the curtains resolutely down. Then
political infighting delayed reconstruction
for more than a decade while costs soared,
hitting the 21 billion peseta mark. From the
outside the building is little changed, but its
innards now boast state-of-the-art acoustics
and an overall cubic area greater than the
Telefónica building on the Gran Vía, at least
according to its architects. The opera house
offers a varied programme, and seat prices
are, by British and American standards,
reasonable, with top seats weighing in at
€100 and a seat in the gods costing €12.

Behind the theatre stands a statue of
Isabel II, erected in 1850. The queen, in an
unusual gesture of royal deference, had it

Horsing Around

The equestrian statue of Philip IV in the
centre of the Plaza de Oriente originally
stood in the Parque del Retiro and has an
interesting history: the original design, by
Florentine sculptor Pietro Tacca, was deemed
too unheroic by Philip's favourite, the Conde
Duque de Olivares, who asked Velázquez to
paint a portrait of the king on a rearing horse
and send it to Florence to show the sculptor
just what was required. Tacca was startled by
the request: no one had ever cast a rearing
horse before. Unwilling to lose the commission, however, he went to Galileo for advice
on the technical problems of balance (make
the rear quarters of the horse solid, and the
front hollow, suggested Galileo). The result
was such a success that, from then on, every
monarch had to have a rearing horse. If
Tacca's king and horse look a bit wooden, it
could be Velázquez's fault: his genius balked
at equestrian portraits – even those in the
Prado look like stage props.

withdrawn, saying that the *madrileños* could put it back after her death, if they found her reign satisfactory. Actually, they didn't – they ousted her in the end – but it seemed unkind to leave her statue rotting in a warehouse.

Real Monasterio de la Encarnación G10

1 Plaza de la Encarnación, **t** *91 454 88 00; metro Opera; wheelchair accessible.* **Guided tours** *only (Spanish only), Tues–Thurs and Sat 10.30–12.45 and 4–5.45, Fri 10.30–12.45, Sun and hols 11–1.45;* **adm** *€3.60, free to EU passport-holders on Wed.*

The Real Monasterio de la Encarnación was founded by Philip III's wife (and cousin) Margarita de Austria in 1611. The nuns at the Encarnación get by with fewer treasures than their cohorts at the nearby Monasterio de las Descalzas (*see* opposite), and their home has gone through more turmoil, condemned to disappear several times in the 19th century, and at one point partially demolished.

The convent was traditionally the home of some of Spain's most regal nuns, and the art collection is their legacy: they managed to nab more than a few canvas gems from their royal relatives, who visited them via a subterranean passageway so as to avoid the plebs on the streets above. One painting, the charming anonymous *The Exchange of Princesses on the River Bidasoa*, depicts the famous big-league Franco-Hispanic princess marriage trade-off during the Twelve Year Truce of 1615: Louis XIII got Anne of Austria, daughter of Philip III, and Philip IV got Elizabeth (Isabelle) of France, daughter of Henry IV. The issue, in the next generation, led to the Bourbons winning the throne of Spain in the War of the Spanish Succession. Other paintings include a *San Isidro*, the city's patron (while he naps, two angels plough; Spaniards say it's a fitting allegory for a capital that lives off the rest of the country); a portrait of Philip III by his court painter, Bartolomé González; and a rather beautiful *St John the Baptist* with an earnest sheep, by Ribera.

In the sculpture room, pride of place goes to the wooden polychrome statues by Gregorio Fernández, master of the 17th-century Spanish blood and guts school of religious art (although he has plenty of rivals): his recumbent, green-faced Christ, distorted in *rigor mortis*, lies in one corner while the still living Christ is viciously flagellated in another. The next hall is lined with portraits of Habsburgs, all copies of works now in the Pitti Palace in Florence (there were a pair of Medicis in the woodpile: the sister of the convent foundress married the Grand Duke of Tuscany, and Marie de' Medicis was the mother of Elizabeth of France, part of the aforementioned princess exchange).

The tour continues to the cloister and **choir**, which also doubles as the convent cemetery; one nun buried here is Luisa de Carajal, a great friend of the first abbess, wh died in the Tower of London in 1614 after going to England to fight against Anglican reform. Note the Herreran walnut stalls (complete with their little Herreran balls) an portraits of the seven archangels with their attributes.

The more fleshy aspects of the faith reach unique epiphany in the convent's **Reliquario** a small ornate room with a frescoed ceiling, and an altarpiece of the *Nativity* by Leonardo's pupil, Bernardino Luini. The wooden cases that line its walls resemble a cosy study, but instead of books hold a worl record-breaking collection of skulls, teeth, toes, hair, fingernails, you name it, with a bit or bob from nearly every saint on the calendar, wrapped up in little boxes with flowers as if they were expensive chocolates. Nearly all these relics were rescued by the Habsburgs from Protestant lands during the Counter-Reformation. Pride of place goe to a droplet of blood from St Pantaleón, a 4th-century Greek doctor, which miraculously liquefies on the day of his martyrdom (27 July) or whenever Spain is in danger.

...idently, he's also a good saint to appeal to ...r lottery numbers; in Rome, if you go ...rough the proper rigmarole, he'll come at ...ght with the winning numbers written on ...iece of paper. Only he's a tricky saint, and ...des it.

...he tour continues to the **church**: behind ...e sombre, boxy granite façade, attributed ... Juan Gómez de Mora, waits a graceful ...terior, one of the prettiest in Madrid, dating ...m a remodelling by Ventura Rodríguez in ...e 1700s, decorated with stuccoes and a ...scoed ceiling called *The Life of St ...gustine*. If you like organ music, the ...nday 11.30 Mass is reputedly a treat, played ...th all the stops out on the original 17th-...ntury instrument. The church bells, ...wever, are charmingly flat.

...alacio del Senado G10

*Plaza de la Marina Española; **metro** Plaza
España or Opera; wheelchair accessible.
ided tours by prior appointment.*

...ust north of the Real Monasterio de la
...carnación, up Calle de la Encarnación, is
...e Palacio del Senado, which also began as a
...nvent in 1581 and was converted in 1820
...o a Neoclassical home for the Senate. In
...91, the senators, who actually have very
...tle political power, caused a national stink
... building themselves a modern extension
...ound the back, complete with all the
...nenities, including an indoor pool. Round
...e corner, the hedonistic senators can take
...eir post-prandial strolls through the
...**dines de Sabatini**, a section of the royal
...rdens that has seen better days.

...eal Monasterio de las
...escalzas Reales I10–11

*...laza de las Descalzas Reales, **t** 91 542 00 59;
...tro Sol or Opera. **Open** Tues–Thurs and Sat
...30–12.45 and 4–5.45, Fri 10.30–12.45, Sun
...d hols 11–1.30; by **guided tour** only, in
...nish; **adm** €5, free to EU passport-holders
...Wed. Note that both monasteries*

*(Encarnación and Descalzas Reales) can be
visited for €6 within a one week duration.*

Originally a palace owned by the kings of
Castile, this was the birthplace of Juana of
Austria, daughter of Charles V. Widowed at
age 19, she decided to make the palace over
into an exclusive convent for blue-blooded
nuns and widows. The first building dates
from 1556 and, although it was substantially
renovated in the late 1700s, the convent
remains properly austere on the outside;
after all, it belongs to the order founded by
Santa Teresa, the discalced or shoeless
Carmelites, sworn to poverty, sandal-wearing
and pious observance. When Juana of Austria
took her vows, however, fashion was not far
behind, and the Royal Barefoots soon
became the richest prestige nunnery in
Christendom, packed full of art and relics
donated over the centuries by nuns not quite
prepared to leave it all behind. The convent's
most important pieces of original artwork
have long since been relocated to the Museo
del Prado, but a few gems still remain – there
are works by Titian, Goya, Lucas Jordán and
Rubens. With 24 resident nuns behind its
walls, the convent is still a functioning
cloister, with a working garden in the interior
patio (one of the few you are likely to find in
congested Madrid) where the nuns grow
flowers, fruits and vegetables. In the 1980s,
the nuns (no longer all royal, although the
convent remains under the special patronage
of Juan Carlos I) converted a section of their
convent into a museum that in 1988 won an
award as the best new one in Europe.

The Interior

To visit you'll have to submit to a guided
tour in rapid-fire Spanish. This begins at the
grand staircase, decorated with excellent
trompe l'oeil frescoes from the mid-1600s by
José Ximénez Donoso and Claudio Coello, in
which Philip IV and his family (including the
Infanta Margarita, the little girl of *Las
Meninas, see* p.103) appear to be looking
down from a balcony.

The enclosed, two-storey **cloister** (in 1999,
restorers uncovered some of its original

fresco decoration) is lined with precious chapels, most with blue-and-yellow tiles from Talavera de la Reina. The first chapel has a gory recumbent Christ with a gaping jewelled hole in his side, where the Host is placed when the statue leads the Good Friday procession. Another chapel, dedicated to the Virgin of Guadaloupe, has 68 oil paintings on glass depicting the strong women of the Bible. Another chapel has an exquisite *belén* (nativity scene) set behind a glass wall, brought to the convent from Naples by Charles III. Finally, the Capilla de la Anunciación (Chapel of the Annunciation) boasts a so-so *Annunciation* painting in the exact spot where Fra Angelico's lapis lazuli *Annunciation* sat before being sent to the Prado.

Next comes the **ante-choir** (entrance-hall to the choir hall), which has another three chapels, including the Virgen del Puig, which displays the very first statue brought to the convent: a simple Virgin and Child. The ante-choir has one of the convent's most curious statues: a St Joseph holding the Child converted into a St Anthony who has ended up with two left hands. The **choir hall** itself is lined in dark wood and is where the nuns sit to hear Mass every day. The Empress María of Austria, one of Charles V's daughters, who moved here after being widowed, was laid to rest here. She has a tomb surrounded by disembodied arm candelabras, like those in Cocteau's film *La Belle et La Bête*. Beneath, a famous statue of the *Virgen Dolorosa* by Pedro de Mena has eyes that seem ready to brim over with tears. María's daughter, the Infanta Margarita, is also enshrined here, though in a smaller, much more modest coffin beneath her mother's. Margarita of the Cross, as she became known, took her nun's vows and spent much of her life here, renouncing her title as Archduchess as well as her right to be buried in the basement of El Escorial.

The nuns have an impressive collection of **tapestries**, including a magnificent series woven in Brussels, the *Triumph of the*

Eucharist designed by Rubens and donated to the convent by Philip II's daughter, the Infanta Isabel Clara Engenia, governor of th Netherlands, as a votive offering for the Spanish victory at Breda in 1626. When the nuns were starving in the anti-clerical 1830 they were about to sell the tapestries to bu food, only to be forbidden by the abbess, w declared that, even if all the nuns perished, the tapestries would belong to the convent until the end of time. There are also several paintings in the tapestry room, one of *St Ursula and the 11,000 Virgins Arriving in Cologne* (the convent has their relics stowe away somewhere – the reliquary must be th size of a boxcar), while another panel, a Flemish-inspired *Presentation in the Temple* was painted on both sides, its back visible thanks to the one and only mirror permitte in the convent.

Another room has a case with spiked sho – not stilettos, but with the spikes inside (the only kind the discalced sisters ever wea – and knotted ropes used for mortification. Beyond is a **room of royal portraits**; one of the little Infantas, daughters of Philip II, shows a rare depiction of the long-lost *alcázar* in the background. There is a full-length portrait of an adolescent Sebastian Portugal, whose timely death enabled his uncle Philip II to claim the crown of Portug (*see* 'If the Cap Fits', p.136). On the back wall hangs a portrait of Charles V's sister Eleanc the one François I agreed to marry. You'll se what changed his mind.

In the **chapterhouse**, decorated with 16th century frescoes of the life of St Francis, the convent keeps its finest sculptures: two oth weepy Virgins, one by Pedro de Mena, who also carved the ultra-realistic *Ecce Homo*. Th dramatic *Magdalen*, a work that looks forward to the *Addams Family*, is attributed to Gregorio Fernández, while over the door the symbolic mural of the *Crucified Nun*. Th next room, the **Hall of the Kings**, preserves stucco frieze under the ceiling and other original features of the royal palace, as wel as more portraits, including many royals

essed up as saints (they fooled everyone
ntil their recent restoration). Note the
arming spiral stair in the corner, a short cut
the upper cloister. This is followed by a
om of Flemish painting, featuring an
usual 16th-century allegory called the *Ship
the Church* by a follower of Bosch, with the
pe at the helm and a crew consisting of
e founders of the religious orders. The royal
mily paddles up in a couple of long boats
hile various sins try to waylay the ship, and
sus and a courtly group of saints wait in
e Port of Salvation. Most of the other
intings are copies of famous works
splayed elsewhere, with the exception of a
autiful *Adoration of the Magi* by Brueghel
e Elder. The **Italian and Spanish rooms** have
Christ Carrying the Cross by Sebastiano del
ombo, a gloomy *St Francis* attributed to
rbarán and *The Tribute Money* by Titian,
o signed his name on the Pharisee's collar.
*he convent's **church** (*open only at Mass
es, 8am and 7pm*), designed by Juan
utista de Toledo, was much altered over
e centuries, especially after a disastrous
e in 1862. One feature that survived is the
mb of the foundress Juana (d.1573), in a
rial chapel designed in part by Juan de
rrera and hidden off to the right of the
esbytery. The marble figure of Juana
aying is by Pompeo Leoni, who sculpted
e similar statues of the royal family for
n Lorenzo de El Escorial.

alle del Arenal H–I11

tro *Opera or Sol.*
Below the Descalzas Reales runs Calle del
enal, the main thoroughfare linking Royal
adrid to central Puerta del Sol. One of the
pital's oldest streets, its name ('sandy')
alls the streams that once ran here and
ve Madrid its watery name (*see p.28*). At
7, the sumptuous **Palacio de Gaviria** (1851)
s built by the eponymous marquis to
rtain Isabel II; although the exterior is
longer what it was, some of the rooms
ide are intact and now contain music bars

(*see p.239*). The disco **Joy Eslava** on the same
street occupies the Teatro Eslava of 1872,
famous for the premier of Garcia Lorca's first
(and disastrous) attempt at drama in 1920, a
saga of cockroach love called *The Butterfly's
Evil Spell*.

Iglesia de San Ginés I11

*C/ del Arenal; **metro** Opera or Sol. **Open**
Fri–Sun 7–10pm; Capilla de Cristo **open** daily
during Mass 9–1 and 6–9.*

The little church of San Ginés was founded
shortly after the Reconquista, but like all the
others in Madrid it was Baroqued in the 17th
century and restored after several fires. A
high-society church in the reign of Isabel II, it
is now dark, very quiet, run by the cultish
Opus Dei and filled with the pungent smell
of incense. One chapel, dedicated to the
Virgen de los Remedios, has a little dried-out
crocodile, dedicated by a certain Alonso de
Montalbán who, like Captain Hook, was
chased by one across the Caribbean until the
Virgin delivered him from its jaws. Two of
Spain's greatest writers have connections to
the church: Francisco de Quevedo (author of
the picaresque novel *El Buscón*) was buried

Spain's Melting Pot

As capital, constantly drawing in people
from all over Spain, Madrid is very much the
national melting pot, and has been for four
and a half centuries. Tried and tested over
the centuries, the *madrileños* have emerged
with top honours as one of the most sane
peoples in the world, who seem uniquely
aware that life is no dress rehearsal. In 1886,
a perceptive French writer named Juliette
Lamber (writing under the pseudonym of
Count Paul Visili) got them down pat:

*Madrid society, unconsciously perhaps, is
democratic; it is frank and sincere, and you
do not find there any stiffness or affecta-
tions. The Castilian arrogance is the covering
for an optimistic self-sufficiency which does
not wound, does not shock, which you will
grow accustomed to, and in which you will
drape yourself unknowingly on your return.*

here, and Lope de Vega, who lived up the street, was married here.

San Ginés' chief prize is hidden away in the adjacent **Capilla de Cristo**, entered by way of Calle de los Bordadores: El Greco's *Expulsion from the Temple*.

The Triángulo de Arte

The Triángulo de Arte

If the Prado wasn't already enough to make Madrid a major art destination, the re-opening of the Centro de Arte Reina Sofía in 1990 and the nation's permanent acquisition of the Thyssen-Bornemisza collection in 1992 removed all doubt. Madrid is rightly proud of its showcase 'golden triangle' – three superb museums all within strolling distance of each other, linked by the Paseo del Prado.

The three collections complement each other neatly. The Museo del Prado is best known for its hoard of masterpieces of Spanish painting from the 12th to the early 19th centuries, and for its rich collections of 15th–17th-century Flemish painting, as well as Italian art by the likes of Titian, Raphael and Botticelli, collected by the kings of Spain. The Museo Nacional Centro de Arte Reina Sofía picks up the thread with its permanent collection of 20th-century art (the centrepiece of which is Picasso's masterwork, *Guernica*). The newcomer on the scene, the Museo Colección Thyssen-Bornemisza, is a remarkable gathering of European and American art spanning eight centuries. Its highlights include early Italian paintings, 17th-century Dutch works, and paintings by 20th-century masters including Braque, Mondrian, Picasso and Warhol. Fortuitously, it manages to fill in a few of the gaps left by the Prado and the Reina Sofía, with collections of Impressionism and Post-impressionism, German Expressionists such as Munch, Schiele and Kandinsky, and a restrained but well-informed selection of Pop Art and geometrical abstracts.

For a walk through the Parque del Retiro and surrounding area, *see* 'A Gardens Walk Around the Retiro', p.181.

1 Lunch

Viridiana, *14 C/ de Juan de Mena*, *t 91 523 78*; *metro Banco de España or Retiro*. **Open** *Mon–Sat 1.30–4 and 9.30–midnight; closed Aug. Diners Club not accepted*. **Expensive**. Although a symbol of the economic boom the late 1980s, Viridiana is no nouveau rich hangout. One of the best wine cellars in the capital, faultless but discreet service and imaginative but classical dishes make for a memorable meal.

2 Tea and Cakes

Ritz, *5 Plaza de la Lealtad*, *t 91 521 28 57*; *metro Banco de España*. Pamper yourself at Madrid's plushest outdoor tearooms in the gardens of the Hotel Ritz.

3 Drinks

El Botánico, *27 C/ de Ruíz de Alarcón*, *t 91 420 23 42*; *metro Banco de España*. A relaxing bar behind the Prado, with outdoor tables.

Highlights

Couples' City: A carriage ride through the Parque del Retiro, pp.106–7

Madrileño's City: Watching the tapestry-makers at the Real Fábrica de Tapices, p.118

Indoor City: The Prado, Thyssen-Bornemisza and Reina Sofía museums, p.98, p.108 and p.113

Outdoor City: The Real Jardín Botánico, p.108

Goya's City: The tapestry cartoons and Black Paintings in the Museo del Prado, p.10

Architectural City: The fabulous tropical emporium at Estación de Atocha, p.117

All grid references in this chapter refer to the map opposite

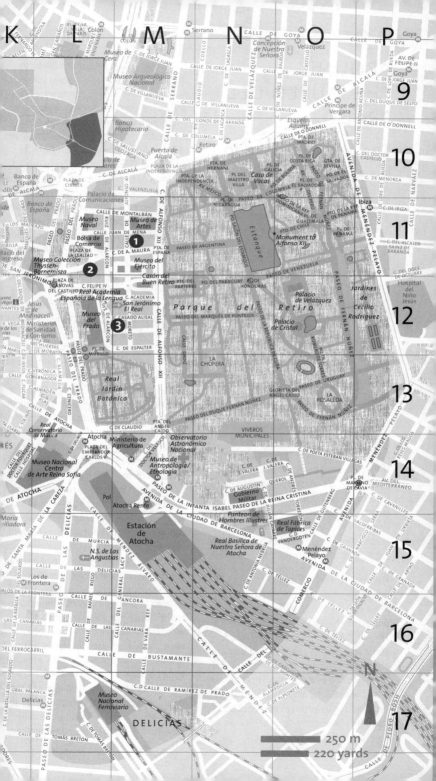

AROUND THE MUSEO DEL PRADO

The Museo del Prado L12

Paseo del Prado, t 91 330 28 00, w museo prado.mcu.es; metro Banco de España or Atocha; wheelchair accessible. Open Tues–Sat 9–7, Sun and hols 9–7; closed 1 Jan, Good Friday, 1 May and 25 Dec; adm €3, free Sun, 18 May, 12 Oct and 6 Dec.

Charles III intended this long, elegant Neoclassical structure to be a natural history museum when it was begun in 1785 by the young architect Juan de Villanueva. But the stuffed elephants never arrived: the building was just completed in 1808 when the French swooped in, made it their barracks and stables, and stripped it bare, even taking part of the roof to melt into bullets. And so it crumbled forlornly until Ferdinand VII, that most hated of kings, decided to do one good deed in his life and act on an idea that had been in the air for centuries. His discerning predecessors had accumulated one of Europe's greatest hoards of art, and although the pictures had been on display in the public areas of the royal palaces and El Escorial, Ferdinand decided that they should be relocated under one roof, and that this one roof (once repaired) should be the Prado's. The collections were opened to the public in 1819. Even repaired, however, the

roof would always bedevil the Prado: the museum was traditionally always closed on rainy days – even in 1993 there were leaks and buckets in the main Velázquez room.

Although the building itself has been restored several times, the collections have changed little since 1819, apart from the addition in 1868 of a mass of religious art confiscated from Spain's suppressed monasteries and convents. Spanish noble families who collected paintings are likely still to have them: the habit of donating to museums never took root here as in the rest of Europe. For the masterpieces of the Prado we can thank the practised eyes of Charles V, Philip and Philip IV. Whatever else history can blame them for, they knew good painting when they saw it. If the collection has survived more or less intact throughout all the tribulations of history, the thanks goes to Philip IV, whose will in 1665 made all the paintings Crown property and prohibited the dispersion of a single one.

There was considerable disgruntlement when in 1993 the government invested an unprecedented (though bargain) sum in acquiring the Thyssen collection while apparently neglecting the Prado's arguably more pressing needs, in particular its nagging space problem. The exhibition areas are only large enough to display a seventh of the collection (though that does amount to 1,000 paintings), and among the 'unseen' canvases are significant works by Spanish masters. Of the 6,000 works not on display, good 3,500 of them are on loan to museums around the world. The Prado continues with major expansion efforts. The biggest project involves an entirely new building: next door to the Claustro de los Jerónimos, Spanish architect Rafael Moneo has designed a new wing, slated to be used for temporary exhibitions, restoration workshops and a research library, and an underground tunnel will connect it to the main building. The Casón del Buen Retiro, closed until the end of 200 is also being expanded with three more basement floors to create more storage

---

Paseo de Arte Ticket

A money-saving Paseo de Arte voucher will allow you one visit to each of the three big museums, the Prado, Reina Sofía and Thyssen, for €7.60; but don't even think about trying to 'do' the three in a single day unless you are the bionic sightseer or likely to be satisfied with a mere snippet of each. With the beautiful gardens of the Parque del Retiro and an assortment of other, but thankfully smaller, museums, this is an area to return to again and again.

nding Your Way Around
e Prado

xpect crowds, especially at weekends, but
n't be dismayed by huge mobs at the
trances: they're likely to be disorganized
ur groups counting heads, and you should
able to pass right through. The earlier you
, the fewer of these you'll have to
ntend with.

he grandiose main entrance is only used
 VIP groups, but there's a secondary
trance (the Puerta de Murillo) at the
uthern end. However, the best place to
gin a comprehensive visit to the collec-
ns is to enter at ground level by the Puerta
 Goya at the north end of the main
ilding, the Edificio Villanueva. The
useum is laid out chronologically, with the
ler paintings on the ground floor. The
ound floor is mostly medieval and
naissance, covering 14th–16th-century
anish, Flemish, German and Italian works.
e first floor covers everything Baroque,
is some of the Goya collection. The rest of
 Goyas are on the second floor.

ace. When it re-opens, it will house the
do's collection of 19th-century painting as
ll as works from the Middle Ages. The
do is also planning to take over the
acio del Buen Retiro (currently the home
the Museo del Ejército), though plans are
 way in the future, as the entire Museo
 Ejército will have to be relocated to the
ázar in Toledo, a changeover that may well
etch into 2004–5. The new Prado-ized
acio will include a more or less intact
ón de Reinos (the throne room from the
ilding's palace days), court paintings from
 17th century and artwork collected by
 Bourbons.

 statue of the first great Habsburg
lector, Charles V, greets visitors in the
 in foyer of the Prado. This was sculpted by
ather and son team, León and Pompeo
ni, who, unbeknownst to the Emperor,
de his armour removable. Underneath
s nude, at least as the sculptors imagined

him, in a rather curious play on the story of
the Emperor's new clothes.

Ground Floor

This floor is mostly medieval and
Renaissance, covering 14th–16th-century
Spanish, Flemish, German and Italian works.
This is where you'll find Hieronymous Bosch,
Fra Angelico, Raphael, Botticelli, Titian,
Veronese, Tintoretto and El Greco. The tour
begins at the Puerta de Goya.

14th–16th-century Spanish Art

The first ground-floor rooms, starting from
the Puerta de Goya, are devoted to medieval
religious works. Don't be in too much of a
hurry to see Velázquez: some of the best
art in the Prado is here, including some stunning 14th- and 15th-century *retablos*:
Archbishop Don Sancho de Rojas by **Rodríguez
de Toledo** and *The Life of the Virgin and
St Francis* by **Nicolás Francés**. The great
Córdoban master **Bartolomé Bermejo**'s
St Dominic Enthroned stands out for sheer
dramatic realism: the saint is shown seated
on a monumental throne surrounded by
figures representing the three theological
and four cardinal virtues.

This rich collection of early Spanish
painting continues with Renaissance-influ-
enced works such as **Fernando Gallego**'s
eerie *Cristo Bendiciendo*. **Pedro Berruguete**
contributes, among much else, an *Auto-da-Fé
Presided Over by St Dominic* that is almost
satirical, with bored church apparatchiks
dozing under a baldachin while the woebegone heretics are led off to the slaughter.
St Peter Martyr, by the same artist, beams
beatifically from beneath the meat cleaver
splitting his skull.

15th–16th-century Flemish and
German Art

Even before Philip II, who valued Flemish
art above all others, the Low Countries' close
commercial and dynastic ties with Spain
ensured that some of their art would turn up
here. Today the Prado's collection of Flemish
art is almost as unmissable as its
Spanish collection.

The works are arranged roughly chronologically, beginning with the 15th-century so-called Primitives, including paintings by **Robert Campin** and breathtakingly detailed work by **Rogier van der Weyden** (1400–64). Weyden's *Descent from the Cross* (c.1435) is astonishing, framed like a scene from a mystery play, in which Gothic stylization is all but forgotten in favour of the realistic visual representation of a whole spectrum of human emotions. Within the tight confines of the composition the figures just float off the surface of the panel. A copy hangs at El Escorial. There are a few more Van der Weydens in the next room, including a sombre, carmine-cloaked *Virgin and Child* and a moving *Piedad* (1450). There are a number of endearing **Hans Memling** paintings, including an *Adoration of the Magi* triptych (1470–2) and a *Virgin and Child between two Angels* (1480–90).

The biggest crowds, though, will be around the works of **Hieronymous Bosch** (1450–1516, known in Spain as 'El Bosco'). His psychological fantasies, including *The Garden of Earthly Delights*, *The Hay Wain*, *The Adoration of the Magi* and the table in the centre of the room decorated with *The Seven Deadly Sins* are too familiar to need any comment. Philip II bought every one he could get his hands on, and it should not be surprising to find the most complex of all Spanish kings as attracted to this dark surrealism as we moderns are. More works by Bosch can be seen in Philip's apartments at El Escorial.

If you like Bosch, you should also get to know his countryman **Joachim Patinir**, some of whose best work can also be found in this section, including *The Rest on the Flight to Egypt* and *The Temptations of St Anthony*. Probably no other museum has such a large complement of terror to balance its own beauty; between Goya (*see* below), Bosch and the other northern painters and the religious hacks, a trip to the Prado can seem like a long ride in a carnival funhouse. If you approach it in this way, the climax will undoubtedly be *The Triumph of Death* by **Pieter Brueghel the Elder** (1525–1569), with its phalanxes of leering skeletons turned loose upon a doomed, terrified world. To Philip II, who is said to have kept a crowned skull on his night table, it must have seemed a deeply religious work. The Dutch, though, in the middle of their war of independence, would probably have been reminded of the horror of intolerance and militant religion that were searing contemporary Europe – much of it emanating from this very city.

German paintings are few, but they are choice. **Albrecht Dürer**'s rather presumptuous *Self-portrait* (1498), for example, is an interesting study, painted at a time when self-portraits were uncommon (artists were considered unworthy subjects), and composed in a style that is often compared to Leonardo da Vinci's *Mona Lisa* (a copy of which hangs in the Italian section, although it was actually painted five years earlier. Also of interest are Dürer's companion painting of Adam and Eve, **Hans Baldung Grien**'s angular Teutonic *Three Graces* and sinister *Three Ages of Man and Death*, and works by **Cranach** and **Mengs**.

14th–16th-century Italian Art

Here the Prado keeps its several paintings by **Raphael** (1483–1520): the tiny, luminous *Holy Family of the Lamb* and other religious paintings, including *Holy Family of the Oak* which Joseph appears to be leering down at the Virgin Mary, and the classic *Holy Family* (1518), which Philip II referred to as 'the pea Other Raphaels include the massive *Transfiguration of Christ* and the fearsome red-cloaked, tight-lipped *Cardinal*. There's also an intensely spiritual *Annunciation* by **Fra Angelico** (1397–1455) and an unusual **Botticelli** (1444–1510) trio of scenes from Boccaccio's *Decameron*, *The Story of Nasta degli Onesti*. **Andrea del Sarto**, **Mantegna**, **Antonello da Messina**, **Veronese**, **Caravagg Bassano**, **Tintoretto** and **Correggio**, among the other Italian masters, are all represente

There are rooms full of works by **Titian** (c.1490–1576), including two portraits of th artist's patron, Charles V, who ruled the

ggest empire of all time but paid the
inter two hitherto unheard-of compli-
ents for the age: he once stooped over and
cked up a brush that Titian had dropped,
d (on another occasion) knighted him.
tian never painted anything small, and
erhaps his biggest canvas of all is *La Gloria*,
colourful, preposterous cloud-bedecked
agining of the Holy Trinity that gently
dges the boundaries of kitsch. Charles
ho is also in the picture, which is some-
mes called his 'Apotheosis') is said to have
zed upon this picture constantly while on
s deathbed. His son, Philip II, another
rvent patron of Titian, apparently spent a
t of time gazing at the sumptuously ripe
male nudes in the Venetian's celebrated
ythologies, or poesies, as he called them.

5th-century Spanish Art

To appreciate the genius of Domenikos
eotocopoulos, better known as **El Greco**
40–1614), there is no substitute for a visit
the museums of Toledo, but the Prado
uses fine examples of what are sometimes
led his 'vertical pictures' – Mannerist
pictions of biblical figures with elongated
nbs and faces – including *The Annunciation*
d *The Adoration of the Shepherds*. El Greco
as also a skilled portraitist and his
bleman with his Hand on his Chest is
rticularly haunting. Other not-to-be-
ssed pieces include the eerie *St Andrew*
d *St Francis*, with their gaunt faces. *The*
ly Face shows Christ's disembodied face in
ld relief against a white rag set upon a
ckground of thick, bloody brown.

rst Floor

he first floor is where you will find every-
ng Baroque, including a mind-blowing
mber of paintings by Peter Paul Rubens, a
rprising number by Anthony van Dyck and
mall collection of Dutch works. The jewel
the crown, however, is indisputably Diego
lázquez, whose masterpieces are appropri-
ly displayed in the very centre of the
useum. Other Spanish masters to be found
this floor include Ribera, Murillo and
Zurbarán. The great Francisco José de Goya y
Lucientes can be found on this floor, too,
though the Goya collection extends up to the
second-floor wings.

17th-century Flemish and Dutch Art

Rubens (1577–1640), a favourite of Philips III
and IV, visited Madrid twice, and is well
represented here. His epic *Adoration of the
Magi* dominates a whole roomful of florid
biblical paintings, and his chubby *Three
Graces* is among other mythological subjects
in an adjacent gallery. A room nearby contains
the famous collaboration of **Brueghel the
Younger** and Rubens, the *Allegory of the Five
Senses*, a complete universe of philosophy in
its five enormous canvases.

Rubens' works are followed by those of
later Flemish masters: delicate portraits by
Anthony van Dyck (1599–1641); complex
studies by **David Teniers** (1610–90), such as
his paintings-within-a-painting of *Archduke
Leopold William in his Picture Gallery*; and,
tucked away in a room full of small canvases,
one of the greatest works of Brueghel the
Younger, the untitled 'snowy landscape'.

The Prado's small Dutch collection consists
mostly of 17th-century hunting scenes, still
lifes and the like, but there is one good
Rembrandt (1606–69), a dignified portrait of
a regal woman thought to be Artemisia, wife
of King Mausolus.

17th–18th-century Spanish Art

By the 17th century, the religious pathology
of the age becomes manifest, notably in a
disturbing painting by **Francisco Ribalta** of
the crucified Christ leaning down off the
Cross to embrace St Bernard. Elsewhere, St
Bernard comes in for more abuse, this time
at the hand of **Alonso Cano**, who illustrates
the old tale of the praying saint receiving a
squirt of milk in his mouth from the breast of
an image of the Virgin.

Other, uneven, works by Spanish Baroque
masters fill a dozen galleries – José de Ribera
(1591–1652), Francisco de Zurbarán (1598–1664)
and Bartolomé Esteban Murillo (1618–1682)

among others. **Ribera** was a follower of Caravaggio's style and he used dark colours, starkly lit, to suggest pious ascetism, pain, suffering and earthy sensual pleasure. His paintings of mythological and religious subjects (such as *St Andrew* and *The Martyrdom of St Philip*) are shot through with sinister undercurrents; he was particularly keen on using scruffy urchins and decaying beggars as models in order to inject warts-and-all realism into his work.

Zurbarán was a Sevillian contemporary of Velázquez, but the style of their work could not be more different. The Prado has some examples of Zurbarán's finely worked still lifes; these have a sacramental quality, with everyday objects laid out like devotional offerings. **Murillo** churned out plenty of sentimental tosh, some of which has found its way here, but his *Holy Family* (1650) is sweet and un-affected, a lovingly painted moment of the toddler Jesus playing with a small dog, gently encouraged by his doting parents.

Velázquez

On a day when there are as many Spaniards as foreigners in the Prado, the crowds around the works of Diego de Silva y Velázquez (1599–1660) can be daunting. Many Spaniards consider their countryman to be the greatest artist of all, and you may find the several rooms devoted to him here, the largest Velázquez collection by far, to be convincing argument. Many of the works have recently been cleaned or restored, making the audacity of his use of light and colour stand out even more clearly.

Almost all of his best-known paintings are here: *The Topers* (*Los Borrachos*, a work inspired by Rubens), *The Tapestry Weavers*

Velázquez

Ever since its opening, the Prado has been celebrated as the place to go to understand the genius of Velázquez (1599–1660). Yet looking at these paintings, it's hard to believe that he was all but unknown in Europe until the Peninsular War (1808–13). Wherever the British found his works (mainly early ones in Seville) they snapped them up; when the Prado opened its doors a few years later, it was an even greater revelation.

Like Picasso, born in Málaga three centuries later, Diego Velázquez was an extremely precocious Andalucian. He was apprenticed in Seville at the age of 10 to Mannerist painter Francisco Pacheco (better known for his biographical writing than his mediocre paintings), who soon recognized the boy's talent; his advice, 'go to nature for everything', would stand Velázquez in good stead throughout his career. When Velázquez became a master artist at age 18, Pacheco married him to his daughter, 'moved by his virtue, integrity and good parts, and my expectations of his disposition and great talent'.

Even then, Velázquez's paintings showed technical mastery few artists ever attain. The Prado's *Adoration of the Magi* (1619), one of his few early works to remain in Spain, is a good example of his young naturalistic style influenced by Caravaggio: the figures are not ideals, but portraits of real people (his wife was probably the model for the Virgin), while the lighting is realistic yet somehow spiritual.

Velázquez made a first brief trip to Madrid in 1622, when he painted a portrait of poet Luis de Góngora. This came to the attention of a fellow Sevillian, the powerful Conde Duque de Olivares, who invited him to return to paint a portrait of Philip IV. The king was six years younger than the artist, but discerning enough to make Velázquez at age 24 his court painter, declaring that no other should paint his portrait. The king would remain Velázquez's greatest admirer and life-long friend, all the more remarkable considering the Gormenghastian stiffness and rigours of the Spanish court. 'The liberality and affability with which he is treated by such a great monarch is incredible,' Pacheco wrote. 'He has a workshop in his gallery and his Majesty has a key to it and

d *The Surrender of Breda*, which the
aniards call *Las Lanzas* (*The Lances*). There
e portraits of court dwarves, such as
ancisco Lezcano, in which he gave his
ters an air of humanity and dignity gener-
y denied them in daily life (dwarves were
mployed as court jesters and were treated
e children, or worse).

Also present are the royal portraits: lumpy,
wildered Philip IV, a king aware enough of
s own inadequacies to let Velázquez
press them on canvas, appears in various
ses – as a hunter, a warrior, or simply
anding around wondering what's for
nner. Of his children, we see the six-year-
d Infante Balthasar Carlos in a charming,
ock-heroic pose on horseback, and again at
e age of 16. It was this prince's untimely
ath soon after the latter portrait that gave
e throne to the idiot Charles II. His sister,
e doll-like Infanta Margarita, appears by

herself and in the most celebrated of all
Velázquez's works, *Las Meninas* (*The Maids-
of-Honour*; 1656), a composition of such
inexhaustible complexity and beauty that
the Prado gives it pride of place. In 1985, a
poll of artists and critics voted it The World's
Greatest Painting. In it, not only does
Velázquez eloquently capture the everyday
atmosphere of the Spanish court (the nearly
life-sized little princess, her bizarre
entourage and, unseen except for in a mirror
in the background, her royal parents, whose
portrait he is painting), but he also turns the
then-accepted artistic limits of perspective
and dimensional space inside out: all the
figures are in focus relative to their proximity
to the light or the Infanta herself, creating an
extraordinary illusion of reality. Velázquez
painted himself in the picture (note how he
seems to be sizing up us, the viewers, as his
subject), but the red cross on his tunic, the

air in order to watch him painting at
sure, almost every day.' Ironically, the
nours and titles that Philip would bestow
Velázquez contributed to his low output,
cing the already slow-working painter
vay from the easel to deal with petty
reaucratic duties. But Velázquez never
emed to mind.

Although he would depict other subjects
any of which were lost in the royal palace
e), Velázquez spent the rest of his career
marily a portrait painter. After studying
e Titians in the royal collection, his brush-
ork become more fluid and looser, making
paintings ever more vivid. He broke with
e canons of Spanish royal portraiture by
sing his subjects in natural positions, elim-
ting superfluous detail to give their
rtraits greater life and directness.

trip to Italy (1629–31), where he absorbed
e lessons of the Venetians and Rubens, led
his mature, fluid style. This is the period of
great equestrian portraits, with their
ty of atmosphere between figures and
dscapes, and his portraits of the court
ls and dwarfs. His great *Surrender of
da* (1635) was as immediate a

contemporary historical painting for its time
as *Guernica* is for ours, only Velázquez's
focus, typically, is on the humane, on the
magnanimity of the Spanish commander,
Ambrogio Spinola, towards Justin of Nassau,
as he presents the key of the city.

The final stage of Velázquez's career dates
from his second trip to Italy (1648–51), when
he was charged with collecting paintings
and antiques for the king and with arranging
fresco painters for the new Palacio de Buen
Retiro. Velázquez's last years in Madrid, while
busy with court duties, resulted in some of
his finest and most subtly beautiful pictures:
his portraits of the sad old king, his second
wife and young children, the *Hilanderas*, as
well as the sublime *Las Meninas*, in which his
brushstrokes dissolve into blurs ('One cannot
understand it if standing too close, but from
a distance it is a miracle,' wrote an early
biographer). In 1660 he accompanied the
king to the border to arrange for the decorations for the wedding of the Infanta María
Teresa to Louis XIV of France, where he
caught a fever and died soon afterwards.

badge of the Order of Santiago, was added by King Philip's own hand, as a graceful way of informing the artist of the honour he was conferring on him.

Goya

The Goya collection is spread over the first and second floors. Like Velázquez, Francisco de Goya y Lucientes (1746–1828) held the office of court painter, in this case at the service of an even more useless monarch, Charles IV. Also like Velázquez, he was hardly inclined to flattery. Critics ever since have wondered how he got away with making his royal patron look so foolish, and the job he did on Charles' wife, the hook-nosed, ignorant and ill-tempered Queen Maria Luisa, is legendary. In every portrait and family scene, she comes out looking half fairy-tale witch, half washerwoman. Her son, later to be the reactionary King Ferdinand VII, is pictured as a teenager, and Goya makes him merely disagreeable and menacing.

Among the other famous Goyas you may compare the *Nude Maja* (on the second floor) and the *Clothed Maja*, whose model may have been the Duchess of Alba (*see* p.169; some art historians guess that the two paintings were designed to be exchanged behind a panel by a hidden mechanism). You'll also find the painter's most famous works, *The Executions of the Second of May* (*Los Fusilamientos del Dos de Mayo*) and *The Executions of Moncloa* (*Los Fusilamientos de Moncloa*), the pair commemorating the uprising of 1808 and its aftermath. The latter, much the better known, shows the impassioned patriots' faces caught in the glare of a lantern, facing the firing squad of grim, almost mechanical French soldiers. Nothing like it had ever been painted before, an unforgettable image and a prophetic prelude to the era of revolutions, mass politics and total war that was just beginning, inaugurated by the French Revolution and Napoleon. The setting is Madrid's Casa de Campo, and the spires of the old town can be made out clearly in the background.

Representing his early work, Goya's remarkable cartoons – designs for tapestries to be made by the Real Fábrica for the king's palaces – provide a dose of joy, with their vivid colours bathed in clear Castilian sunshine. These can be found on the second floor at the Puerta de Murillo end of the building. Most, such as *The Parasol* and *The Fiesta of San Isidro*, are idealized scenes of festivals or country life, and the creatures inhabiting them seem less Spaniards than angels.

In stark contrast are some of the Prado's greatest treasures, its collection of Goya's Black Paintings, late works painted on his kitchen wall following his mysterious illness. These works are separated from the others as if it were feared they would contaminate the sunnier paintings upstairs. All the well-known images of dark fantasy and terror are here: *Saturn Devouring one of his Sons*, *Duel with Cudgels*, *The Colossus (Panic)* and even nightmarish vision of the same San Isidro festivities that the artist painted so happily when he was healthy.

The Paseo del Prado L10–

Metro Atocha or Banco de España.

The Paseo del Prado, the leafy boulevard that ties the Triángulo de Arte together, was yet another innovation of the 'mayor-king' Charles III. As a son of the Enlightenment, Charles was dismayed at the haphazard, higgledy-piggledy way Madrid had grown up, and decided to give his capital a proper broad avenue, lined with worthy scientific institutions. A tree-lined path through the meadow (*prado*) near the Monasterio de San Jerónimo was selected for glory, and in 1775 architect José de Hermosilla laid out the paseo, a project that involved a massive amount of landfill and levelling. Some of the sweat was provided by speeders: Madrid's first traffic laws had just been put on the books, penalizing reckless coachmen with ten days' labour on the paseo project. By the 19th century, the paseo was a roaring success – it was the place to see and be seen in

adrid, and everyone from all walks of life
ongregated there in the evening. Six lanes
f motor traffic have since changed all that,
obably for ever.

Magnificent fountains by Ventura
odríguez frame what was called the 'Salón
el Prado' – from the Fountain of Cibeles in
e north (*see* p.140) to the **Fountain of
eptune** in the south, in front of the Prado,
ith a smaller **Fountain of Apollo** in
etween. Hermosilla's model for these was
ome's Piazza Navona, and here the foun-
ins served the same purpose as there, as
e spina of an ancient circus, for the fash-
nable carriages to go round and round.
eptune, where the supporters of Atlético de
adrid frolic to celebrate victories, features a
atue of the sea god holding his trident;
ring the 'Hunger Years' of the 1940s, he
so sported a sign, added by a local wag:
ther give me something to eat or at least
ke away my fork!'

ehind the Prado

This neighbourhood, the Barrio de los
rónimos (or the Retiro), has been the fash-
nable centre of Madrid for over a century,
d consequently has attracted quite a few
useums. In fact, museums are about all
ere is to interest the visitor these days, for,
steful as it is, this is one of the duller
rners of Madrid.

asón del Buen Retiro M12

*C/ de Alfonso XII, **t** 91 330 28 00; **metro**
tiro or Atocha. **Closed** for renovation until
e 2004; when reopened, opening times as
seo del Prado.*

he Casón del Buen Retiro was originally
e ballroom of the Palacio del Buen Retiro,
other building the Prado is revamping to
pand its exhibition space. In the past (and,
all likelihood, the future), this building
used the Prado's collection of 18th- and
th-century Spanish art, including painters
ch as Mario Fortuny, Joaquín Sorolla, José
Madrazo, Federico de Madrazo, Francisco

Pradilla and Vicente López. The restoration
involves fixing the roof and excavating two
subterranean levels for art storage. When the
museum was last open, it contained enough
little-known gems to make it worth a visit.

San Jerónimo el Real M12

*19 C/ de Ruíz de Alarcón, **t** 91 420 35 78; **metro**
Retiro or Atocha; wheelchair accessible. **Open**
daily 9–1 and 5–8.30.*

The area's oldest and certainly most
woebegone monument is the monastery of
San Jerónimo el Real, founded by Ferdinand
and Isabel in 1505, when there was nothing
else at all on this side of town. It was here
that the local nobles and the Cortes swore
their fidelity to the kings of Spain, and its
importance as a venue for royal and state
ceremonies was the factor that made Philip II
build an apartment in the vicinity, which
later evolved into a royal palace. Like the
palace itself, the monastery took so many
licks in the Peninsular War that much of it
was demolished. Only the church and some
of the ruined cloister were spared; the former
was completely restored and given a pair of
pseudo-Gothic towers. It remains the setting
for royal pageants, most recently the corona-
tion of Juan Carlos in 1975, although it still
manages to look worn out and dilapidated.

Real Academia Española
de la Lengua M12

*17 C/ de Ruíz de Alarcón, **t** 91 420 14 78; **metro**
Retiro or Atocha. Closed to the public.*

Opposite is Spain's equivalent of the
Académie Française, the Real Academia
Española de la Lengua, which fits perfectly
into this haughty neighbourhood. Both the
French and Spanish institutions are devoted
to defending the purity of their respective
language and writing a dictionary. Both
academies were founded by Bourbons, this
one by Philip V in 1714; but unlike their French
counterparts, the 40 academicians of
Castellano refrain from noisily promoting
national laws to keep out 'los hot dogs'.

Museo del Ejército (Army Museum) M11

*1 C/ de Méndez Núñez, t 91 522 89 77; **metro** Retiro or Banco de España; wheelchair accessible. **Open** Tues–Sun 10–2; adm €1, free Sat.*

At the time of writing, the Prado was planning to take over this museum in order to house 17th-century court paintings and artwork collected by the Bourbons, although this may not happen until long into the future. At present, the abandoned-looking museum pokes its scores of rusting old cannons menacingly out at the surrounding apartment blocks. Like the Casón del Buen Retiro, the building was originally part of the Palacio del Buen Retiro, a ceremonial annexe called the Salón de Reinos, dedicated to Spain's empire and used by Philip IV to hang many of Velázquez's equestrian portraits as well as *The Surrender of Breda*. Like the building itself, most of the exhibits have also seen better days: armour and arms from the conquistadors, and from the nearly invincible infantry that made Spain a European power in the days of the Catholic Kings. One of El Cid's swords is here, as is that of Boabdil el Chico (the last Moorish king of Granada, overthrown by the Catholic Monarchs), among rooms full of shiny military bric-a-brac. The Carlist and Napoleonic Wars are covered, and the Civil War, too – you can get the army's side of the story, to music ranging from the *Ride of the Valkyries* to *Shaft*.

Museo Naval L11

*5 Paseo del Prado, t 91 379 52 99; **metro** Retiro or Banco de España. **Open** Tues–Sun 10–2; closed Aug; adm free.*

This museum occupies a corner of the Ministry of Defence. Whatever relics of the Age of Exploration were not locked away in Seville's Archive of the Indies ended up here. Some of the most fascinating are the maps and charts, not simple sailors' tools, but lovely works in which art and scholarship are joined; the 1375 *Atlas Catalán* is one of these. Juan de la Cosa's *Mapa Mundi* of 1500 is the earliest Spanish map to show parts of the American coast. Another, made by Diego Rivera just 29 years later, has almost all of the Americas' Atlantic coasts, and some of the Pacific, a tribute to the hard work of Spanish explorers.

Much of the museum is given over to ship models. Some are wonderfully detailed and precise, offering real insight into the complexity and artfulness of the age of sail. Columbus' *Santa Maria* is one of these, and is a reminder of the Admiral of Ocean Sea's achievement to see how small and frail his craft really were.

Museo de Artes Decorativas M11

*12 C/ de Montalbán, t 91 532 64 99; **metro** Retiro or Banco de España; wheelchair accessible. **Open** Tues–Fri 10–5, Sat, Sun and hols 10–2; adm €2.50, free Sat after 2pm and Sun.*

Here you'll find a comprehensive collection of furniture, costume, ceramics and work in wood, textiles, gold and silver from the 15th to the 20th century – six floors of it, in fact. Every aspect of Spanish design is covered, with complete rooms furnished in various styles. The Gothic hall has leather walls and charming painted Mudéjar ceilings (the museum has exceptionally fine ones, from every period), as well as intricate reliquaries, carved chests and a 15th-century ivory horn called the Oliphant. Another curiosity is the raised *estrado*, a platform where noble Spanish women of the 15th and 16th centuries would lounge the day away, embroidering and playing music. From the 19th century come an array of fans, jewellery, Lalique glass, Art Nouveau furnishings, a little theatre of biblical scenes framed in dried flowers and yet another collection of holy bone shards. A favourite exhibit is the lovely 18th-century Valencian kitchen on the top floor, covered with whimsical tiles of food, kitchen workers and naughty cats.

Parque del Retiro N10–13

Metro Retiro, Atocha, Menéndez Pelayo or Ibiza; wheelchair accessible. Guided walks leave daily at 10am from the Puerta de Alcalá

In 1636 the Conde Duque de Olivares
decreed that a stately pleasure dome be built
at the eastern end of Madrid to distract
Philip IV while his bankrupt empire crumbled
to pieces. This royal preserve included a
fortress and palace (both long gone) and a
park. Apart from growing smaller – it once
extended westwards to the Paseo del Prado –
the Retiro has changed essentially little since
the 17th century: an elegant, formal garden,
perfect for the decorous pageants and
alliances of the Baroque era. Good king
Charles III was the first to open parts of it up
to the public, in 1767, but with a strict dress
code: men had to comb their hair and not
wear capes or hairnets, while women had to
wear shawls instead of the more seductive
mantillas. After several decades of repairs
and replantings following the Peninsular
War, the whole Retiro was opened to the
public in 1868 and has been the much loved
patrimony of the citizens of Madrid
ever since.

If possible, visit the Retiro in spring, when
the tulips and horse-chestnut trees are in
bloom; failing that, come on any Sunday,
when all Madrid comes to drink *horchata* in
the cafés and see the flowers, concerts and
other impromptu entertainments. To take a
carriage ride through the park, wait at the
little cabin marked '*Servicio de simones*' near
the entrance opposite Calle de
Antonio Maura.

Among the 400-odd acres of the Retiro are
ol fountains, a Japanese garden and,
towards the south, a seemingly endless
expanse of quiet paths among old shady
trees and gardens where you can easily
forget you're in the centre of a major metropolis, although the rustlings of busy couples
in the privacy of the undergrowth will
remind you that you are hardly alone.

The Estanque N11

A favourite thing to do in the Retiro is rent
canoes or paddleboats on the Estanque, the
broad lagoon in the centre of the park. No
king ever did less to earn such a grandiose
memorial than **Alfonso XII** (1874–86), but

that's him up on horseback decorating the
eastern end of the lake, in a monument
erected by his equally ineffectual son,
Alfonso XIII, in 1922. In the 17th century, this
was a favourite spot for royal diversions,
water pageants and plays. One of the best
remembered was a royal performance of
Calderón's *Polifemo y Circe* and *Los Incantos
de Circe* in 1663; artificial islands were built
for the action, while the audience sat around
the edge of the Estanque. The whole affair
took nine hours, including battles, sea
voyages in miniature galleys and Odysseus'
trip to the Underworld.

Buildings in the Park

An eclectic assortment of buildings dot the
Retiro and host a regular schedule of exhibitions and shows. There's the pink **Casa de
Vacas**, where cows were kept back in the
1800s to provide visitors with the freshest of
milk, and the **Palacio de Velázquez** (1883, by
Ricardo Velázquez Bosco; *t 91 573 62 45; open
Mon and Wed–Sat 11–8, Sun and hols 11–6*),
designed for a mining exhibition; it incorpo-
rates the decorated coloured bricks and tiles
that the architect would later employ in the
Ministerio de Agricultura (*see p.116*).
Velázquez Bosco also designed the
enchanting glass and iron **Palacio de Cristal**
(*t 91 588 61 37, open Tues–Fri 10–2 and 4–6,
Sat and Sun 11–5*) in 1887 for the Philippines
Exposition, using London's Crystal Palace as a
model. Manuel Azaña was elected President
of the Republic here in 1936. Both these *palacios* are now under the wing of the Reina
Sofía museum and are used as space for
temporary exhibitions; they tend to be even
more cutting-edge than the main Reina
Sofía building.

Angel Caído O13

At the southern end of the park, seek out
the monument to the *Angel Caído* ('Fallen
Angel', 1878) by Ricardo Bellver, shown
tumbling head first from heaven. Madrid is
proud to be the only city anywhere to have a
statue of Satan himself. Before Lucifer fell to
earth on this spot, it was occupied by the

Royal Porcelain Factory, founded by Charles III in 1760. According to the *madrileños*, it was doing so well (you can see some examples of the plates made here in the Museo Municipal; *see* p.160) that it began to compete with British porcelain-makers, which is why the British Army officiously declared it damaged beyond repair in the Peninsular War and knocked it down.

Observatorio Astronómico Nacional M14

3 C/ de Alfonso XII, t 91 527 01 07, w www.oan.es; metro Atocha. Open Mon–Fri 10–2; adm free.

On a hill towards the south entrance to the Retiro stands the Observatorio Astronómico, a beautiful Neoclassical building by Juan de Villanueva. This was commissioned by Charles III, in 1785, although he never had a chance to peep through one of its telescopes – he died before it was begun in 1790, and after years of neglect and extensive damage caused by the French, it wasn't completed until 1845. The result resembles a Palladian villa, with its Corinthian porch and rotunda, although the four parallelepipeds attached to the corners mark it as a Spanish building. The museum, with a Foucault's pendulum suspended from the rotunda, has a collection of old telescopes, including two built by Herschel, and other astronomical instruments. But if you want to look at the stars you have to make an appointment.

Real Jardín Botánico L–M13

2 Plaza de Murillo, t 91 420 30 17; metro Atocha; wheelchair accessible. Open June–Aug daily 10–9, Sept–May daily 10–dusk; adm €1.50; free guided tours in Spanish only, group tours must be arranged in advance.

This particularly special urban oasis was commissioned by Charles III, and developed by architect Juan de Villanueva and botanist Casimiro Gómez Ortega. The goal was to nurture species from Spain's colonies, and find new herbal remedies. After decades of neglect, the gardens were completely restored according to the original plans in the 1980s, and feature an estimated 30,000 plants, many of them from far-flung corners of the globe; the more exotic flourish in a magnificent hothouse, while ex-Prime Minister Felipe González's bonsai collection gets a shady pavilion all of its own.

Along the south end of the Jardín Botánico runs the Cuesta de Claudio Moyano, a street where, on fine days (and especially on Sundays), **secondhand bookstalls** offer their tempting and sometimes bizarre wares, maybe even the one title you've been searching for all these years.

AROUND THE THYSSEN-BORNEMISZA

Museo Colección Thyssen-Bornemisza L11

Palacio de Villahermosa, 8 Paseo del Prado, t 91 420 39 44, f 91 420 27 80, w www .museothyssen.org; metro Banco de España; wheelchair accessible. Open Tues–Sun 10–7; adm €4.80, €6.60 includes temporary exhibition. If you want to take a break, make sure you get a stamp ('sello') on your wrist at the information desk.

The directors of the Reina Sofía, reeling from the media response to the controversies surrounding their early policies, were glad to have the spotlight eased off them for a while in October 1992, when everyone's attention switched up the road to the Palacio de Villahermosa. Thanks to the persuasiveness of his wife, Carmen 'La Tita' Cervera, a former Miss Spain, Baron Hans-Heinrich Thyssen-Bornemisza had already decided on Madrid as the temporary home for the cream of his unique collection of art (Madrid having outbid other cities, including London, represented by none other than Prince Charles). In 1993, the arrangement was made permanent: the Spanish government purchased the

llection for the extremely reasonable sum
44,000 million pesetas (€264,000,000).
espite the recession, and the further
illions required to convert the palace into
ouilding to house the paintings per-
anently, the acquisition seemed to
present an unmissable opportunity to
oost Madrid's, and Spain's, already high
ofile on the international art scene.
The collection, started in the 1920s by the
esent baron's father, Baron Heinrich
yssen-Bornemisza, is idiosyncratic, eclectic
d fun, and offers a fascinating insight into
e personal taste of two men who shared
e same magpie compulsion. When the
der baron died and the paintings were
read out among his heirs, the present
ron diligently went about buying them
ck from his kin, and then kept adding and
ding, until the collection's old home, the
la Favorita in Lugano, was bursting at
e seams.

ike a prized and precious stamp collection,
e museum contains a little of everything –
ere's an entry on practically every page of
history, from the religious works of 13th-
ntury Italy to the brash output of Europe
d the USA in the 1960s and 70s – with the
o Barons' particular favourites represented
larger quantities (they liked 19th-century
nerican painting; you might not). A stan-
rd bearer of art for the modern world, the
esent Baron Thyssen's hoard is widely
garded as the world's finest private art
lection after that of the British royal
mily. He has claimed that he learned all he
ows about art simply by hanging his
tures up and looking at them; with an
proach as honest and pragmatic as this it
vholly consistent that he decided to make
ossible for the general public to share
enjoyment.

o create the gallery spaces, architect
fael Moneo (who is currently building an
dition to the Prado) was given a shell of a
Iding, and the result avoids the slightly
tiseptic quality of many modern
useums, the walls washed in a warm cross
ween salmon and terracotta (the

Finding Your Way Around the Thyssen-Bornemisza

The chronological sequence of works begins on the top floor (reached by the lift or stairs towards the centre of the building) and works its way, anticlockwise, downwards. The sequence was arranged like this so that the modern works could benefit from being hung in the high-ceilinged ground-floor rooms. In the basement is a café and a space for temporary exhibitions.

Baroness's favourite colour – she insisted on it) and bathed in a very pleasing balance of natural and artificial light.

In the entrance, you are welcomed by two pairs of full-length portraits: of Queen Sofia and King Juan Carlos I, and of the Baron and Baroness, Titi in a remarkable winged cocktail dress with a smudgy canine at her feet.

Second Floor

The collection opens with one of its highlights, a treasure trove of gems of **Primitive and medieval Italian religious art**, including a hauntingly simple and lovely 13th-century statue of the *Madonna and Child*, and 14th-century gilded panels of exquisite beauty by the likes of Duccio di Buoninsegna and Simone Martini.

These are followed by **15th-century works from the Low Countries**, among them Jan van Eyck's stirring and brilliantly executed monochrome *Annunciation Diptych* (c.1435–41), depicting the Angel Gabriel and the Virgin Mary with the Holy Spirit fluttering above her head in the form of a dove. Only rather then as 'real' figures, van Eyck shows them as stone sculptures, reflected in the shiny black stone behind them: for the time a unique work of art depicting art. *Clothing the Naked* (c.1470) by the Master of St Gudule offers an interesting illustration of the development of perspective techniques: a courtyard recedes, like a stage set, behind the figures in the foreground. Rogier van der Weyden's tiny, immaculate *Madonna and Child Enthroned* (c.1433), in which the Virgin sits in a stone alcove carved with New

Testament scenes, is a fascinating point of reference for his large, slightly later work, *The Descent from the Cross*, which hangs in the Prado. Beside this is Petrus Christus' symbolic masterpiece, *Our Lady of the Dry Tree* (c.1450), hung with 15 letter As, each representing an Ave María.

The next room contains **15th-century Italian works** such as Bramantino's spooky, cadaverous *Resurrected Christ* and Ercole de' Roberti's charming mythology, *The Argonauts Leaving Colchis* (c.1480), a rarefied work from the Humanist court of Ferrara. Another member of the same school, Cosmè Tura, contributes an almost surreal *St John the Evangelist on Patmos*.

Early Renaissance portraits form another high point of the collection. There are plenty of familiar faces here, including Holbein's *Henry VIII* (c.1534–6), Memling's *Young Man at Prayer* (c.1485), Campin's uncompromisingly crisp *Stout Man* (c.1425) and Antonello da Messina's *Portrait of a Man* (c.1475–6), whose eyes fix you with his direct, intelligent gaze. There is also a *Portrait of Giovanna Tornabuoni* (1488) by Domenico Ghirlandaio, one-time tutor to Michelangelo, who includes a Latin inscription behind the sitter's elegant neck: 'If art could portray character and virtue, no painting in the world would be more beautiful.' Isabel la Católica's favourite painter, the Hispano-Flemish Juan de Flandres, contributes the exquisite, wistful *Portrait of an Infanta* (c.1496), a Spanish princess minus all the usual trappings; it could be Catherine of Aragon or, more poignantly, Isabel's daughter and heir to the throne, the young Juana the Mad.

Rafael Moneo designed the long and windowed **Villahermosa Gallery**, running the length of the building, to recall similar painting *gallerias* in Italian palaces. Most of the works here are portraits – the special favourite of the first Baron Thyssen. Here another Raphael, *the* Raphael, painted the *Portrait of a Young Man* (c.1515), believed to be Alessandro de' Medicis.

Off the gallery, a row of rooms contains **16th-century paintings**. The first is dedicated to the Italians. Vittore Carpaccio's delightful *Young Knight in a Landscape* (1510) is one of the Thyssen's most famous works, remarkab for its richly detailed allegorical backdrop. Carpaccio's fellow Venetians are here, too: a late *Sacra Conversazione* (c.1510) by Giovanni Bellini, a lushly coloured work against a serene background; and *La Bella* (1525) by Bellini's pupil Palma Vecchio, renowned for h talent for painting beautiful women. Venetian Sebastiano del Piombo's masterful *Portrait of Ferry Carondelet* (1512) was long attributed to Raphael. One of the great quirl painters of the Renaissance, Piero di Cosimo shows the Virgin and Angel tickling a laughing baby Jesus. In the *Virgin, Child and John*, Leonardo's pupil Bernardino Luini demonstrates his skill in his master's charac teristic *sfumato*, or smoky shadows. In stark contrast, Domenico Beccafumi's *Virgin and Child with SS. John and Jerome* is a near Day-Glo example of the startling colours of Tusc Mannerism, the same used by Michelangelo in the Sistine Chapel.

Among the 16th-century German works i the next two rooms are five scenes of a stri ingly vivid *Crucifixion* by Derick Baegert, fro a painting cut up centuries ago. Dürer's *Jes among the Doctors* (1506) is a brilliant, oppressively compact composition built around a central motif of two pairs of hand the youthful ones of Jesus and the sinewy ones of one of the six suspicious-looking priests that seem to be closing in on him. I the same room is a range of works by the Cranach clan: an intense *Virgin and Child with Grapes*, *Portrait of Emperor Charles V* with his huge overbite and a sultry *Nymph the Spring* by the elder Lucas, and the funny cross-dressing *Hercules and Maids of Omphale* by his brother Hans. From the sar school is another of the Thyssen's signatur works, Hans Baldung Grien's stylish, enig-matic *Portrait of a Woman* (1530), using an extremely limited palette; his *Adam and Ev* rather unusually shows Adam enjoying Eve charms just before the Fall.

Dutch paintings from the same century f the next room, starring Marten van

eemskerck's memorable *Portrait of a Lady*
inning (1531), and the quirky Joachim
tinir, whose *Rest on the Flight to Egypt* is
ore concerned with the scenery than the
minal religious subject. Patinir's followers
ould simply leave out the biblical figures
d paint empty landscapes.

The **great masters of 16th- and 17th-
ntury painting** are in the following rooms:
ery late *St Jerome in the Desert* (1575) by
tian is an excellent example of his late
yle, painted with broad brushstrokes and a
lour tonalism, radical for the age, that
ould reverberate down through the late
orks of Cézanne. Titian's freedom of
ndling more immediately inspired
toretto (*Paradise*; 1583) and El Greco,
hose *Annunciation* painted while still in
nice was directly influenced by Titian's and
akes an interesting comparison to the one
the same room that he painted for
adrid's Monasterio de la Encarnación.

The **Baroque collection** kicks off with *St
therine of Alexandria* (1597), an early
ravaggio that has been compared to a
mish still life. His later style, with its revo-
ionary realistic depiction of biblical figures
d dramatic lighting, had its greatest
lowers in José de Ribera (*Lamentation*) and
attia Preti (*The Concert*, all in earth tones).
ese are followed by brighter canvases by
urillo and Claude Lorraine before the
lection takes a diversion into 18th-century
nice; there are views by Canaletto and
ncesco Guardi, Giambattista Tiepolo's
minous *Death of Hyacinth*, complete with
e fatal badminton racket, and one of
nre-master Pietro Longhi's most delightful
orks, *The Tickle* (1755).

ubens dominates among the Flemish and
tch Baroque paintings, which include one
the museum's many interesting juxtaposi-
ns: Matthias Stom's *Supper at Emmaus*
633–9) and Hendrick ter Brugghen's *Esau
ling his Birthright* (c.1627). Both lend
ense drama to climactic biblical moments
casting them in candlelight.

First Floor

A series of rooms is devoted to **17th-century
Dutch paintings**, the best and most
endearing of which show jolly, ribald genre
scenes from peasant life, such as Frans Hals'
skittish *Fisherman Playing the Violin* (c.1630).
These are followed by **Rococo and
Neoclassical works**, including a Watteau
(*Pierrot Content*; 1712) and portraits by
Reynolds and Gainsborough, which number
among the very few English paintings in
Madrid outside of the Museo Lázaro
Galdiano. Next comes an unusual collection,
possibly the only one of its kind in a
European museum: paintings by **19th-
century American artists**. It's a mixed bag,
from chocolate-boxy autumnal sunsets by
Frederic Edwin Church, John Frederick
Kensett and Jasper Francis Cropsey to an
innovative still life by John Frederick Peto,
Tom's River (1905), displaying a bold sense of
composition years ahead of its time. One
curiosity is the *Portrait of Washington's Cook*
by Gilbert Stuart, whose famous portrait of
the first president adorns classrooms across
the United States. In contrast are the paintings by American painters who lived in
Europe most of their lives, James McNeill
Whistler and John Singer Sargent; the latter,
a close friend of Sorolla, painted in a similar
style of loose brushstrokes shot with light
(*The Venetian Onion Seller*).

Among other **19th-century European works**
are three late Goyas, including *Asensio Julià*
(1798), a portrait of the artist who worked
with him in San Antonio de la Florida, and
the delightful laughing *El Tío Paquete*,
painted just before Goya left for Bordeaux.
There is a fine shimmery late work by Corot,
*Setting out for a Walk in the Parc des Lions in
Port-Marly*, and another by John Constable,
The Lock (1824), full of silvery highlights and
rich colours, a fitting prelude to the selection
of **Impressionist paintings**. This is sadly
rather slim (although it does contain a lovely
Renoir, his *Woman with a Parasol in a
Garden*). The **Post-impressionist and Fauve
painters** are better represented: a few glori-
ously lurid Van Goghs; a Cézanne *Portrait of a*

Farmer (1901–6), relaxing cross-legged in dappled blue shade; Degas' gauzy snapshot-like *Swaying Dancer*; a lovely portrait by Toulouse-Lautrec, *The Red Head in a White Blouse*; and some riotously coloured works by Dufy, Derain and Vlaminck.

The Thyssen's collection of **Expressionist painting** is particularly strong. Some of its leading exponents are here, including Ernst Ludwig Kirchner (1880–1938), Max Beckmann (1884–1950) and Egon Schiele (1890–1918); Schiele's *Houses next to the River* seem to have eyes instead of windows. The iconic early 20th-century **Blaue Reiter movement** is represented by typically symbolic horsey works by Franz Marc and August Macke. Although he exhibited with the Blaue Reiter, American-born Lyonel Feininger developed an original prismatic Cubism all his own, which he mostly applied to marine and urban scenes; see his *Ships and Lady in Mauve* (1922).

The neurotic years of the Weimar Republic led to the final stage of German Expressionism, the **Neue Sachlichkeit** (New Objectivity); Otto Dix's quasi-photographic *Hugo Erfurth with a Dog* stands out, its precision in tempera a throwback to the early Renaissance. From Christian Schad there is his discomforting *Portrait of Doctor Haustein* (1928), a tense, psychologically charged work in which the doctor of the title stares out at the viewer, his very smooth hands clasped off-centre, while behind him looms the menacing, distorted shadow of his mistress with a hint of smoke at her lips. Doctor Haustein's infidelity was one of the factors that pushed his wife to suicide; he himself took poison in 1933 rather than be captured by the Gestapo. The same room contains George Grosz' *Metropolis* (1917) with all the frenetic movement of Fritz Lang's famous film of the same name, and Ludwig Meidner's troubling *House on a Corner in Dresden*.

Ground Floor

A radical change in atmosphere marks the beginning of the collection clumped together as the **Experimental Avant-gardes**. Cubism is represented by its three brightest

stars, Georges Braque, Pablo Picasso and Juan Gris, and the individual spin-offs they inspired, Léger, the Delaunays and the Czech master Frantisek Kupka. The Russian pre- and post-Revolution Avant-garde are well represented, and there is plenty of space to appreciate the scale of the Mondrians – two of them, *Composition I* (1931) and *New York City, New York*, left unfinished when he died in 1942 – and Filonov's astoundingly complex untitled canvas.

A section entitled '**The Synthesis of Modernism**' contains Chagall's delightful, dreamlike *The Rooster* (1929), and more paintings by Picasso (the classicizing *Harlequin with a Mirror*; 1923) and Braque, plus glittering works by Ernst, Klee, Kandinsky, Léger and Miró, followed by American Modernists: Mark Rothko, Georgia O'Keeffe, Jackson Pollock and emigré Surrealist Arshile Gorky.

Along with a fine Magritte (*Key to the Field* and other Surrealist works, Baron Thyssen got his hands on an excellent Dalí, his *Dream Caused by the Flight of a Bee Around a Pomegranate a Second before Awakening* (1944), but it is the very last section that contains perhaps the most striking works of all: Edward Hopper's *Hotel Room* (1931); a characteristically disturbing Francis Bacon (*Portrait of George Dyer in a Mirror*; 1968); an unforgettable Lichtenstein (*Woman in the Bath*; 1963), in which every dot really is painted by hand to look like a screen print; Hockney (*In Memoriam of Cecchio Bracci*; 1962); a startling Tom Wesselmann (*Nude No.1*; 1970); and last of all, one of the best works in the museum – Richard Estes' multi-layered slices of New York (*Telephone Booths*; 1967).

Plaza de la Lealtad L11

The large buildings on the circular Plaza de la Lealtad (Loyalty Square), opposite the Thyssen, were designed to blend in with its Neoclassical stateliness: the **Ritz Hotel** with its delightful tea garden, built in 1908 at the special request of Alfonso XIII (whose

mous wedding was marred not only by a
omb, but also by the lack of suitably posh
oms in which to lodge his guests); and the
olsa de Comercio, or Stock Exchange, which
ometimes has free art exhibitions as well as
permanent one on the institution itself. In
e centre of the square, a patriotic **obelisk**,
ected in 1840 to a design by González
elázquez, is the chief monument to the
ctims of the 2 May uprising – in fact, their
mains are in the urn. The gates are usually
cked – perhaps to prevent over-curious
urists singeing themselves on the eternal
ame that burns in front of the tomb.

ROUND THE
EINA SOFÍA

Museo Nacional Centro
e Arte Reina Sofía L14

*C/ de Santa Isabel, t 91 467 50 62, f 91 467
63, w museoreinasofia.mcu.es; metro*
ocha; wheelchair accessible. **Open** *Mon and*
ed–Sat 10–9, Sun 10–2.30; closed 1 Jan, 24,
and 26 Dec; free **guided tours** Mon and
ed at 5pm, Sat at 11am; **adm** €3.10, free Sat
ter 2.30pm, Sun, 18 May, 12 Oct and 6 Dec.
With the continuing success of ARCO,
adrid's annual contemporary art fair
unded in the early 1980s, and with prom-
ng work emerging from local artists, the
adrileños' active interest in modern art has
ver been at such a high. It was partly in
der to satisfy this popular passion that the
anish government set about providing
eir capital with a world-class 20th-century-
: museum, to replace the old Museo
añol de Arte Contemporáneo.
Conversion of the defunct General Hospital
hich dates back to 1781) began in 1980, and
e Centro de Arte Reina Sofía was inaugu-
ed by the shy but much loved queen in
86. Cynics muttered that the timing of the
ening was no more than a vote-catching
y in this, an election year, since the

Finding Your Way Around the Reina Sofía

The paintings, sketches and sculptures occupy the second and fourth floors of the building and are grouped chronologically and according to stylistic or conceptual affinity; you'll find you have to weave about a little to follow the intended order of the rooms. The first part of the collection is displayed on the second floor (rooms 1–17) and covers the final years of the 19th century until the end of the Second World War. Later works are upstairs on the fourth floor (rooms 18–45). Temporary exhibitions (and there are often several going on at once) can be found in Espacio UNO on the ground floor and on the third floor.

---

building wasn't actually ready – the air-conditioning, for example, was woefully inadequate. After this abortive inauguration, it was back to the drawing board, and, four years and several more millions of pesetas later, a second opening ceremony was held. The building, graced by its three new land-mark glass lifts (or 'crystal towers'), was by now fully equipped to house both temporary exhibitions and a permanent collection of art: all it lacked was a quorum of internation-ally famous paintings. It was two more years before the Reina Sofía really made its debut as an art centre to be reckoned with: in 1992, Spain's golden year, Picasso's *Guernica* was moved here (*see* 'Controversial Moves').

One of the Reina Sofía's greatest assets is the huge amount of space it has at its disposal. As well as having plenty of room for its permanent collection, it has large gallery spaces for temporary exhibitions. There is also an excellent bookshop, a decent café, an oasis of a courtyard garden, a library, a music archive and education unit, and enough supplementary resource areas fully to justify its status as an energetic multimedia community arts centre.

Second Floor

The Reina Sofía's permanent collection contains works by every one of Spain's

Controversial Moves

In 1992, Picasso's *Guernica* was moved to the Reina Sofía from the Prado's annexe, the Casón del Buen Retiro. This was done in spite of Picasso's own instructions left with New York's Museum of Modern Art, that it should return the painting to Spain when liberty was restored there and that it should hang in the Prado, outwardly as a gesture towards the modernization of that collection, but also as the ultimate exorcism of the Civil War and Franco. His wish was granted in 1981, and millions of Spaniards made the pilgrimage to the Prado to see a part of their history denied them under 40 years of dictatorship. When the Spanish government proposed the removal of the painting to the Reina Sofía, there were bitter objections from Picasso's surviving relatives, but these were over-ruled in the interests of the fulfilment of a master plan: the Prado was to hold the Old Masters, the Casón del Buen Retiro the 19th-century art and the Reina Sofía the 20th-century works, with *Guernica*, arguably the 20th century's most famous painting, taking pride of place. The superseding of Picasso's will has, however, led to three other places staking a claim to his masterpiece: Malaga as his birthplace, Barcelona as the city where he grew up and began his career, and Bilbao, with the nearest museum to *Guernica* itself.

celebrated 20th-century artists, which together amount to solid evidence, if any were needed, to back up the nation's claim to the title of contemporary creative super-power. Pablo Picasso, Salvador Dalí, Joan Miró, Juan Gris, Julio González, Antoni Tàpies, José Gutiérrez Solana and Antonio Saura are all represented.

The opening rooms set the scene for the Avant-garde works to come; Anglada-Camarasa's *Portrait of Sonia de Klamery, Countess Pradère* rubs glittering shoulders with the sombre portraits of **Ramón Casas**. The next room is entirely devoted to the paintings of **Solana**; in his *Tertulia at Café de Pombo* (1920) we are given a sombre glimpse of that typically *madrileño* institution of the late 19th and early 20th century – the *tertulia*, the regular gatherings and discussion of the intelligentsia in the cafés. The Café de Pombo on the Puerta del Sol was one of the most famous until the Civil War; Solana includes himself in the coterie.

The curvy, colourful works of **Sonia Delaunay**, and severely graceful lead sculptures of **Jacques Lipchitz** come next, along with works by other members of the early Avant-garde. In the adjacent gallery, increasingly mature paintings by **Juan Gris** line the walls, dominated by the coolly confident *Portrait of Josette*, his wife. A tiny room, not much more than a hallway, displays the superb fluid traceries, deconstructed busts and skin-skeletons in bronze and iron of **Pablo Gargallo** (1881–1934), who introduced Picasso to metal sculpture and in turn was influenced by Cubism.

Gargallo's arch *Mask of Greta Garbo with Lock of Hair* flicks an insouciant glance as you pass through to the galleries containing some early, supernatural-looking **Miró** portraits. These are divided from his later works by a gallery devoted to the remarkable sculpture of **Julio González** (1876–1942), one of the first to render iron as an artistic medium and to speak as much with void space as with solid material. The space is shared with the delicate sculptures of the American Abstract Expressionist **David Smith**, who described González as the 'father of all sculpture in iron in this century'.

It is easy to be distracted from these with *Guernica* just a room away. The lead-up to the painting has **Picasso**'s stern-faced *Woman in Blue* (1901) presiding over an adjacent gallery of his early work. This painting had a lucky escape from oblivion when Picasso disowned it after it failed to receive much recognition at a show; years later it was discovered by a private collector. Also here is his eerie *Still Life (Dead Birds)* (1912). Usually a hefty knot of people are gathered

ound *Guernica*, placed dramatically alone
ong one long wall of the central gallery
ee 'Guernica').

Alexander Calder's (1898–1976) delightful
onstellation (1940), an airy wood and
re mobile of abstract spheres, floats
onchalantly in a nearby room, along
th works from other early Surrealists:
an Arp's bold wood reliefs, **André Masson**'s
rebral paintings and, finally, the lyrical
intings of **Vassily Kandinsky**, founder of
ostract Expressionism.

Dalí's works are also given a whole room to
emselves; particularly outstanding are *Girl*
the Window, *The Invisible Man* and *The*
eat Masturbator. Some of his early paint-
gs show him dabbling in the Cubist style –
scinating precursors to the better-known
eces. A product of his collaboration with
an Ray, an intriguing, dreamy oil and
aster sculpture, *Portrait of Joella*, sits in the
xt room along with works by other
embers of the Surrealist movement,
cluding the bleakly nostalgic Spanish
tist **Oscar Domínguez** (1906–57).

Dalí's collaborations with the experi-
ental film-maker **Luis Buñuel** (they met as
udents in Madrid's Residencia de
tudiantes; *see* p.148) – *An Andalucian Dog*
29) and *The Golden Age* (1930), co-scripted
th Dalí – are screened in Room 12.

ignificant numbers of Spanish artists took
residence in Paris between the wars, and a
ection of their output, including sweetly
stalgic works such as the evocative *Joy of*
Basque Country (1920) by **Daniel Vázquez**
az, are grouped together in a gallery
voted to the various movements which
olved in Spanish art after the First World
ar. In an interesting juxtaposition, three
rks – by **José de Togores i Llach** (*Nudes on a*
ach*; 1922), **Rosario Velasco** (*Adam and Eve*;
2) and **Balbuena** (*Nude*; 1932) – each
hibit an obsessive, almost architectural
erest in the smooth rendering of the
man form. The unsettling *Accident* (1936),
Alfonso Ponce de León, uncannily presages
own death later that year.

Guernica

In 1936, Picasso, then living full time in
Paris, was commissioned by the Republic to
supply a painting for Spain's pavilion at the
Paris World Exhibition of 1937. He dawdled,
unable to decide what to paint, then in May
1937 began work on *Guernica*, in immediate,
outraged response to the events of the
previous month. When the German Condor
Legion practised its new theory of saturation
bombing on the Basque town of Guernica in
April 1937, Franco most likely had not been
informed. Nevertheless, the Nationalists
were forced to create an elaborate lie – they
said the Communists had planted bombs in
the sewers – and it became the official
version until Franco's death. Picasso was
determined to show the truth: his use of
black and white gives the painting the
immediacy of a newspaper photo.

Guernica is much more than a moment of
terror caught in the glare of an electric bulb.
What seemed so mysterious, shocking and
revolutionary in 1937 now seems quite
familiar and eloquent to us, so much have
our ways of seeing changed since it was
painted. Picasso's preliminary sketches
displayed in the adjoining gallery of his
earlier works show that the fallen horse and
rider in the centre were in the artist's mind
from the beginning. In them we can see the
image of Guernica's destroyers: the man on
horseback, the bully, the crusader, the
caudillo, the conqueror meeting a bad end
from his own designs. The meaning is clear –
with such an atrocity as this, the man on
horseback has finally gone too far.

The penultimate rooms of the first part of
the museum's permanent collection are
given over to the Asturian painter **Luis**
Fernández, also a prolific art theoretician; the
slim, elegant sculptures of **Alberto Sánchez**;
and the vivid, schematic compositions of
Benjamín Palencia.

The final room on this floor is dedicated to
sculpture; although it focuses on **Miró**'s
bronzes, including the sublimely simple

Wind Clock (1967), other notable pieces include **Angel Ferrant**'s mobiles and sculptures made from 'found objects', and **Ramón Marinello**'s wonderful *Figures in Front of the Sea* (1936) – organic plaster and wood reliefs in simple white.

Fourth Floor

Up on the fourth floor (take the speedy glass lift for wonderful views), the museum picks up the story in the 1940s when the Spanish art scene was characterized by a desire to rebuild and regroup in the wake of the Civil War. Postwar trauma is evident in some of the earliest works exhibited here, but, as the 40s gave way to the 50s, a more liberal mood of catharsis took hold. Among the works from this period are boxy sculptures by the quixotic Basque master **Jorge de Oteiza**; bristling, spiky pieces by **Pablo Serrano**; flamboyant, blazing paintings by the Andalucian **José Guerrero**; and light, filmy, obscure compositions by **Manuel Mompó** – as well as the large geometric canvases of the co-operative **Equipo 57**.

All these jostling Avant-garde theories are put into their European context in the next series of rooms. The bathos of **Francis Bacon**'s bleak figures contrasts with the Minimalist showmanship of **Yves Klein**'s slashed canvases and monochrome paintings, while organic **Henry Moore** sculptures complement the three-dimensional pieces, such as *Spatial Conception*, *The End of God*, by **Lucio Fontana**. **Antonio López García** (1936–), a leading member of the Madrid Realism movement which was instrumental in the renewal of Madrid's art scene in the 1960s and 1970s, has some meticulous urban portraits of Madrid, placed alongside the life-sized sculpted figures of **Francisco López Hernández** (he died in 2002).

Nearby, the works of the Basque **Eduardo Chillida**, one of Spain's greatest sculptors, are scooped from wood and terracotta, or wrought from iron and stone. After the ripped, rucked and daubed fabric works by **Millares** and the turbulent, jolting paintings of **Antonio Saura**, the series culminates in a

room devoted to texture-obsessed **Antoni Tàpies**, from his early sculptures made out of junk to his later stark monochromes.

The **Equipo Crónica** group jibe at American mass culture in works such as *Painting is like Hitting* (1964), a Pop Art painting which has two black-and-white TV baddies fighting it out amid a shower of paint tubes. **Eduardo Arroyo**'s dark, cartoonish night paintings keep them company. A side room is devoted to the multicoloured invitation cards to so-called 'concerts' by the quirky, politically provocative **Zaj** group.

But Minimalism strikes back with the bright clear canvases of **Ellsworth Kelly**, the huge formal iron cubes of **Donald Judd** and **Soto**'s rather staggering *Yellow and White Extension*, before **Schnabel**'s vast, lucid *Buen Retiro Ducks* series, painted as a gift to the Spanish people.

Plaza Emperador Carlos V L14

***Metro** Atocha.*

The Paseo del Prado (*see* p.104) ends at the Plaza Emperador Carlos V. It's not immediately apparent, but this square represents one of civic-minded Madrid's most significant environmental victories of the 1980s. Not so long ago, the entire plaza was buried under a ghastly, multi-level highway interchange *madrileños* called the 'scalextric' after the model racing-car circuit. The scalextric was Mayor Tierno's pet peeve, and he saw it dismantled just before he died, as part of his decade-long Operation Atocha.

The traffic is still pretty bad, speeding around another fountain, a replica of the **Fuente de la Alcachofa** designed by Ventura Rodríguez in 1781 for the bottom end of the Paseo del Prado; the original was dismantled and shuttled off to the Retiro when the Estación de Atocha was built. A mermaid and a triton hold the Madrid coat-of-arms while four children support a granite artichoke, an allegory of wisdom, which lies at the core of subject and can only be discovered by peeling away the layers and dipping them in butter

Ministerio de Agricultura M14

Another of 19th-century Madrid's great art pieces, the ministry was designed in 1893 by Ricardo Velázquez Bosco, who married Neo-Mudéjar to Belle Epoque in a shotgun wedding. This centre of farm bureaucracy is decorated with flying horses and colourful ceramics by Zuloaga, one of the masters of the art. Like the sublime Palacio de Comunicaciones at the top of the Paseo del Prado (see p.140), it elevates what might seem merely functional to an opulence assumed by the more outrageous Babylonian potentates.

Estación de Atocha L14–N15

In 19th-century Madrid, trains and their passengers required pizzazz too, and they got it in the cast-iron and glass Atocha station, designed by Alberto del Palacio in 1892. After 100 years of faithful service it was earmarked for a facelift, including major re-modelling to provide a terminal for the new high-speed Madrid to Seville AVE link. Rafael Moneo was put in charge of the project, and in 1992 the old Atocha station reopened as a shining new temple to rail travel, complete with an indoor shopping and eating emporium. Its centrepiece is an acclimatized tropical garden, with nervous-looking goldfish swimming in pools beneath soaring palm trees. Steam filters down onto this mini urban jungle through ducts in the roof. The effect is spectacular; it's a pity, then, that the glass panels in the ceiling don't admit enough light (hence the banks of artificial lights), and that the designer chose exotic palms rather than local ones, so many of the trees are struggling to survive. If you're catching a Cercania train or a slow train to the south, the newer Atocha station with its rotunda, also designed by Moneo, is adjacent.

Museo de Antropología/ Etnología M14

*68 C/ de Alfonso XII or Paseo de la Infanta Isabel II, **t** 91 530 64 18; **metro** Atocha. **Open** Tues–Sat 10–7.30, Sun and hols 10–2; **adm** €2.40, free Sat afternoon and Sun.*

In the merry-go-round of Madrid's museums, this was formerly the Museo de Etnología. Few visitors make it here and more likely than not you will find yourself alone among the Amazonian shrunken heads, African initiation bonnets, Mongolian tents and subdued cheers of the bored, card-playing guards.

Its permanent exhibitions on physical and cultural anthropology are mostly gleaned from Spain's colonies, with an especially interesting section on the Philippines. Most of the truly bizarre artefacts, including a stylish Inuit raincoat made from seal intestines and a bell-bedecked bottom pad, good for shimmying, come from the original 19th-century Cabinet of Curiosities of Dr González Velasco, the museum's founder, a surgeon and one of Madrid's most famous eccentrics. According to dark rumour, he embalmed the body of his young daughter and would prop her up in his carriage for rides down the Paseo del Prado.

Panteón de Hombres Ilustres N14–15

*3 C/ de Julián Gayarre; **metro** Menéndez Pelayo.*

Started in Spain's topsy-turvy 19th century, the project of providing a suitable, central-ized last resting place for the nation's great men never really got off the ground, unable to get past the politically sensitive problems of deciding who actually rated (opinion changed with each change of government) and the fact that the remains of most of the eligible neutral candidates, such as Cervantes, Calderón de la Barca and Velázquez, were long lost. Designed after Pisa's Campo Santo, the pantheon has a

number of elaborate tombs, some of whose residents were, in the age-old Madrid custom, later relocated.

Real Basílica de Nuestra Señora de Atocha N15

*1 C/ de Julián Gayarre, t 91 551 38 04; **metro** Menéndez Pelayo.*

Next to the Panteón is the Real Basílica de Atocha, a bland, neo-Baroque structure rebuilt after the Civil War. The cult of the Virgin of Atocha is one of the oldest in Madrid. The story goes that a figure of the Virgin was discovered in the esparto grass (*atocha*) shortly after Madrid was captured by the Moors, and became a rallying point among the local Christians. One, Gracián Ramírez, fearing he would be killed in the battles, slit the throats of his wife and daughters to keep them from falling into the hands of the infidels. When he survived, however, he was filled with remorse and went to pray to the Virgin – only to find his family miraculously restored to life. As with the Virgin of the Almudena, the Virgin of Atocha was given a big boost after the Reconquista, thanks to the royal patronage of Alfonso VI. A few *madrileños* still keep up the custom of making a special visit before their wedding, to pray for a happy marriage.

Real Fábrica de Tapices (Tapestry Factory) O15

*2 C/ de Fuenterrabia, t 91 434 05 51; **metro** Menéndez Pelayo; wheelchair accessible. **Open** Mon–Fri 10–2; closed Aug; **adm** €2.50.*

A bit further along, Calle de Julián Gayarre leads to a handicrafts workshop fit for kings. In all Madrid's royal residences, as well as the Ritz Hotel, hang tapestries made here. Ever since Philip V founded it in the 1710s as Spain's answer to Paris' Gobelins, the weavers of the Real Fábrica have served the Spanish élite's love of fine, pictorial tapestries – not only decorative, but a positive asset to any draughty palace during the chill Castilian winters. Its best-known productions, of course, are those woven to Goya's designs before he became court painter, the cartoons for which are now hanging in the Prado.

Much of the work that comes to the factory in these centrally heated days is repairs of older works, which require an impressive amount of skill, matching colou▮ and intricate designs. You may watch the master weavers (there are only 42 now, compared to 400 before the Civil War) at work on their 18th-century looms any weekday morning, and those with gargantuan bank accounts can even order a genui▮ tapestry as a souvenir.

Las Delicias

Museo Nacional Ferroviario (National Railway Museum) L17

*61 Paseo de las Delicias, t 91 506 83 33, **w** www.museodelferrocarril.org; **metro** Delicias; wheelchair accessible. **Open** Tues–S▮ 10–5.30; closed Aug and hols; **adm** €3.*

Five blocks south of Estación de Atocha station was yet another, the Delicias statio▮ its cast-iron skeleton designed by Gustav Eiffel and built in 1880, and its name a brav▮ euphemism for a once notably undelightfu▮ fleabag corner of Madrid. The city is busily remaking this whole area into a family attraction, beginning with the station itsel▮ now a train museum with RENFE's oldest and proudest warhorses (some from the 1840s) shined up to look as good as new.

Planetario (Planetarium) Off ma▮

*16 Avenida de Planetario, Parque Enrique Tierno Galván, t 91 467 38 98; **metro** Ménde▮ Alvaro; **bus** No.148; wheelchair accessible. **Open** Tues–Sun 11–1.45 and 5–7.45; **adm** €3▮*

Further south, the old train tracks have been replaced by the Parque Enrique Tierno Galván, site of Madrid's new planetarium, with all sorts of exhibitions on all things astronomical, and the popular **IMAX cinem▮** (*see* 'Children and Teenagers' Madrid', p.266▮

Santa Ana
and Huertas

1 Lunch

Lhardy, *8 Carrera de San Jerónimo*, *t 91 522 22 07*; **metro** *Sol or Sevilla*. **Open** *Mon–Sat 1–3.30 and 8.30–11, Sun 1–3.30pm*. **Expensive**. A Madrid institution, founded in 1839 and nearly unchanged. The dining rooms upstairs feature French and *muy castizo madrileño* cuisine. Downstairs, clients help themselves to sweet or savoury delicacies, then pay at the door.

2 Tea and Cakes

La Suiza, *2 Plaza Santa Ana*; **metro** *Sevilla*. **Open** *Sun–Thurs 7.30am–midnight, Fri 7.30am–1am, Sat 7.30am–2am*. Has fantastic displays of pâtisserie and a bar where you can while away the morning with your *café con leche*.

3 Drinks

Viva Madrid, *7 C/ de Manuel Fernández y González*; **metro** *Sevilla or Antón Martín*. **Open** *daily 1pm–2am*. One of Lorca's old haunts, which retains its gorgeous tiled façade; inside there are more coloured tiles, carved wood and caryatids, plus the obligatory free-flowing beer taps.

250 n
220 yards

Santa Ana and Huertas

This pie wedge of a neighbourhood of narrow dark streets grew up after 1560, just after Philip II made the city the capital. Located outside the walls until 1654, it had low rents (initially) and small houses, and became the congenial home to Madrid's first theatres, its Golden Age writers and playwrights, bordellos and taverns, booksellers, printers and *pícaros* – those out-of-work soldiers and other landless ne'er-do-wells whose roguish adventures are colourfully recounted in the picaresque novels of the day. The neighbourhood's most caustic writer, Francisco de Quevedo, wrote the best of these picaresque tales, *El Buscón* (*The Swindler*), which is probably the second-best Golden Age novel after *Don Quixote*, whose author lived just round the corner.

Today the district is sometimes called the Barrio de las Letras or de los Literatos, and the distinction isn't entirely limited to the glory days of the reign of Philip IV: the area has produced two winners of the Nobel Prize for literature, José Echegaray and Jacinto Benavente. But most people call it Huertas and Santa Ana for its most important street and square. Don't expect many museums or monuments here: bars and theatres are still the main landmarks, although in the evenings they can be packed with more tourists and swindlers than *madrileños*.

For a walk through this area, *see* 'A Literary Walk Around Santa Ana', p.177.

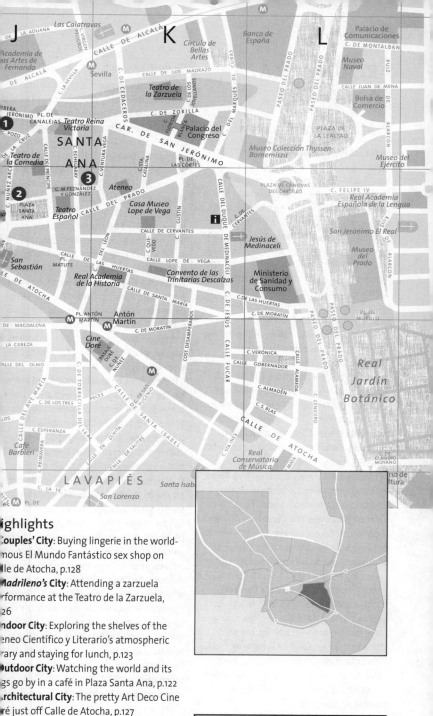

Highlights

Couples' City: Buying lingerie in the world-famous El Mundo Fantástico sex shop on Calle de Atocha, p.128

Madrileno's City: Attending a zarzuela performance at the Teatro de la Zarzuela, p.126

Indoor City: Exploring the shelves of the Ateneo Científico y Literario's atmospheric library and staying for lunch, p.123

Outdoor City: Watching the world and its dogs go by in a café in Plaza Santa Ana, p.122

Architectural City: The pretty Art Deco Cine Doré just off Calle de Atocha, p.127

All grid references in this chapter refer to the map above

AROUND PLAZA SANTA ANA

Plaza Santa Ana J12

***Metro** Sol, Antón Martín or Sevilla.*

The centre of the labyrinth is Plaza Santa Ana, one of the main nodes of tourist Madrid; the southern, Calle del Prado, side in particular is lined with tiled cafés, bars and restaurants. The actual square has been cleaned up. There's no more grass to conceal syringes and condoms, and a couple of playgrounds means the plaza is attracting more families these days. Advertising mega-stars Saatchi & Saatchi have even opened up an office here – you can't get much more cosmo-sophisticated than that!

The square was yet another gift to the city from the '*rey de las plazuelas*', Joseph Bonaparte, who demolished the convent of Santa Ana to clear the space. The current **Teatro Español** (1802) occupies the site of the Corral del Príncipe, one of Spain's earliest theatres (*see* 'Early Theatre'), and is decorated with busts of Spanish playwrights. A bird takes flight from the hands of Lorca in a simple statue in front. On the western side of the square is the Riviera-style **Tryp Reina Victoria**, a long-time favourite of visiting *toreros*; a plaque honours one of the greatest, Manolete. The **Cervecería Alemana**, their (and of course Hemingway's) favourite drinking hole, has a fascinating display of photos and other taurine memorabilia.

Running north of the square, Calle del Príncipe holds the **Teatro de la Comedia** (1875), one of the best places in Madrid to see the classics of the Golden Age, in a handsome pseudo-Moorish interior. The next street to the east, **Calle de Echegaray**, has a string of old bars, many preserving their beautiful ceramic décor from the 1920s (*see* 'Santa Ana and Huertas' in the 'Nightlife' chapter, pp.240–42).

Early Theatre

Plaza Santa Ana was once the address of the Corral del Príncipe (1583), one of the first purpose-built theatres in Spain. Not as wild as the OK Corral (in Spanish the word conjures up any kind of open-air pen, or courtyard), it was nevertheless famous as being one of the rowdiest places in the city.

Theatre in Madrid began as soon as Philip made it the capital of Spain and the seat of his court. As most of the people who moved to the city lived off the bounty of the court, they had plenty of time to kill during the day and it wasn't long before the impromptu dramas held in the courtyards of the grande houses developed into a more professional art form, the profits divided between the performers and playwrights and the charitable bodies that owned the *corralas*. Much to the amazement of northern Europeans who were used to working for a living, the plays usually began at noon.

Here at the Corral del Príncipe and at the nearby Corral de la Cruz, which stood just to the west but was demolished in 1859, many of the dramas of the Golden Age were premiered to a famously hard-to-please audience, attracted in part by the presence of the actresses (unlike in Shakespearian England, the female parts in Madrid were played by women). While distinguished guests sat in special compartments or balconies along the sides of the *corralas*, the cheapest places in the pit were filled by the so-called 'musketeers', the local tradesmen, who came to each performance armed with noise-makers and bells to disrupt a play whenever it failed to meet their approval. If the catcalls became too menacing, the playwright sitting in the wings would hastily revise the end. Lope de Vega, in particular, was renowned for paying the musketeers to heckle the works of his rivals. A theatre has stood on the site of the Corral del Príncipe ever since, currently the Teatro Español (180

Ateneo Científico y Literario de Madrid K12

Calle del Prado, t 91 390 60 00; metro Antón Martín or Sevilla. Open daily 9am–11.30pm.

Madrid's Athenium or Ateneo was founded in 1820 to promote the arts and sciences, but was closed down by the reactionary Ferdinand VII in 1835 because he didn't want anyone promoting any such thing. When the Ateneo was allowed to reopen, it quickly became one of the cultural bastions of the city, and now wears a magnificently shabby patina of scholarship. The delightful old-fashioned library with individual reading lamps has a collection of volumes second only to the Biblioteca Nacional; another asset is its popular, very cheap, cafeteria.

Casa Museo de Lope de Vega K12

C/ de Cervantes, t 91 429 92 16; metro Antón Martín or Sevilla. Open Tues–Fri 9.30–2, Sat 10–2; closed hols and Aug; adm €1.50 (guided tours only), free Sat.

One of the few tangible souvenirs of Spain's Golden Age left in the neighbourhood is the Casa Museo de Lope de Vega, where that 'phoenix of Spanish wits' spent the last 25 years of his life. The house was restored according to an inventory of goods and furnishings found there upon his death. One of the rooms is, appropriately for a man of Lope's busy libido, a harem, while another contains personal memorabilia. Perhaps the nicest bit is his little garden, diligently restored to its 17th-century appearance. Although Cervantes and Vega were bitter enemies (old gossip says it was over the favours of actress Elena Osorio), the two lived and died on the same street. But **Cervantes' house**, at the corner of Calles Cervantes and León, was knocked down in 1833, in spite of a huge protest at the time, led by the great historian Mesonero Romanos. It's now replaced with a plaque.

Convento de las Trinitarias Descalzas K12

C/ de Lope de Vega; metro Antón Martín.

What molecules remain on earth that once comprised Miguel de Cervantes lie buried somewhere or other in the church of San Ildefonso, in the Convento de las Trinitarias Descalzas, a grim and forbidding place with tiny barred windows founded in 1612. Both Cervantes and Vega had daughters who became nuns here. Because of its literary connections, the Spanish academy managed to have the church spared twice when it was threatened with demolition.

A jollier place than the convent is the tiny and very old fashioned *frutería*, on the same street at No.14, surrounded with little netted bags of oranges and bunches of gossiping locals.

Jesús de Medinaceli K12

Plaza de Jesús; metro Antón Martín.

The church of Jesús de Medinaceli is one of the ugliest in Madrid. It was built in 1920 to replace the church of the monastery of the Trinitarias Descalzos, whose monks devoted themselves to charitable causes, chiefly by raising money to liberate Spanish soldiers captured by Barbary pirates. In 1580 they raised the ransom to free Cervantes.

The original Jesús de Medinaceli was the parish church of the theatre district in the 17th century. Sunday Mass here was a fashion parade as rival actresses sought to outdress one another, much to the delight of their followers if to the outrage of more pious *madrileños*. The church is named for its much venerated 16th-century statue of Jesus, which had also been captured by Algerian pirates, who demanded its weight in gold as its ransom. But when the funds were raised and the statue was put on the scales, it was miraculously found to weigh only as much as a single coin. Hundreds of *madrileños* come on the first Friday of each month to kiss its feet.

CARRERA DE SAN JERÓNIMO

East of the Puerta del Sol, the Carrera de San Jerónimo is the main street from old Madrid to the Prado and the Retiro. Laid out as the processional route to the royal monastery of San Jerónimo (*see* p.105), it is now mostly a dull and respectable row of banks and offices.

Just off the street, however, colourful bars line **Calle de la Victoria**, and tempting old shops wait to wreak havoc on your figure. Among the most famous, on Calle del Pozo (which runs off Calle de Victoria) is the **Antigua Pastelería del Pozo**, founded in 1830 and devoted to exquisite cakes. **Casa Mira**, at 30 Carrera de San Jerónimo, is a temple to *turrón* (nougat) and still going strong after six generations.

Lhardy J11

*8 Carrera de San Jerónimo; **metro** Sol. **Open** Mon–Sat 1–3.30 and 8.30–11, Sun 1–3.30pm.*

Most famous of all is a Madrid institution: Lhardy, founded in 1839 by Emilio Lhardy, a friend of French writer Prosper Mérimée. Mérimée was a keen observer of life and art (besides writing the story of *Carmen*, he was France's inspector of historical monuments) and he told Lhardy just what the capital of Spain needed: chocolate éclairs. Mérimée, of course, was right, and not long after cornering the market in French pastries, Lhardy discerned a crying need for more substantial fare, and his confectioner's evolved into the city's best restaurant. Lhardy's home-delivery business was so good that wealthy *madrileños* fired their cooks and built their palaces with only the most rudimentary of kitchens. The 'white room' upstairs, a favourite for 19th-century trysts,

The Phoenix of Spanish Wits, Lope de Vega

Lope de Vega (1562–1635) was born in Madrid only a year after it became the capital, and by the time he died he had completely revolutionized its favourite pastime. With packed theatres almost every day of the week, demand for novelty was insatiable, and Vega filled it almost single-handedly: he wrote 20 pages every day of his life, and boasted that over 100 of his plays were written and staged within 24 hours. On his own he quintupled the number of dramatical works in the language, penning some 1,800 plays (426 have survived; the names are known of 300 others) and over 400 *auto sacramentales* (short allegorical plays). That's not all: Vega's non-dramatic works, including over 1,500 sonnets, fill 21 volumes. It was Cervantes who gave him his other nickname, the 'Monster of Nature'.

Cervantes was sore because Vega made his attempts at drama obsolete. Vega revolutionized Spanish drama, derived until then from Roman interpretations of Greek tragedy: he abolished the role of the classical chorus and instead used a character (usually a clever servant, the *gracioso*) to comment on the action. He reduced the traditional five acts to three, and made the classical unity of time and place between the acts irrelevant. He replaced the stilted hendecasyllabic blank verse then used with metered prose that led to a new lyricism and drama on the stage. As Shakespeare later did, he often went back to history for plots that offered crowd-pleasing parallels to the mood of national greatness. His lighter plots (especially in the *cape y espada*, or cloak and sword plays), with all their tragi-comic complications, incident, misunderstandings, love entanglements and ultra sensitivity to *pundonor* or 'points of honour', often using contemporary *madrileños* as characters, became the essence of Spanish *comedia*. In his treatise *The New Art of Writing Plays in Our Time* (1609) Vega reveals the secrets of his craft, the first of which was to please the audience. No other writer matched his intuitive understanding of Golden Age Spain. Because

as practically monopolized by the nympho-maniac Isabel II. Lhardy hasn't changed uch in a century, and still maintains the adition of allowing customers to help emselves to the delicious consommé from e grand old silver samovar at the back of e shop (see 'Eating Out', p.225).

alacio del Congreso Las Cortes) K11

aza de las Cortes, Carrera de San Jerónimo, 91 390 65 25, w www.congreso.es; metro anco de España or Sevilla; wheelchair acces-le. Guided tours on Sat 10.30 and 12.30, cept in Aug; adm free; bring your passport.

It is hard to miss the dowdy but imposing rtes (or Palacio de los Diputados; 1850), the me of the Spanish parliament. Knots of le guards toting machine guns and aviator nglasses are a hint of serious business oot, but many cities one-tenth Madrid's

size have larger and more elegant post offices; from it we can see how little Spaniards thought of their corrupt govern-ments of the 19th century.

Today, important sessions of the Cortes are broadcast on the radio, and it was on one such occasion on 23 February 1981 that Civil Guard Colonel Tejero and his right-wing die-hard zealots stormed in, shooting off their pistols while the nation listened (the bullet holes are pointed out on the tour). Tejero held the Cortes hostage for 24 hours, finally surrendering when it became clear that the majority of the army supported the King and democracy. The following day saw the biggest demonstration in the city's history, led by the leaders of all the political parties, marching arm-in-arm down Calle de Alcalá. Although democracy triumphed, the attempted coup did succeed in shaking up Spain's politicians, who have since donned kid gloves on issues sensitive to the army;

the haste in which they were written, the ays are uneven, but the best – Fuente vejuna (All Citizens are Soldiers), El Major calde, El Rey (The King, the Greatest Alcalde) d El Cabellero de Olmedo (The Knight from medo) among them – have never left e repertoire.

One great source for Vega's work was his vn singularly messy private life. The son of embroidery shop owner, he received a sic humanistic education at Madrid's perial Jesuit College, but he left university follow a beautiful actress, Elena Osorio. hen she left him for a duke in 1588, he rote such outrageous scandal about her at he was taken to court and exiled from stile for eight years. During this time, he ducted a 16-year-old, Isabel de Urbina, ughter of Philip II's marshal, and was rced to marry her; after sailing with the vincible Armada, he moved to Valencia, here he wrote his first plays. When his wife ed in childbirth in 1595, he sold everything d moved to Madrid, where he immediately used another scandal by openly living with

a widow. His most enduring mistress, the beautiful actress Michela de Córdoba, gave him five children, while he remarried, much to the amusement of his fellow literati, Juana, the daughter of a wealthy pork butcher, who gave him two children as well. From 1605 he was employed as a confidential secretary and panderer by the Count of Sessa.

In 1610, his domestic life began to unravel. Juana miscarried, became ill and died in spite of Vega's diligent care; their son died at the same time, as did Michela. These sorrows made Lope take up religion and seriously contemplate the priesthood. Alarmed, the Count of Sessa encouraged an actress to seduce Vega and bring him round to his old scandalous ways. But there were to be more sorrows. During their 12 years together, his last mistress, Marta de Nevares, lost her sight and sanity before she died. Vega also lived to see his only surviving son lost at sea and his daughter abducted and abandoned. The heartbreak may have led to his death the next year in 1635, which plunged all Madrid into mourning.

Miguel de Cervantes

A soldier, courtier and poet, Miguel de Cervantes (1547–1616) came from the same Renaissance mould as Walter Raleigh and Philip Sidney. Cervantes, however, was as adventurous in his writing as in his life, constantly innovating and experimenting in nearly every genre without financial success, until he embarked on a satire of the romantic ballads of his day, which was to grow into *Don Quixote*.

Cervantes was the fourth of seven children of a poor barber-surgeon in Alcalá de Henares, who travelled about Castile cutting hair, setting bones and letting blood. While living in Madrid, Miguel was strongly influenced by a progressive-minded schoolmaster, a follower of Erasmus, who instilled an avid love of reading in his pupil. At age 21, Cervantes published his first poem (on the death of Philip II's queen, Elizabeth of Valois).

Like many ambitious young Spaniards, Cervantes went to Italy, enlisting in the infantry in Spanish-held Naples. He first saw active service in 1571, joining the allied Christian fleet led by Philip II's brother Don Juan against the Ottoman Turks, at the famous Battle of Lepanto. In spite of a raging fever, Cervantes insisted on taking his place on deck and fought with exemplary courage, receiving three gun wounds, two in the chest and one that maimed his left arm, leaving it useless for the rest of his life. In spite of that handicap, he remained a soldier for the next three years, fighting in Tunis and Navarino. When he left the army in 1575 and sailed to Spain, it was with warm letters of commendation from his commanders and Don Juan himself. His career seemed to be made. Instead, he and his brother Rodrigo were captured by pirates and sold in the slave market in Algiers.

Although Rodrigo was ransomed after two years, Miguel (regarded as extra valuable because of his letters) remained a slave for five years. He made four daring attempts to escape, but thanks to his perceived importance he was never severely punished. Finally, in 1580, just before his master Hasan

---

Tejero may bear the ultimate responsibility for the failed talks with Basque terrorists during ETA's recent and sadly short-lived truce.

The Cortes' most beloved feature are its two bronze lions, made from melted-down Moroccan canons captured by Generals Prim and O'Donnell in 1860. They are named Daoiz and Velarde (after the heroes of the 2 May 1808 uprising) and, judging by their distressed expressions, have just eaten something bad.

Teatro de la Zarzuela K11

4 C/ de los Jovellanos, t 91 524 54 00; metro Banco de España or Sevilla.

Located just behind the Cortes, the modest, rosy Teatro de la Zarzuela (1856) outsparkles the Cortes architecturally and (most of the time) for entertainment value as well, with its productions of Madrid's home-grown art form (a lively mix of classical opera and soap opera), ballet and other music and dance. The building is based on the layout of La Scala in Milan.

HUERTAS AND CALLE DE ATOCHA

Calle de las Huertas J–L12

Metro Antón Martín.

Bar-lined Calle de las Huertas was not so long ago the place where there were '*más putas que puertas*' ('more whores than doors'). The numbers were impressive: in the 18th century, an estimated 800 brothels in Madrid served a population of 150,000.

In Plaza Matute, don't miss the curvaceous asymmetrical Modernista **Casa Pérez Villan** (No.10), built in 1906 by Eduardo Reynals. The **Palacio de Santoña** is further west along Calle de las Huertas, on the corner of Calle d

asha decided to sell his unsold slaves in onstantinople, his family and the Trinitarian rothers raised the necessary 500 gold :udos to set him free (he would later ctionalize his adventures in the Captive's le in *Don Quixote*).

Back in Spain, Cervantes spent the rest of s life in and out of petty jobs and prison. ·ices had risen and his impoverished family ·ruggled to get by. The great victory of ·panto was yesterday's news and the Crown nored Cervantes' petitions and job ·quests; the steadiest work he managed to ·et was as a commissary to gather food from ·willing villages for Philip II's Armada. This ·volved long travels in Andalucia, and nego- ·ations so complex he was excommunicated · several occasions by the Church for · istakenly touching its possessions. He later ·ad the thankless task of collecting unpaid ·xes, but discrepancies in the books landed · m in jail.

Meanwhile he turned to his pen to live. He ·rote a score of plays (the performances of ·hich, he observed, were neither pelted with vegetables nor booed off the stage, but only two have survived) and a pastoral novel, *Galatea*, which Cervantes himself pronounced a failure. Finally, in 1604, he enjoyed nearly instant fame with the publi- cation of the first part of *Don Quixote*; it was so popular that within a month the first pirated edition was on sale, and English and French translations soon followed.

Yet Cervantes still struggled; it seems that he may have given most of his profits to his only child, Isabel de Saavreda, born out of wedlock in the early 1580s. He took an administrative post for the Crown, and moved from Valladolid to Madrid along with the Court in 1606. He had another success, in 1613, with the ribald and satirical *Exemplary Novels*. In 1615 he published the second part of *Don Quixote*, after another author horned in and wrote a mediocre sequel. His name was a household word, but when Cervantes died on 23 April 1616, a visitor described him as 'old, a soldier, a gentleman and poor'. It was a dark day for literature altogether: Shakespeare died on the very same day.

íncipe. Built by Pedro de Ribera in 1734 and ·ecorated with his characteristic ornate ·rtals, it now houses Madrid's Chamber of ·ommerce. At the western end of Huertas ·ands the church of **San Sebastián**, where ·pe de Vega was buried in 1635. Like most ·mous corpses in Madrid, however, his body ·as lost even before the church was burnt ·wn in the Civil War.

·eal Academia · e la Historia K12

*C/ del León, **t** 91 429 06 11; metro Antón ·artín. **Open** only for researchers, call for ·formation.*

·Amid all the bars, the Academia Real de la · storia (Royal Academy of History) main- · ins a stiff, disapproving respectability. The ·cademy was founded by Philip V in 1738, but · is building was originally designed by Juan · e Villanueva in 1788 as a place where the ·onks of El Escorial could sell their prayer books; a century later the academy took it over. It maintains a small museum with some paintings by Goya, Iberian and Roman antiquities, and religious art of the Middle Ages, plus a 500,000 volume library.

Calle de Atocha I12–L13

Metro Antón Martín.

Calle de Atocha, running south of Huertas, was blazed as the main route from the Plaza Mayor to the Basílica of Atocha. It's now flamboyantly seedy. Tucked away in Pasaje Doré, a narrow shop-lined arcade perfumed with the fleshy smells of the surrounding meat and fish stalls, you'll find Madrid's oldest cinema, the **Cine Doré** (1922). Now the Filmoteca (p.250) shows old art films most nights, and outdoors on the pleasant terrace on balmy summer evenings.

The first part of *Don Quixote* was printed in 1604 at a printer's that stood at 87 Calle de Atocha, which may some day be a museum

dedicated to Cervantes. A plaque at No.94 marks the house of the author of *The Three-Cornered Hat*, Pedro Antonio de Alarcón. But what this stretch of Calle de Atocha is best known for is the now legendary BIGGEST sex shop in the world, **El Mundo Fantástico**, with its tempting Las Vegas-style entrance and doorman.

La Latina, Embajadores and Lavapiés

7

La Latina, Embajadores and Lavapiés

Fanning south of the former cathedral of San Isidro are Madrid's *barrios bajos* (low neighbourhoods), named not for their morals but for their location on the slope down to the Manzanares. They grew up quickly in the 18th and 19th centuries to house the burgeoning population, especially the tradesmen and workers who began to make the once parasitical capital into a city that earned its own way in the world.

Today the *barrios bajos* lend the city much of its distinct character; unlike most European capitals, the heart of Madrid has not yet been totally given over to *los yuppies*. These colourful neighbourhoods retain a mix of people who have been there for generations, the 'true sons and daughters of Madrid' or *castizos* (*see* 'The Real McCoy', p.132), mingled with newcomers both

1 Lunch

Malacatín, 5 C/ de la Ruda, t 91 365 52 41; *metro* La Latina. **Open** Mon–Sat 1–3.30pm; closed 15 July–15 Aug. Cash only. **Moderate**. For a genuine Madrid experience, book their renowned *cocido* (€15) for lunch and ask what time to show up.

2 Tea and Cakes

Pastelería Licorería El Madroño, 10 C/ de Caravaca, t 91 539 41 78; *metro* Lavapiés. **Open** Sun–Thurs 10–2 and 6–midnight, Fri and Sat 10–2 and 6–2. Birthplace of the *licore de madroño*, distilled from the fruit of the strawberry tree, as well as some unusual cakes.

3 Drinks

Casa Montes, 40 C/ de Lavapiés, t 91 527 00 64; *metro* Lavapiés. **Open** Tues–Sat noon–4 and 8–midnight, Sun noon–4pm. One of the oldest, most traditional bars in this area with an excellent selection of wines.

Spanish and foreign. How long they can resist gentrification probably depends on how long *madrileños* stay in love with their cars – the city's policy of pedestrianizing the streets makes parking difficult. For the time being, trendy *madrileños* are only another element in a vibrant mix.

The *barrios bajos* have only a few monuments to see. However, they really come into their own on Sunday mornings for the Rastro market, and during the summer festivals, the *verbenas*, and the more spontaneous neighbourhood parties that happen on weekend evenings in the bars, which include some of the most traditional in Madrid (*see* 'Nightlife', p.242, and 'Eating Out', pp.227–8).

For a walk through this area, taking in some of the more, and less, traditional bars, *see* 'A Bar and Tapas Walk', p.174.

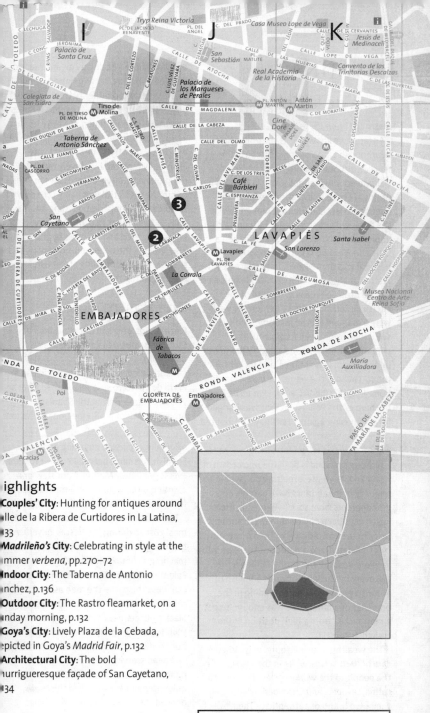

Highlights

Couples' City: Hunting for antiques around Calle de la Ribera de Curtidores in La Latina, p.133

Madrileño's City: Celebrating in style at the summer *verbena*, pp.270–72

Indoor City: The Taberna de Antonio Sánchez, p.136

Outdoor City: The Rastro fleamarket, on a Sunday morning, p.132

Goya's City: Lively Plaza de la Cebada, depicted in Goya's *Madrid Fair*, p.132

Architectural City: The bold Churrigueresque façade of San Cayetano, p.134

All grid references in this chapter refer to the map above

LA LATINA

Plaza de la Cebada H13

Metro *La Latina.*

As far as we know, this is the only neighbourhood in Europe named after a Latin teacher, although no ordinary one: Beatriz Galindo not only taught Isabel la Católica her conjugations, but also became one of the queen's closest confidantes. Along the way she amassed enough money to found a charitable hospital that took her nickname, La Latina, in Plaza de la Cebada. In 1900 the hospital was demolished and replaced by the Teatro La Latina, which specializes in musicals.

Plaza de la Cebada was the site of the Puerta de Toledo until 1656, when the walls were expanded for the last time, and ever since then it has been a colourful and piquant corner of Madrid. Goya's *Madrid Fair* (in the Prado) was set here, and for centuries the square was the venue for public executions. In 1824, Liberal General Rafael de Riego, the hero of the Peninsular War, was hanged for his uprising against Ferdinand VII, but put on a bad show by dying a coward. Madrid's beloved dandy by day and bandit by night, Luis Candelas, did rather better in 1837, befo one of the biggest crowds ever to witness a execution in Spain, when he spoke his last words with a smile: '*Sé feliz, patria mía*' ('Be happy, my country'). The scaffold was eventually replaced by a lovely **market**, designed in the style of Les Halles in Paris, but in the 1950s this was sadly torn down fo the present lumpish yet bustling agora with piles of fresh meat, fish and produce, knowingly eyed and prodded by the locals. also shelters the neighbourhood pool, and the bars and surrounding streets are hopping at night.

The Rastro I13–H14

Plaza de Cascorro and C/ de la Ribera de Curtidores; **metro** *La Latina.* **Held** *Sun 9am–2pm.*

Madrid's legendary market begins up in **Plaza de Cascorro**, a square named after a village in Cuba; during the Spanish–American War of 1898, Eloy Gonzalo (whose

The Real McCoy

Although Madrid is both the microcosm of Spain and its greatest melting pot, where the majority of inhabitants have parents or grandparents from somewhere else, there has always been an attachment to authenticity. In the bad old days of the 17th century, this translated into a neurotic obsession with *limpieza de sangre*, or purity of blood: the discovery by the Inquisition of a Jewish or Moorish great-grandparent hiding in the branches of a family tree was enough to get a man sacked from a high position in the church or court.

The wealthy, as usual, found ways to take care of themselves, while in the 19th century the people in the working-class *barrios* – La Latina, Lavapiés and Chamberí – developed their own brand of authenticity. Their denizens are the real McCoy, the *castizos*, 'true born' children of the city, similar to the Cockneys in London. The word *castizo*, which originally applied to anything distinctly Spanish, has since been taken over for what ever is genuinely Madrid, from stew or a painting by Goya to the ultimate *castizo* art form, the zarzuela (*see* 'La Zarzuela', p.248).

The *castizo* neighbourhoods are at their most *castizo* during the fiestas, or *verbenas*, beginning with San Isidro in May and reaching a climax with the Virgen de la Paloma in August. Then everyone in Madrid can dress the part – the men as *chulos* (from *chaul*, the Arabic for lad) in flat caps, tight black trousers, neck scarves and waistcoats, their female counterparts as *chulapas* in ful flounced skirts, flowery shawls with fringes and head scarves, set back to reveal the *de rigueur* carnation in the hair. They dance a quick-stepping dance called the *chotis*, derived they say from the Scottish jigs danced in Madrid by British troops in the Peninsular War, with a bit of the Wild West saloon stomp thrown in.

atue you see) offered to go on a suicide
ssion to torch the fort there, asking only
at his comrades drag his body back. You see
m standing with his petrol can and the
pe he tied about his waist. Gonzalo had
lunteered because he was raised in a
arby orphanage and had no family to
ourn him; although his fellow solders did
anage to rescue him after he was shot, he
ed a few weeks later. According to a
pular saying, if you enter the Rastro
thout the courtesy of greeting Eloy
onzalo, you will leave disappointed and
mpty-handed.

Eloy, in effect, marks the beginning of El
astro, Spain's best-known and longest-
nning outdoor market. *Rastro* pungently
anslates as 'stain' for the blood that trickled
wn the street from the slaughterhouses
at once stood in Plaza de Cascorro. The
ins passed directly from abattoir to the
nners (the *curtidores*). One thing it's hard
be nostalgic about in Madrid is the pong
at must have once hung over this area.
Nowadays, the Rastro can provide you with
erything from bargain fashions to electric
extension cables, peacock feathers, second-
hand flamenco dresses and plastic flowers,
while in the side streets you may find not
only some genuine antiques, but also
reputedly stolen goods (perhaps very recent
stolen goods: beware that the Rastro is
renowned for its pickpockets). **Calle de la
Ribera de Curtidores** is the main Rastro
street, filled with general fleamarket stands
– jewellery, clothes, music, arts and crafts,
ladies' knickers and so on. The side streets are
more product-specific: at Plaza del General
Vara del Rey, you'll find all kinds of used
clothing, from Mao jackets to worn-out
Levi's; antiques and used furniture are on
Calle de Rodas and in Galerías Piquer on
Ribera de Curtidores. As you move south
toward the Glorieta de Embajadores, you'll
find power tools, kitchen supplies and
bicycle accessories.

During the other days of the week, Calle de
la Ribera de Curtidores and its tributaries are
a fertile field for poking around **antique and
furniture shops**; check out streets such as
Calle del Carnero, de Arganzuela, de Mira el
Río Alta and de Mira el Río Baja.

But *castizos* have always had their own
eculiar fashion sense, since the days of their
andified ancestors, known either as
anolos (*see* 'Plaza de Lavapiés', p.135) or
ajos, a word derived from the old May Day
stivities, when everyone dressed in their
est. While other European men duly
nformed to the late 18th-century style of
irted frock coat, wig and tricorn hat, the
ajos pulled their long hair back in hairnets,
ore short, many-buttoned jackets over
mbroidered shirts, wrapped themselves in
ng cloaks and wore large-brimmed hats.
eir female equivalent, the Majas, dressed
full mid-calf skirts, embroidered bodices,
hite stockings with a dagger in the garter
nd a black lace mantilla over their compli-
ted hair.

Goya's depictions of Madrid's Majos were
popular that even the nobility liked to
ose for him in the costume. One of his
vourite subjects was the festive pilgrimage
or *romería* of San Isidro, showing the Majos
and Majas dancing Madrid's beautiful native
dance, the bolero; performed with castanets,
with intricate ballet-like toe work and a good
deal of flexible upper-body work, its very
difficulty condemned it to fall from popularity. You'd have to be very lucky to see it on
Madrid's dancefloors today, among the more
popular sevillanas and paso dobles.

As the song goes, 'It ain't what you do, it's
the way that you do it'. From the days of the
Majos, *castizo* has also been about attitude, a
swaggering easygoing jauntiness, a streetwise cockiness and quick sharp wit. Thanks
to Franco and modern mass culture, this
saucy attitude has been diluted, although
not lost altogether; if your Spanish is up to
scratch, you can hear the verbal rapiers of the
descendants of the Majos and Majas
in any neighbourhood bar in La Latina
and Lavapiés.

Puerta de Toledo G14

Metro *Puerta de Toledo.*

From Plaza de la Cebada, Calle de Toledo descends to the Neoclassical Puerta de Toledo, isolated in a hornets' nest of traffic buzzing around the Ronda de Toledo. This gate in the 17th-century walls was begun as a triumphal arch by Joseph Bonaparte to mark the beginning of his reign, but it was finished by Ferdinand VII to celebrate the ending of it and the start of his own calamitous rule. The arch is covered with much Latinizing about the excessive and tyrannical Gauls. It has been restored, not because anyone likes it, but as a stern history lesson.

Mercado Puerta de Toledo H14

Between Ronda de Toledo and Plaza Campillo Mundo Nuevo; *metro* Puerta de Toledo.

The arch to a hated king ironically nick-named 'the Desired One' had fishmongers for neighbours, holding court in the Mercado Puerta de Toledo. Since it's within easy walking distance of the Rastro, it seemed logical in the late 1980s to replace the fish with antique shops, and in its inaugural year over a million people visited the new Mercado de Anticuarios. A decade later, most of the shops were empty, a victim, they say, of misman-agement. Over-design may also have had something to do with its current desolation, an effect heightened by the piped-in Musak. You could shoot a modern film version of *Theseus and the Minotaur* here; a tourist office is said to be lurking in its depths, but take a ball of twine if you go in search of it. Another case of design gone wrong is adjacent: the singularly uninviting **Puerta de Toledo Complex** (1985–7), a social service and cultural centre designed by Juan Navarro Baldeweg.

Virgen de la Paloma G14

Calle de la Paloma; *metro* Puerta de Toledo.

This is the spiritual focus of La Latina and the seat of Madrid's unofficial patroness, La Virgen de la Paloma. The church replaces the convent of the Virgen de las Maravillas, where a pet dove (*paloma*) made a singular impres-sion by piously following a religious processio In the 18th century, a forgotten painting of the Virgin was rediscovered on the convent wall. This became such a popular focus of local devotion that a chapel was built to house it, which in 1913 was replaced by the handsome Neo-Mudéjar church you see no designed by Lorenzo Alvarez Capra. During the first church burnings in 1931, the paintir was hidden away and replaced by a copy. A couple of years later even the copy was stole by a local shoemaker, who kept it safe durir the Civil War. On 15 August the surrounding streets witness the Verbena de la Paloma.

Puente de Toledo Off maps

C/ de Toledo; *bus* No.18 or 23 from C/ de Toledo; *metro* Marqués de Vadillo.

This handsome nine-arched bridge over tl Manzanares, in the midst of a traffic clover-leaf, was designed by Pedro de Ribera for Philip V and completed in 1732. A pair of ornate shrines, one dedicated to San Isidro and another to his wife, Santa María de la Cabeza, recall the festive pilgrimage or *romería* that crosses this bridge on San Isidro's day on 15 May, the subject of several of Goya's finest paintings in the Prado.

EMBAJADORES

Calle de Embajadores I13–

Metro *La Latina or Embajadores.*

This *barrio* and its main street, Calle de Embajadores, a lively narrow street dotted with old shops, got their names in the 15th century, when a plague in the centre of Madrid sent the resident ambassadors fleeing here to safety.

San Cayetano I13

17 C/ de Embajadores; *metro* La Latina.

Along the upper part of the street, the twin-towered Baroque church dedicated to

n Cayetano, the patron saint of the *barrio*,
as founded by the Theatines in the
th century. Although the interior was
mpletely burnt out in the Civil War, the
iginal red-brick façade flush with the street
s survived, floridly encrusted with columns
d barnacle ornamentation by José de
urriguera (1761), a member of the family
ho perfected the art and gave their name
the style. Like the Virgen de la Paloma, the
ugust *verbena* here is a chance for some
ild foot-stomping.

ábrica de Tabacos J14–15

etro Embajadores.

At the foot of Calle de Embajadores, two
and buildings face off: a Neo-Mudéjar
stituto de Enseñanza Media Cervantes
81) and the Fábrica de Tabacos, nothing
ss than Europe's oldest tobacco factory,
unded in 1809 in what had started out as a
stillery. Although Carmen, Spain's most
mous cigar-roller, was a Sevillana, Madrid's
garreras were a feisty and proud lot who
ve the *barrio* much of its character. In the
th century, they composed a fifth of the
tire working population of Madrid. They
ere also the city's most organized work
rce, and went on strike to gain benefits,
otably in childcare and schools, that few
ale workers ever managed to achieve.

a Corrala J14

' *de Tribulete; metro Lavapiés.*

La Corrala (1839–80) is an example of a
pical 19th-century tenement block. Its
mpanion building has been destroyed,
aving the once intimate inner courtyard
tween them the present wide open space.
is type of housing, once dominant in
adrid and other Spanish cities, led to a
ose-knit existence that had little room for
ivacy and 'personal space' and all our
ntemporary defences. As many of Madrid's
erettas, or zarzuelas, are set in these social
eehives, La Corrala's empty lot provides the
erfect setting for performances in July and
ugust, and the chance for swanning about
full *castizo* attire (*see* 'La Zarzuela', p.248).

The ruined church opposite La Corrala, **San
Fernando**, was burnt in the Civil War and left
standing as a monument as well as a canvas
for anarchist spraypainters. The school once
connected to the church was demolished to
create **Plaza de la Corrala** and its pleasant
playground, a rare commodity in these parts.
The statue presiding is of Mexican poet
Augustin Lara, author of Madrid's anthem,
which you'll hear over and over and over
again at the summer fiestas: 'Madrid,
Madrid, Madrid/Pedazo de la España en que
naci...' (Madrid, Madrid, Madrid/Bit of Spain
where I was born...).

LAVAPIÉS

Plaza de Lavapiés J14

Metro Lavapiés.

This is a lively square with an hourglass
figure. The name translates as 'wash feet',
and it may have derived in some way from a
fountain in the centre. Some writers have
spelled it El Avapiés, and find the origin of its
name in the Hebrew *aba-puest*, 'the place of
Jews'. This was certainly true in the Middle
Ages: the square was the centre of Madrid's
ghetto until 1492, when Ferdinand and Isabel
issued their order to convert or leave Spain.
Those *conversos* who remained were forced
to change their names and, as most chose
Manolo (Manuel) for their firstborn sons, the
neighbourhood became known as the Barrio
de los Manolos. As they were sharp dressers,
Manolos in the late 18th century became a
madrileño synonym for Majos (*see* 'The Real
McCoy', p.132). Around here, you may well
notice that the *castizos* are now something
of a minority: Northern Europeans, Africans,
Americans, artists and others have moved in
and change is afoot. The main synagogue
once stood on the site of the **Teatro Olímpia**.
This, one of the playhouses of the Centro
Dramático Nacional, has attracted a number
of fringe theatre companies to the area.

At 45 C/ del Ave María, just off the square,
you can visit the one neighbourhood

If the Cap Fits

Calle de Sombrerete ('Little Hat Street') in Embajadores recalls the strange story of Sebastian of Portugal, the heir to that throne, who went to fight in Morocco at the age of 21 and was apparently killed in the battle of Alcazar-el-Kebir (1578), although his body was never identified. His disappearance allowed his uncle, Philip II, to claim the crown of Portugal. The Portuguese, however, refused to believe Sebastian was dead, and rumours circulated that he would return to them after seven years of penance. Although some remains, reportedly his, were buried in Lisbon in 1582 in the presence of Philip II, most of the Portuguese still weren't convinced, and the first 'Sebastians' began to appear in 1585.

The most celebrated one was a pastry cook named Gabriel de Espinosa, who was put forward by a former confidant of the real Sebastian, the Portuguese friar Miguel dos Santos. Santos was also a confidant of the young Anna, illegitimate daughter of Philip' half-brother Don Juan of Austria, convincing her that she should marry the pastry-cook Sebastian and help him regain the throne of Portugal, and liberate Jerusalem. The project had support in high places, most notably from Henri IV of France.

Philip, not surprisingly, wasn't having any of this and, after parading friar Santos through Madrid in a silly pointed hat, had him hanged in the Plaza Mayor, while the ha was ceremoniously taken down this street and left on a pile of dung. The false Sebastia received similar treatment, and Anna was locked up in a convent.

constant: **Café Barbieri**, virtually unchanged since it opened its doors in 1902, and as popular as ever with both elderly *castizos* and newer arrivals. Another neighbourhood waterhole, the pleasant **Bar Lavapiés** (at the corner of C/ de Lavapiés and C/ de la Cabeza), by all rights should be haunted, but isn't; its building was originally the prison of the Inquisition.

Plaza Tirso de Molina I13

Metro Tirso de Molina.

At the top of Calle de Lavapiés is a leafy triangular plaza dedicated to the Golden Age playwright Fray Gabriel Téllez (1583–1648), who wrote under the name Tirso de Molina. Fray Gabriel entered the Mercedarian Order at the age of 17, and spent his last 25 years in a monastery that once stood on the square. In 1836, Liberal Minister Mendizábal confiscated and demolished it along with hundreds of others. Mendizábal's expropriation of Church property smacked too much of Republicanism for the victors of the Civil War, and his statue, which originally embellished the square, was replaced in 1943 with Tirso de Molina's. Inspired by Lope de Vega's brisk, naturalistic style, Tirso de Molina at his best provided far deeper psychological insights, and created the most famous of th period's characters in his play *The Seducer o Seville*: the hero-cum-villain Don Juan Tenori the original of Mozart's Don Giovanni.

This is a good place to find a reasonably priced meal, or a memorable one, at the historic **Taberna de Antonio Sánchez** (*see* p.228), just south at 13 Calle de Mesón de Paredes. Founded in 1830, the tavern was bought in 1920 by a famous bullfighter, wh hung up his cape to pick up the brush, and took lessons from Ignacio Zuloaga, one of th most successful painters of the day. The wa are covered with Sánchez's portraits of mata dors, many of whom stop in and chat with the current owner, himself an ex-torero.

Palacio de los Marqueses de Perales J12–13

C/ de la Magdalena; metro Tirso de Molina.

Just off the square is the area's most striking building, the Palacio de los Marqueses de Perales (1734), designed by Pedro de Ribera, with a fine Baroque door. One of the scions of the house had the misfortune to be governor of Madrid in 180 his defences of the city were found to be so inadequate, owing to corruption and ineffi- ciency, that the furious citizenry attacked this palace and killed him.

New Madrid

New Madrid

When Madrid, a walkable little city while it remained snug within its walls, began to expand in the late 18th century, it was to a different scale altogether. The proportions were set by the Plaza de Cibeles and, over the next 200 years, the city spread into a grid of impossibly wide boulevards and traffic-filled plazas. Most of this is not much fun for walking, and the best approach is to pick out what you'd like to see – and there are some gems – and bus- or metro-hop between them. If you're in the market for a modern office building and want to see what some of the more fashionable Madrid architects have put up in the past two decades, a cruise up the Paseo de la Castellana is in order.

1 Lunch

Gran Café Gijón, *21 Paseo de Recoletos*, **t** *9 521 54 25*; **metro** *Banco de España or Colón; wheelchair accessible.* **Open** *Sun–Fri 9am–1.30am, Sat 9am–2am.* **Moderate**. The legendary haunt of Madrid's intellectuals, the Gijón has been in business since 1888.

2 Tea and Cakes

Embassy, *12 Paseo de la Castellana*, **t** *91 57 48 77*; **metro** *Serrano or Colón.* **Open** *Mon–S 9.30am–1am, Sun 9.30am–11pm.* The fashi able tearoom in this diplomatic corner of Madrid since 1931, with plenty of atmosphe

3 Drinks

Teatríz, *15 C/ de Hermosilla*; **metro** *Serran* **Open** *daily 1.30–4 and 9–1.* Now something of an institution, Teatríz's 1980s Philippe Starck interior still packs the Salamanca smart set in.

Highlights

Couples' City: The intimate, sunlit canvases by Joaquín Sorolla at the Museo Sorolla, p.14

Madrileño's City: Hanging out at night along Paseo de la Castellana and its *terrazas* p.146

Indoor City: The Museo Arqueológico Nacional, the finest in Spain, p.143

Outdoor City: The Museo de Escultura al Aire Libre, p.146

Goya's City: A whole roomful, in the Museo Lázaro Galdiano, p.147

Architectural City: The world's fanciest po office, the Palacio de Comunicaciones, p.140

All grid references in this chapter refer to the map opposite

CALLE DE ALCALÁ

Plaza de Cibeles L10

Metro *Banco de España.*

Three of Madrid's most important streets, the Paseo del Prado, the Paseo de Recoletos and Calle de Alcalá, meet at Madrid's most glorious roundabout, the Plaza de Cibeles.

Cibeles Fountain

Streams of traffic swirl around Ventura Rodríguez' fountain (1780), in which jets of water dance around the great mother goddess Cibeles in a carriage drawn by lions. Although it often dismantles and moves them, Madrid loves its fountains. This one is a special favourite of Real Madrid supporters, who celebrate their club's victories with total-immersion baptisms and high jinks that in 1994 resulted in the breakage of one of Cibeles' arms. One wonders if they would have dared to take such liberties had they known that Cibeles' cult was famous in antiquity for requiring self-castration of her priests. These days, whenever Cibeles is threatened by a Spanish football victory, she is given full police protection.

Palacio de Comunicaciones

Museum open *Mon–Fri 9–2 and 5–7, Sat 9–2;* **adm** *free.*

The Plaza de Cibeles is considered *la madrileñísima* (the most Madridy) of all, perhaps because it's the most unlike any other square, in Spain or anywhere on the planet. One reason for this is the elaborate, fantastical marble pile on the southeastern side, which is nothing more than the city's main post office, the Palacio de Comunicaciones, designed by Antonio Palacios (1904). Ever since it was built, the *madrileños* have been making fun of what they immediately dubbed 'Nuestra Señora de Comunicaciones', but buying a stamp has never felt so glamourous, and posting a letter through one of the magnificent slots, one for each region of Spain, offers a quaint sense of civic order and wellbeing in a cocka-mamie world (the world outside Madrid's post office, that is). You can bask a little longer in the old-world magic at the post office's **museum**, with a huge collection of stamps, old phones and switchboards, and postal employee uniforms through the ages.

Other Buildings on Plaza de Cibeles

The three other buildings that share the Plaza de Cibeles with the post office weigh nearly as much. One, the **Palacio de Buena-vista** on the northwest corner, was built for Goya's lover, the Duchess of Alba, in 1777, but now contains the Army. Spain's central bank, the **Banco de España** (1882, by Eduardo Adaro; *2 Paseo del Prado*), with elaborate façade and fancy clock, houses works of art ranging from the 16th to the 20th centuries, but they are visible only if you write in advance to the bank's Chief of Protocol.

The third, the **Palacio de Linares** (*2 Paseo de Recoletos, t 91 595 48 00; exhibitions open Mon–Fri 11–2 and 5–8, Sat 11–7, Sun and hols 11–2*), at the northeast corner, is one of the last of many extravagant mansions that made the Plaza de Cibeles–Paseo de Recoletos axis a Millionaire's Row in the early 1890s. It was built by a banker, the Marqués de Linares, who had the curious misfortune of falling in love with and marrying his half-sister, a fact he only learned in his father's deathbed confession. Accorded a special dispensation by the Church, the two were permitted to live under the same roof but in separate quarters, and the palace was designed to give each spouse a floor of their own. Long boarded up and forlorn, the palace was refurbished and reopened as part of the 1992 celebrations as the Casa de América, a venue for concerts, movies and exhibitions of works from Latin America.

Puerta de Alcalá M10

Metro *Retiro.*

East of Plaza de Cibeles, Calle de Alcalá continues to Plaza de la Independencia and its centrepiece, the stately Neoclassical

erta de Alcalá (1778). This is one of Madrid's
mbols, a sort of triumphal arch with no
umph to commemorate. Before the city's
st set of walls was demolished in the
th century, this was the actual gate on the
ad to the university town of Alcalá de
enares. It was also the same road from
nich most foreign travellers entered
adrid. A good first impression was in order
d, after rejecting several designs,
arles III, who commissioned it, finally
ose one by Francesco Sabatini.
Actually he absentmindedly chose two
signs, and, not wanting to offend or
uble the monarch any further, Sabatini
ed both, one on each side, although even
day most *madrileños* who pass it daily
main unaware of its asymmetry. The
anite of the body contrasts nicely with the
nite Colmenar stone and granite decora-
n, and it shines at night in the floodlights.

scuelas Aguirre 010

etro Retiro or Goya.

Once past the gate, Calle de Alcalá skirts
e Parque del Retiro and an equestrian
atue of General Baldomero Espartero, hero
the first Carlist War – and briefly head
ncho in Spain (1841–3) after a *pronuncia-
ento* – astride his famously well-endowed
rse. Nearby is one of the finest Neo-
udéjar buildings in Madrid, the Escuelas
uirre (1887), with its tower designed by
nilio Rodríguez Ayuso.

laza de Toros
Monumental de las
entas Off maps

*7 C/ de Alcalá, arena t 91 725 18 57;
etro Ventas; 1.5km walk from Plaza de la
dependencia; wheelchair accessible.
useum open Tues–Fri 9.30–2.30, Sun 10–1;
m free. Box office open Fri–Sat 10–2 and
8, Sun 10–1 (or bullfight).*

Rodríguez Ayuso also designed the other
ndmark on long Calle de Alcalá, the almost
winsome Plaza de Toros Monumental de las
Ventas (1929): the busiest and most prestigious, the biggest (with seating for 23,000)
and, according to the *madrileños* at any rate,
the most beautiful bullring in Spain, in Neo-
Mudéjar brick brightened with colourful
tiles. Around the back by the stables is the
recently re-arranged **Museo Taurino**, the
largest and most complete museum of bullfighting, with special exhibitions on famous
toreros such as Manolete, who met the horn
in this ring in 1947.

PASEO
DE RECOLETOS

North of Cibeles, the tree-lined Paseo de
Recoletos is named for the Augustinian
Convento de los Recoletos and was planned
as an extension of the Paseo del Prado back
in the 1770s, but it only made it off the
drawing board as a proper street in the
1840s, after the dissolution of the monasteries. It became the *sine qua non* of fashion
in the 1850s, although only a few of the fancy
mansions (**Nos.13 and 15**) built here have
survived. Because of Madrid's topography,
when the city was ready to grow, it had to go
north, and what started as an exclusive residential promenade is now the base of the
city's busiest axis.

Banco Hipotecario M10

*10 Paseo de Recoletos; **metro** Banco
de España.*

Ostentation wasn't a dirty word in 19th-
century Madrid, and one prime example is
the primrose yellow Italianate Banco
Hipotecario, set back from the street. Built on
the site of the Convento de los Recoletos, the
bank occupies the mansion of its founder,
the flamboyant speculator and developer the
Marqués de Salamanca (*see* 'The Marqués de
Salamanca', p.145). When finished in 1850, his
palacio housed his dazzling 17th-century art
collection, not to mention the first private

flush toilet in Spain. The Marqués' parties were legendary, and did their bit in persuading monied Madrid to leave the crowded city centre and its almost nonexistent plumbing behind for the luxurious mansions in Salamanca (see 'Salamanca', below). The building now houses the headquarters of BBVA, one of Spain's banking heavyweights.

Gran Café Gijón L9

21 Paseo de Recoletos, t 91 521 54 25; metro Banco de España or Colón; wheelchair accessible. Open Daily 7am–1.30am.

One of Madrid's most celebrated cafés, the Gijón was founded in 1888 by a native of Gijón in Asturias, who made a fortune in Cuba. It was a favourite haunt for spies, including Mata Hari, during the First World War (Spain was neutral, and the embassies of the main players are all nearby). In the 1920s, the spies were replaced by writers, and the café became legendary for literary *tertulias* that attracted the likes of Lorca and Neruda. The Gijón was refurbished one last time, in 1948, with the plush seats and gilded mirrors you see today, and became the one place in Madrid where politicians and the intelligentsia from both the right and left felt free to meet and talk. This *tertulia* tradition continues today in the late afternoon, at some of the specially reserved tables. More than hot air, the chat has spawned fine literature, including *The Hive*, a novel about its regulars, by Nobel Prize-winner Camilo José Cela. In 1951, the Café Gijón Short Novel literary prize was established, and since the a number of books have appeared about th goings-on at these tables.

Biblioteca Nacional and Museo del Libro M9

20 Paseo de Recoletos, t 91 580 78 00, w www.bne.es; metro Serrano or Colón; wheelchair accessible. Library open Mon–Fr 9–9, Sat 9–2; adm free. Museum open Tues–Sat 10–9, Sun and hols 10–2; adm free.

This florid pile was built by Isabel II to house the National Library. Nicknamed the 'Prado of Paper', its collection includes ever work printed in Spain since 1712 as well as rare ancient manuscripts, drawings by the Grand Masters and the first ever Spanish grammar (Spain was the first language to have one, back in 1492). It has recently opened a Museo del Libro dedicated to the history of books and the media.

Museo de Cera (Wax Museum) L9

41 Paseo de Recoletos, t 91 319 26 49; metro Colón; wheelchair accessible. Open daily 10–2 and 4.30–8; adm €12.

As an antidote to the overall tastefulness of the area, Madrid's wax museum awaits, with a score of tableaux that will whip you through the whole history of Spain in less than an hour, plus over 450 'almost alive' celebrities, as boast its advertisements. Gluttons for punishment can take the terror train and ride the virtual-reality flight simulator.

Plaza de Colón M8

Metro Colón.

Recoletos ends where its old gate once stood, in the broad crossroads of the Plaza de Colón, dedicated to Genoese seaman Cristoforo Colombo, who, in one of the mar self-made mysteries that surround his life, used the alias Colón when he arrived in

---

St Clare of the Soaps

The church of San Pascal, on the left-hand side of Paseo de Recoletos as you head north, once belonged to a convent on this site, but was rebuilt in the 1850s. It's as nondescript as any in Madrid, but is known for its chapel dedicated to St Clare, patron saint of television (owing to a TV-like vision she once had in Assisi), who has an enviable reputation for finding parts in TV dramas for her devotees. If you'd like a walk-on part in *The Bill* or *Days of our Lives*, pop in to light a candle.

ain. The upper part of the square, the **rdines del Descubrimiento**, were planted in e 1970s, replacing the old royal mint. The eat blocks of sandstone decorating it are l part of a modern Monument to lumbus, carved with reliefs and quotes om the admiral's journals; at night its lowing fountains are lit to resemble the ils of his ships – the *Niña*, *Pinta* and *Santa aria*. Below the gardens, with an entrance nderneath the 'waterfall-at-the-end-of-the- orld', is the **Centro Cultural de la Villa** 91 575 60 80), a municipal arts centre with theatre. Though it offers all sorts of eatrical programming, it's especially nown for its children's shows. Completing e ensemble is the original Neo-Gothic lumbus monument, erected in 1885.

Museo Arqueológico Nacional M9

C/ de Serrano, t 91 577 79 12; metro Serrano Retiro; wheelchair accessible. Open es–Sat 9.30–8.30, Sun 9.30–2.30; closed ls, 1, 3 and 10 Nov, 6, 24 and 31 Dec; adm €3, ee Sat after 2.30pm, Sun, 18 May, 12 Oct and Dec.

By any measure, this is the only compre- nsive archaeological museum in the untry and, if you can read a little Spanish, e explanations will provide a thorough ucation in the obscure comings and ings of Spain's shadowy prehistory. Not at the museum is limited to Spain – there a surprisingly good collection of Greek ses, and an Egyptian room full of ummies and gaping schoolchildren, along ith some very fine jewellery and engraved als. Many of the Greek and Egyptian relics ere actually found in Spain, testimony to e close trade relations ancient Iberia joyed with the rest of the Mediterranean orld. The museum continues to be active in quisitions as well; recently an extensive ew collection of shields and coins, many ting back to the era of the Austrian kings, as added to the holdings.

Second Floor

The museum tour begins on the second floor, which covers the Palaeolithic, Neolithic, Copper, Bronze and Iron Ages in Iberia, and then moves on to Northern Africa, Egypt and the near east. Among the urns and pottery shards you will find the **sarcophagus of Amenemhat**, which belonged to a Nubian priest of Ancient Egypt, along with all the funerary accoutrements that accompanied him into the afterlife. The Iberians of the Bronze Age were at least up-to-date in metalworking, and the collection of small expressionistic **bronze figurines** shows a fine talent; these are similar in many ways to the famous bronzes from the same period found in Sardinia. Spain's entry into the literate world is chronicled in a host of **inscriptions** from all over the country. There are some in Iberian, a non-Indo-European language that may have been related to Basque, but died out completely with the advent of the Romans; not surprisingly they haven't completely deciphered any of them. From the **Roman era**, there are indifferent mosaics and copies of Greek sculpture, along with larger-than-life statues of emperors. The bronze tablets from AD 176, inscribed with the laws and orations of Septimus Severus, would have been set up in public places – a landmark in the development of political propaganda. The practice was begun by Augustus and used by several of the more energetic emperors that followed. There are also working models of the Roman catapult and ballista (a kind of gigantic crossbow), if you've ever wondered how they did the business.

Third Floor

Moving up to the third floor you will find a decent reproduction of the Altamira caves, as well as relics dating back to Roman, Visigothic and Islamic Iberia, the latter focusing on the marvellous carvings and craftsmanship of Muslim Andalucia.

A visit to this museum, however, is really a pilgrimage to the first and greatest of the great ladies of Spain, *La Dama de Elche*. Nothing we know of the history and culture

of the Iberians can properly explain the presence of this beautiful 5th-century BC cult image. As a work of art she ranks among the finest sculptures of antiquity. Pre-Roman Spain was one of the backwaters of the Mediterranean and, while it would be sacrilege in Spain to suggest that this lady was the work of a foreign hand, the conclusion seems inescapable. The dress and figure are reminiscent of some eastern Mediterranean image of Cibeles, and the Greeks could often capture the same expression of cold majesty on the face of an Artemis, Ariadne or Persephone. Elche, where the bust was discovered, was then in the Carthaginian zone, and that meant easy access to all the Mediterranean world; an artist from anywhere could conceivably have turned up to execute the high priests' commission. Nevertheless, many experts disagree, and find in *La Dama*'s unapproachable hauteur something distinctly Spanish. She holds court these days from a large glass case on a pedestal in the museum's main hall; when the hordes of schoolchildren run up, pressing their noses on the glass and shouting, as thousands of them do every day, you will see the lady's expression intensify into a look of chilly disdain that is a wonder to behold. She shares the room with her less formidable cousins, the very few other Iberian goddesses that have ever been found, including the 4th-century BC *Dama de Baza* and the *Dama de Cerra de los Santos*.

Spanish **early Christian art** is one of the museum's surprises. The architectural sculpture and mosaics show a strong, original sense of design, and a tendency to contemplative geometry that is almost Islamic. The Visigoths haven't much to offer outside the **Treasure of Gurrazar**, a collection of barbaric bejewelled crowns and crosses in glittering gold found in the Visigothic capital, Toledo. King Reccesvinth's rich crown (c.650) has his name dangling from it in gold enamelled letters; to the mainly illiterate Visigoths, these must have seemed like magic symbols. A small number of Moorish and medieval Christian works complete the collection.

Fourth Floor

A refreshing surprise awaits on the top floor: the modern age. Though it may seem incongruous in an archaeological museum, you can admire cases of porcelain from the **17th-century** kitchen of Isabel Farnese, glass vitrines filled with **Counter-reformation age** jewels owned by the Austrian kings and queens, and a rifle adorned with garnets and amethysts from the beginning of the **Bourbon age**. There is also a lovely collection of items from the beginning of the **scientific age**, including periscopes, compasses, globes and an astrolabe used for observing the cosmos.

The Altamira Replica

Outside, near the gate, a small cave has been dug to house replicas of the famous Upper Palaeolithic paintings of Altamira, in Cantabria: flowing and vigorous bisons, bulls and other animals in red and black from the same 'school' as Lascaux. The museum has gone to great lengths to copy the atmosphere of the real cave – the lighting is so realistically dim, you can barely make out the pictures.

SALAMANCA

The Paseo de Recoletos runs along the west end of the fashionable Barrio de Salamanca. When the last city walls were knocked down in the 1860s and the spacious grid of streets of the *ensanche* (extension) was laid out by Carlos María de Castro, the response to the sudden availability of hundreds of new building sites was decidedly underwhelming; no one had the money to do anything, with the exception of the Marqués de Salamanca, who left the quarter his name (see 'The Marqués de Salamanca').

Much of Salamanca's cheerless waffle iron of swanky avenues bears an eerie resemblance to the well-dressed neighbourhoods around New York's Park Avenue, with a scattering of old mansions wearing a certain Victorian panache, illegally parked cars with diplomatic licence plates, trendy show-offs peering in the windows of the glittering

he Marqués de Salamanca

During a long and busy career, the Marqués e Salamanca (1811–83) reigned supreme as adrid's first and probably most roguish bber baron and sometime Liberal Finance inister. Born in Málaga and a member of e Cortes by the time he was 26, the arqués made his first million when he anaged to obtain the national monopoly salt, and used the profits to found the nk that has since become the Banco de paña. In 1851, he built Spain's first railway, e line to Aranjuez, and dabbled in the stock arket – not always following the rules. He ent bankrupt twice, and was forced to ave Spain under a cloud when his financial andals and insider deals with the govern- ent became too outrageous; at one point rlist supporters pillaged his house and utilated his gold-plated private railway car. But the Marqués was above all a survivor, vice ruined and three times rich', and on s third comeback from financial and polit- al exile in France, he invested tremendous

sums in his slice of the new *ensanche*, building houses that were the last word in luxury at the time – complete with lifts and indoor plumbing – all linked to the Puerta del Sol by Madrid's very first tram, which proved such a success that the city was obliged to extend the service and create public trans- port in the city. The Marqués was famous for his grand gestures: once while showing important investors around, an employee took him aside and warned that there was a serious flaw in the cement of the house he was about to visit. The Marqués turned the potential embarrassment into a public rela- tions coup by pointing out the fault to the investors and burning the house down in front of them.

Since, to a developer's eye, squares take up valuable space, Salamanca has only one, the Plaza del Marqués de Salamanca, presided over by a statue of the same. It's the least the *barrio* could do: the venture ruined him yet again, and he died ignored in a small suburban house.

---

utiques, and bored concierges walking her people's Pekineses.

The main reason to come here is to shop ead for Calles Serrano, Goya, Claudio Coello, lázquez and Ortega y Gasset) at some of e big-name stores. *See* the 'Shopping' apter, p.254.

oncepción e Nuestra Señora 09

de Goya (corner of Núñez de Balboa); etro Velázquez.

One exception to the generally staid chitecture of Salamanca is the early th-century church of the Concepción. esigned by Eugenio Jiménez Corera and sús Carrasco, it's where Art Nouveau meets eo-Gothic, with numerous references to the eat cathedral of Burgos (the fretwork spire d the star vaulting in the interior, r example).

Fundación Juan March 07

77 C/ de Castelló, t 91 435 42 40; metro Núñez de Balboa; wheelchair accessible. When there's an exhibition, the museum is open Mon–Sat 11–9, Sun and hols 11–3; closed Aug; adm free.

This foundation was established in 1955 by Barcelona's equivalent of the Marqués de Salamanca, the tycoon Juan March, who was also one of the great financiers of the Nationalist cause in the Civil War. Unlike the Marqués, however, March's swindles eventually caught up with him in the 1970s and he served time. Besides an excellent permanent collection of contemporary Spanish art, the foundation organizes major retrospectives, concerts and exhibitions throughout the year.

PASEO DE LA CASTELLANA

Metro *Colón, Rubén Darío or Gregorio Marañón.*

When people say Madrid resembles the capitals of Latin America, they're often thinking of the Paseo de la Castellana. Although the word *paseo* evokes the leisurely promenades of the 19th century, when this street was lined with fancy mansions, today's Castellana is designed for thundering herds of cars and resembles a trophy thoroughfare, where banks, insurance offices and corporate internationals vie to upstage one another with shiny new headquarters designed by the latest fashionable architects. It wasn't planned as such: the Castellana grew up from Charles III's genteel Paseo del Prado, and naturally kept its width and pretensions as it became the Paseo de Recoletos; then, like a mighty shoot, it shot north along with the burgeoning city. Although sadly stripped of its trees in recent decades, it now enjoys something of the social success of the 19th-century Paseo del Prado; in the summer, the business of business is swept aside in the evenings as the *terrazas* take over, some of the more elaborate outdoor bars doubling as nightclubs for poor wretches who can't get away to Ibiza.

Architecture along the Castellana M8–6

The Castellana starts in the Plaza de Colón and the parade of showcase headquarters soon begins. Just up on the left are the **Torres Colón** (by Antonio Lamela; 1967–76), twin towers built from the top down in a then-experimental technique and now joined together under a green crown. Further up, you'll find the brick and stone **Bankinter** (1973–6) at No.29, by Rafael Moneo and Ramón Bescos, a building considered something of a prototype for contemporary

architecture in Madrid, stalwartly modernist and yet in the Spanish tradition, with a gentle touch of eclecticism. To the left of Bankinter a truncated pyramid squats on a lawn, another work by Lamela.

Opposite, at No.24, the **Banco Santander** headquarters spreads across three 19th-century apartment buildings that once housed royalty, but now contain one of the most exciting contemporary interiors in Spain, designed by Hans Hollein in 1993 (you can peek into the atrium from the Calle de Ortega y Gasset entrance). Next to this at No.34 is the cupola-crowned Andalucian-style **ABC** building (1926), former headquarters of the conservative newspaper of the same name, but since 1995 a fancy-pants shopping centre, adroitly combining three buildings with another pair of façades on Calle de Serrano; the old ABC restaurant (entrance Calle de Serrano), with its leaded Art Nouveau roof lights, is especially pretty. The slim, slick black building across the Castellana is **La Unión y el Fénix** (1968) insurance headquarters by Madrid's most prolific architect of the Franco years, Luis Gutiérrez Soto.

Museo de Escultura al Aire Libre (Museum of Outdoor Sculpture) M6

41 Paseo de la Castellana, beneath Paseo de Eduardo Dato; metro Rubén Darío.

This project was set up in the 1970s when the highway engineers who designed the Calle de Juan Bravo overpass – linking Salamanca to the leafy district of Chamberí thought the extra space they created on the edges should be filled in with sculpture. Works were duly donated by Joan Miró, Henry Moore, Julio González and Eduardo Chillida, whose *Stranded Mermaid*, a six-ton cube suspended from the flyover, steals the show. The nearby area is packed on summer nights, with an array of cheerful summer bars and *terrazas*.

Glorieta Emilio Castelar M5

etro Rubén Darío.

The next big node on the Castellana, Glorieta Emilio Castelar, encompasses both the fountain, the **Fuente Castellana**, that gave the street its name, and a **monument to Emilio Castelar**. A famous speaker, he briefly became prime minister during the First Republic in 1873, a tenure he used to abolish slavery in Spain. The monument (1908) was paid for by public subscription, and shows Castelar speaking to a distinguished audience that includes the suitably impressed figures of Demosthenes and Cicero.

Showcase bank and insurance buildings surround the *glorieta*, including Madrid's first experiment in architectural high-tech, the rusty barrel-vaulted **Bankunión** (José Antonio Corrales and Ramón Vázquez Molezún; 1972). Best of all, set back on an embankment (at No.50, on the corner of Calle de General Oroá), are the cantilevered prisms of the **Catalana Occidente** building (1987) by Rafael de la Hoz, a pioneering work of four-dimensional architecture. In an engineering tour de force, the outer floor is suspended on steel cables from the concrete roof slab. The floating lightness of the building is enhanced by walls made of two layers of glass that deflect the sunlight and heat.

A block in on the east side of the Castellana, at 75 C/ de Serrano, you'll find the only building that really stands out in Salamanca: the **US Embassy** (1955), done in that style only possible to American embassies, half fortress and half kitchen appliance.

Museo Sorolla L5

Paseo del General Martínez Campos, t 91 310 17 31; metro Rubén Darío or Gregorio Marañón. Open Tues–Sat 10–3, Sun and hols 10–2; adm €2.40, free Sun.

This delightful museum over in Chamberí takes you back a century in the Valencian painter's home, with its refreshing Moorish garden. Joaquín Sorolla (1863–1923) was one of the most fashionable international painters of his day, specializing in large, highly coloured, sun-filled outdoor scenes in the country or by the beach – often with his wife and family as models, all dressed in billowing white – to which his broad, vigorous brushstrokes were especially adapted. His house and studio have remained very much as he left it when he died, and offer a charming insight into the man, his times and his art.

Museo Lázaro Galdiano N5

122 C/ de Serrano, t 91 561 60 84; metro Gregorio Marañón or Núñez de Balboa; wheelchair accessible. Closed for expansion until mid 2004. At time of research admission times and price unconfirmed. Check at the tourist office for an update.

At the time of writing this museum was closed for renovation, but due to re-open in mid 2004. If you're able to visit, you'll notice that Lázaro Galdiano, who died in 1948, had a better eye and deeper pockets than the other Madrid collectors whose homes have been turned into museums. In the 37 rooms of art, he assembled one work by nearly every important Spanish painter, including beautiful 15th- and 16th-century triptychs by the masters of Astorga and Ávila, a self-portrait by the excellent Renaissance master Pedro Berruguete, an apocalyptic *Vision of Tondal* and *St John of Patmos* by Hieronymous Bosch, a *Descent* by Quentin Metsys, two works by Magnasco, a Rembrandt portrait and, something you won't see much of in any other Spanish museum, English paintings, including works by Gainsborough, Turner and Reynolds. There's nearly a whole room of Goyas, including two early 'Black Paintings', which originally hung in the Duchess of Osuna's El Capricho (*see* 'Sports and Green Spaces', p.263), as well as a collection of his prints, drawings and lithographs.

Galdiano's tastes were remarkably eclectic and on the ground floor artefacts from the Moors, Byzantines, Persians and Celts share

space with medieval enamels, swords and armour, little Renaissance bronzes, early clocks and watches, and two exceptional treasures: the gold and enamel Gran Sagrario de Limoges (c.1300) and an engraved goblet made for one of the nuttiest Habsburgs, Rudolph II of Prague.

Residencia de Estudiantes M4–5

23 C/ del Pinar, t 91 563 64 11; metro República Argentina or Gregorio Marañón. Open for frequent exhibitions.

This rather plain brick building is the celebrated 'resi', as everyone calls it. It features frequent exhibitions. Founded by Alberto Jímenez Fraud in 1911 to offer an open university education to all and a forum for writers, academics and artists, the revolutionary resi soon became the most important institution of its kind in Spain, publishing its own magazine and attracting notice from intellectuals and artists from around the world, who lectured or performed here. Under Franco, the Residencia became part of the CSIC, a scientific research council; in the 1980s, it decided, along with the Ministry of Education and Culture, to re-create Fraud's original vision.

AROUND NUEVOS MINISTERIOS

Museo de Ciencias Naturales M3–4

2 C/ de José Gutiérrez Abascal, t 91 411 13 28; metro Nuevos Ministerios or Gregorio Marañón; wheelchair accessible. Open Tues–Fri 10–6, Sat 10–8, Sun 10–2.30; adm €3

On the east side of the Castellana, an equestrian statue of Isabel la Católica guards a landscaped oasis around the last relic of Madrid's 1881 Exhibition of Industry and the Arts, a brick building with an iron skeleton crowned with a round Neo-Renaissance dome. Two of its pavilions house the Museo de Ciencias Naturales, with all sorts of buttons to push and other kinds of interactive educational doodads that children love, although in Spanish only.

Among the bones of dinosaurs and other extinct creatures is a stuffed Indian elephant named Pizarro, who travelled around America and Spain in a carnival show, defeating every bull and other animal pitted against it, and losing a tusk in the process. In 1863, the mayor of Madrid offered Pizarro the old botanical gardens (then used as a zoo) for his retirement. On one memorable occasion when he found his feed uninspiring, Pizarro walked into the street and raided a nearby shop.

Nearby, south along the Castellana, a **giant hand** by Botero rises out of the median to greet passing commuters. Just beyond it you'll find the building that threw down the design gauntlet to the other banks and insurance companies, the audacious upside-down pyramid of **La Caixa** at No.61, designed by José María Bosch Aymerich in 1968.

Nuevos Ministerios L2

Metro Nuevos Ministerios.

Until 1930, the Plaza de San Juan de la Cruz marked the end of the Castellana. The Republic's Minister of Public Works, Indalecio Prieto (whose statue was erected here in 1984), carried the street through by knocking down a race course that stood in the way, making room for the long grey bunker of the Nuevos Ministerios, which contains three ministries in a building as outsized as Spain's first lesson in totalitarianism, El Escorial. Planned by dictator Primo de Rivera and his wonderfully named architect Secundino Zuazo, building began during the Republic; when Franco came to power, Zuazo returned from exile to rework the project to fit in with the régime's more conservative mindset. The park in front, originally designed for people, has been given over to cars; the recently glassed-in **gallery** in front holds exhibitions

architecture. A recent **statue of Largo
 ballero** (prime minister during the
 public) stands on the pavement outside,
 mouring his role as Minister of Labour
 m 1931 to 1937, while an equestrian **statue
 Franco**, the last one in Madrid, stands
 ser than the two men ever did in life, at
 e west end of Plaza de San Juan de la Cruz.
 A 10-minute walk east of Nuevos
 nisterios, you'll find **El Viso** ('the vantage
 int'), a garden community of Art Deco
 o- and three-storey houses laid out in the
 20s and 30s, when this was the outskirts
 Madrid.

RBANIZACIÓN
 ZCA

tro Nuevos Ministerios or Lima.
 Back in the mid-1950s, the government
 me up with a project with the inedible
 me of Urbanización AZCA (Asociación
 na Comercial A) as a centre for business
 at might relieve some of the congestion in
 e centre. The inspiration came from the
 ited States: self-contained traffic-free
 azas on various levels, combining offices,
 using, shopping and public areas, with a
 l array of bars, restaurants and clubs to
 ep it hopping at night.
 The plan hibernated until the 1970s, when
 e skyscrapers burst forth. As commercial
 erests took over, the original scheme of
 ilding in harmony went by the board, as
 d much of the planned housing. AZCA does,
 wever, have plenty of shopping, including
 enormous El Corte Inglés department
 re and shopping centre patronized by
 adrid yuppiedom, and a smattering of
 staurants, cafés and discos.
 Originally designed to hold a modern opera
 use, the central **Plaza Picasso** has a monu-
 ent to the artist and a garden where office
 rkers sit out during lunch, pouring out of
 e AZCA's three skyscrapers: the **Banco
 bao-Vizcaya** of 1980, with its genteelly
 sty awnings, designed by one of Madrid's

most influential architects, Saénz de Oíza.
This is the only building in the city equipped
with shock absorbers in its foundations, to
counter the vibrations of the
Atocha–Chamartín train tunnel underneath.
Madrid's tallest building is here as well, the
slim, white, aluminum-clad 43-storey **Torre
Picasso** (1988), the last work by Minori
Yamasaki, the same Japanese architect who
built the World Trade Center in New York. A
helipad on top does a brisk trade, although
the entrance resembles a giant mouse hole.
The cylindrical **Torre de Europa** at the north
end of AZCA (Miguel Oriol e Ibarra; 1982),
home of the Caja de Madrid, has an art exhibition space underneath, the Fundación
Mapfre Vida, open daily. On the opposite side
of the Castellana, another eye-catcher is the
office block at **No.110** topped with a glass
pyramid hat, where the managers of the Abu
Dhabi Investment Agency deliberate.

Estadio Santiago Barnabéu Off maps

*C/ Concha Espina; **metro** Santiago Barnabéu.*
 Just north of AZCA, you'll find the striking
Estadio Santiago Bernabéu, home of Real
Madrid since the late 1940s, when Franco
heavily supported the club to give the
madrileños something to be proud of during
the years of hunger (and to trounce arch-
rival Barcelona). The stadium was expanded
and given a muscular concrete case in 1982,
when Spain hosted the World Cup. It can
hold 105,000 fans, and often does. Opposite
is a brightly coloured mural by Miró crying
out for a scrub, decorating the Palacio de
Congresos, built by Franco in 1964 to
commemorate his 25 years in office.

Puerta de Europa Off maps

Metro Plaza de Castilla.
 Up past a rather long dull stretch of offices
stand the most controversial but certainly
the most attention-grabbing of all the
projects along the Castellana: the Kuwait
Investment Office Towers (or, more properly,

the Puerta de Europa, as the KIO, embroiled in a financial scandal, was unable to finish the project), completed in 1996 and designed by the New York firm Burgee and Associates. You can't miss them – the pair tilt towards one another like blind grubs in love, 15 degrees off true, dwarfing the fountain, roundabout and new bus depot below. Diehard modernists may find them facile, grossly commercial and inelegant (not to mention an exact copy of a project in Toledo, Ohio), but the *madrileños* are quite fond of

them; if you don't agree that they represent the 'New Spain', they do signal a revival of the 12th-century knack for building leaning towers (other good examples are in Pisa and Bologna, in Italy, and there's a good tilting church, Santa María del Sar, in Santiago de Compostela). It's fun to watch the window-washers in action, inching along a purpose-built metal bar that fits into the aluminium tracks that run up the corners of the towers.

Gran Vía, Malasaña and Chueca

Gran Vía, Malasaña and Chueca

The Gran Vía is the Madrid of the bright lights, the main shopping and business area, replete with awkward skyscrapers, grand imperial cinemas with enormous hand-painted billboards, hamburger joints, banks – and swarming with traffic and people late into the night. Part of the excitement comes from the area's wildly eclectic array of early 20th-century architecture along the Calle de Alcalá and Gran Vía. North of the Gran Vía are the two flavoursome old districts of Malasaña and Chueca, once seedy and druggy but now two top night-time destinations. Chueca is firmly established as the city's gay district.

1 Lunch

Salvador, *12 C/ de Barbieri*, **t** *91 521 45 24*; *metro Chueca*. **Open** *Mon–Sat 1.30–4 and 9–11.30*. **Inexpensive**. A famous neighbourhood hangout that has remained true to its bullfighting roots since it opened in 1941. They serve stalwartly traditional, cheerful food.

2 Tea and Cakes

Café de Círculo de Bellas Artes, *42 C/ Alcalá*, **t** *91 521 69 42*; *metro Banco de España*. **Open** *Sun–Thurs 9am–1pm, Fri and Sat 9am–3am*. Madrid's celebrated fine-arts centre has a large café which looks rather like a ballroom, but is one of the most relaxed places to linger in the city centre.

3 Drinks

Museo Chicote, *12 Gran Vía*, **t** *91 532 37 67*; *metro Gran Vía*. **Open** *Mon–Sat 8am–3am*. An Art Deco haven which never closed during the Civil War and, in recent years, has had its original 1940s furnishings immaculately restored. Chicote was famous for his cocktails and this was his bar.

ighlights

Couples' City: The evocative Museo
mántico, p.161

Madrileño's City: Checking out the city's
anges in the Museo Municipal, p.160

Indoor City: The Círculo de Bellas Artes, for
exhibitions or just a drink, p.156

Outdoor City: Neighbourhood atmosphere
in the colourful Plaza de Chueca, p.162

Goya's City: The great paintings in the Real
Academia de Bellas Artes de San Fernando,
p.154

Architectural City: The lovely Modernista
Sociedad General de Autores, p.162

All grid references in this chapter refer
to the map above

CALLE DE ALCALÁ

One of the 10 streets radiating from the Puerta del Sol (see p.74), broad, dignified Calle de Alcalá sweeps out past the Hotel Paris to the northeast. In the Middle Ages, its path was blazed by shepherds, herding their massive flocks between Extremadura and the summer pastures in the north. By the 18th century, however, this transhumance trail was one of the most elegant streets in all Europe, lined with superb palaces, and even today it maintains its panache – at least here on its west end – even though many of the private mansions were replaced with plush and pompous bank buildings in the late 19th century.

Real Academia de Bellas Artes de San Fernando J11

13 C/ de Alcalá, t 91 524 08 64; metro Sol or Sevilla; wheelchair accessible. Open Tues–Fri 9–7, Sat–Mon and hols 9–2.30; adm €2.40, free Wed; free guided tour Wed 5pm (Spanish only).

One of the most beautiful homes on Calle de Alcalá was the Palacio Goyeneche, designed for a banker by José de Churriguera in 1710. When it became home of the Real Academia de Bellas Artes de San Fernando in 1773, the 'enlightened' academicians found Churriguera's lavish Baroque froo-froos frivolous, and stripped them away. The building has looked like Cinderella after the ball ever since.

Founded by Ferdinand VI in 1752, the city's fine arts academy has a collection of art that makes a fine appetizer or dessert to the feast served at Madrid's Big Three. And like the Prado and Thyssen, the personality of the collectors shines through in unexpected ways: the academicians, in short, may have considered themselves enlightened, but their tastes weigh very much towards the unusual, the whimsical and the downright funny.

Temporary exhibition space and the Calcografía Nacional (see below) are on the mezzanine level between the ground and first floors, and the permanent collection is on the first and second floors. The collection is displayed in vaguely chronological order, with older works (14th–18th centuries) on the first floor and newer works (18th–20th centuries) upstairs, though there is some overlap. Goya is on the first floor. The itinerary begins at the staircase to your right as you enter the breezeway of the museum; follow the signs up to the first floor.

First Floor

The collection begins with a room full of moody, dramatic **Riberas** and **Alonso Canos**, nearly all on religious themes, including an unorthodox *Assumption of the Magdalen*, who by most accounts never assumpted anywhere. Cano also weighs in with *Death of a Franciscan*, a sombre scene, at least on the earthly plane, but thanks to the artist we see the friar riding off merrily to his reward in a chariot drawn by white horses. There are five remarkable life-size portraits of monks by **Zurbarán**, beautiful works full of early-Renaissance precision; in contrast, his *Blessed Alonso Rodríguez* is an unusually busy picture in which the subject is being branded by Jesus and Mary, sitting in heaven and holding their hearts out like ray guns. Then there's *La Abundancia*, by **Martin de Vos**, in which one child frolics with a fiery salamander and another holds a miniature triceratops in his hand – probably the first instance of a dinosaur in art.

Along with the quirky works there are fine paintings by **Murillo**, **El Greco** and **Velázquez** (portraits of Philip IV and Mariana of Austria) and dark works by the Venetian **Bassano dynasty**, who specialized in nocturnal scenes. One room has small paintings by **Bellini** and **Correggio**, next to the delightful *Spring*, a portrait of a man entirely composed of flowers, the only work in Spain by Italian proto-Surrealist **Arcimboldo**, who painted for the Habsburgs in Austria and Prague.

In **Rubens'** *Susanna and the Elders* (c.1608) the dirty old men are not content with their

al role as Peeping Toms, but pinch her
ughy pink flesh, while the same artist's *St
ustine between Christ and the Virgin*
ws the Virgin doing some pinching of her
n, while Augustine rolls his eyes in either
belief or ecstasy. **Jans Jannsens'** *Roman
arity* (a theme taken up by Steinbeck at
end of *The Grapes of Wrath*) is equally
morable, with a loving rendition of the old
n's dirty feet. The last two paintings in the
m are by that most uncanny of 17th-
tury painters, **Alessandro Magnasco** of
noa, who used his precocious quick-stroke
hnique to highlight the nightmares of his
eased age. One painting looks like a self-
trait in a wizard's hat, and the other, the
nciscan Chapter, shows the friars appar-
ly writhing and dissolving in a whirlwind
Vitus dance.

est of all are the excellent **Goyas**,
luding two self-portraits (one young, one
ubled and deaf), one of Ferdinand VII,
king silly on a horse two sizes too small
him, and another of the detested minister
nuel Godoy, slumped contemptuously in a
ir in the middle of a battle. There are also
nting scenes in his 'Black Style': *Bullfight,
uisition, Flagellants, Madhouse* and his
nous and rather eerie *The Burial of the
dine*, showing the riotous fiestas that
rk the end of carnival. The sardine burial
tinues to this day in Madrid, with a mock
eral party that bears a coffin containing a
ge papier-mâché sardine through the
eets to the Casa de Campo, where it is set
ght. It commemorates the occasion when
starving townspeople of Madrid received
ng-awaited consignment of fish only to
cover that it was completely rotten, and
only thing to do was burn it on the spot.
he soft contours of **Bartolomé Esteban
rillo** are on display in *Resurrection of the
d*, and a big, swooping *Ecstasy of St Francis
Assisi*. There is a significant collection of
ntings by **Mengs**, among the lovelier of
ich is the portrait of the Marquesa de
no, with a parrot. There are also paintings
Van Dyck and David Teniers, and a
e **Fragonard**.

Second Floor

As peculiar as much of this is, none of it
really prepares you for the anti-Christmas
crib at the top of the steps. Like the Italians,
the Spaniards love elaborate Nativity scenes
populated by a host of extras, but it took a
pervert like Charles IV, who wanted to
achieve the ultimate 5,950-piece display in
the Palacio Real, to commission **José Gines** to
sculpt figures illustrating the Massacre of
the Innocents. At least the maddened
mothers seem to be getting their own back,
as they bite, stab and tear the eyeballs out of
the cruel men.

As an antidote, there are charming sun-
filled paintings by **Sorolla**, **Andrés Segovia**'s
guitar, a goofy Greek fantasy of the
Colossus of Rhodes by **M. Degrain** and
Family of Skeletons by **J. López**, all happily
holding hands.

Calcografía Nacional

Another, perhaps lesser-known part of the
Real Academia is the Calcografía Nacional,
the national print collection. Founded in 1789
by the Count of Floridablanca as the Real
Estampería (Royal Print Collection), it is
Spain's most important centre for the study
of etchings, engravings and other related art-
printing processes. Its over 8,000 copper,
steel and zinc plates can be viewed if one
makes a written request in advance. Some of
Goya's copper plates are exhibited on a
rotating basis, and on display in other rooms
you will find lithographic machines and
other printing tools.

Architecture along
Calle de Alcalá J–K11

Metro Sevilla or Banco de España.

Next door to the Real Academia, at No.11,
the Finance and Interior Ministries occupy
the former **Casa Real de la Aduana** (Royal
Customs House), another project of mayor-
king Charles III, who commissioned it from
Francesco Sabatini in 1761. Sabatini borrowed
heavily from Rome's Palazzo Farnese for the
façade; the elaborate door, by Pedro de

Ribera, installed here in 1944, comes from a palace destroyed in the Civil War.

Just east from the academy at No.15 you'll find the sumptuous Riviera-style **Casino de Madrid**, since 1903 a private club, though the original men-only rule is no longer in force. If you ask nicely at the door they may just let you have a peek at Madrid's most extraordinary flowing stairway, so beautiful that you may want to join the club or compromise your virtue with a member just to swan down it (*visits can be arranged, generally for groups, by calling in advance,* **t** *91 521 87 00*).

The building squeezed into the sharp corner opposite, now housing the **Banco Español de Crédito**, was designed in the 1880s by Catalan José Grassés Riera, who introduced some of Barcelona's Modernista curves and whimsy into a city more used to Castilian symmetry. This was the first major commercial block in Madrid. Next to it, the **Banco de Bilbao** (Ricardo Bastida; 1910) supports not one, but two bronze quadrigas straight out of *Ben Hur*, ready to fly over the Calle de Alcalá in an airborne circus. Further down, on the corner of Calle de Cedaceros, the **New Club** (1899) was the first private English-style club in Madrid, designed by Grassés Riera in one of his tamer moods.

Next on the street, at No.25, is the massively domed church of the convent of **Las Calatravas**, built between 1670 and 78 for nuns of the eponymous military order. One of Madrid's better Baroque churches, it still possesses one last breathlessly overwrought altarpiece by José de Churriguera.

The point of the V where Calle de Alcalá meets the Gran Vía is filled by the **Edificio Metropólis**, performing the same landmark role as the Flatiron building in New York. Designed in 1905 by Jules and Raymond Fevrier in the French Belle Epoque bathyscope style, the Metropólis set the snazzy tone for future projects along the Gran Vía, with its cylindrical prow of Corinthian columns, ring of statues and dome picked out with gilt falderol, topped by a Winged Victory, who looks as if she's waiting to crown the winning charioteer on the Banco de Bilbao.

Círculo de Bellas Artes

2 C/ del Marqués de Casa Riera **t** *91 360 54 (* *(corner of Alcalá);* **metro** *Banco de España.* **Exhibitions open** *Tues–Fri 5–9pm, Sat 11–2 c* *5–9, Sun 11am–2pm; closed Aug;* **café open** *Sun–Thurs 9am–2am, Fri and Sat 9am–4ar* **adm** *€1.*

Opposite the Metropólis is another attention-grabber. The Círculo is one of Madrid's best, if most eccentric, Art Deco structures concocted by Antonio Palacios (1919–26), architect of the cream-cake Palacio de Comunicaciones (*see* p.140). Originally another private club devoted to the arts (hence the statue of Athena), the Círculo is now open to the public for a small fee. Its cool vanilla marble interior has a delightfu airy bar (which also serves a very reasonab priced *menu del día*), while the other floors feature exhibition halls, theatres, a lavish ballroom and classrooms. The Círculo publishes *Minerva*, a monthly magazine w exhaustive (and slightly exhausting) coverage of the myriad cultural activities o offer here.

Further along, at No.49, is another, less exotic work by Palacios, the **Banco Central Hispano** (1910), while, opposite, the brick church of **San José** (1742) was the last work Pedro de Ribera and is famous for having witnessed the wedding in 1802 of Spain's future nemesis, Simon Bolívar, the great liberator of South America.

Casa de las Siete Chimeneas K10

Plaza del Rey; **metro** *Banco de España.*

The supposedly haunted House of the Seven Chimneys was designed by Juan de Herrera as a country retreat in 1577 (some s it was intended for a lover of Philip II), whe Madrid ended at the Puerta del Sol. The ghost is a young lady in white, and her skeleton, with some late 16th-century coin was found hidden in the walls during a 19t century restoration. Among the famous wl have stayed here, in 1623, was the future

arles I of England, coming down for a
view of the Infanta Maria (*see* 'A Spanish
tch'). The house is now used as an annexe
he Ministry of Culture. The sculpture in
square is by Eduardo Chillida.

HE GRAN VÍA

oughed through 14 pokey medieval
eets of old Madrid between 1910 and 1930,
Gran Vía was a smash hit from the start
h the *madrileños*. Planned as an elegant
isian boulevard in the Baron Hausmann
de, it evolved instead into a quirky cosmo-

politan architectural ratatouille of office
blocks, hotels and music halls, reminiscent of
big commercial streets in Latin America. The
Gran Vía is always bustling, even on Sundays,
when everyone heads over for an afternoon
or evening at the cinema. Many of these old
movie palaces hide behind elephant-sized
hand-painted posters; the artists, a specialized guild, use house-paint for their portraits
of the stars and can crank them out in a
couple of days. The fact that the Gran Vía
isn't straight, as was originally planned (two
church properties in the way forced it to have
an elbow), adds to the visual impact. And
don't forget to look up: there is a plethora of

Spanish Match

pain in the 17th century made itself the
e homeland of the picaresque, the inspira-
n for the first novels, and Spaniards set
fashions and the manners for all Europe
he age of Baroque. Life was a stage, and a
n wasn't a man until he'd gone out and
d an adventure – even if he was the son of
ng. The Casa de las Siete Chimeneas, just
th of the Gran Vía and Calle de Alcalá,
ce belonged to John Digby, Earl of Bristol,
pain on government business, and in
rch of 1623 it received a very unusual
ger – none other than the 21-year-old
ce of Wales, the future Charles I. Charles
travelled to Spain incognito, with his
nd the Duke of Buckingham, using the
nes 'John Brown and Tom Smith'. The Earl,
o was keeping an eye on Charles for his
her, James I, wrote home that the pair
re 'sweet boys and dear virtuous knights,
rthy to be put in a new romanso'.
he visit had a purpose: Spain and England
re enjoying a rare period of peace, and
re was talk of marrying Charles to the
anta Doña María. Naturally, he wanted to
e a look at her first. Riding to Spain was
easy part; getting into the court of
ip IV, who didn't much care for Protestant
etics, proved much harder. Charles first
y his Infanta when their coaches passed in
adrid street; later, go-betweens managed

to contrive a meeting during the *paseo* on
the Prado – Charles would know her by the
blue ribbon in her hair.

When word of this got out, Charles' presence could no longer be kept a secret; more
and more English were arriving all the time
to see the show, including King James' celebrated fool, Archie Armstrong. Finally the
King consented to a state entrance for
Charles in the biggest spectacle Madrid had
to offer, a gala bullfight in the Plaza Mayor
with all the court in attendance, watching
from the balconies.

Charles apparently liked what he saw
(according to Olivares, he devoured the
Infanta with his eyes 'like a cat does a
mouse'), for he tried without success to
surprise her in the Casa de Campo, where she
and her friends were out at dawn gathering
May dew. But this is history, not a *romanso*,
and politics and religion made it a match
never to be. Charles stayed in Madrid for six
months; he met Velázquez and Van Dyck, and
went back home with presents from the
royal family that included paintings by Titian
and Correggio, an elephant, an ostrich and
five camels. This began Charles' own career as
an art collector, and he amassed quite a
remarkable collection before he lost his head.
His philistine Roundhead successors had no
use for such trumperies and sold them off at
a ridiculous price – to the King of Spain.

giant doodads, as if Gargantua's bric-a-brac cabinet had spilled on top of them.

Grassy K10

1 Gran Vía; **metro** *Banco de España or Sevilla.* **Museum open** *Mon–Sat 10–1 and 5–8.*

The aforementioned Metropólis building at the corner of Calle de Alcalá was echoed just up at the next wedge-shaped corner, in a building of 1916 belonging to Madrid's most prestigious jewellery makers, Grassy, with its big sign for Piaget. Downstairs, it has a small museum dedicated to Art Nouveau clocks.

Museo Chicote K10

12 Gran Vía, **t** *91 532 37 67;* **metro** *Gran Vía or Banco de España.* **Open** *Mon–Sat 8am–3am.*

Another 'museum' on the Gran Vía is Chicote, Madrid's premier cocktail bar, designed in 1931 by Luis Gutiérrez Soto, who would go on to build many of Franco's show-case buildings. The interior, down to the seats and even some of the waiters, remains the same as ever. Famous as the only bar in Madrid that never closed during the Civil War, it was the favourite oasis of war correspondents, of Hemingway and of every celebrity who ever passed through Madrid.

Telefónica and Around J10

28 Gran Vía, museum entrance on C/ de Fuencarral; **metro** *Gran Vía; wheelchair accessible.* **Museum open** *Tues–Fri 10–2 and 5–8, Sat, Sun and hols 10–2;* **adm** *free.*

The phone company building was Madrid's first skyscraper, designed in 1929 by American Lewis Weeks and Ignacio de Cárdenas. It rises 266ft, and comes complete with little Herreran turrets just to remind us that we're in Madrid. In the 1920s, dictator Primo de Rivera hired the Bell Telephone Company of America to construct a state-of-the-art phone system for Spain. During the Civil War, it proved its worth when commanders from both sides could ring up their front lines to see which villages had been captured. A small museum on the ground and first floors is devoted to the history of telephones and surprisingly excellent contemporary art exhibitions.

Opposite Telefónica, note the **1904 building**, covered with busts. The streets to the south of here, especially Calle de la Montera, are Madrid's red light district. If y take Montera and turn immediately to the left, you'll come to one of the churches tha caused a crick in the Gran Vía, the Neoclassical **Oratorio del Caballero de Gra** designed in the late 18th century by Prado architect Juan de Villanueva, with a hand-some basilican interior.

This humming mid-section of the Gran V between Telefónica and Plaza del Callao, completed under the Republic, has a pair c buildings by Palacios, the offices at **No.27** a the **Hotel Avendia**.

Plaza del Callao to Plaza de España I10–G9

Metro *Callao or Plaza de España.*

Plaza del Callao has more fine Art Deco buildings, the **Palacio de la Música** (35 Gra Vía), the brick **Palacio de la Prensa** (4 Plaza del Callao) and the **Cine Callao**, with its lav interior and its exterior resembling flocked wallpaper. South of Plaza del Callao, the bu pedestrian-only **Calle de Preciados** links th Gran Vía to the Puerta del Sol, with its boutiques, buskers, beggars and branches the omnipresent El Corte Inglés and FNAC chains.

Best of all is the Edificio Carrión (41 Gran Vía), better known as the **Capitol**, for the cinema it houses, a lovely streamlined Art Deco building of 1932 by Luis Martínez Feduchi and Vicente Eced.

The last segment of the Gran Vía has few pretensions. **Calle de los Libreros**, off to the north, is famous for its secondhand book-shops. Round the corner, on Calle de la Flor Alta, is a grand, if dilapidated, **Neoclassical façade** designed in 1722 by Ventura Rodríg for the Count of Altamira. But it was all tha was ever completed.

ALASAÑA

 the north of the Gran Vía and east of the
e-grand Calle de San Bernardo lies the
uant neighbourhood of Malasaña, a
ble of crowded streets, which are by day
ne to locals and by night thronged with
llers. In the past this was one of the
rest districts in the city, called the Barrio
Maravillas, 'of Marigolds', but also, more
msically, 'of Wonders', in the same way
t the beggars of Paris had their Cours de
acles. Under Franco this neighbourhood
narvels hit rock bottom and was at the
nt of being bulldozed, when the residents
ed in protest to save it. In the 1960s, its
culously low rents combined with the
venient location began to attract hippies
other alternative types. Although quiet
ay – it is one of the last genuine residen-
areas in the centre – Malasaña still lives
ts reputation as the epicentre of the
vida years, and every other doorway
ms to be a club. The town hall has cleaned
place up recently, and cleared out many
he badly parked cars, turning the area
 a more or less pedestrian zone.

n Placido 19

 de San Roque, t 91 522 37 74; **metro** Callao.
is is the church of a convent founded in
 by a frisky noblewoman who wanted to
ome a nun while keeping her lover, the
verful and extremely wealthy Jerónimo
Villanueva, state minister to Philip IV.
anueva built a love-nest next door to the
vent, linked by a secret passageway. This
ky-panky, however, was only the begin-
 of a scandal worthy of the *National
uirer*: the passage was used by the
prous king himself when he fell in love
 a beautiful young nun, Sor Margarita de
ruz, who only managed to deter his
vanted attentions by lying in a coffin,
ching a crucifix and pretending to be
d. It gave Philip IV the shock of his life, but

led to his pious commissioning of Velázquez
to paint *Christ on the Cross*, which Philip then
donated to the convent (it now hangs in the
Prado). Before long these shenanigans in the
convent attracted the attention of the
Inquisition, which sent a messenger to Rome
with the tale of royal indiscretion. The
messenger didn't make it: the indefatigable
Conde Duque de Olivares, Philip's right-hand
man, had him kidnapped along the way. The
convent's father confessor, who used sex to
exorcise nuns supposedly possessed of the
devil, fared less well and was imprisoned by
the Inquisition for life.

The church, rebuilt in the 20th century, may
no longer have its Velázquez or lusty nuns
but it does have a gory *Recumbent Christ* by
Gregorio Fernández, an *Annunciation* by
Claudio Coello and polychrome saints by
Manuel Pereira. Perhaps there's some poetic
justice in the fact that this is now a red
light district.

San Antonio
de los Alemanes 19

16 Corredera de San Pablo, t 91 522 37 74;
metro Callao.

Calle del Pez ('of the fish', named for the
ponds that were here in the 16th century)
leads to the district's other church, the brick
Baroque San Antonio de los Alemanes,
founded in 1607 as part of a hospice by
Philip III to care for the many down-and-out
Portuguese who immigrated to Madrid in
search of work, when Portugal was under the
Spanish Crown (1580–1640). It was later
given to the Germans who accompanied one
of the unfortunate brides of the unfortunate
Charles II. Today it retains its charitable
mission and is run by the Hermandad del
Refugio. The interior is entirely frescoed: the
Apotheosis of St Anthony in the dome was
painted by Francisco Rizzi and Juan Carreño
de Miranda, and the walls are by Luca
Giordano, with more on St Anthony, mingled
with a handful of royal portraits.

Plaza de Dos de Mayo and Around I8

Metro Tribunal.

A few blocks north, the heart of Malasaña is the Plaza de Dos de Mayo, named for the famous events that took place that day in 1808 (*see* 'Dos de Mayo'). The square, with its classical statues of Velarde and Daoiz (both of whom were killed in the battle) is lined with pleasant *terrazas*. A popular late-night party rendezvous, in the daytime it reverts to its Dr Jekyll normality and niceness, with just a few flecks of graffiti to betray its night-time antics. The church just to the south of the square, the **Iglesia de las Maravillas**, has a Virgin with marigolds (*maravillas*) on the altar.

Like any good *barrio* in Madrid, Malasaña has its quirky shops and quirky shop signs. Masterpieces of the genre, in tiles, may be found at 28 Calle de San Vicente Ferrer at the **Laboratorio de Especialidades Juanse**, with its advertisements from 1925 of ailments that the Juanse crew promised to relieve (unfortunately no longer available), and the adjacent **Antiqua Herrería** (the 'Old Eggery'), where the tiles show contented chickens.

The next street south, **Calle del Espíritu Santo**, has a fine old neighbourhood feel. In the 17th century it was famous for its brothels, which were impressively decimated one night by a bolt of lightning.

CHUECA

East of Malasaña, its sister *barrio* of Chueca has prospered in its role as the capital's gay district. It, too, has an older name, the Barrio de los Chisperos, which referred to the area's many blacksmiths, although the word later became synonymous with any low-class, low-down inhabitant of Madrid. In the heyday of the movida, Chueca gained a sinister reputation for hard drugs. Madrid's gay community has managed to clean it up, and co-exists in an exemplary fashion with the elderly residents who have stuck here

Dos de Mayo

During the reign of the useless Charles IV (1788–1808), Spain came increasingly under the power of Napoleon. In March 1808, French troops entered Madrid, while the royal family fled to France. The government was ready to cave in, but the *madrileños* rebelled.

A crowd in the Puerta del Sol began to protest at the apparent abduction of the royal family and were fired on by French troops. A young officer, Pedro Velarde, ran to the square now called Plaza de Dos de Mayo in Malasaña, which was then the site of the Montleón artillery barracks (only the entrance arch survives). He convinced Captain Daoiz to disobey the French order to close all the barracks and instead to distribute weapons to the citizenry to defend themselves against Napoleon's army. A fierce, desperate fight of several hours ensued, in which the *madrileños* never really had a chance. One casualty was a local 17-year-old seamstress, Manuela Malasaña, who was summarily shot for defending herself with her scissors (according to the most popular account); the district now bears her name.

through thick and thin. The bars, restaurants and fancy and quirky shops (not all of which are exclusively gay by any means) are among the hippest in the city.

Museo Municipal J8

78 C/ de Fuencarral, t 91 588 86 72; metro Tribunal. Open Tues–Fri 9.30–8, Sat–Sun 10–2; closed hols; adm free.

Colourful Calle de Fuencarral is one of Chueca's main streets, a slice of real Madrid and a perfect setting for this excellent museum. Housed in the 18th-century Hospicio de San Fernando, with an exuberant, almost orgasmic Churrigueresque portal by Pedro de Ribera, the museum was opened in 1929 but has been renovated and greatly expanded in recent years. More *madrileños* come here than tourists, and you can sense their growing civic pride as you

tch them scrutinizing the old maps and
nts, pointing out landmarks and
cussing how their city has changed.
ne collection is large, and you can learn as
ch as you care to about Madrid; exhibits
right back to the Palaeolithic era. There
paintings of the city from various
iods, and the excellent **1656 street plan** of
drid, by Pedro Texeira. Spaniards love to
ke room-sized **models** of their cities, and
re is a remarkable one here, commis-
ned by Ferdinand VII from Colonel León
de Palacio, that accurately reproduces the
drid of the 1830s on a scale of 1:864,
nplete with every balcony and window,
ntain and garden, closed in by walls with
ates. Also here are Pedro Berruguete's
pid *Virgin and Child* and the Renaissance-
ceresque **burial effigies** of the ubiquitous
triz Galindo ('La Latina'), Isabel's enor-
usly influential Latin teacher, and her
band, Francisco Mirez, equally specialized
bombardments) and known as 'El
llero'. Then there's Goya's ***Allegory of
drid***, which has a history that demon-
tes the interesting times he lived in (*see*
Allegory of Madrid').

ehind the museum, Ribera's **Fuente
a Fama**, the fountain equivalent of his
rway, was moved here to serve as his
nument. Another monument here is the
ha, a celebrity nightclub housed in Luis
iérrez Soto's **Cine Barceló** of 1930, one of
buildings that hint of the cool, stream-
d architecture Madrid might have had if
Depression, Civil War and dictatorship
not intervened.

useo Romántico K8

/ de San Mateo, **t** 91 448 10 45; **metro**
unal or Alonso Martínez; wheelchair
essible. Closed for reforms at time of
arch. Scheduled to re-open December 2004.
nis atmospheric museum was founded by
Marqués de Vega-Inclán in 1924 with the
of re-creating a typical abode of the
y 19th century (the building actually goes
k to the mid-1700s). He didn't do a bad

An Allegory of Madrid

Goya's *Allegory of Madrid* in the Museo
Municipal has a chequered history that
reflects both the painter's fundamental
indifference to politics and his keen aware-
ness of which side his bread was buttered
on. In the original version, commissioned by
the city in 1810 to preside over its sessions,
Goya painted a portrait of then king Joseph
Bonaparte in the oval frame supported by
the angels, next to Madrid's coat-of-arms. In
1812, when King Joseph took to his heels, the
city asked Goya to replace the portrait with a
book labelled *The Constitution of 1812*. When
Joseph returned in 1813, Goya was asked to
repaint him.

In 1814, the King was replaced again by the
Constitution, but this had to be smudged out
and replaced with a portrait of the hated
Ferdinand VII by one of Goya's followers. In
the same year Goya was lucky to be exon-
erated from the charge of 'accepting
employment from the usurper', but only
because he had never worn the medal
Joseph Bonaparte had given him; he further
patched things up by painting his famous *Los
Fusilamientos del Dos de Mayo* and *Los
Fusilamientos de Moncloa*, now in the Prado.

As for the *Allegory*, it had to be repainted in
1829 after a soldier stabbed the painting
with his bayonet. In 1841, when the Liberals
took power, the *Constitution* re-appeared.
Studying the layers of paint, the mayor of
Madrid in 1861 asked that they all be scraped
off to reveal Goya's original intention. But
when the restorers reached the portrait of
Joseph Bonaparte, it was too much to
stomach and so they replaced it with the
words 'Dos de Mayo'. And so it has remained.

job, with a collection of paintings from the
period, including a *St Gregory* by Goya and
other works by *costumbrista* painters who,
like Goya, delighted in scenes of festivities.
You can also peruse the personal memorabilia of the Romantic poet Mariano José de
Larra, who cut a great potential career short
at age 27 by shooting himself in 1837 with
the pistols on display.

Sociedad General de Autores K8

*4 C/ de Fernando VI; **metro** Alonso Martínez.*

Madrid's best and most beautiful Art Nouveau building, the Palacio Longoria, is now better known as the Sociedad General de Autores, for the association of writers and artists who own it. Designed in 1902 by Catalan architect José Grassés Riera for a banker, the undulating structure eschews all right angles and straight lines, with a result that looks ever so creamy and edible. If the doorman will admit you, step inside to see the wonderful spiralling stairway, inset with a rainbow-hued, domed, stained-glass ceiling, the colours echoed in the daisies, inset with coloured glass petals, which seem to grow out of the banisters.

Calle de Hortaleza J10–K8

***Metro** Chueca.*

Calle de Hortaleza, whose name recalls the gardens that once lined it, is now a good place to buy a muscle enhancer, glittering disco balls or a fluffy alien. The street also has another church by Pedro de Ribera, **San Antón**, although later architects have stripped away his signature lavish stone frosting. St Anthony Abbot (San Antonio Abad) is always depicted with a pig, and this is a good place to be on his saint's day (17 January), when the millions of *madrileños* with dogs, and a surprising number of other household pets, show up to have them blessed.

Plaza de Chueca K9

***Metro** Chueca*

East of Hortaleza, Calle de Gravina leads to Plaza de Chueca, the symbol of the neighbourhood's revival, where the local transvestites walk their poodles and stop off for a *vermut aperitivo* with the other locals at the zinc and tile **Taberna de Angel Sierra**. Colourful Calle de Barbieri crosses the square and is the address of the funky **San Antón market**. Near the bottom of Calle de Barbieri

(No.5) is the Art Deco **Hotel Mónaco**, a famous kitsch palace, converted in 1919 by Frenchman into a lovers' hideaway before turned into Madrid's society brothel, frequented by King Alfonso XIII. The favou royal room at No.30 had not only mirrors a paintings, but also enough space for a stri quartet to serenade his amours.

Las Salesas L9

***Metro** Colón.*

To the east, the atmosphere changes ag in the *barrio* known as Las Salesas, tucked behind the big barracks on Plaza de Cibele Only a couple of blocks east of Plaza de Chueca, **Calle del Almirante** is snobby and full of trendy boutiques and art galleries, including the **Moriarty Gallery** (No.5), a ho spot during the movida. Just north, on Ca del Marqués de la Enseneda, is a Modernis building by Riera, the **French Institute** (190 adorned with his favourite elephant-head motifs.

On Calle de Bárbara de Braganza is the church that gave the neighbourhood its name, **Las Salesas Reales**, originally part o convent founded in 1747 by Barbara de Braganza, wife of Ferdinand VI, and design by a French architect, François Carlier. The Queen wanted to establish a cosy niche fo her widowhood (only she died first) and spent so much money on the project that *madrileños* say '*Bárbara reina, Bárbara obre bárbaro gusto, bárbaro gasto*' (Barbara que Barbara work, barbaric taste, barbaric was The adjacent convent is now Madrid's law courts, but the church survives in its origin Rococo state (if you're lucky enough to fin open), with much green marble, frescoes a the tombs of Queen Barbara (she was chil less so could not be buried in El Escorial) a Ferdinand VI, designed by Sabatini. Anothe belongs to General Leopoldo O'Donnell, w was publicly and intimately prominent during the reign of Isabel II (the queen on famously huffed to her minister Naváez: 'love the institution of the monarchy, but O'Donnell loves me for myself').

To the West

To the West

The western end of Madrid has its largest parks, where you'll find most of the trees that substantiate the town's claim to be the second most wooded city in the world. It also has one of Goya's masterpieces, in the Ermita de San Antonio de la Florida, and some surprises: a genuine Egyptian temple, an amusement park, a lighthouse without a light and yet another royal palace.

Highlights

Couples' City: Waltzing around the ballroom at the Museo Cerralbo, p.167

Madrileño's **City**: Riding the rollercoasters in the Parque de Atracciones in the Casa de Campo, p.170

Indoor City: The treasures in the Museo de América, p.171

Outdoor City: Taking the *teleférico* from the Parque del Oeste to the Casa de Campo, p.170

Goya's City: His pantheon, the Ermita de San Antonio de la Florida, p.168

Architectural City: The transplanted Egyptian Templo de Debod, p.167

---

1 Lunch

Casa Mingo, *2 Paseo de la Florida, Parque del Oeste*, **t** *91 547 79 18*; **metro** *Argüelles.* **Open** *daily 11am–midnight. Cash only.* **Moderate**. An authentic Asturian *sidrería* and roast chicken emporium, unchanged over the decades, with plenty of outdoor tables.

2 Tea and Cakes

Café Bruin, *48 Paseo del Pintor Rosales*, **t** *91 541 59 21*; **metro** *Argüelles.* Long-established and excellent purveyor of ice cream and other refreshments.

3 Drinks

La Tabernilla, *2 Calle Cristo*, **t** *91 541 41 12*; *metro Noviciado.* **Open** *daily 1–1.* There's a great atmosphere in this tiny bar on a pedestrian side street around the corner from the Conde Duque cultural centre.

All grid references in this chapter refer to the map opposite

AROUND PLAZA DE ESPAÑA

Metro Plaza de España.

The broad Plaza de España, marking the western end of the Gran Vía, is yet another open space created by Joseph Bonaparte when he demolished the San Gil barracks, but its current appearance is a legacy of the Franco era. Infected with a typical case of dictator's edifice complex, Franco wanted to out-top the Telefónica building on the Gran Vía (*see* p.158) with a skyscraper to prove to the world that his regime could get one up: the resulting **Edificio España** (Joaquín and José María Otamendi; 1953) is even more Baroque than the phone building, with 26 floors of limestone and brick. There's a hotel and swimming pool on the roof, which is decorated with little Herreran towers, like spikes to keep pigeons off. Its nickname is El Taco, although in this case it means 'the stopper' rather than a Mexican snack.

Pleased with the result, Franco commissioned the same fraternal duo to outdo themselves four years later with the building of El Taco's neighbour, the ugly 32-floor **Torre de Madrid**, to take over the kudos as the tallest building in Spain. As an antidote to the bombast, take a look at the luscious Modernista **Casa Gallardo** apartments by Federico Arias Rey (who studied in Barcelona) on the northwest corner of the big square.

The centre of the Plaza de España, much beloved by local winos, has a fountain and olive grove, and what for most tourists is the main attraction: a back-handed **monument to Cervantes**. Its goofy bronze figures of Don Quixote and Sancho Panza from 1928 have become a favourite for cheesy snapshots.

Centro Cultural Conde Duque G–H8

11 C/ del Conde Duque, t 91 588 58 34; metro Plaza de España, San Bernardo or Noviciado; wheelchair accessible. **Open** *Tues–Sun 11–9.*

This is the former royal barracks, the gargantuan Cuartel del Conde Duque. It wa designed in 1717 by Pedro de Ribera, with hi signature elaborate doorway, at the behest of Philip V, who reorganized the army and created the Compañías Reales de Guardias de Corps. For this noble legion, an appropriately noble edifice was required, and de Ribera delivered. The place is humungous, with three giant courtyards. It suffered yea of fires and decline before it was purchased and restored by the city in the 1980s. It now hosts a lively culture centre, including an excellent modern art gallery, the **Museo Municipal de Arte Contemporáneo**. In the summer it is one of the precious few places in Madrid that remains alive with activity.

Comendadoras H8

Plaza de las Comendadoras; metro San Bernardo or Noviciado.

Just east of the Centro Cultural, on a little plaza just off C/ de Amaniel, you'll find the home of the last few Comendadoras, nuns who form something of a ladies' auxiliary the lofty knightly Order of Santiago – henc the little red cross they wear on their habit Their convent, with its old-fashioned Flemi Habsburg slate towers, is attributed to Manuel and José del Olmo and dates from 1679, while the attractive church is embellished with several references to the patron saint of the order, St James the Moor-Slaye including an equestrian statue over the entrance and a large painting over the alta by Luca Giordano. Hanging banners record the names and dates of the Knights' victor during the Reconquista.

lesia de Montserrat 18

*C/ de San Bernardo; **metro** San Bernardo Noviciado.*

ot far from the Comendadoras, this urch was founded in 1642 by Philip IV for nks from Montserrat in Catalonia, when y were forced to flee their own monastery ring a separatist revolt. Due to financial ficulties, the church took so long to build t it mostly bears the 18th-century imprint edro de Ribera, who completed the door lavishly ornate tower. Its treasure is a er eerie Christ made out of hide and man hair, like the famous Buffalo Jesus in gos, and dressed up in bits of lace. Today old people's home shares the monastery h the monks.

lacio de Liria G8

*C/ de la Princesa, **t** 91 547 53 02; **metro** za de España. **Open** Fri morning by ance written request (the current waiting is six months long).*

ehind the Centro Cultural is the 18th-tury Palacio de Liria, the home of one of most venerable noble families of Spain, Dukes of Alba. The palace was built by tura Rodríguez and Sabatini for the Duke Berwick and Liria, James Stuart Fitz-James, married a ducal sister, but it was badly naged by bombs in 1936 and has since n sumptuously restored. The bombs put a ous dent in one of Spain's great collec-s of art and treasures, but what remains g in the galleries is seriously impressive, u are one of the lucky handful of visitors h the forethought to have written ahead nths in advance. There are excellent works ra Angelico, Titian, Andrea del Sarto, brandt, Rubens, Velázquez and El Greco ong many others; portraits of the Stuarts ainsborough, Reynolds, Romney and stable; and the famous full-length trait by Goya of the beautiful 13th chess of Alba, in which she is seen ting to the words 'Only Goya'.

Museo Cerralbo G9

*17 C/ de Ventura Rodríguez, **t** 91 547 36 46; **metro** Plaza de España. **Open** Tues–Sat 9.30–3, Sun 10–3, closed hols; **adm** €2.40, free Wed and Sun.*

When the Marqués de Cerralbo died in 1922, his will decreed that his house and its treasures, accumulated during a lifetime as a travelling magpie, should become a museum. The Marqués further dictated that not a thing should ever be moved from the gloriously cluttered state in which he left it. The walls are dotted with minor **paintings** by Ribera, Tintoretto, Palma Giovane, Magnasco, Zurbarán and Valdes Léal; a fine *St Francis* by El Greco; and a curious picture of the Marqués in a collage of lottery tickets. The intricately decorated **Sala Arabe** has suits of Western and Japanese armour, and an ornate opium pipe, with instructions for use. The **bathroom** fixtures are lovely, and there's a very cosy little **library and dining room** where guests could enjoy paintings of porcupines and vipers; plus lots of ambient bric-a-brac, furniture, some awful chandeliers and scores of ticking clocks.

Best of all are the two delightful rooms decorated by otherwise little-known Máximo Juderías Cabellero in 1891–3: the **Salón de Confianza**, frescoed with *The Four Seasons*, where the Marqués played bridge while nymphs peeked down into his hand; and a superb **ballroom**, dedicated to dance with a whirl of gilt stuccoes and a remarkable mix of realistic-historical-mythological scenes on the walls.

Templo de Debod F9

*Parque de la Montana, **t** 91 366 74 15; **metro** Ventura Rodríguez or Plaza de España. **Open** April–Sept Tues–Fri 10–2 and 6–8, Sat–Sun 10–2; Oct–Mar Tues–Fri 9.45–1.45 and 4.15–6.15, Sat and Sun 10–2; closed hols; **adm** free.*

The little park just beyond the Museo Cerralbo wears an unexpected ornament: a sandstone Egyptian temple of the

4th century BC. It's nothing very elaborate, but it is genuine. In 1968, the Egyptian government sent it, block by block, as a token of appreciation for Spanish help in the relocation of monuments during the building of the Aswan dam.

However far it has strayed from the Nile, the little temple seems cheerfully at home, facing a reflecting pool, surrounded by palms, orientated to the same sunrise, looking over the peculiar city below. Inside, some of the reliefs and a later altar dedicated by Cleopatra's dad have survived the temple's vicissitudes: it was moved at least twice in Egypt before arriving in Madrid, and spent a number of years under water, which washed out its murals.

In July 1936, this spot was occupied by the Montaña Barracks, scene of one of the earliest and bloodiest events of the Civil War. When the government decided to arm the popular militias, they found that the bolts for most of the rifles available were locked away in these barracks, held by a group of rebellious officers and Falangists. After a brief siege, miners from Asturias managed to blow a hole in the walls. The barracks were then stormed by a mob, who killed most of those inside, throwing many alive from second-storey windows.

PARQUE DEL OESTE

Paseo del Pintor Rosales; metro Argüelles.

In 1808 what is now the Parque del Oeste became a battlefield when the *madrileños* rose up against the French. The park was laid out in the early 1900s, but it had to be completely replanted after the Civil War left it a wasteland. All this now seems far, far away as you stroll through its beautifully landscaped grounds. A rose garden in the centre, **La Rosaleda**, is the scene each spring of Madrid's international rose exhibition. Nearby is the *teleférico* (*see* p.170) to the Casa de Campo.

Ermita de San Antonio de la Florida (The Goya Pantheon) D

5 Paseo de la Florida, t 91 542 07 22; **metro** *Príncipe Pío; wheelchair accessible.* **Open** *Tues–Fri 10–2 and 4–8, Sat–Sun 10–2; closed hols; **adm** free.*

From the centre of the Parque del Oeste, Calle de Francisco y Jacinto Alcántara descends to the train tracks, passing next t a little garden with a ceramic copy of Goya *Tres de Mayo*, marking the first burial place the 43 victims of the execution in 1808. A pedestrian flyover through the railyards of the woebegone Estación de Príncipe Pío w take you to the narrow island between the tracks and the river, where two identical Neoclassical chapels stand, both dedicated the same St Anthony. The one you want is opposite the seated statue of the painter; other is a replica, built when the original w made into the Goya Pantheon. Around 13 June, the replica is the focus of the week long *verbena* dedicated to St Anthony, whe the *paseo* is closed off for the festivities.

The original church was designed by Phi Fontana for Charles IV, and contains one o the milestones of Spanish art. In 1798, Goy was commissioned to do a series of frescoe on the upper walls, ceiling and dome, and genius of 'magical atmospheres' did them a way never seen before in any church. St Anthony, in the dome, is clearly recognizab (he is bringing a corpse to life to bear witn in a dispute), but that is Goya's only conce sion to the usual conventions of religious The scores of figures covering the ceiling have the same faces as the people in his ce brated cartoons, only instead of angelic *madrileños* they have become angels in fac Every one has the quality of a portrait; the peaceful rapture expressed in their faces h at its source nothing the Church could giv but a particular secret perhaps known onl to Goya. He painted the whole thing in 120 days; the restorers in 1996 took three time as long, but the frescoes are now more

ancisco de Goya y Lucientes

very century and a half, it seems, an artist born in Spain who is destined to re-invent nting. Between Velázquez (1599) and asso (1881) there was Francisco de Goya y cientes, born in an Aragonese village in 6. Goya lived his life in two distinct stages, wildly different as to seem like that of two ferent artists, and separated by a strange erlude. In 1775 he came to Madrid, and nt the next 14 years doing little but toons for the Real Fábrica de Tapices (see 8). 'Cartoons', however, seems a sleading word: they had to be complete ntings, perfect in line and colour, each the l size of the tapestry that would be copied m it. Some of these were over 20ft wide, d the indefatigable Goya managed 63 of m. Most are now in the Prado, and their ourful, dreamlike scenes are as much of a elation to many visitors as the more nous paintings that came later.

he strange interlude's name was María vetana, Duchess of Alba. Goya met this utiful and alarming widow at the court und 1786, and rumours of their affair scanzed Madrid. Goya may have used her as model for the naked and clothed Majas in Prado. Partly due to the Duchess's influ-e, Goya became court painter in 1789, with alary of 15,000 reales. For a few years the st was at the top of the world; friends nd him 'intoxicated by fame'. Then, in 1792, picked up a serious disease, perhaps hilis, that left him stone deaf.

uring his convalescence, Goya began to tch small fantasy scenes to take his mind his sufferings, probably unaware that he

was beginning one of the strangest voyages ever taken through the Western mind. For the rest of his life, the fantastical world would be his stock in trade. The first work of the new Goya was the incredible series of engravings, now in the Prado, called *The Caprices* (*Los Caprichos*). Done in the shadow of the French Revolution and Napoleon, they evoke a world strangely akin to that of Goya's contemporary William Blake. The inscription for one of these engravings could serve as a motto for the rest of Goya's work: 'The sleep of reason produces monsters.' Next came his grotesque portraits of the royal family; then *The Disasters of War*, sparing none of the brutality of the Peninsular War; and finally the apocalyptic vortex of the Black Paintings, painted on the walls of his country house just outside Madrid, the Quinto del Sordo ('House of the Deaf Man'), and now also in the Prado.

Rulers from Charles IV (who thought the portraits were all too true) to Joseph Bonaparte to the horrible Ferdinand VII all recognized Goya's talent and let him do as he liked, even though Ferdinand once told him, 'If we did not admire you so much, you would deserve garotting.' In 1824, the King allowed his painter to move to Bordeaux for health reasons; perhaps he had suffered too much Spain and needed somewhere foggy and drear. Goya worked right until the end, always innovating and perfecting his technique, and died in Bordeaux in 1828 at the age of 82. If his last works are any indication, if he'd survived any longer he might have invented Impressionism.

---

utiful than ever. An audiovisual guide ers surprising close-ups.

oya was buried here after his body was ught back from Bordeaux. His body, that ut not his head: legend has it that he ed the executor of his will to separate his ll and bury it in a secret place with the t of the Duchess of Alba (*see* 'Goya'), who deceased him by 26 years. Goya died in 8 and, when the body was moved from

Bordeaux in 1880, the head was already missing. Like those of most famous *madrileños*, the Duchess's tomb has been lost over the years; the church she was buried in was demolished, along with the frescoes that Goya painted around her tomb, of men carrying her body to its last rest. In the frescoes she was said to have resembled his famous Maja. Or so they say.

From the church, it's a short walk to the Puente Reina Victoria, spanning the **Río Manzanares**. Madrid's great environmentalist mayor, Tierno Galván, added the pleasant mile-long walk along the bank.

CASA DE CAMPO

Metro Batán or Lago; teleférico (t 91 541 75 70, w www.teleferico.com; wheelchair accessible) from Parque del Oeste Apr–Sept daily 11–8, Oct–March noon–8 (tickets single €3, return €4.50); bus No.33 from metro Príncipe Pío.

When the Habsburgs decided to make Madrid their capital, they didn't give much thought to amenities. One of their tricks was to chop down every tree of the forests that once surrounded Madrid, sell them as firewood all over Castile and use the money to embellish their palaces. Philip II, an avid hunter like most of his kin, soon regretted this, and he had this tract of several square miles reforested. There was no altruism in Philip's motives, but the Casa de Campo was the happy result, a stretch of quiet, green countryside for picnics and outings, in spite of a slightly shady reputation for illicit goings-on. During the summer, the big **outdoor pool** and **boating lake** are packed with sizzling *madrileños*.

If you don't suffer from vertigo, take the **teleférico** from the Parque del Oeste for the views, not only of the Casa de Campo but also of the Manzanares and the Palacio Real with the city beyond.

Parque de Atracciones Off maps

t 91 526 80 30, t 91 463 29 00. Open winter Sun–Fri noon–11pm, Sat noon–1am; summer Sun–Thurs noon–11pm, Fri and Sat noon–3am; adm adults €20.90, children €11.80.

Kids love the Parque de Atracciones, a permanent funfair offering thrills and chills on the 'Flume Ride', 'Top Spin' and 'Looping Star' rollercoasters. The 'Tornado', a triple loop-the-loop rollercoaster in which punters are strapped in without a proper floor, is one of the scariest in Europe.

Zoo-Acuario de Madrid Off maps

t 91 512 37 70; wheelchair accessible. Open daily 10–6; adm adults €12.75, children €10.3

The combo zoo-aquarium has over 2,000 animals representing 150 different kinds of mammals, from African monkeys to koala bears, and 100 different kinds of birds. There a separate dolphin pool, ostrich zone and snake den. The star is Chulín, the first panda to be born in captivity in the West. Although rarely visible, the panda has surroundings that are at least roomy. The zoo also has a 1.8 million-litre tropical aquarium, filled wit hammerheads and other sharks.

ARGÜELLES

The prosperous residential and shopping area of Argüelles was named, like La Latina after one of Isabel I's tutors, in this case Agustín Argüelles. It was the last home of the great chronicler of Madrid, Benito Pére Galdós, who died here in poverty in 1920, ju before Argüelles evolved into a fancy subu of decorative flats. In spite of furious protests, **Galdós' house** at 7 Calle de Gaztambide was bulldozed in the 1970s an replaced by a plaque. Just up on the same street, the former home of another residen Chilean poet Pablo Neruda, is now a natio monument: the huge brick **Casa de las Flor** is an innovative low-cost apartment block from the 1930s designed by Secundino Zuazo. The advent of the Second Republic had fired architects across Spain to design more functional, socially responsive buildings, and the Casa de las Flores, where eacl flat is filled with natural light and air, was one.

Ministerio del Aire E6

*de la Princesa; **metro** Moncloa.*

The neighbourhood's biggest pile is the
Ministry of Air, designed by Luis Gutiérrez
Soto in 1942 after designs by Hitler's pet
architect Albert Speer, but altered after the
Führer's defeat into something that looks so
much like El Escorial that it was immediately
dubbed the 'Monasterio del Aire'. Although
Franco adored it, Soto, an Art Deco master in
the 1930s, found it extremely embarrassing –
in the next decade he would be the first
architect in Madrid to embrace
functionalism, after a visit to the States.

Plaza de Moncloa F5–6

metro Moncloa.

Opposite the Ministerio del Aire, at the
head of Calle de la Princesa, is a circular eagle-
shaped **monument to Franco's war dead**,
which the local council now uses as offices.
At the top of the square, Franco's **Arco de la
Victoria** celebrates his victory in the Civil War.
It also has a practical purpose: inside are the
archives of the Universidad Complutense,
the campus of which begins just beyond.

Faro de Moncloa F5

*Open summer Mon–Fri 9.30–2 and 4.30–7.30,
winter Mon–Fri 10–2 and 5–7, weekends
(all year) 10–6; **adm** adults €1, children €0.50.*

This is Madrid's inland lighthouse,
designed by Salvator Pérez Arroyo to be
exactly 92m high as part of the 1992 celebrations. A lift will whizz you up to the
observation platform for fine 360° views, but
buy a drink from the vending machine before
you ascend, as the Faro is the one dry spot in
this city of bars.

Museo de América E4

*Avenida de los Reyes Católicos, t 91 549 26
00; **metro** Moncloa; wheelchair accessible.
Open Tues–Sun 10–3; **adm** €3, free Sun.*

The museum is cool, elegant and beautifully designed. On display is one of Europe's
largest collections of artefacts from the

Aztecs, Incas, Maya and other indigenous
New World cultures, many of them plun-
dered in the time of the conquistadors, but
many others acquired much later by more
honourable means.

Among the most beautiful are **gold ornaments** from Colombia and Costa Rica, some
over 1,000 years old, and ancient Peruvian
and Chilean **textiles**. The museum holds an
extremely rare post-Classic Mayan codex, the
Códice Tro-Cortesiano, a 112-page document
in hieroglyphs, relating, among other things,
news of the Spanish arrival; because of its
fragility a replica is on display. **Spanish
engravings** depicting indigenous South
Americans as fantastical giants, headless
monsters or cheerful cannibals give a fascinating insight into the popular state of mind
at the dawn of the Age of Exploration, and a
series of 16th- to 18th-century **maps** graphi-
cally illustrates the rapid growth of Western
knowledge of this alien territory.

Ciudad Universitaria D2–3

***Metro** Ciudad Universitaria.*

Miguel Primo de Rivera always liked to
think of himself as a great benefactor of
education, and it exasperated him that
Spain's university students spent most of the
1920s out in the streets calling him names.
He began this sprawling, suburban campus
in Moncloa in 1927, partly to appease them
but mostly to get them out of town.

This institution, the nation's largest, began
as the Complutensian University, founded by
Cardinal Cisneros in Alcalá de Henares. After
it moved to Madrid, its buildings were originally north of the Gran Vía. Primo de Rivera's
new campus was unfinished when the Civil
War broke out; in the battles for Madrid, the
university found itself in the frontline,
providing a potent symbol of the nature of
the war as Franco's artillery pounded the
halls of knowledge to rubble. Franco rebuilt
them after the war in a stolid, authoritarian
style. Today the campus is well kept, but as
dull for visitors as it must be for the students
who attend it.

PALACIO REAL DE EL PARDO Off maps

Cenitra de El Pardo, t 91 376 15 00; metro Moncloa then bus No.83 (30mins) from Paseo de Moret nearby every 10–15mins; wheelchair accessible. Open Mon–Sat 10.30–5, Sun 10–1.30; closed when used by a visiting head of state; adm €3.

El Pardo, 13km from central Madrid, once offered the richest hunting grounds in central Castile, and the first hunting lodge on this site was built by Henry III in the 1390s. Charles V and his son Philip made it into a palace, apparently the first in Spain to sport slate Flemish towers. It was burnt down and rebuilt by Sabatini for Charles III, and hung with Goya's sweet tapestries.

Now used to lodge visiting presidents and princes, El Pardo was used by Franco as his residence throughout the dictatorship, and the palace offers a rare glimpse of how the dictator worked, with his office left as it was when he died. The beautiful hills and woodlands are still full of game, and mostly off limits to visitors.

As a footnote, *pardo* means 'dun', and got the name from a huge dun-coloured bear killed there by King Alfonso XI. It made such an impression, according to some, that it was placed on the coat-of-arms of Madrid.

The current king of Spain, Juan Carlos I, and his family live on a simpler scale in the **Palacio de la Zarzuela** (*no access*) nearby. The original palace, where Philip IV was entertained by the ancestors of Madrid's famous operetta, was burnt during the Civil War, but rebuilt in the 1950s to house the heir to the throne.

Walks

A LITERARY WALK AROUND SANTA ANA 177

A GARDENS WALK AROUND THE RETIRO 181

A BAR AND TAPAS WALK

The easiest and most famous place for a *tapeo* ('tapas crawl') is undoubtedly around Plaza Santa Ana, where virtually every doorway belongs to a bar or café. This walk, however, covers less touristy corners of the city, particularly the piquant districts of Lavapiés and La Latina, where timeless neighbourhood bars rub shoulders with the latest hip nightspots which have sprouted up over the past couple of years. It also takes a swoop into the swankier neighbourhood of Los Austrias, where tapas have reached new gastronomic heights, and a quick dander through the mayhem of the Plaza Mayor, before heading back to the shabby-chic and multicultural *barrio* of Lavapiés. Don't even think about leaving your hotel before 9pm, unless you particularly want all the bars and restaurants completely to yourself. You can break this walk up into sections and try it on different nights, if you don't want to be sipping your 19th *vermut* at 9am.

Leave La Latina metro station and walk down past the Mercado de la Cebada towards Plaza de la Cebada, which connects with Plaza de la Humilladero. **El Viajero [1]**, 11 Plaza de la Cebada (*see* p.228), a café, bar and Uraguayan restaurant on three floors, with a breezy rooftop terrace, is a very lively, laid-back spot and a great place for some dinner, but you'll need to get there early for a coveted roof seat. This nub of adjoining squares is a very popular place to come for a drink and a snack after the Rastro fleamarket on Sunday mornings; there are dozens of bars, and people mill around on the streets listening to impromptu music from the buskers on the square. At the corner of Calle del Almendro is **La Carpanta [2]**, No.22 (*see*

p.222), run by a well-known acting family, so there is always the chance you'll bump into a celebrity or two. **La Taberna del Zapatero [3]**, Calle del Almendro 27 (*see* p.223), is one of a new breed of gourmet tapas bars, with a delicious range of inventive titbits to match an excellent wine list.

Running parallel with Calle del Almendro, Calle de la Cava Baja, an almost unbroken thread of restaurants and bars. **Casa Lucio [4]**, at No.35 (*see* p.218) on the left, is a good stop-off for a glass of wine. Calle de la Cava Baja opens out into little Plaza de la Puerta Cerrada; across the square to the left you'll find the venerable (and pricey), tile-lined **Casa Paco [5]** at No.11 (*see* p.223), a very traditional old *taberna* which offers fine *charcuterie* and steaks. Take a short detour down Calle del Nuncio to find the delightful **Café del Nuncio [6]** at No.12 (*see* p.222), with a lovely terrace overlooking a pretty little

Start: Metro La Latina.
Finish: Near Metro Antón Martín or at Pasadizo de San Ginés (metro Sol or Opera).
Walking time: All night!
Suggested start time: 9pm.

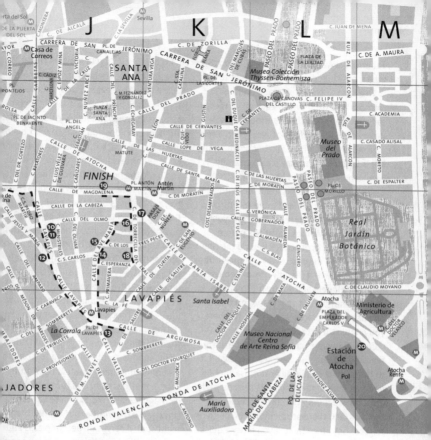

...sage, the Escalinata del Nuncio. It's a ...at stop for a cocktail, with a very relaxed ...osphere.

...turn to Plaza de la Puerta Cerrada: ...ding up from here is Calle del Conde de la ...a, which passes the quietly elegant Plaza ...Conde de Barajas. Calle Conde de la Pasa ...ds into the Plaza San Miguel, which circles ...market of the same name. There are ...ens of *tabernas* and bars here, but the ...of them all is the **Cervecería La Plaza [7]** ...p.239), with its terrace seating over- ...king the market and tasty tapas like ...atas ali-oli* and *pisto con huevos*.

...ving up through the passage which joins ...Plaza San Miguel with the altogether ...nder, noisier Plaza Mayor. There's more to ...elegantly arcaded square than the ...ensive touristy café-bars, though: to the ...as you enter the square, underneath the ...eally painted Casa de la Panadería, is **La**

Torre de Oro [8] at No.26 (*see* p.223). This noisy, hectic Andalucian tapas bar has deli-cious *pescaditos fritos* (whitebait) and other delights, served by cheerful waiters. Sit out on the square and enjoy the street life.

Leave the Plaza Mayor by Calle de Toledo (on the opposite side of the square, to the right of the tourist office). Just down on the right is **Taberna San Isidro [9]** (*see* p.242), a crusty old-fashioned local where you can enjoy an invigorating swig of *sidra de barril*.

Keep walking down Calle de Toledo, heading for the Lavapiés district, and take the third left down Calle de la Colegiata. Pass Plaza de Tirso de Molina and turn right down Calle de Lavapiés, the backbone of the neigh-bourhood's nightlife. Lavapiés has yet to succumb to gentrification; the hip young kids in their flashy clothes are still outnumbered by neighbourhood stalwarts and oddballs. On the left, just down the street, is the

Taberna del Avapiés [10] at No.5 (see p.228), which has chilled *vermut* on draught (try it with a tapa of *boquerones* and another of *anchoas* and spear one of each on your cocktail stick – pungent, but delicious), as well as plenty of seats for the foot-weary and a very nice selection of wines. Further down on the left is **La Redicha [11]** (see p.242), a family-owned neighbourhood bar which is welcoming despite the gloom and a good place for a tipple of *vino* before setting off again. Just beyond here, on the right, you'll see little **Casa Montes [12]** at No.40 (see p.228), with racks of bottles behind the tiny bar. There's no room, so everyone spills out onto the street – a friendly mix of bemused locals, foreigners and young hipsters. The *tapas* are simple but very tasty, and this is one of the few places left in the city where you might still get something on the house.

Calle de Lavapiés culminates in the dusty, nondescript Plaza de Lavapiés; leading off it to the left is the Calle de Argumosa, nick-named Costa Argumosa for its seaside party atmosphere during the summer, when all the bars (and there are plenty) open up their terraces onto the street. If you fancy a quick detox stop by **El Granero del Lavapiés [13]** (see p.228) at No.10 for a freshly squeezed juice, this is one of the few vegetarian restaurant-cafés in these parts.

Another of the neighbourhood's institutions is on Calle del Ave María, which leads uphill from the Plaza de Lavapiés. On your right you'll find **Café Barbieri [14]** at No.45 (see p.242), a very mellow, old-fashioned café with big windows and burnished mirrors, where you can enjoy a cocktail with a cheerful, friendly crowd in the evenings. Just up on the left at No.44 (see p.242) is **La Peluquería [15]**, set in an old hairdressing salon. It's a laid-back little place, zanily decorated with plenty of comfy sofas and other fleamarket finds, showing regular exhibitions of local art on the walls. It serves coffee and homemade cakes, as well as the usual stronger stuff. A couple of streets beyond La Peluquería is the crossroads with Calle del Olmo: this street has plenty more trendy

hangouts, including **La Ventura [16]** at No.7 (see p.246), stuck behind an anonymous doorway with no sign. It's currently one of the places to hear the best DJs in Madrid spin, and, if you don't feel like dancing, there are floor cushions and sofas to relax on in the lounge at the back. Calle del Olmo runs into Calle de Torrecilla del Leal; at the junction, you'll see the pretty Art Deco **Cine Doré [17]** (see p.127), which has its own popular café-bar, although it's only open until midnight. Calle de Torrecilla del Leal has plenty of down-to-earth neighbourhood bars, but gay bars and trendy music hangouts are opening up along here, too. **La Lupe [18]** at No.12 (see p.269) is a lively gay bar which has occasional (and equally lively) drag acts after dark, attracting a mixed camp/non-camp crowd. It also has a good late-night bar with very reasonably priced drinks, inventive lighting, friendly staff, and DJs playing mainly electronic sounds. If you're looking for something different, turn uphill towards the Antón Martín metro station and turn left onto Calle de Magdalena; at No.27 there's **La Recoba [19]** (see p.227), another atmospheric late-night spot. It serves up decent pizzas and crêpes until late, to the sound of live tango music and singing.

Serious clubbers will want to hop in a cab and head down to Estación de Atocha, where the city's largest and wildest multi-level terazza, **La Vieja Estación [20]** (see p.241), can be found in a big chasm right next to the station from May to September. With bars, dancefloors and an Argentine restaurant spread over several layers, this is one of the best places in the city for dancing out beneath the stars.

A night out in Madrid wouldn't be complete without a visit to the famous **Chocolatería San Ginés [off maps]**, 11 Pasadizo de San Ginés (see p.223; just off Calle del Arenal), which has been serving up thick hot chocolate and freshly fried *churros* for more than a century.

Finally, it might be time for bed.

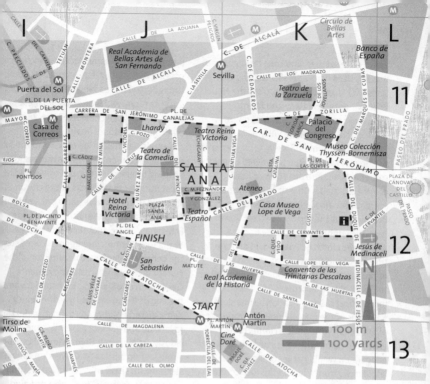

LITERARY WALK
ROUND
SANTA ANA

y the end of the 16th century, Spain's
den Age was in full swing, and the brand-
 capital was its glittering showcase. The
ngle of narrow streets threading off the
za Santa Ana, known as the Barrio de los
eratos, packed with theatres, bordellos
 bars, was the raucous heart of the city's
tural life. Cervantes and Lope de Vega
d, bickered and died here; the players
tted and preened; and the aristocrats
ne in droves to taste the low life at the
erns, scattering coins in their wake. From
 end of the 19th century until the party
ded with the Civil War, the area saw
ther brilliant revival, as writers, artists
 intellectuals set up shop in the cafés,
 took the age-old Spanish custom of the
tulia (part conversation, part argument)
ver greater heights.

Leaving Antón Martín metro, walk uphill
along Calle de Atocha; on your right, at the
corner of Calle de San Sebastián, you'll see
the small and apparently unimpressive
church of **San Sebastián**, a grim 20th-century
reconstruction of the 16th-century original.
And yet, this small, plain church has been
linked with a startling number of the city's
most celebrated writers, architects and
artists, including Cervantes, whose death

Start: Metro Antón Martín.
Finish: Plaza Santa Ana (metro Sevilla).
Walking time: About two hours, not
including lunch, museum or coffee stops.
Lunch and drinks stops: Lhardy, see p.225;
Casa Manolo, see p.226; Taberna Dolores, see
p.227; Pizzería Cervantes, 8 C/ del Léon, see
p.226; Ateneo, 21 C/ del Prado; Los Gabrieles,
see p.241; La Venencia, see p.241; Viva Madrid,
see p.241; Cervecería Alemana, see p.241; Las
Bravas, see p.226.
Suggested start time: Lunchtime, perhaps
taking in lunch at Lhardy and winding up at
Plaza Santa Ana for the evening.

was registered here, and Lope de Vega, who was baptized here, as well as having connections with dozens of others, from the Nobel Prize-winners Echegaray and Jacinto Benavente to the architects José de Churriguera and Juan de Villanueva.

Jacinto Benavente (1866–1954), a dramatist whose plays were often premièred round the corner in the Teatro de la Comedia, is commemorated with a statue in the nondescript, traffic-filled **Plaza de Jacinto Benavente** at the top of the street. From here, turn right down Calle de Carretas, which leads into the **Puerta del Sol** (*see* p.74), the hub of the city, where 10 streets converge under the famous giant Tio Pepe sign and the clock atop the former Casa de Correos (post office) is Spain's national timepiece. The steps of the long-demolished monastery of San Felipe were once an important gossiping point, where courtiers, writers and hangers-on would gather to discuss the latest news from court. In the 19th century, dozens of animated cafés and bars opened in and around Sol to continue the tradition; art, politics and revolution were heatedly discussed until gagged by Franco's regime, and the cafés closed, most of them forever.

Head down **Carrera de San Jerónimo**, to the right of the Tio Pepe sign as you face it. Although now lined with florid banks and dreary official government buildings, this was once part of the grand 'Ceremonial Route' of the Habsburg and Bourbon monarchs. Take a few steps down Calle de la Victoria to the right, where a plaque commemorates the site of the **Fontana de Oro** (now an Irish pub), perhaps the most celebrated café of all, where politics were thrashed out in the heady 1820s and long after; the life of the café is intimately chronicled in Pérez Galdós' historical novel *La Fontana de Oro*. The Fontana de Oro may have changed beyond recognition, but one of its contemporaries remains virtually the same at No.8 Carrera de San Jerónimo: **Lhardy**, a restaurant, confectioner's and tapas bar, was opened in 1839 by Emile Lhardy, at the behest of Prosper Mérimée, who was

desperate to find some decent French cooking in the city. It has retained its sumptuous décor, last redone in 1884. In one of t upstairs room, with gorgeous Japanese décor, Primo de Rivera plotted the coup tha made him dictator of Spain.

Plaza de Canalejas was once surrounded convents and monasteries; nowadays it's a bustling intersection flanked by two of the most floridly ornate banks in the city and t splendid **Hotel Asturias** (*see* p.211). Continu down the street to the corner of Calle de Echegaray, where another celebrated haun of the 19th-century intelligentsia once stoc the **Cervezería Inglesa**. One survivor of the vibrant literary and artistic movement Generation of 98, which flourished toward the end of the 19th century, is the **Teatro Reina Victoria**, sumptuously tiled in dazzlin royal blue and gold. Opposite it is the deliciously Art Nouveau **Union Músical Españo** a music shop with racks of wooden cabinet stuffed with sheet music, and a beautiful carved entranceway. The **Centro de Salud**, a few doorways down, wasn't always so gloomy; in 1896, the first films made by the celebrated Lumière brothers were screene here to the amazement of everyone in Madrid, including the royal family.

If you take a left down Calle de Zorilla, which runs behind the Cortes (Parliament Building), and then left onto Calle de los Jovellanos, you'll come across the peachy Neoclassical façade of the **Teatro de la Zarzuela**, built in the mid-1850s and still on of the best places to see Madrid's homegrown operettas. Opposite, **Casa Manolo** is tiny old-fashioned spot and a great place f some *chocolate y churros*, or to try out a fe traditional tapas. Make your way back to Carrera de San Jerónimo and skirt past the lions guarding the grim, grey façade of the **Cortes** building, heading towards the crea meringue of the **Palace Hotel**, which open its fabulous doors in 1913.

Turn right up Calle del Conde Duque de Medinaceli, and you'll find the dour, mode façade of the church of **Jesús de Medinace** It's worth stepping in, however, to see the

wds who queue patiently, fans fluttering, touch the miraculous statue of Jesús de dinaceli placed high above the altar. This urch replaced an earlier chapel which ned a scandalous notoriety during the lden Age thanks to the jewelled and wdered actresses (not a few of whom re also mistresses of Lope de Vega) who ended its eleven o'clock Masses on ndays, to the delight and distraction of the gregation if not the priests. Opposite is Cerería de Jesus, a tiny shop devoted to gious ornaments and paraphernalia, with ealth of fabulous kitsch. In the little plaza ront of the church, a string of old-hioned tiled bars provide a different kind ustenance; the furthest to the left is the ebrated Taberna Dolores, dating back to 1920s and thickly covered with colourful s. It serves excellent tapas.

troll up Calle de Cervantes: on the right at 11 you'll find the modern little two-storey ne of Lope de Vega, the interior tastefully tored as the Casa Museo de Lope de Vega p.123). This peaceful spot is where Lope Vega spent the last 25 years of his life, rning out several plays a week, while naging to juggle his complicated and ndalous love life. Despite this, towards end of his career he acquired an almost tly reputation and adoring crowds would her around him on the street, kissing his ds and begging for his blessing.

nort, narrow Calle de Quevedo leads off to left, almost opposite Lope de Vega's se. Quevedo, a crippled 17th-century poet satirist with a famously acerbic tongue, d at a now demolished house near the rance to the street. Luis de Góngora, now gnised as one of the greatest poets of Golden Age, boarded in the house until evedo bought it for the pleasure of turfing his rival. Góngora made short work of e de Vega in an exchange of satirical ses, but couldn't match the vicious wit of evedo. Góngora lost his bottle and eventu-buried himself in the countryside, oting himself ever after to sentimental, toral poetry.

Calle de Quevedo meets Calle de Lope de Vega. The upper section of the street is flanked by the grim, forbidding walls of the **Convento de las Trinitarias Descalzas**, where the daughters of both Cervantes and Lope de Vega took the veil. Cervantes, who lived nearby in Calle del Léon, is buried here – although, in the old Madrid tradition of mislaying the famous dead, no one quite knows where. This was one of the few religious institutions spared during the massive clear-outs of the 1830s, when the finance minister Mendizábal passed his bold laws confiscating Church property in order to bump up the empty coffers of the government. It's an odd twist of fate that Cervantes should be buried on the street named after his arch-rival Lope de Vega and that Lope de Vega's home is situated on a street named after Cervantes, whom he despised.

Continue walking uphill and turn right onto Calle del Léon, an old street with several restaurants and bars. At No.8, **Pizzería Cervantes** is a centuries-old taberna and still good for a light snack and drink if you don't want to go the pizza route. Further down on the right, **Cervantes' house** once stood at the corner of Calle de Cervantes marked now by another plaque (round the corner at 2 Calle de Cervantes). Like Lope de Vega, Cervantes was a prolific writer and it was in this house that he wrote the second part of the enormously successful *Don Quixote*, after reading the dreadful sequel circulated by a hapless forger intent on making a quick buck. Poor old Cervantes, unhappily married, sickly and plagued by financial problems, eventually died in 1616, virtually destitute. His house once overlooked a small square, now long gone, known as the Mentidero de Representantes, one of the dozens of recognized gossip centres around the city; *mentideros* such as this one were an important source of scandal and news in an age when knowing who was in and who was out of favour was of vital importance.

Calle del Léon leads into Calle del Prado, just past the corner on the left you'll see the grand doorway of the **Ateneo Científico y**

Literario de Madrid (*see* p.123), one of the city's most illustrious cultural institutions. The original building stood on Calle de la Montera, but it was reopened on Calle del Prado because this street held dozens of the most popular café-bars which were the informal meeting places of the city's intellectuals and artists. Nowadays, the Ateneo has its own excellent (and surprisingly cheap) café, as well as one of the finest libraries in Spain. The oval lecture theatre was the springboard for many of Madrid's most talented writers, who would give their first public readings here.

Turn right out of the entrance and walk up Calle del Prado, then turn right onto Calle de Echegaray, one of the most animated streets in the neighbourhood, packed with lively bars and restaurants. The most photographed must be the ex-gypsy brothel **Los Gabrieles**, at No.17, with wall-to-wall tiling including a copy of a Velázquez painting, *The Topers*. Further down on the right is lovely, studiously unfashionable **La Venencia**, a small, dusty bar with peeling bullfighting posters which still serves sherry straight from the barrels stacked above the bar. A small passage with a long name leads up to the left: Calle Manuel Fernández y González is lined with more bars, all with outdoor terraces in summer. The best known is **Viva Madrid**, a survivor from the turn of the last century, with old paddle fans, wooden beams and huge tiled images of Madrid a century ago.

The small street emerges on Calle del Príncipe, once a vortex of Madrid's artistic community, with its theatres and countless café-bars. The area is still the heart of Madrid's theatre district, but the old cafés that saw interminable *tertulias* at the end of the 19th century have sadly disappeared, including the celebrated El Gato Negro, which once sat next to the Teatro de la Comedia at No.14. It was a favourite with the flamboyant Catalan painter Santiago Rusiñol, who held court here during his visits to the capital. The Corral del Príncipe, after which the street is named (one of the first

theatres in Madrid, constructed in 1583), wa destroyed, and replaced with the infinitely more respectable Teatro del Príncipe, which was in turn replaced by the current buildin the **Teatro Español**, which overlooks Plaza Santa Ana, still the hub of *madrileño* nightlife. The theatre has preserved its Neoclassical façade by Juan de Villanueva, the architect of the Prado. Its austerity marked a turning-point in theatre-going at tudes: the old *corrales* – both the Corral del Príncipe and the Corral de Cruz, which once stood nearby – were anarchic places, where raucous audience participation often led t quick plot changes in mid-performance. Th Teatro Español in its most recent incarnati has seen the premières of some of Spain's most enduring modern dramas, including Lorca's ground-breaking *Yerma* in 1934, wh he and his leading actress had to endure homophobic catcalls from the outraged audience.

The tiled **Cervecería Alemana** on Plaza Santa Ana, famously associated with Hemingway, was also a popular meeting place for intellectuals and artists, although now it is firmly on the tourist map and can get very crowded. There are more pretty til this time depicting the major southern cit of Seville, Córdoba and Granada, on the opposite corner of the square (to the right the Reina Victoria as you face it), covering t **Villa Rosa**, a popular 19th-century haunt which once offered flamenco shows. This building leads the way into Calle de Núñez de Arce, which in turn has a tiny passage leading off to the left: Callejón de Alvarez Gato, the birthplace of the now ubiquitous Spanish tapas dish *patatas bravas*. These were apparently invented (and patented – they hold patent No.357942) at the striden orange bar studded with distorting mirror on the right, **Las Bravas**.

Emerging from Callejón de Alvarez Gato onto **Calle de la Cruz**, turn left. This street i named for another of the old theatres, whi rivalled but never eclipsed the Corral del Príncipe: the Corral de Cruz reached the height of its popularity under Philip IV, wh

s having an affair with one of its most glit-
ng actresses, María Calderón; she bore
n an illegitimate child, later known as Juan
Austria. Turning left down Calle de Espoz y
na will bring you out onto the Plaza del
gel, where you'll find the **Café Central**, one
Madrid's most atmospheric jazz venues, set
converted mirror shop at No. 10.

nis is where the walk ends: it's time to
d back to the lively bars of the Plaza
ta Ana (which nudges onto the Plaza del
gel) and engage in a *tertulia* of your own.

GARDENS WALK
ROUND THE
ETIRO

his parks and gardens walk is best taken
en the city streets are sweltering in
mmer, or in spring when the gardens are
heir most colourful and fragrant. It circles
district once completely covered by the
acio del Buen Retiro, the pleasure palace
igned for Philip IV in the 1630s. It was
t on the cheap, abused by the French
ing their occupation, and by the mid-19th
tury only the much remodelled Casón del
en Retiro and the building housing the
seo del Ejército remained of the complex.
gardens, however, have survived rela-
ly unchanged, although one casualty was
aviary, which gave the palace its scornful
kname of 'the chicken-coop' from the
ke, fed-up citizenry.

he walk begins at the imperious statue of
eles in her chariot, ambles through the
y promenades and perfectly manicured
dens of the Parque del Retiro, and circles
und to the quiet, secluded Real Jardín
ánico near the Prado. Restaurants and
s have been included in the walk, but
might like to pack a picnic (*see* p.257 for
ps and delicatessens) to enjoy in
shade.

he Banco de España metro stop will bring
out at the **Plaza de Cibeles**, with a large

marble statue of the goddess poised above
the noisy, traffic-filled hub. On the opposite
side of the square are two palaces: the
grandest, on the right, is the city's fantastical
Palacio de Comunicaciones (*see* p.140), which
outshines every other public building in the
city. To the left of it, across Calle de Alcalá, is
the **Palacio de Linares** (*see* p.140), one of the
most flamboyant palaces to be built along
the new Paseo de Recoletos when the rich
began their exodus from the old city in the
19th century. As part of the Columbus celebrations of 1992, it was converted into the
Casa de América, housing a lovely garden
with a fine Catalan restaurant, the **Paradis
Madrid**, a perfect spot to fortify yourself for
a stroll.

Walk down broad, busy Calle de Alcalá,
which will bring you to the Plaza de la
Independencia, with the extraordinary triple-
arched **Puerta de Alcalá** (1778). Huge cherubs
swarm over it, giggling podgily. Yet, along
with the bear and the strawberry tree (*see*
'Bear Necessities', p.75), the gate has become
one of the symbols of Madrid, and accomplished its stated aim of impressing foreign
visitors entering the city.

The Puerta de Alcalá is next to the main
entrance to the Parque del Retiro, for more
than three centuries Madrid's favourite
picnic spot and refuge from the summer
heat. Once through the 19th-century **Puerta
de la Independencia**, a wide, sandy path
leads to the **Fuente de los Galápagos**, a huge
fountain covered with cavorting putti,
dolphins, frogs and turtles made for the first
birthday of Ferdinand VII's elder daughter,
the future Isabel II. This originally splashed

Start: Metro Banco de España.
Finish: Plaza Jesús (metro Antón Martín or
Banco de España).
Walking time: About three hours, not
including lunch, museum or coffee stops.
Lunch and drinks stops: Paradis Madrid, *see*
p.224; café overlooking the lake in Parque del
Retiro; café-bar on C/ de Claudio de Moyano;
El Botánico, *see* p.241; Ritz, *see* p.225; Taberna
Dolores, *see* p.227.

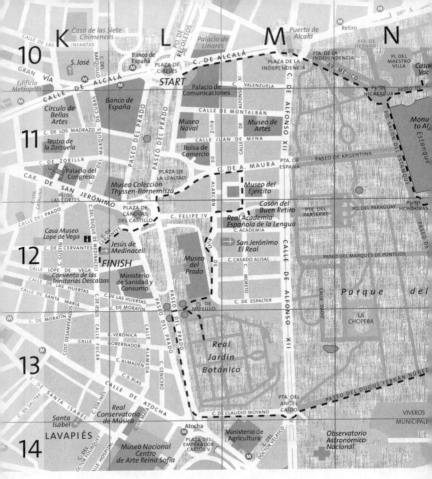

away at the top of Calle de la Montera, but was moved here in 1919 to get it out of the way of the new Gran Vía.

Beyond lies one of the few survivors of the original 17th-century park, the **Estanque**, a rectangular lake crammed with carp. The Buen Retiro (literally 'good retreat') park was inaugurated in 1632, with a magnificent water-borne pageant on the Estanque depicting the story of Orpheus and Eurydice. Nowadays, you can put on your own mini-pageant by hiring a rowing boat. The preposterous monument hogging one whole side of the lake is dedicated to one of Spain's more lacklustre and ineffectual monarchs, **Alfonso XII**, who surveys the park with a very regal air from the top of his enormous bronze horse. Just across from the boating lake, on the other side of the Paseo de

Colombia, you'll see the 19th-century **Casa Vacas**, a grand cowshed now run by the cit as a cultural centre, with an eccentric, if usually entertaining, selection of changing art exhibitions, and puppet shows in summer for kids. The side of the lake that faces Alfonso XII is much more down-to-earth, where a host of flamenco dancers, fortune-tellers and portrait-painters enter tain the passing crowds. There are plenty o cafés and snack bars dotted around the pa where you can stop for a cold drink under t shade of a parasol, but the **café** overlookin the lake is one of the breeziest.

Just beyond this café, turn left towards t **Palacio de Velázquez**, a pretty glass and iro pavilion heavily decorated with multi-coloured floral tiles by Daniel Zuloaga. It's now used by the Centro de Arte Reina Sofí

the left, the **Paseo del Duque de Fernán Núñez**, was laid out for coaches in 1874 and is the annual scene of the city's enormous book fair, held in late May or early June. On the other side of this wide street are the formal **Jardines de Cecilio Rodríguez** (open Mon–Fri 8–5), named for the indefatigable municipal gardener who was also responsible for the pretty rose gardens – **La Rosaleda** – near the southern end of the park. The hundreds of different roses here are heavenly in late spring when in full bloom.

At the corner of La Rosaleda, Ricardo Bellver's statue of the **Angel Caído** (*Fallen Angel; see p.107*) tumbles dramatically from heaven; it's the only known monument to evil in the world. The Paseo del Duque de Fernán Núñez continues down from here to the exit at the corner of the Calle de Alfonso XII. Just before you leave the park, you'll see the dome of the elegant Neoclassical **Observatorio Astronómico** (*see p.108*), commissioned in 1785 by Charles III and designed by Juan de Villanueva.

Calle de Claudio de Moyano, better known as Cuesta de Moyano, is the street that runs downhill to the Glorieta de Atocha and is prettily lined with wooden-slatted stalls selling new and secondhand books; some are open all week, but it's busiest on Sunday mornings. There's another **outdoor café-bar** at the bottom of the street, on the left, in a leafy glade which can't quite block out the rushing traffic. Still, it offers splendid views of the monumental, colourfully tiled **Ministerio de Agricultura**, designed by the architect of the pavilions in the Parque del Retiro, Ricardo Velázquez Bosco. It's crowned by an allegory of Glory flanked by winged horses.

Head up the Paseo del Prado, keeping the **Real Jardín Botánico** (*see p.108*) on your right. The main entrance is opposite the southern entrance to the Prado in the little Plaza de Murillo, with its dashing statue of the painter brandishing his palette. The first botanical gardens were commissioned by Ferdinand VI and established on the banks of the Río Manzanares. The plants were gathered by the King's botanist and surgeon, José

temporary art exhibitions. It's named for 9th-century architect, Ricardo Velázquez co, who also designed the graceful, light-d **Palacio de Cristal** (reached by the path osite the main entrance to the Palacio de ázquez). A stunningly lovely pavilion ected in a small lake, its vast, glassy inte- is the perfect backdrop to the large allations which often feature in the art ibitions held here. A huge jet of water ots up from the centre of the lake, king it another pleasantly cool spot to se for a while. (There's usually an ice- m stand just by the lake, too.)

e section of the park beyond the Palacio ristal is full of shady trees, dotted with oracing lovers, young people practising chi or yoga, avid sunbathers and families oying a picnic. The wide promenade to

Quer, who managed to acquire more than 2,000 plants, mainly for medicinal purposes. Charles III commissioned the current, grand setting, which was designed by the royal architect Sabatini and Juan de Villanueva, although much of it was destroyed in the Peninsular War in 1812. The Villanueva greenhouse and the surrounding arbours managed to survive the years of neglect and destruction and, after extensive renovations, the gardens were restored to their former glory and reopened in 1981. It's a delicious oasis, studded with fountains and statues (although the traffic is never completely drowned out). More than 30,000 plants are on display, from the *madroño* or arbutus, which features in the city's symbol, to examples of the vines found in different regions of Spain. A useful plan can be obtained at the entrance desk. If you turn right as you leave, there's a pleasant café overlooking the Plaza de Murillo: the smart **El Botánico**.

Skirting the back of the Museo del Prado and heading down Calle de Ruiz de Alarcón, you'll pass the church of **San Jerónimo el Real**, which, despite its moth-eaten appearance, was founded by Ferdinand and Isabel in 1505 (although most of what you see is 19th-century pseudo-Gothic) and has become a popular spot for high-society weddings ever since King Juan Carlos was crowned here in 1975. Very controversially, plans are afoot to afix a glassy modern cube to the church and turn it into offices and another exhibition space for the Prado. Next to the church is the aristocratic building belonging to the **Real Academia Española de la Lengua**, where the

learned officials are all busily engaged in producing a dictionary that bears little relation to the *castillano* you'll hear on the stree

Turn right onto Calle de Felipe IV, and hea up to the **Casón del Buen Retiro**, which was once the ballroom of the original Palacio R del Buen Retiro. It was substantially remod elled in the 19th century and, until recently was used to show the Prado's collection of 19th-century art. The building is being enlarged – three new floors are being built underground – and it opened in late 2002. Across from the Casón del Buen Retiro (on Calle de Méndez Nuñez) is the **Museo del Ejército**, now the city's army museum, but also another of the rare survivors of the ori inal Palacio del Buen Retiro. Although it ha also been substantially remodelled, it has nonetheless retained the ornamental Salón de Reinos, or throne room, of the original palace.

Walk straight out of the exit to the Muse del Ejército, and then turn left down Calle Antonio Maura. This leads to the small Plaː de la Lealtad (Loyalty Square), flanked on o side by the stately **Bolsa de Comercio** (Stoc Exchange) building and on the other by the opulent **Ritz Hotel**. The Ritz's luxurious terrace amid peaceful gardens is a good place to end this walk for the suitably atti and moneyed, but an equally good spot is the old-fashioned, tiled **Taberna Dolores** (cross the Plaza de Cánovas del Castillo an walk up Calle de Cervantes, taking the firs left onto the Plaza Jesús).

Day Trips

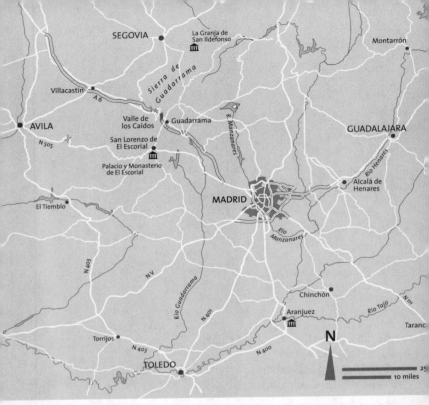

Beyond the caprice of Charles V and Philip II, Madrid's location made it the logical site for Spain's capital. Not only is it roughly central to the country as a whole, but its growth filled a vacuum at the centre of a region containing many of the most important cities of 16th-century Spain. Philip's new capital thus had a sort of ready-made Ile-de-France around it, a garland of historic and lovely towns, each with something different to offer the visitor and easy to escape to whenever Madrid's traffic and endless museum corridors become too much. Everyone goes to Toledo, of course, and romantically beautiful Segovia also comes in for its share of travellers. You may also conveniently use Madrid as a base for visiting the royal palaces at Aranjuez or El Escorial.

EL ESCORIAL AND VALLE DE LOS CAÍDOS

The giant palace-monastery complex of San Lorenzo de el Escorial was built by the mystic (and megalomaniac) Philip II as a mausoleum for his father and a retreat for himself. It contains great works of art from the Habsburg collections and is well worth visit from Madrid. The trip can be combine with a visit to the Valle de los Caídos, Franc freakish monument to the Civil War dead.

San Lorenzo el Real de el Escorial

Open *April–Sept Tues–Sun 10–6, Oct–March Tues–Sun 10–5; closed hols; **adm** €6, free for EU passport-holders on Wed.*

The Spaniards aren't shy; they matter-of-factly refer to Philip II's combination

etting There

Train

rains to El Escorial (*cercanías* line C8a or
ionales line R1, direction Ávila; 1hr; trains
east once hourly during the day) start
m Madrid-Atocha, and also stop at
drid-Chamartín. The trains arrive at the
ghbouring village of El Escorial and are
t by local buses for the monastery. The
ernative to this short bus ride is a gentle
n walk uphill from the station, along a
grant avenue shaded by chestnuts.
neral RENFE information: **t** 902 24 02 02;
canías information: **t** 91 506 61 37.

Bus

eep in mind that the proper name of the
vn beside the monastery is San Lorenzo de
scorial, and it appears that way in bus
edules. The bus (Nos.661 and 664; every
f-hour in the morning, every hour there-
er, daily; 1hr) is run by Herranz, **t** 91 890 41
from bay 3 of the Intercambiador de
nsportes (next to the Moncloa metro stop
Madrid) to the stop in Plaza Virgen de
acia in San Lorenzo, very near the
nastery. Herranz also has a once-daily
vice (20mins) from San Lorenzo to the
le de los Caídos, allowing enough time to

see the place. Tickets are sold from a little
office in a bar on C/ de Reina Victoria.

Tourist Information

2 C/ Grimaldi, **t** 91 890 53 13. **Open** Mon–Thur
11–6, Fri–Sun 10–7.

Eating Out

Beef from the Sierra de Guadarrama has
been given its own denomination of origin –
if you're a meat-eater, there's nothing finer.

Charolés, *24 C/ de Floridablanca*, **t** *91 890 59
75*. **Expensive**. Steeped in tradition, this is the
town's best restaurant. Its Wednesday *cocido*
is a grand affair and an event in itself.

Parrilla Príncipe, *6 C/ de Floridablanca*, **t** *91
890 16 11*. **Open** Wed–Mon 1–4 and
8.30–midnight. **Moderate**. An intimate,
restful haven located inside an 18th-century
palacete, with lovely views of the monastery.
Excellent meat and fish in a spot that, for all
its elegant, English-style décor, attracts a
surprisingly varied crowd.

Babel Café, *7 C/ Juan de Austrias*, **t** *91 896
04 43*. **Inexpensive**. A laid-back café with
delicious home-cooked food, plus Internet
access and a play area for kids.

El Croché, *6 C/ de San Lorenzo*. An old-world
café that's perfect for a coffee.

---

ace-secretariat-monastery-mausoleum as
e eighth wonder of the world'. Any
lding with a façade 66oft wide and 2,673
ndows is entitled to some consideration,
t it's not so much the glass and stone of El
orial that make it remarkable, but the
urotic will of the king who conjured it up.
spite all the effort Philip expended in
mping out heretical opinions in his long
gn, he seems to have entertained on the
quite a few of his own, possibly picked up
ring his years spent in the Low Countries.
found geomancers to select the proper
e for the millennial temple, astrologers to
k the date for laying the corner stone (on
April 1563) and hermetic philosophers to
p with the numerical mysticism that is
pposedly built into every proportion of
e building.

An '*escorial*' is a slagheap – there once was
some sort of mine on this site – and so the
proper title of Philip's dream-house translates as the Royal Seat of the Royal St
Lawrence of the Slagheap. The reasons for
the dedication to San Lorenzo are unclear.
Supposedly Philip won a victory on the
saint's day in 1557, at St Quentin in Flanders,
and vowed to build him something in return;
this is unlikely, as the dedication wasn't
made until 10 years after El Escorial was
completed. An even less probable tale has
Philip's architects planning this rectangle of
buildings and enclosed courtyards as an echo
of the saint's gridiron attribute (San Lorenzo
was roasted alive on one; he is supposed to
have told the Romans: 'You can turn me over
now; I'm done on this side'). While San
Lorenzo is not one of the most popular

saints, there's an obscure legend that he brought the Holy Grail to Spain, and this may help to explain the tangled web of esotericism behind Philip's work.

Philip's original architect, Juan Bautista de Toledo, had worked on St Peter's in Rome; you may find that these two chilly, overblown symbols of the Counter-reformation have much in common. Work commenced in 1563, but Bautista died four years later, and El Escorial was entrusted to his brilliant pupil, Juan de Herrera, who saw the task through to its completion in 1584. It kept him busy; even though Herrera had little time to spare on any other buildings, his reputation as one of the great Spanish architects was made. By creating the *estilo desornamentado* ('unadorned style'), stripping the Renaissance building to its barest essentials, he captured perfectly the nation's mood of austere militancy.

You can explore the complex independently, but we recommend you take one of the official tours as, without any guidance, you may miss out on a lot of intriguing details, such as the many manifestations of Philip's obsession with mystical patterns in designing and building the place. You may also find, as you make your way from chamber to chamber and up and down dim stone staircases, that you quickly lose all sense of direction, and fail to appreciate, for example, the strategic location of the royal mausolea and Philip's apartments in relation to the Basílica.

Palacio de los Borbones and Nuevos Museos

The official tours begin in the northeastern quarter of El Escorial, a quarter never used by Philip II, but converted by the Bourbons Charles III and Charles IV into a royal residence. These two do not seem to have had any interest in Philip's conception of El Escorial, but used it only as a sort of glorified hunting-lodge. Not surprisingly, they refurbished these rooms as a similar, though smaller version of the Bourbon Palacio Real in Madrid. The **Bourbon apartments**, with

their tapestries after works by Goya and others, have now been restored to their former splendour, and they form a pleasant contrast to the austerity of their surroundings. One of the most interesting rooms is the **Hall of the Battles**, with its fresco nearly 62m long representing every detail of the 1431 Battle of Higuerela, a victory of King Juan II over the Moors of Granada.

Downstairs there is an exhibition of some of the machinery and tools used to build the complex, plus architectural drawings and scale models tracing the progress of the construction work through its various stages of completion. Upstairs again, the **Nuevos Museos** occupy a long corridor along the eastern walls, with windows looking out over intricate knot gardens. Much of Philip's collection of paintings is displayed here, including works by Bosch, Patinir, Titian, Veronese, Ribera, El Greco and Dürer; later additions include a Velázquez.

Palacio de Philip II

Such is the reputation Philip earned for himself – the evil genius of the Inquisition and all – that it comes as a genuine surprise to visit the little palace he tacked onto the back of El Escorial for himself. Few kings anywhere have ever chosen a more delightful abode: a few simple rooms reminiscent of the interiors from paintings of Vermeer, with white walls, Delft-blue tiles and big windows opening onto gardens and forests on all sides. These rooms suggest that Philip's famous self-isolation had less of the monkishness about it than the desire of a cultured, bookish monarch to ensure the necessary serenity for the execution of the royal duty he took so seriously. Aesthete and mystic, he approached politics with the soul of a clerk, and each of all the long list of mistakes he made was decided upon with the greatest of care.

Here he also endured the wasting disease that killed him, stinking so badly that neither servants nor visitors could bear his presence. He made sure his bed was situated right above the High Altar of his Basílica, and had

py-hole cut in the bedchamber wall so
at he could observe the endless Masses
wn below. With only that crowned skull on
night table to keep him company, here he
vaited the reward of the virtuous.

he art and furnishings of the apartments
ay not necessarily be an accurate represen-
:ion of Philip's tastes, but there is a copy
ilip had made of Bosch's *Hay Wain*, one of
favourites, the original of which hangs in
e Prado. In the **Throne Room**, be sure to see
e marvellous inlaid wood doors, decorated
th trompe-l'oeil scenes and architectural
ıtasies, done by an anonymous German
:ist of the 16th century; they are among
e most beautiful things in El Escorial.

ınteón Real and Biblioteca

ın opulent but narrow staircase leads
wn to the **Panteón Real**, situated beneath
e Basílica's High Altar. All manner of stories
ve grown up around this pantheon of bad
ıgs. Charles II, it is said, spent whole days
wn here, ordering the gilded marble
mbs to be opened so that he might gaze
his mummified ancestors. As in the
sílica, the most expensive stone from
ound the Mediterranean was used in its
nstruction; the red jasper of the pavement
d pilasters is so hard it had to be cut with
amond-tipped saws. The adjacent room is
led, charmingly, the **Pudrería** (the 'rotting
amber'), where Habsburg and Bourbon
tentates spent 20-odd years mouldering
til they became sufficiently dried out for
eir interments. Royal relations fill a maze of
rridors beyond the Panteón, guarded by
ormous white heralds with golden maces.
n Juan, victor of Lepanto, is the best
own of them, though the tomb everyone
tices is the tall, marble wedding cake that
ıs built to hold 60 baby princes and
ncesses; it is now more than half full. Don
an, the father of the current king, Juan
rlos I, is the Panteón's most recent addition.
n Juan got in, despite never having ruled,
gely on the say so of his son. Beyond are
e **Sacristía** (sacristy) and **Salas Capitulares**
apter houses), which house some of the
:orial's collections of religious art.

One other section that may be seen is the
Biblioteca (library), entered by a stair near
the main gate. Philip's books meant as much
to him as his paintings: here lies one of the
largest collections of Latin, Greek, Hebrew
and Arabic philosophical and mystical works
in Europe. Philip's agents watched over all
the book-burnings of the Inquisition, and
saved from the flames anything that was
especially interesting. That his hoard of
40,000 volumes survives almost unchanged
since Philip's day is due only to the benign
neglect of the generations that followed;
18th-century travellers reported that the
monks watching over the collection were all
illiterate. The frescoes of 1590–2 that cover
the vaulted ceiling, by the Italian Pellegrino
Tibaldi, are an allegory of the seven liberal
arts, portraying seven of the famous philosophers and scientists of antiquity. The large
globe of nested spheres in the centre of the
library is Philip's orrery, used in making astronomical calculations.

Basílica and Patio de los Reyes

Once inside the huge, square church, you
will quickly become aware of the heightened
atmosphere of a holy-of-holies. With very few
windows, the Basílica was purposely kept
dark as a contrast to the airiness of the rest
of El Escorial. No church in Spain is colder
inside; even in the hottest days of July the
thin air seems pure distilled essence of
Castile. Just inside the entrance, in the
narrow **lower choir**, note the unusual ceiling
and its 'flat vaulting', an architectural trick of
very shallow vaulting that creates the illusion of flatness. It was far too daring for
Philip II, who ordered Herrera to support it
with a column. The architect complied, but in
wood and plaster, which he dramatically
kicked away in the presence of the king to
prove his skill, only to earn his famous
scolding from Philip: 'Juan de Herrera, Juan de
Herrera, with kings one does not play games.'

From here, the eye is drawn to the bright
retablo, framed in darkness. Its paintings are
by several then-fashionable Italian artists,
including Pellegrino Tibaldi, who like Juan

Bautista was a pupil of Michelangelo. Above them all is a golden figure of Christ on the Cross, and at its foot a tiny golden skull that stands out even across the great distance; its hollow eyes seem to follow you as you pass through the Basílica. These are really only of gilded bronze; if they weren't, they wouldn't be here. Originally the Basílica was full of real gold ornaments, and the precious stones of the Tabernacle were some of the most valuable that the Spanish royal house possessed. Napoleon's troops did a thorough job of looting El Escorial in 1808, making off with them all. Connoisseurs that they were, they left the artwork in peace. Notable are the gilded **bronze ensembles** to the sides of the altar, the families of Charles V and Philip II (with all three of his wives) at prayer. Beneath the high altar is the *primera piedra*, the cornerstone of the Escorial.

The west doors of the Basílica open onto the **Patio de los Reyes**, which is El Escorial's main courtyard, named after sculptures by Monegro representing six mighty kings of Judea which adorn the church's western façade. On the far side of the courtyard is the west gate, the main ceremonial entrance to El Escorial, and to the right and left are the boys' school, '*colegio*', and the monastery, which are both still in use, and are not open to the public. The two statues in the centre represent David and Solomon.

Valle de los Caídos

Death is the patron saint of Spain.
Váldez Léal

If you're one of those who came to El Escorial expecting freakishness and gloom, don't be disappointed yet. From the town, there's a regular bus service to Francisco Franco's own idea of building for the ages. The Valley of the Fallen is supposedly meant as a memorial to soldiers from both sides of the Civil War, but it was old Republicans and other political unfortunates languishing in Franco's jails who did the work in the 1950s, blasting a 262m tunnel-like church out of the mountainside and erecting a 125m stone

cross above. The crowds of Spaniards who come here in a holiday mood on any weekend seem to care little for history or politics; they linger at one of Spain's most outrageous souvenir stands, then take the children up the funicular railway to the base of the cross. For local colour, there'll be a few ancient widows in black who come every week, and perhaps a pair of maladjusted teenagers in Falangist blue shirts. If you find yourself in the area around 20 November, make the trek: it's the anniversary of the Generalísimo's death, attracting a strange mixture of followers.

The **cross**, held up by faith and structural steel, is claimed to be the largest in the world. Around its base are a series of titanic sculptured figures in some lost, murky symbolism: lions, eagles and pensive giants lurch out above you. The view takes in the hills and valleys for miles, as well as the monastery Franco built for the monks who look after the Basílica below.

This cave **church** is impressive, in the way the palace of a troll-king might be. The nave goes on and on, past giant, disconcerting Fascist angels with big swords, past dim chapels and holy images, finally ending in a plain, circular altar. José Antonio Primo de Rivera, founder of the Falangists, is buried here, as is Franco. Franco's tomb is a plain stone slab on the floor near the altar, opposite José Antonio's. The gentlemen behind you in sunglasses and Hawaiian shirts are, you haven't guessed, plain-clothes policemen, waiting for someone to try and spit on the old Caudillo.

SEGOVIA

Segovia is within easy reach of Madrid as a day trip, though as one of the most beautiful cities of Spain it is a place where you may wish to spend more time. Three distinct cultures have endowed this once-prominent town with three famous monuments. The Romans left Segovia a great aqueduct, and the age of Emperor Charles V (Carlos I of

Getting There

By Train

Unless you've a hankering for slow, uncomfortable train journeys, Segovia is better reached by bus. There are nine trains every weekday and seven daily at weekends from Madrid-Atocha (*regionales* line R2, via Villalba de Guadarrama; return €9; 2hrs), leaving at 2mins past the even hours, plus 3.02pm. All trains pass through Madrid-Chamartín about 15mins after leaving Madrid-Atocha. The journey takes you through some rugged, craggy scenery, and there are good views of the huge cross of the Valle de los Caídos as the train approaches Los Molinos. Segovia station is in the modern part of town, about 20mins' walk from the old city, or a short ride by local bus. RENFE information: **t** 902 24 02 02.

By Bus

La Sepulvedana (**w** *www.sepulvedana.com*, Madrid **t** 91 530 48 00, Segovia **t** 921 42 77 07), a comfortable, modern fleet, runs 15 buses (1hr 15mins; €5.50) every weekday (fewer at weekends) from 11 Paseo de la Florida, Madrid, to Segovia's bus station on the central Paseo de Ezequiel González. Segovia also has bus connections to La Granja.

Tourist Information

10 Plaza Mayor, **t** 921 46 03 34, **f** 921 44 27 , (**open** *Mon–Fri 9–2 and 5–7, Sat and Sun 10– and 5–8*). If it's closed, there's plenty of information posted up on the doors and window.

1 Plaza del Azoguejo (by the viaduct), **t** 921 44 02 05, **f** 921 462 29 14 (**open** *Mon–S 8–8, Sun 10–8*).

Eating Out

Segovia

More than anywhere else in Castile, Segovia takes dining seriously, and the streets around the Plaza Mayor and the aqueduct are packed with dimly lit *típico* restaurants, each with a window heaped

Spain) contributed an equally famous cathedral. The third, Segovia's Alcázar, should be as well known. Though begun by the Moors and rebuilt in the Middle Ages, its present incarnation is pure 19th-century fantasy, a lost stage set from a Wagnerian opera. Segovia has its other monuments – a unique style of Romanesque church and the *esgrafiado* façades of its old mansions – but the memory the visitor takes away is likely to be mostly a fond impression. The delicate skyline silhouetted on a high narrow promontory between two green river valleys gives the city the appearance of a great ship among the rolling hills of Castile.

When the Emperor Trajan built the aqueduct in the early 2nd century, Segovia was already a venerable city. Under Rome, and later the Visigoths and Moors, it attained little distinction, but it survived. After it fell to the Christians in the 11th century, Segovia blossomed in the great cultural and economic expansion of medieval Castile. Its Romanesque churches and palaces were built on the profits of an important textile industry, and by the time of the Catholic Kings it was one of the leading cities of Spai

The Cathedral

Open *March–Oct daily 9–6.30, Nov–Feb dail 9–5.30;* **adm** *€4.95.*

The cathedral has been called the 'last Gothic cathedral' of Spain; most of the wor was done between 1525 and 1590, though parts were not completed until the 18th century. Segovia's old cathedral had been burnt during the Comunero revolt, and Charles V contributed much to its replacement as an act of reconciliation. Juan Gil de Hontañón designed it, expressing the national mood of austerity in grandeur in much the same way as El Escorial. The best parts of this cathedral are the semicircular **eastern end**, where an exuberant ascent of pinnacles and buttresses (which surely inspired Gaudí in his Sagrada Família in Barcelona) covers the chapels behind the main altar, the unique squarish **bell-tower** and an elegant **dome** over the choir. The

h a luxurious display of produce. Here
ster *asadores* of reputation, bedecked in
bons and medals, serve up Spain's best
hinillo (roast suckling-pig, traditionally
y 21 days old and so tender that you can
it with the blunt edge of a plate), along
h roast milk-fed lamb and other formi-
bly heavy Castilian specialities. Less
ensive places can be found on Calle de
n Bravo and the Plaza de San Martín.
sitive souls should lay off the *sopa castel-*
a (spicy garlic soup served with a poached
g), especially in the cheaper places, where
made with enough grease to lubricate a
omotive. It's not bad, though.

asa Duque, *12 C/ de Cervantes,* t *921 46 24*
Expensive. With a renowned *asadore.*

lesón de Cándido, *5 Plaza del Azoguejo,*
1 42 59 11; wheelchair accessible.
ensive. Heading the list for 50 years or so,
h its picturesque exterior (shown on most
Segovia's tourist brochures), beside the
educt. The late Señor Cándido was the

expert – he used to write cookbooks on
Castilian cuisine – and he played host to all
the famous folk who have ever passed
through Segovia (autographed photos on the
walls, of course, to prove it).

Restaurante José María, *off the Plaza
Mayor at 11 C/ de Cronista Lecea,* t *921 46 11 11,*
t *921 46 02 73. **Moderate**.* The young
contender in Segovia (try the breaded frogs'
legs, another local treat). José María, who
started his career as an apprentice under
Cándido, is passionate about Castilian wines.

Tasca La Posada, *19 C/ Judería Vieja,* t *921 46
21 71. **Moderate**.* Traditional Castilian cuisine –
try the local dish *cochinillo asado* (roast suckling pig). The front bar is good for tapas.

La Granja

Zaca, *La Granja,* t *921 47 00 87. **Open** only for
lunch; **booking** essential at the weekend.
Moderate.* If all that roast flesh from Segovia
is palling, then it's worth thinking about
lunch in La Granja. Stews are the speciality.

er two are Renaissance elements that
n perfectly; in an age of architectural
nsition it was the greatest part of Juan
s accomplishment to make a harmonious
nbination of such diverse elements. The
hitect chose to be buried in the spare,
ll-lit interior.

here's little to see on the inside – a
nment on the hard times 16th-century
govia had come into – and the small
seum (*adm €1*) inside is almost painful to
t. See the **cloister**, though, if it's open; this
art of the original cathedral, built in the
belline Gothic style by Juan Guas and
ved here and reassembled after it
vived the fire.

cázar

za de la Reina Victoria Eugenia, t *921 46 07*
Open summer daily 10–7, winter daily
-6; adm €3.

he Alcázar, jutting out on its cliffs over the
nfluence of the Río Eresma and the smaller
mores, was one of the great royal

residences of Castile when Segovia was at
the height of its prominence during the 12th
and 13th centuries. By the 19th, though, the
old, forgotten castle had declined into a
military school; in 1862, some young cadets
set fire to it, in the hope they might be
transferred to Madrid. No one, it seems,
bothered to record the name of the architects who oversaw the Alcázar's restoration
in the 1880s. Even worse, some writers have
sniffed that the job they did is 'not authentic'.
Just because these forgotten heroes of the
picturesque saw fit to turn the Alcázar into a
flight of fancy worthy of the Mad King
Ludwig, with pointed turrets and curving
crenellated walks, some people find fault.

The people of Segovia who look after the
castle have joined in the fun, fitting out the
interior in a fashion that would make the
characters of any Sir Walter Scott novel feel
quite at home. There are plenty of 14th-
century cannons and armour, an harquebus
or two, stained glass and dusty paintings of
Visigothic kings. Some of the interiors
survived the fire; there are fine *artesonado*

ceilings in the **Sala de las Piñas** and in the **Throne Room**, built by Enrique IV but furnished as it might have been in the days of Ferdinand and Isabel.

Old Quarters and Romanesque Churches

Between the Cathedral and Alcázar lies the oldest district of Segovia. The *esgrafiado* **work** on some of the houses is a local speciality; a coat of stucco is applied, then scraped away around stencils to make decorative patterns. The streets meander languidly; to meander along with them is a treat, and fortunately the old town is small enough for you never entirely to get lost.

The medieval parish churches are everywhere. In small Plaza de San Esteban just north of the Cathedral stands the finest and most representative of Segovia's late Romanesque churches, the 13th-century church of **San Esteban**, with a lively belltower in the Italian style. The arcaded porch around two sides of the church is the trademark of Segovia's Romanesque architecture. Across the plaza is the **Palacio Episcopal** (Archbishop's Palace; *t 921 46 09 63; open Fri and Sat 10–2 and 5–7*), its plain façade enlivened only by the reliefs of a serpentwoman and other curious medieval fancies over the entrance. You should also hunt down **San Andrés**, a solid, simple work from the 12th century on the Plaza Merced; the church of **La Trinidad** on the Plaza de Doctor Laguna, off Calle de la Trinidad, with an interior restored to something like its original appearance; and **San Martín** on Calle de Juan Bravo (with a tiny museum attached); and **San Juan de los Caballeros** on the Plaza de Colmenares. Both of the last are smaller versions of San Esteban (though both are older), with the characteristic arcades and towers. The **Casa de los Picos**, on Calle de Cervantes, is another Segovia landmark, a 14th-century mansion with a façade like a waffle-iron, with protruding stone diamonds, a style copied in many later buildings in Spain and even one famous church in Naples.

One of Segovia's finest churches is outside the walls, near the centre of the new town, on Avenida de Fernández Ladreda. Built in the 12th century, **San Millán** is also the oldest but the capitals of its arcade, charmingly sculpted with scenes from the Bible and from everyday life, have survived much more clearly than at the other churches. This structure is thought by many to be the finest example of the Segovian Romaneque style.

The Aqueduct

Nothing else remains from Roman Segóbriga, but for the city to have merited such an elaborate water-supply it must have had nearly as many inhabitants in the 1st century AD as it does now, 50,000. Trajan, one of the Spanish emperors of the Roman Empire, most likely ordered its construction. Its two-storey arcade rises 29m over the busy Plaza Azoguejo below, making it the tallest surviving Roman aqueduct.

The Romans, antiquity's master plumbers, did not build it there just to show off. An aqueduct's purpose is to bring water from a distant source, in this case the Río Frío, over 15km away. Over the length of it a constant downward slope must be maintained to sustain the flow, and wherever it crosses a valley like this an arcade must be built to keep the flow level. The actual water-course, a channel cut into the stone and lined with lead, is at the very top. What you see here is only a small part of the system; the Romans built an underground water-course from here to the Alcázar, and from the other end you can follow the arcade, ever shallower as the ground rises, up Calle Fernán García from the Plaza Azoguejo and right out of the city.

Note the notches cut into the rough stone on the arcade; these allowed for attaching scaffolding for the higher levels, and for blocks and tackles to hoist up the heavier stones. The Romans never cut corners; this was built for the centuries to come, and most likely would have survived unchanged had not several of the arches been destroyed in a siege by the Moors in the 11th century. Some 400 years later, Queen Isabel hired the

onks of El Parral monastery to oversee the construction; when they had finished, they placed the little statue of Hercules that d stood in a niche over the centre with an age of the Virgin Mary.

alley of the Eresma

Do not by any means leave Segovia thout a walk through the valley of the esma. Through either of the old Mudéjar tes in the city's northern walls, the road ds down to the river through willow and plar woods dotted with wild flowers. lowing the road under the walls of the ázar, you cross the river and arrive at the urch of La Vera Cruz, standing on a low hill open countryside.

Vera Cruz

rretera de Zamarramala, t 921 43 14 75. en summer Tues–Sun 10.30–1.30 and 0–7, winter Tues–Sun 10.30–1.30 and 0–6; closed Nov.

This is one of the most interesting rviving Templar foundations. The church s built in 1208, and with the dissolution of e Templars in 1312 it became a regular rish church. The last few centuries have en it abandoned and its relic of the True oss (*la vera cruz*), a sliver of wood, moved to e nearby village of Zamarramala. Like any Templar churches, this one is round, th 12 sides; at its centre is the two-storeyed amber, the 'inner temple', where the mplar secret rites took place, as opposed to e 'outer temple' which belonged to the mmon Church rituals.

None of the paintings or furnishings is as l as the Templars, but one 15th-century ture of the Last Supper, with the apostles ated at a round table, is worth a look. You ay climb the bell-tower for one of the best ws of Segovia and the Alcázar, taking in a mber of churches and monasteries nearby this holy valley, now largely unused. lose by is the **Convento de las Carmelitas scalzas** (*open June–Sept daily 10–1.30 and 8, Oct–May daily 10–1.30 and 4–6.30*), a

17th-century convent with the tomb of the gentle St John of the Cross.

El Parral

***Open** Mon–Sat 10–12.30 and 4–6, Sun 10–11.30am; Gregorian chant at noon.*

Retrace your steps from La Vera Cruz to the river and continue up the opposite bank. On the way you'll pass the remains of the **Moneda**, or mint, where American gold and silver were turned into coins before 1730. El Parral's founder, Juan Pacheco, Marqués de Villena, apparently chose this site because it had brought him luck – he had killed three men here in duels. In its day, El Parral was famous throughout Spain for its woods and gardens. The place is still lovely, and the long-neglected church has been restored, with a number of interesting tombs of famous Segovians (and some of the Marqués' illegitimate children).

La Granja de San Ildefonso

***Palace open** summer Tues–Sat 10–6, Sun 10–2; winter Tues–Sat 10–1.30 and 3–5, Sun 10–2; **adm** €5, free for EU passport-holders on Wed; **gardens open** summer daily 10–8, winter daily 10–6.*

La Granja ('the farm'), 11km southeast of Segovia on the N-601 and linked by bus, is one of the works of Philip V, he of the insatiable appetite for palaces. The building has a certain Rococo elegance of the sort American millionaires love to copy, but its fame has always been its **gardens**. Philip originally conceived La Granja as a scaled-down version of Versailles (his father, Louis XIV's, palace) and the gardens, laid out in the 1740s, completed the picture. There are some 28 hectares (70 acres) of them, with remarkable fountains everywhere, decorated with pretty pagan deities. However, there is only one day of the year when they all work, and it's worth watching them come alive: 25 August. The **palace** itself is furnished in 18th-century French style, and contains an impressive collection of Spanish and French tapestries and some spectacular cut-glass chandeliers.

ARANJUEZ

***Palace open, t** 91 891 07 40 April–Sept Tues–Sun 10–6.15, Oct–March Tues–Sun 10–5.15; **adm** €3, free for EU passport-holders on Wed; **gardens open** April–Sept Tues–Sun 8am–8.30pm, Oct–March Tues–Sun 8–6.30.*

There has been a royal residence in Aranjuez since the days of Philip II. His palace, built by Bautista and Herrera, the architects of El Escorial, burnt down in the 17th century, and we can only wonder what sort of pleasure-dome those two grinds could have created. Philip V began the replacement at the same time as he was building his palace at La Granja. It is hard to tell the two apart. Like La Granja, Aranjuez is an attempt to emulate some of the grandeur of Versailles; it isn't surprising, with Louis XIV meddling in Spain's affairs at every step, that the junior Bourbon wanted to show that he, too, was somebody. Aranjuez is a natural

location for a palace. The water of the Río Ta makes it an oasis among the brown hills, o the threshold of La Mancha. Centuries of ro attention have given the area more trees than any other corner of Castile, and even today it is famous in Spain for its strawberri and asparagus. A small town has grown up around the palace since the 16th century.

As at La Granja, the prime attractions her are the **gardens**, full of sculptural allegory, with fountains in the most surprising place shady avenues and walks along the Tajo, an even an informal garden of the sort that were called 'English gardens' in the 18th century. They'll drag you through a guided tour of the **Palacio Real**, packed full of chan deliers and mirrors, with collections of porcelain, fancy clocks and court costume c the period. Among the gardens is another small palace, the **Casa del Labrador**, modell on the Petit Trianon, and along the river a **museum of boats**; conscientious Charles III

Getting There

By Train

Cercanías line C3 trains from Madrid-Atocha run to Aranjuez roughly every half-hour and take 45mins. To make a special outing of it, you could pay the extra to take the Tren de la Fresa (strawberry train), a real steam train that chuffs from Atocha's AVE platforms to Aranjuez and back weekends from mid-May to October and once a day during the summer months, leaving at about 10am and returning at around 7pm. A local bus will take you right from Aranjuez station to the palace; if you'd rather walk, turn right out of the station, then left down the avenue. RENFE information: **t** 902 24 02 02, **w** *www.aranjuez.net*.

By Bus

Buses from Madrid, run by Autominibus, **t** 91 530 46 06, leave hourly from Estación Sur, C/ de Méndez Álvaro (metro Méndez Álvaro).

Tourist Information

9 Plaza de San Antonio, **t** 91 891 04 27.

Eating Out

The boom in tourism over the last decade has meant that most restaurants can't get local strawberries and asparagus (but this is what people come here to eat). And they figure prominently on most of the town's restaurant menus. Most of them are expensive, though, and you may settle for *fresas co nata* (strawberries and cream) from one of the little stands around town, although the cream won't be real either. Many restaurant have elegant settings along the riverfront.

Casa José, *32 C/ Abastos,* **t** *91 891 14 88.* ***Expensive****. A special-occasion restaurant with an intimate atmosphere and quality traditional cuisine. Try the *sopa de ajo* (garl soup with poached egg and croutons).

Casa Pablo, *42 C/ de Almíbar,* **t** *91 891 14 51* ***Moderate***. Makes a change from the usual fare, with inventive, international, nouvelle inspired cuisine, making it very popular.

La Rana Verde, *1 C/ de Reina,* **t** *91 891 17 40* ***Moderate.*** On the riverfront. Paying the ext for one of the fish or game specialities here preferable to the simple set menu.

ilt the structure as part of a forgotten
oject to make the Tajo navigable, but his
ccessors turned it into a boathouse, and
eir pleasure craft are on display.

OLEDO

No city in Spain has seen more, or learnt
ore, or stayed true to itself for so long
rough the shifting fortunes of a discour-
ing history. Under the rule of Madrid the
urper, though, the last 400 years have
en murder for Toledo; its pride humbled, its
ents and achievements dried up, this city
th little political or economic function is
tirely at the mercy of the tourists. It would
a ghost town without them. It isn't
edo's fault that it has become a museum
y, but it carries out the rôle with consider-
le grace. Its monuments are well
ubbed, its streets lively and pleasant, with
eautiful setting on a plateau above the
Tajo. El Greco made Toledo his home for
arly 40 years, and the city contains many
his strange, intensely spiritual works.

istory

oledo was a capital of sorts when the
mans found it, a centre for the local
ltiberian tribes called the Carpetani. As a
man town, Toletum did not gain much
tinction, but scanty remains of temples
d a circus, still visible just north of town off
e Avenida de la Reconquista, indicate it
ust have been fairly large. The Visigoths
ade it their capital in the 6th century; their
lace may have been on the site of the
ázar, but they were not great builders,
d relatively little is left from their two
nturies of rule.

he city fell to the Moors in the year 716.
re, long before the Crusades, the Christian
d Islamic worlds first met, in a city
nowned throughout the Mediterranean
learning. A school of translators grew up
er the centuries in which Arab, Jewish and
ristian scholars transmitted Greek and

Arabic science, as well as Islamic and Jewish
theology and mysticism, to the lands of the
north. Conveniently close to the mercury
mine at Almadén, Toledo became a centre for
the study of alchemy. Schools of occult
philosophy and mathematics proliferated,
attracting students from all over
Christian Europe.

The chroniclers claimed a population for
Moorish Toledo of some 200,000 people,
over three times as large as it is today. Even
so, it was never a centre of political power,
and to the sultans and emirs of Al-Andalus it
meant little more than the central bastion of
their defensive line against the rapacious
Christians of the north. In a moment of in-
attention they lost it to Alfonso VI and El Cid.

The conquest of the city in 1085 was never
reversed, and tipped the balance of power
irreparably against the Moors. For a long
time, Toledo under Castilian rule continued
its role as a city of tolerance and scholarship,
and its Moorish and Jewish populations
easily accommodated the Christian settlers
introduced by the Castilian kings. After the
accession of Ferdinand and Isabel, however,
disasters followed thick and fast. The Church
and the Inquisition were given a free hand,
and soon succeeded in snuffing out Toledo's
intellectual lights. The expulsion of the Jews,
and later the Moors, put an end to the city's
long-established culture, and the permanent
establishment of the capital at Madrid
ended for ever the political importance
Toledo had enjoyed in medieval Castile. To
make matters worse, Toledo had been a focal
point of the Comunero revolt, and suffered
greatly after its suppression. By the 18th
century the city had become an impoverished backwater and, except for the famous
siege of the Alcázar during the Civil War, little
has happened there since. Long ago, Toledo
made its living from silk and steel; the silk
industry died off with the expulsion of the
Moors, and the famous Toledo blades,
tempered in cold water from the Tajo, are
only a memory, except for the cheap versions
the tourists buy.

Circo Romano

Calle Escalona

Museo Hospital de Tavera

AVENIDA DE CARLOS III

AVENIDA DE LA RECONQUISTA

CALLE DE LA DIPUTACIÓN

PASEO DEL CIRCO ROMANO

PASEO DE CANÓNIGOS

Paseo de Merchán

PASEO DEL CRISTO DE LA VEGA

PZA. ALFONSO VI

Tourist Office

Puerta de Bisagra

AVENIDA PUENTE DE LA CAVA

C/ LA CARRERA

PASEO DE RECAREDO

Puerta del Cambrón

CUESTA DE LA GRANJA

Santiago del Arrabal

PZA. SOLAR ANTEQUERUELA

LAS CARMELITAS

CALLE REAL

SANTA LEOCADIA

CALLE AZACAR

Monasterio de S. Juan de los Reyes

Puerta del Sol

C/ CARRETAS

Mezquita del Cristo de la Luz

CALLE GERARDO

LOS REYES CATÓLICOS

PZA. PADILLA

PZA. STA. CLARA

PZA. CARMELITAS

PZA. S. VICENTE

LOS ALFILERITOS

CLÉRIGOS MENORES

Hospital de Santa Cruz

Museo de Arte Contemporáneo

ESTEBAN ILLÁN

S. CLEMENTE

Post Office

PZA. AMADOR DE LOS RIOS

TOLEDO DE OHIO

Museo de la Cultura Visigótica

PZA. DE ZOCODOVER

Sinagoga de Sta. Maria la Blanca

CALLE ANGEL

PZA. BARRIO NUEVO

Santo Tomé

PZA. DE VALDECABALLEROS

ALFONSO XII

Palacio Arzobispal

PZA. MAGDALENA

CALLE CERVANTES

Sinagoga del Tránsito and Museo Sefardí

Palacio de Fuensalida

Taller del Moro

LA TRINIDAD

PLAZA MAYOR

Alcázar

Casa Museo de El Greco

PASEO DEL TRÁNSITO

Ayuntamiento

PLAZA AYUNTAMIENTO

Cathedral

Posada de la Hermandad

GRAL. MOSCARDO

RIO TAJO

PZA. DE SAN CRISTÓBAL

PZA. DEL REY D. PEDRO

AVE. MARIA PLEGADERO

PZA. FUENTES

PZA. SAN JUSTO

CUESTA DE SAN JUSTO

N

PZA. DE STA. CATALINA

C/ SACRAMENTO

PZA. SAN LORENZO

LAS RECOGIDAS

CARRERAS DE SAN SEBASTIÁN

PZA. DON FERNANDO

PZA. DE SAN LUCAS

San Lucas

PASEO DE LA CANDELARIA

RIO TAJO

CARRETERA DE CIRCUNVALAC

300 metres
300 yards

PZA. ANDAQUE

Around the Plaza de Zocodover

The name, like the souk of a Moroccan city, is from the Arabic for market, and this square – triangle, really – has always been the centre of Toledo. A traditional market is still held here on Tuesdays. On the long, eastern edge of the triangle, the stately building with the clock is the seat of the provincial government, rebuilt after it burnt down during the Civil War. From the archway under the clock, stairs lead to Calle de Cervantes and the enormous, fascinating museum contained within the 1544 Hospital de Santa Cruz.

Hospital de Santa Cruz

3 C/ de Cervantes, t 925 22 10 36. Open Tues–S 10–2 and 4–6.30, Sun 10–2; adm €1.50.

Set in a building by Enrique de Egas with wildly decorated façade, a little bit of every thing has been assembled here: archaeological finds from Toletum, painting and tapestries, Toledo swords and daggers. The building itself is worth a visit, its long airy halls typical of hospitals of the period, with beautiful ceilings and staircases.

etting There

Train

here are nine trains a day at one- to two-
urly intervals from Madrid-Atocha
ssing through Chamartín) to Toledo's
rming Mudéjar-style station east of town
ionales line 9f; 60–85mins). Any city bus
l take you from the station into the
tre. RENFE information: t 902 24 02 02.

Bus

mpresa Galiano Continental, t 91 527 29
has departures every half-hour from
ación Sur, C/ de Méndez Álvaro (metro
ndez Álvaro). In Toledo, call t 925 21 58 50.

urist Information

st outside the Puerta de Bisagra,
5 22 08 43, f 925 25 26 48, on the road
m Madrid.

ting Out

ining in Toledo is largely a matter of
iding overpriced tourist troughs.
xpensive restaurants are not as hard to
d as you might think; there's a small
ony of them along the C/ de Barrio Rey,
t off the Plaza de Zocodover. Make sure

you try Toledo's old speciality, *mazapán*,
made from almond paste and sugar.

Asador Adolfo, *6 C/ de la Granada*, *t 925 22
73 21*. **Expensive**. Considered to be Toledo's
best restaurant and the place to go for truly
flamboyant dining.

La Lumbre, *3 C/ de Real del Arrabal*, *t 925 22
03 73*. **Expensive**. Mixes local cooking with
French-inspired dishes; this is one place
where vegetarians generally have plenty to
choose from.

Casón de los López de Toledo, *3 C/ Sillería*,
t 925 25 47 74; **Expensive**. One of the most
beautiful buildings in Toledo, you enter via a
vaulted foyer leading to a ground floor café
serving coffee and snacks. Upstairs there is a
choice of dining rooms. There are magnificent antiques and paintings throughout. The
market-based menu features fine Castilian
and Continental cuisine.

Hostal del Cardenal, *24 Paseo Recaredo*,
t 925 22 08 62. **Moderate**. You'll get your
money's worth at the fine restaurant here. As
elsewhere in Toledo, stuffed partridge is a
speciality, well-hung and gamey the way the
Spaniards like it.

La Abadía, *3 C/ Núñez de Arce*. **Inexpensive**.
Can get a bit hectic – but that's all part of
the appeal.

nish medicine was quite advanced in the
h century (most of the physicians were
vish and exempt from the persecutions)
d the surroundings were held to be an
portant part of the cure. Notable among
displays are Don Juan's huge standard
m his flagship at the Battle of Lepanto,
ntings by El Greco, some eccentric holy
nes by the 16th-century Maestro de
ena, a sculptural frieze from a pre-Roman
edo house and a lovely 15th-century
mish tapestry, the Tapiz de los Astrolabios.
st round the corner of Calle de la
ncepción, the chapel of **San Jerónimo** is
e of the best examples of Toledo's 16th-
tury Mudéjar churches.

The Alcázar

*2 Cuesta de Carlos V, t 925 22 16 73.
Undergoing major reforms and will not be
open to the public until late 2007.*

Romans, Visigoths and Moors all had some
sort of fortress on this spot, at the highest
point of the city. The present plan of the big,
square palace-fortress, the same that stands
out so clearly in El Greco's famous *View of
Toledo*, was constructed by Charles V, though
rebuilt after destructions in the Napoleonic
Wars and again in the Civil War. The second
siege was a bitter one. Toledo declared for
the Republic in July 1936, but a number of
soldiers, civilians and Guardia Civil barred
themselves inside the Alcázar with the idea
that the coup would soon be over. Instead,
what they got was a two-month ordeal, with

Republican irregulars keeping them under constant fire. Finally Asturian miners succeeded in collapsing most of the fortress with dynamite charges. Still the defenders held out, under the leadership of Colonel José Moscardó, in the ruins and underground tunnels, until a relief column finally arrived in September.

Mezquita del Cristo de la Luz

Cuesta del Cristo de la Luz. Open Thur–Mon 10–2.30 and 1.30–7; adm €1.50.

The church of Cristo de la Luz is in reality a mosque built around 980 and incorporating elements of an earlier Visigothic church. When Alfonso VI captured the city (the story goes), he and El Cid were making their triumphal entrance when the king's horse knelt down in front of the mosque and refused to move. Taking this as a portent, the king ordered the mosque to be searched, and a niche was discovered, bricked up in the walls, with a crucifix and a lamp that had been miraculously burning since the days of the Visigoths. The tiny mosque, one of the oldest surviving Moorish buildings in Spain, is an exceptional example of their work.

The Cathedral

Open daily 10.30–2 and 4–6.30; museum open Tues–Sat 10.30–1 and 3.30–6, Sun 10.30–1; adm €4.95.

This isn't a building that may be approached directly; most of its bulk is hidden behind walls and rows of old buildings, with corners peeking out where you least expect them. The best of its portals, the **Puerta del Reloj**, is tucked away in a small courtyard where few ever see it, at the end of Calle Chapinería. The façade, on Plaza Ayuntamiento, is a little disappointing. Too many cooks have been at work, and the great rose windows are hidden behind superfluous arches, over three big portals where the sculpture is indifferent but grandiose. Before too long, the interest fades; look across

the square and you'll see one of Spain's mc beautiful city halls, the 1618 **Ayuntamiento** by El Greco's son, Jorge Theotocopoulos.

Don't give up on the cathedral yet, however; few Gothic churches in Spain car match its interior, unusually light and airy and with memorable works of art in every corner. Some 800 fine **stained-glass windo** from the 15th and 16th centuries dispel the gloom. Sculpture takes the place of honou before painting, unlike in most other cathe drals of Spain. Some of the best work is in **t** Old Testament scenes around the wall of t **Coro**, at the centre of the Cathedral (note t interesting versions of the Creation and st of Adam and Eve). The Coro's stalls are famous, decorated with highly detailed scenes from the conquest of Granada, don just three years after the event by Rodrigo Alemán. Behind the Coro is the freestandin **Chapel of the Descent**, dedicated to San Ildefonso; with its golden pinnacle it seem to be some giant monstrance left in the ais Another oddity is the 30ft-tall painting of *St Christopher* on the south wall.

The **Capilla Mayor**, around the main altar contains some fine sculpture. A famous statue on the left-hand wall is that of Mart Alhaga, a mysterious shepherd who guide Alfonso VIII's army through the mountains before its victory at Las Navas de Tolosa, th disappeared; only the king saw his face, an he directed the sculptor at his work. On the right, another statue honours the memory Alfaqui Abu Walid. When Alfonso VI conquered Toledo, he promised this Moori alcalde that the great mosque, on the site the cathedral, would be left in peace. While he was on a campaign, however, the bishop and the king's French wife Constance conspired to tear it down; upon his return the enraged Alfonso was only dissuaded from punishing them by the entreaties of t generous Moor. Behind the altar, the beau tiful *retablo* reaches almost to the vaulting

But even in a cathedral where so much is unusual, the **Transparente** takes the cake. Early in the 18th century, someone decided that Mass here would seem even more

scendent if somehow a shaft of light
ld be directed over the altar. To do this a
e was chopped in the wall of the Capilla
yor, and another in the vaulting of the
bulatory. The difficult question of how to
oncile this intrusion was given to the
lptor Narciso Tomé and his four sons; in
eral years' work (completed in 1732), they
nsformed the ungainly openings into a
oque spectacular, combining painting,
lpture and architecture into a cloud of
nts, angels and men that grow magically
of the cathedral's stones – many of the
res are partly painted, partly sculpture
d to the walls.

ear the Transparente, the ratty old bit of
h hanging from the vaulting is a **cardinal's**
– cardinals in Spain have the privilege of
ging them wherever they like before they
It is one of several in the cathedral.
hough the numbers of those faithful to
Mozarabic liturgy have dwindled, their
ss is still regularly celebrated in the large
pel in the southwest corner of the cathe-
l, the **Mozarabic Chapel**, built by Cardinal
neros, a friend and protector of the
zarabs. The story goes that, after the
istian conquest of Toledo, a dispute arose
ween the city's long-established
istians and the officious Castilian prelates
r which form of the liturgy would be used
Masses: the ancient Mozarabic form
cended from the time of the Visigoths, or
modern, Church-sanctioned style of the
of Europe. Alfonso, as any good Crusader
ght have done, elected to hold a trial by
nbat to decide the issue. The Mozarabic
mpion won, but the churchmen weren't
sfied, and demanded a trial by fire. So
y ignited some prayerbooks. The Roman
sion was blown from the flames by a
den wind, while the Mozarabic wouldn't
n. Alfonso decreed that the two versions
he faith would coexist on an equal
ting. Unfortunately, the chapel, the only
ne of the oldest surviving Christian ritual
Western Europe, is usually locked up tight.
ther sections of the cathedral are open by
arate admission, from the enormous

souvenir stand inside the Puerta del Mollete.
The **Treasury** has little of interest, though the
3m-high silver reliquary does not fail to
impress. In the **Sala Capitular**, a richly decorated room with a gilt *artesanado* ceiling, you
can see some unusual frescoes and portraits
of all Toledo's archbishops. El Greco painted
the frescoes and altarpiece of the **Sacristy**,
and there are other works of his, as well as a
Holy Family by Van Dyck and a gloomy representation of the arrest of Christ by Goya that
makes an interesting contrast to his famous
Los Fusilamientos de Moncloa in the Prado.

Museo de los Concilios y de la Cultura Visigótica

*C/ de San Román, t 92 522 78 72. Open Tues–Sat
10–2 and 4–6.30, Sun 10–2; adm €0.60.*

Here the 13th-century church of San Román
has been converted into a museum of
Visigothic culture, the only one of its kind in
Spain. '*Concilios*' refers to the several General
Councils of the Western Church that were
held in Toledo in the days of Visigothic rule,
but the majority of the museum's exhibits
are simple Visigothic relics, jewellery and religious artworks. Some of the buckles, brooches
and carved stones show an idiosyncratic
talent, but the lesson here is that the artistic
inspiration of Spain did not really change in
the transition from Roman to Visigothic rule
– there was simply far less of it. The building
itself is much more interesting, half-Christian
and half-Moorish, with naïve, original frescoes of the Last Judgement and the 12 Apostles
in a garden. Painted angels and saints peer
out from the ceilings and horseshoe arches.

The Judería

As long as the streets continue to slope
downwards, you'll know you're going in the
right direction. The Judería, Toledo's Jewish
quarter before 1492, occupies a narrow strip
of land overlooking the Tajo in the south-
western corner of the city. El Greco lived here,
and the back streets of the Judería hold a

concentration of some of old Toledo's most intriguing and interesting monuments.

Santo Tomé

The church of Santo Tomé, on the street of the same name, is unremarkable in itself, but in a little chamber to the side, surrounded by souvenir stands, they'll show you El Greco's *El Entierro del Conde de Orgaz* (*The Burial of the Count of Orgaz*). A miracle was recorded at this obscure Count's burial in 1323: SS. Stephen and Augustine themselves came down from heaven to assist with the obsequies, and this is the scene El Greco portrays. A group of the Count's friends and descendants had petitioned Rome for his beatification, and it is perhaps in support of this that El Greco received the commission, over 200 years later. The portrayal of the burial has for a background a row of gravely serious men, each one a notable portrait in itself (the artist is said to have included himself, sixth from the right, and his son, the small boy in the foreground, and some commentators have even claimed to find Lope de Vega and Cervantes among the group of mourners). Above, the earthly scene is paralleled by the Count's reception into heaven. This painting is perhaps the ultimate expression of the intense, somewhat twisted, spirituality of 16th-century Castile. It is an exaltation of the mysteries of power and death, and the longer you look at it, the more disturbing it becomes.

Casa-Museo de El Greco

3 C/ de Samuel Leví, **t** *925 22 40 46.* **Open** *Tues–Sun 10–2 and 4–6, Sun 10–2;* **adm** *€2.40.*

This is where the painter lodged for most of the years he lived in Toledo. The city itself, as seen from across the Tajo, was one of his favourite subjects (though his most famous *View of Toledo* is now in the Metropolitan Museum of Art, New York). The best parts of the restored house are the courtyard and tiled kitchen. Only a few of El Greco's paintings here are of special merit – notably a portrait of St Peter, another favourite subject.

Taller del Moro

C/ del Taller del Moro, **t** *925 22 71 15.* **Open** *Tues–Sat 10–2 and 4–6.30, Sun 10–2.*

Just round the corner from Santo Tomé church, the Taller del Moro (Moor's Workshop) gets its name from the days it spent as a shop for the cathedral workmen. The building itself is an interesting work of Mudéjar architecture; inside is a collection of the sort of things the craftsmen made.

Sinagoga de Santa María la Blanca

Plaza de Barrionuevo, **t** *925 22 72 57.* **Open** *Sat–Thurs 10–2 and 3.30–6, Fri 10–2 and 3.30–7;* **adm** *€1.50.*

Not surprisingly, in a city where Jews played such a prominent and constructive role for so long, two of Toledo's best buildings are synagogues, saved only by good luck after centuries of neglect. La Sinagoga de Santa María la Blanca (c.1180), so called from its days as a church, is stunning and small, a glistening white confection of horseshoe arches, elaborately carved capitals and geometric medallions that is rightly considered to be one of the masterpieces of Mudéjar architecture.

Sinagoga del Tránsito

Paseo del Tránsito, **t** *925 22 36 65.* **Open** *Tues–Sat 10–1.45 and 4–5.45, Sun 10–1.45;* **adm** *€4.50.*

Just as good, though in an entirely different style, is the other synagogue, built by Samuel Leví, treasurer to King Pedro I (the Cruel) before that whimsical monarch had him executed. The synagogue is much later than Santa María la Blanca, and shows the influence of the Granada Moors – the interior could be a room in the Alhambra, with its ornate ceiling and carved arabesques, except that the calligraphic inscriptions are in Hebrew instead of Arabic, and the Star of David is interspersed with the arms of Castile and León. The building now houses the **Museo Sefardí** (Sephardic Museum), assembled out of a few surviving relics found around the city. Elements of Jewish life and

...eek Fire

...orn in 1541 in Venetian-ruled Crete, ...menikos Theotocopoulos was trained as ...icon painter, but had more talent than his ...ive island could hold. By the time he was ...he was in Titian's workshop in Venice, ...hough it was the elongated, linear, ...stical style of another Venetian, ...toretto, that proved the greatest influ-...e on the young painter. In 1570 he was in ...ne, coming into contact with the works of ...chelangelo and the great central Italian ...nnerists (Pontormo, Rosso Fiorentino), ...ose strange, startling colours, unrealistic ...spectives and exaggerated, often tortured ...es were to be reflected in his own art.

...iego de Castilla, dean of canons of Toledo ...hedral, gave El Greco his first major ...nmission: a triptych for the high altar of ...edo's Santo Domingo de Antiguo (central ...nel in Chicago and two outer panels in the ...do). It was with this great altarpiece that ...perfected his unique, highly personal style of elongated forms, a nervous line and figures that rise up like flame, all perceptions heightened to a fervent rapture and honed to the spiritual essential of truth. Not everyone was ready for it.

El Greco never found favour with that otherwise discriminating art patron Philip II, who panicked at the sight of the *Martyrdom of San Maurizio* that the Cretan had painted for a chapel in El Escorial in 1587. The painter refused all hints that supplication or an offer to soften the colours might win approval, and in a huff he took his brushes off to Toledo, where he spent his last 37 years.

Incapable of doing anything halfway, he lived as extravagantly as a lord, buying a 24-room palace in the former Jewish quarter and paying a guitarist to accompany his every meal. Although he never lacked for commissions from the Church or for portraits (usually of clergymen), after his death all of his worldly possessions fitted into a single trunk. He had spent it all.

...ture are displayed with explanatory notes, ...eacquaint Spaniards with a part of their ...itage they have quite forgotten.

...onasterio de ...an Juan de los Reyes

...V de San Juan de los Reyes, **t** *925 22 38 02.* ***en** daily 10–2 and 3.30–7;* **adm** *€1.50.*

...efore the conquest of Granada, Ferdinand ...d Isabel built a church here with the inten-...n of making it their last resting-place. The ...hitect was Juan Guas, working the ...pendicular elegance of Isabelline Gothic ...perfection in every detail. Los Reyes ...ólicos wanted no doubt as to whose ...nument this was: their F and Y mono-...m, coats-of-arms and yoke-and-arrows ...nbols are everywhere, even on the stained ...ss. One of the side chapels contains one of ... most grotesque, emaciated statues of ...us in Spain. The **exterior** of the church is ...ous, with its western wall covered with ... chains of prisoners released from the Moors during the Granada campaigns. The **Cloister** is another of Toledo's architectural treasures, with elegant windows and vault-ings on the lower level. If you go up to the second floor and gaze up from the arches you will see the hilarious collection of **gargoyles** added by restorers in the 1880s – all manner of monsters, a farting monk and a frog riding a fish; see if you can find the cat.

Outside the Walls

Start at the **Puerta del Sol**, north of the Plaza de Zocodover, a pretty gatehouse from the 12th century. In the 14th century, the Knights of St John rebuilt it and added the curious relief medallion, much commented on as a late example of Toledan mysticism; it shows the sun, moon and a large triangle around a scene of San Ildefonso, patron and 4th-century bishop of Toledo, receiving a chasuble woven by angels from the hands of the Virgin. According to local legend, it was presented in return for a treatise the saint

wrote on the meaning of the Immaculate Conception.

Further down, in the old quarter called the Arrabal outside the Moorish walls, is another fine Mudéjar church, a joyous excess of pointed arches and towers done in brick, the 11th-century **Santiago del Arrabal**. In the 1480s, this was the church of San Vicente Ferrer, the anti-Semitic fire-eater whose sermons started regular riots and helped to force the expulsion of the Jews.

Here the modern road curves around the **Nueva Puerta de Bisagra**, more like a palace than a gate, with its pointed spires and courtyard. Charles V built it, strictly for decoration, and added his enormous coat of arms in stone after the Comunero wars, to remind the Toledans who was boss.

Just outside the gate, the city's tourist office is on the edge of a large park called the Paseo de Merchán, on the other side of which stands a 16th-century charitable institution converted into a museum, the **Museo Hospital de Tavera**, Avenida de los Duques de Lerma (*open daily 10.30–1.30 and 3.30–6*), lovingly guarded by three old ladies. Cardinal Tavera was a member of the house of Mendoza, a grandee of Spain and an adviser to Charles V. His collection, including his portrait, also contains several works by El Greco and the memorable *Bearded Woman* by Ribera; it shares space with objects and furnishings from the Cardinal's time.

Where to Stay

With some 50,000 hotel rooms in Madrid, there are always enough to go around. If it's reliability or familiarity you're looking for, there are all the world's big chains to choose from, or you could stay at any of a hundred other three-, four- or five-star hotels – all pleasant and well-staffed, and many have benefited from a recent refurbishment to comply with tighter new laws. A number of tasteful classy hotels has also boosted the quality quota of accommodation in the city. Children under two stay for free in all Spanish hotels.

At the top end of the scale, Madrid has well over a third of all the luxury hotels in Spain. You could always pamper yourself at the Ritz, but only, needless to say, if money is no object – if you'd be inclined to wonder whether any hotel suite can possibly be worth €1,000 a night (the 'royal suite' is even more expensive) then this is definitely not your kind of place. At the other extreme, finding a good, inexpensive room for the night is not a problem if you're prepared to share a bathroom; otherwise you'll be hard pressed to find a double for under €30.

Price Categories

The price categories for a double room are as follows:

luxury	over €180
expensive	€100–180
moderate	€60–100
inexpensive	€30–60
cheap	under €30

Booking Agents

If you haven't got the time or the inclination to find accommodation yourself, there are a couple of agencies who will work it all out for you:

Brújula Agency, *Estación de Atocha, C/ Atocha s/n*, **t** *91 539 11 73*. Books accommodation in Madrid and the surrounding region for a fee of €2.50. They will also provide you with a map and directions for getting to the hotel. There is a branch at Estación de Chamartín (**t** *91 315 78 94*).

Viajes Aira, *Terminals 1 and 2 of Aeropuerto de Barajas*, **t** *91 305 42 24*, **f** *91 305 84 19*. There is no booking fee, but they only offer hotels in the moderate–expensive range and don't provide maps or directions.

Web Sites

There are a good dozen Web sites on which you can peruse Madrid's wealth of hotels; some sites offer online booking options. A good few places to start are:

1st Choice Hotels and Resorts, **w** *www.1stmadridhotels.com* Mainly two- to four-star hotels. Online booking available for some.

10 Selected Hotels, **w** *www.madrid.hotels.msk.ru*. The title is misleading as there are far more hotels listed, some with online booking, and lots of photos.

All Madrid Hotels, **w** *www.madrid-hotels-spain.com*. With customer reviews, plus online booking for some.

Gulliver's Madrid Hotels, **w** *www.gulliversmadridhotels.com*. This Internet site has a good choice of hotels and special discount rates, especially in the expensive–luxury range.

Spain-Barcelona Hotels, **w** *www.spain-barcelona-hotels.com*. A misleading name: an endless list of hotels, hostels and some apartment hotels in Madrid.

Travel-in Madrid, **w** *www.travel-in-madrid.com*. An elegantly designed, magaziney site offering online booking and a more editorial focus.

Old and Royal Madrid

Expensive

(46) Hotel Santo Domingo **** H10
13 Plaza de Santo Domingo, **t** *91 547 98 00*, **f** *91 547 59 95*, **w** *www.hotelsantodomingo.net*; **metro** *Santo Domingo*.
Not far from the buzzing Gran this stylish establishment has some priceless 17th-century old masters in the lobby and comfortable, elegant rooms. Facilities include jacuzzi baths a parking, and it is well placed fo the area's nightlife.

**(47) Hotel Tryp Ambassador ** H10
5–7 Cuesta de Santo Domingo, **t** *91 541 67 00*, **f** *91 559 10 40*, **w** *www.solmelia.com*; **metro** *Santo Domingo*.
Right in the centre but tucked i a quiet street between the Pala Real, Teatro Real and Gran Vía, t luxurious establishment is arguably the capital's best-kept secret. The attractive central gla atrium makes the hotel an oasi of light and calm in the summe months. All rooms have satellite TV and minibar.

Moderate

**(81) Hostal Persal ** J12
Plaza del Angel 12, **t** *91 369 46 43*, **f** *91 369 19 52*, **w** *www.hostal persal.com*; **metro** *Sol*; *wheelcha accessible*.
A recent facelift has brightened up this old-fashioned hotel situated in a lovely square near Plaza Mayor. The spacious room have TV, air-con, brightly tiled bathrooms and small balconies.

(51) Hotel Carlos V * I11
5 C/ Maestro Victoria, **t** *91 531 41 00*, **f** *91 531 37 61*, **e** *recepcion@ hotelcarlosv.com*, **w** *www.hotel carlosv.com*; **metro** *Sol*.
Family-run and friendly, despite being part of the Best Western chain, this is an otherwise unex ceptional place, popular partly, doubt, because of its location – mere hop from El Corte Inglés. Airport shuttle service.

**(52) Hotel Europa ** I11
4 C/ del Carmen, **t** *91 521 29 00*, **f** *521 46 96*, **e** *info@hoteleuropa.n* **w** *www.hoteleuropa.es*; **metro** *S* A solid, good-value hotel with

ctacular views straight onto
Puerta del Sol. There's a
y mirrors-and-gold motif in
hallway, and the rooms have
ky cream bedspreads,
stionable art work and all
usual amenities. There's a
ty Andalucian-style central
o, restaurant, café and
ndry service.

6) **Hotel Paris ✶✶** J11
de Alcalá, t 91 521 64 91, f 91 531
8; metro Sol.

chandeliered hotel lobby
ked with china bric-a-brac has
old-fashioned grandeur, but
friendly staff soon make
tors feel right at home. Two
s away from the Puerta del
the best of the wooden-
red rooms look onto the
rtyard garden and keep the
nd of traffic at bay. All rooms
e TV and safe. There's a money
ange and laundry service.

6) **Hotel Plaza Mayor ✶✶** I12
de Atocha, t 91 360 06 06, f 91
06 10, e ifo@h-plazamayor
n, w www.h-plazamayor.com;
ro Tirso de Molina or Sol.

utifully renovated hotel in an
stone building just across the
et from one of the quieter
es of the Plaza Mayor. All
ns have air-con and TV.
re's a sophisticated bar-café
currency exchange.

expensive

3) **Hostal Americano ✶✶** I11
uerta del Sol, 3° and 4°, t 91 522
2, f 91 522 11 92; metro Sol.
main plus here is the location,
rlooking the Sol fountain. The
rior is basic and could do with
vamp – especially the lounge
a with its black vinyl seating.
rooms have TV, telephone and
ate bath.

4) **Hostal Cruz Sol ✶✶** I12
aza de Santa Cruz, 2°, t/f 91 532
7; metro Sol.
the lovely arcaded Plaza de
ta Cruz behind the Plaza
yor, this hostal is bright and
t with en suite bathrooms
air-con.

(50) **Hostal Las Fuentes** H11
10 C/ de las Fuentes, 1°D, t 91 542 18
53, f 91 542 18 54, e reserva@
hostallasfuentes.com, w www
.hostallasfuentes.com; metro Opera.
A classically castizo building in a
classic castizo neighborhood, with
the Plaza de Oriente, Palacio Real
and Teatro Real just a stone's
throw from this quiet street.
Spacious rooms with private bath,
air-con and telephone. There's
Internet hookup and room service.

(57) **Hostal La Macarena ✶** H12
8 Cava de San Miguel, t 91 365 92 21,
f 91 364 27 5, w www.macarena@
silserranos.com; metro Opera
or Sol.
Just off the Plaza Mayor. One of
the most atmospheric places to
experience Madrid, tucked in a
street full of ancient bars and
restaurants (including fake
Mexican eatery El Cuchi, whose
awning proclaims, memorably,
'Hemingway Never Ate Here'), and
tall buildings pitched at such a
slope they look as though they'll
topple over at any minute.

Cheap

(55) **Hostal La Perla Asturiana ✶✶**
I12
3 Plaza de Santa Cruz, t 91 366 46
00, f 91 366 46 08, e perlaasturiana
@mundivia.es, w www.perla
asturiana.com; metro Sol.
In a grand old building looking out
on to Atocha and the Plaza de
Santa Cruz to the back of the
Plaza Mayor. Sunny common
rooms brimming with the occasional school group. Rooms have
bathroom, TV, telephone and fan,
and the salon has computers with
Internet access.

The Triángulo
de Arte

Luxury

(76) **Hotel Ritz ✶✶✶✶✶** L11
5 Plaza de la Lealtad, t 91 701 67 67,
f 91 701 67 76, w www.ritz.es;
metro Banco de España.
Wheelchair accessible.

Consistently rated among the best
hotels worldwide. A stay at the
Ritz is all about being pampered –
from the renovated and sumptuous rooms to the fabulous
restaurants and 'place-to-be-seen'
garden terrace. The hotel is close
to the Prado and is just a stone's
throw from the Retiro and the
boutiques lining the streets of
Salamanca. The décor includes
embroidered linen sheets, hand-
woven carpets and antique
furniture. All the facilities you'd
expect from a five-star hotel.

Inexpensive

(75) **Hotel Mora ✶✶** L11
32 Paseo del Prado, t 91 420 15 69,
f 91 420 05 64; metro Atocha.
Clean and recently reformed,
the Mora is good value, and well
located opposite the Prado. All
rooms have TV, telephone and
safe. There's a bar-cafeteria and
currency exchange.

(79) **HSR Coruña ✶** L12
12 Paseo del Prado, 3°dcha, t 91 429
25 43; metro Banco de España.
So close to the Prado you could
practically spit on it. Old-fashioned rooms with somewhat
sparse furnishings, though all
rooms have a TV.

(74) **HSR Principado** L11
7 C/ de Zorrilla, 1° dcha, t 91 429 81
87, f 91 369 40 60; metro Banco
de España.
Old-world décor in an old-world
corner of the city, up the street
from the splendid Teatro de la
Zarzuela, the Congreso de los
Diputados and the Thyssen-
Bornemisza. The rooms are
simple and monastic, with carved
wooden headboards and severe
Spanish white lace designs on
the bedlinen and bath towels.
All rooms have private bath and
TV. Excellent value for the
neighbourhood.

(80) **HSR Sudamericana ✶** L12
12 Paseo del Prado, 6°izqda, t 91
429 25 64; metro Banco de España.
One of the friendliest and quietest
lodgings in Madrid, occupying a
fine old building with leafy views

Hotels and Hostels

Map Key

towards the Prado. Bathrooms are shared with washbasins in each room.

Santa Ana and Huertas

Luxury

(61) **Tryp Reina Victoria** **** J 14 Plaza Santa Ana, **t** 91 531 45 00, **f** 91 522 03 07, **w** www.solmelia. com; **metro** Sevilla; wheelchair accessible.

Well-established, convenient and comfortable, this hotel is a bull fighters' favourite. Minibuses carrying clutches of them, resplendent in their fighting regalia, regularly pull up outside the wedding-cake façade. The nicest rooms overlook the Plaza Santa Ana. Facilities include parking, currency exchange, coffee shop and safes in all rooms.

(77) **Palace Hotel** ***** K12 7 Plaza de las Cortes, **t** 91 360 80 00, **f** 91 360 81 00, **e** madrid@ westin.com, **w** www.palace madrid.com; **metro** Banco de España; wheelchair accessible.

In a perfect location between the Prado and Sol, turn-of-the-20th-century architecture meets the latest facilities in one of Madrid's largest luxury hotels. But it's far from impersonal, and restaurants and bars in the stunning public areas make the Palace a bustling friendly place to stay or just to have Facilities include business centre, gym, bodega with over 200 wines, hairdresser, cigar menu, airport shuttle, and so on.

Expensive

(73) **Hotel Suecia** **** K11 4 C/ del Marqués de Casa Riera, **t** 91 531 69 00, **f** 91 521 71 41, **w** www.hotelsuecia.com; **metro** Sevilla or Banco de España.

Tucked away in a quiet corner of the old city, the Suecia has colourful upbeat rooms and a pleasant terrace on the 7th floor

sunbathing and relaxing.
ilities include bar, restaurant,
ysitting, no-smoking floor,
rency exchange and trans-
ng service.

1) Hotel Villa Real *** K11
laza de las Cortes, **t** *91 420 37*
f *91 420 25 47,* **e** *info@derby*
els.es, **w** *www.derbyhotels.es;*
tro Banco de España.
eelchair accessible.

hough only built in 1990, the
a Real has captured the
oclassical feel of the elegant
ghbourhood. It's ideally situ-
d for the main museums and
Puerta del Sol. A member of
Small Luxury Hotels of the
rld group. Facilities include
uzzis, babysitting, parking and
ort shuttle.

oderate

58) **Hotel Asturias ** J11
/ de Sevilla, **t** *91 429 66 76,* **f** *91*
40 36, **e** *asturias@chh.es,*
www.chh.es; **metro** *Sevilla.*
eelchair accessible.

t up from Sol, and well placed
the Santa Ana area. The rooms
e are spacious and bright.
tside rooms have good views,
can be noisy. All rooms have
and safe. There's also a cafe-
a and restaurant.

0) **Hotel Inglés *** J11
/ de Echegaray, **t** *91 429 65 51,*
420 24 23; **metro** *Sevilla or Sol.*
h 150 years of history under its
t, this family-run hotel lies
idistant from the shopping
as of Preciados and Carmen
l the bars of Santa Ana.
re's a relaxed and very
nfortable atmosphere in the
lic areas and sunny rooms,
those overlooking Echegaray
lf can be noisy at the weekend.
ilities include car park, bar,
et agency, fax service, laundry
l room service.

32) **Hotel Moira *** J12
del Príncipe 26, **t** *91 369 71 20,*
429 74 60, **w** *www.hotelmiau.*
n; **metro** *Sol.*

A classy new hotel with Japanese-feel décor of pale greens and cream. Overlooks one of the buzziest squares in the city which means rooms at the front can be noisy on a Saturday night. All rooms have TV and air-con, and there is discount parking available across the street.

Inexpensive

(62) **Hostal Alhambra ** J11
6 C/ de Espoz y Mina, **t** *91 521 31 14,*
f *91 532 70 78,* **w** *www.hostal*
alhambra.com; **metro** *Sol.*
Sadly the hotel doesn't quite live up to its grand name and the entrance hall is discouragingly shabby. However, the tiles in the bathrooms are remarkably evocative of the great Granada institution. All rooms have air-con, private bath and TV – something you can't say for the Alhambra.

(83) **Hostal Biarritz ** J11
2 C/ de Victoria, **t** *91 521 92 12,*
f *91 522 19 01.*
Light airy hostal with good-size rooms, some with balconies and in an excellent position for restaurants, nightlife and shopping.

(78) **Hostal Cervantes ** K12
34 C/ de Cervantes, 2°, **t** *91 429 83*
65, **f** *91 429 27 45;* **metro** *Antón Martín.*
In a quieter side street close to the buzzy nightlife of the Huertas and Santa Ana area, an easy-going ambience is the tonic in this small, owner-managed hotel. Recently reformed, the rooms have plenty of natural light, en-suite bath and TV. There is also Internet access available for guests.

(89) **Hostal Dulcinea** K12
19 C/ de Cervantes, 2°, **t** *91 429 93*
09, **f** *91 369 25 69,* **e** *donato@tele*
line.es; **metro** *Antón Martín.*
Great old building with a vast lobby dominated by a wonderfully old-fashioned (and fully functional!) wrought-iron elevator. All rooms have bath and TV, just like at its sister hostal across the street, the Corbero.

(84) **Hostal Lido ** J11
5 C/ de Echegaray, 2°, **t** *91 429 62 07.*
There are ten sparkling rooms at this excellent value hostal on one of Madrid's most happening streets. There are en-suite baths, heating (and fans) and fridges, which make it a favourite for those travelling on the cheap, especially with singles costing just €23.

(63) **Hostal San Isidro** J12
17 C/ del Príncipe, **t** *91 429 15 91,* **f** *91*
429 58 55, **e** *info@hostalsanisidro*
.com, **w** *www.hostalsanisidro.com.*
There are shiny wood floors and dollhouse-style bedframes and bedspreads in this sweet inn, in the middle of one of Santa Ana's main thoroughfares. All rooms have private bath, TV and air-con.

(64) **Hostal Tineo** J11
6 C/ de Victoria, **t** *91 521 49 43,*
e *info@hostaltineo.com,* **w** *www*
.hostaltineo.com; **metro** *Sol.*
Typical musty Spanish hostal décor, with unbearably shiny bedspreads, but the location and price make it worth it. Rooms have private bath and TV, and there's a laundry service.

(69) **Hotel Santander ** J11
1 C/ de Echegaray, **t** *91 429 95 51,*
f *91 369 10 78;* **metro** *Sevilla or Sol.*
High-ceilings, a jumble of furniture from all over and the light-filled, although sometimes noisy, exterior rooms make the Santander a firm favourite of many budget travellers. Obliging staff and a great location close to shops and bars mean it's best to call ahead and reserve. All rooms have TV, telephone, air-con and safe. Additional facilities include fax, laundry and room services.

(88) **HSR Corberó ** K12
34 C/ de Cervantes, 1°izqda, **t** *91 429*
41 71, **f** *91 369 25 69,* **e** *donato@*
hostalcorbero.com, **w** *www.hostal*
corbero.com; **metro** *Banco*
de España.
Better than most in this price range with good-size doubles.

(65) **HSR Maria Raloba** ** J11
8 C/ de Espoz y Mina, 3°, t 91 532 43
03; *metro* Sol.
Probably the best-value option in
this area, with new owners and a
new name. The rooms are large
with fabulous balconies, giving
views, opposite, of rooftop
gardens and, down the street to
the left, the Puerta del Sol's landmark Tío Pepe advert.

(60) **HSR Vetusta** * J12
3 C/ de Huertas, 1°, t 91 429 64 04;
metro Sol.
This hotel has a balcony dripping
with greenery and good-size
rooms with functional, if boxy,
built-in bathrooms.

Cheap

(72) **Hostal Madrazo** K11
10 C/ de los Madrazo, 1°, t 91 429 45
75; *metro* Banco de España.
In a tranquil, elegant neighbourhood, this hostal is bare-bones,
but the quality–price ratio is
astounding. Rooms with or
without bath. Guests have use of
dining facilities and microwave.

La Latina, Embajadores and Lavapiés

(59) **Hostal La Vera** * J12
21 C/ de Magdalena, 2°dcha, t/f 91
369 17 38; *metro* Antón Martín.
Inexpensive.
In a picturesque building once
owned by the cousin of the Duque
de Alba, this hostel is sweet and
homey, with a teeny living room
and equally teeny rooms. Try to
avoid the interior rooms without
windows and request one looking
out on to bustling C/ de
Magdalena.

(87) **Hostal Oriente** ** H11
23 Calle Arenal, 1°, t 91 548 03 14,
f 91 547 84 53, w www.
hostaloriente.com.
A bright, squeaky clean hostal
right off the lively Plaza Isabel 11.
The rooms are reasonably sized
and facilities include TV, telephone,
safe-deposit box and air-con.

(58) **Hotel Reyes Católicos** ***
G12
18 C/ del Angel, t 91 365 86 00, f 91
365 98 67, w www.reyescatolicos
.com; *metro* Puerta de Toledo.
Moderate.
Set in a pleasant old neighbourhood near the centre; small,
personal, and a good bargain for
the services offered, which include
a café, fax service, car rental,
currency exchange and disco. All
rooms have air-con, TV and safe.

New Madrid: Castellana and Salamanca

Luxury

(21) **Hotel Adler** ***** N8
33 C/ de Velázquez, t 91 426 32 20,
f 91 426 32 21, w www.iova-sa.com,
e hoteladler@iova-sa.com; *metro*
Velázquez.
Ideal for travellers who want to be
near the shopping action, but
away from the traffic hub. The
building retains all its 19th-century
charm (try the suites with marvellous wrought-iron terraces looking
out on the avenue), but has been
completely refurbished inside,
with some nice touches such as
huge marble bathrooms, brocade
curtains and Regency furniture.
There's a bar and restaurant.

(9) **Hotel Emperatriz** **** M5
4 C/ de López de Hoyos, t 91 563 80
88, f 91 563 98 04, e emperatriz@
mad.servicom.es, w www.hotel-
emperatriz.com; *metro* Rubén
Darío; *wheelchair accessible.*
A deluxe hotel in a deluxe location. Facilities include currency
exchange, hairdresser and everything else you expect for the price.

(6) **Hotel Miguel Angel** ***** L5
29–31 C/ de Miguel Angel, t 91 442
00 22, f 91 442 53 20, w www.
occidentalmiguelangel.com;
metro Gregorio Marañón.
One of Madrid's plusher hotels in
one of Madrid's plusher, less
touristy neighbourhoods. With
two restaurants (one, La Broche,
has three Michelin stars), a

splendid summertime garden
dining room, laundry service,
health club (exercise bikes can be
delivered to your room!), pillow
menu, etc, it is high luxury.
Swanky, modern-style décor.

(12) **Hotel Santo Mauro** *****
36 C/ de Zurbano, t 91 319 69 00,
f 91 308 54 77, w www.
ac-hoteles.com; *metro* Rubén
Darío; *wheelchair accessible.*
Built as a palace late in the 19th
century, the classicism of the
public areas of this small-but-
perfectly-formed luxury hotel
contrasts with the contemporary
Postmodernism of the rooms.
Tucked away in a residential
neighbourhood, the hotel is
frequented by the rich and
famous who also like their privacy.
This is the hotel where David
Beckham and family stayed while
house-hunting in the autumn of
2003, reputedly running up a
€600,000-plus bill over 11 weeks.
Facilities include car park, swimming pool, garden and sauna.

(14) **Hotel Villa Magna** ***** M6
22 Paseo de la Castellana, t 91 57
75 00, f 91 575 95 04, w www.villa-
magna.es, w madrid.hyatt.com;
metro Rubén Darío; *wheelchair
accessible.*
The Villa Magna's modern – albeit
bland – surroundings are more
than made up for by the quality
service and facilities on offer at
this hotel away from the city
centre. The establishment of
choice for many visiting sports
stars and celebrities, the Villa
Magna is also home to one of
Madrid's most famous, and justly
so, restaurants, Le Divellec. Other
facilities include fitness centre,
business centre, babysitting, car
rental and limousine service.

(20) **Hotel Wellington** ***** N7
8 C/ de Velázquez, t 91 575 44 00,
f 91 576 41 64, e wellington@hotel
wellington.com, w www.hotel-
wellington.com; *metro* Retiro
Discreetly upmarket, and well-
placed for the expensive shops
that line Velázquez and nearby
Retiro park, the Wellington's

cess is based firmly on good fashioned service. Enter its nd portals and leave behind cares. Downstairs is the disco – unusual in Madrid – there is a swimming pool.

pensive

5) **Gran Hotel Velázquez ****
7
/ de Velázquez, **t** 91 575 28 00,
575 28 09, **e** velazquez@chh.es,
ww.chh.es; **metro** Velázquez.
old-world, smaller luxury hotel
seems a bit past its prime,
ugh weekend rates drop
siderably, making it something
splurge-steal. There's a
ndry service, satellite TV, car
k, currency exchange, bar
restaurant.

0) **Hotel Castellana
tercontinental ****** M5
aseo de la Castellana, **t** 91 700
0, **f** 91 319 58 53, **e** madrid@
rconti.com, **w** www.interconti
n; **metro** Rubén Darío.
eelchair accessible.
ular with business travellers,
hotel is perhaps the best
e at the top end of the scale.
best rooms overlook the inte-
garden, itself one of the
tal's best-kept secrets, with
jazz in summer. The rooftop
-terrace-bar offers wonderful
vs. Other facilities include a
aurant, babysitting, gym,
ort transfer and laundry.

) **Hotel Melia
nfort Los Galgos ****** N5
C/ de Claudio Coello, **t** 91 562
0, **f** 91 561 76 62, **e** melia
fort.galgos@solmelia.es,
ww.solmelia.es; **metro** Núñez
alboa; wheelchair accessible.
dern, comfortable, with excel-
facilities (parking, currency
hange, bar and restaurant),
certainly well-located.
usually for a Spanish hotel, it
has non-smoking floors.

9) **Hotel NH Alcalá ****** O9
C/ de Alcalá, **t** 91 435 10 60, **f** 91
11 05, **w** www.nh-hoteles.com;
ro Príncipe de Vergara.
ndly staff provide a warm

welcome at this popular hotel. The courtyard garden looked onto by the quieter interior rooms is a verdant reminder of the nearby Retiro. One suite has been given an ultra hip makeover by local designer Agatha Ruíz de la Prada. Facilities include car park,currency exchange, no-smoking rooms, bar and café.

(13) **Husa Serrano Royal Hotel **** M7
8 C/ del Marqués de Villamejor, **t** 91 576 96 26, **f** 91 575 33 07, **w** www.husa.es; **metro** Rubén Darío.
If you want to be in the smart, Salamanca area, this is probably as good value as you're going to find. Part of the prestigious Husa Hotel chain, rooms are classily immaculate with TV, air-con and phone. There's also a bar, café and business centre.

Moderate

(17) **Hotel Bauza **** O8
79 C/ de Goya, **t** 91 435 75 45, **w** www.hotelbauza.com; **metro** Goya. Wheelchair accessible.
Slickly decorated in the Philippe Starck mould, this well-appointed hotel is suitably upbeat and modern, and offers excellent value. Facilities include in-room Internet access, laundry service, library and restaurant.

(5) **Hotel NH Zurbano *** L5
79–81 C/ de Zurbano, **t** 91 441 45 00, **f** 91 441 32 24; **metro** Gregorio Marañón; wheelchair accessible.
North of the centre, near to the shopping and office complexes which line the Paseo de la Castellana, this unabashedly modern, spacious hotel is popular with business people during the week. As a result, discount rates on weekends add up to a great deal for a break away from the usual tourist route. Facilities include babysitting, non-smoking rooms, bar and restaurant.

(18) **Hotel Rafael Ventas *** O9, off maps
269 C/ de Alcalá, **t** 91 326 16 20, **f** 91 926 18 19; **metro** Carmen; wheelchair accessible.

Bright, breezy and very modern, this hotel is near the bullring and attracts a number of *toreros*. The staff are very helpful. There's a car park, garden, swimming pool, café and bar.

(11) **Hotel Tryp Escultor **** L6
3 C/ de Miguel Angel, **t** 91 310 42 03, **f** 91 319 25 84, **w** www.solmelia. com; **metro** Rubén Darío.
This small hotel is fairly basic, but comfortable nonetheless. It is set in one of Madrid's most exclusive residential areas, not far from the delightful Museo Sorolla. There's an excellent restaurant 'Errazu' specializing in Basque cuisine, plus babysitting, car park and bar-cafeteria.

(16) **HSR Don Diego *** N8
45 C/ de Velázquez, **t** 91 435 07 60, **f** 91 431 42 63; **metro** Velázquez.
Located in a stunning building with wrought-iron balconies, the interior has had a welcome revamp and the rooms are cheery and quiet. The hotel is handy for El Retiro park and shopping. Facilities include a lively bar-cafeteria.

(22) **HSR Galiano *** L–M8
6 C/ de Alcalá Galiano, **t** 91 319 20 00, **f** 91 319 99 14; **metro** Colón. Wheelchair accessible.
The peculiarities of the Spanish system of categorizing hotels makes this a three-star hostal. However, this charming former palace knocks spots off most of the city's hotels with its intimate, old-world feel. There's a car park.

(7) **La Residencia de El Viso *** N5
8 C/ de Nervión, **t** 91 564 03 70, **f** 91 564 19 65, **w** www.laresidenci-adelviso.com; **metro** República Argentina; wheelchair accessible.
A charming hotel with 12 rooms in one of Madrid's poshest and most picturesque residential neighbour-hoods to the north of Salamanca. A refreshing antedote to the giant chains that dominate the lodging landscape. Built in the 1930s, it has been well adapted. With restau-rant, café and interior patio, where you can enjoy a quiet drink under the shade of a magnolia tree.

Gran Vía, Malasaña and Chueca

Luxury

(23) Hotel Orfila *** L8**
6 C/ de Orfila, t 91 702 77 70, t 91 702 77 72, e inforeservas@hotel orfila.com, w www.hotelorfila .com; metro Colón.
The only hotel in Madrid that belongs to the Relais et Chateaux chain, the Orfila is also arguably Madrid's most beautiful hotel, a sensitively converted 19th-century palacete. There's an idyllic garden, tearoom and restaurant. The décor is restrained luxury, with antique furniture, oil paintings and delicate silk wallcoverings.

(86) Intur Palacio San Martín ** I11**
5 Plaza de San Martín, t 91 701 50 00, f 91 701 50 10, w www.intur.com.
Two 15th-century noblemen's houses have been tastefully restored, retaining much of the original character. The result is fabulously plush and tasteful with wood panelling, stucco ceilings and a gracious central courtyard. There are non-smoking rooms, gym, pay movies and parking, and several of the rooms have stunning views of the city.

Expensive

(45) Hotel Emperador ** H10**
53 Gran Vía, t 91 540 06 57, f 91 547 28 17, w www.emperadorhotel.es; metro Santo Domingo; wheelchair accessible.
Home to the only remaining rooftop hotel pool in Madrid, commanding stunning views up and down the Gran Vía, the Emperador is at the heart of the capital's traditional shopping centre. Just a short walk from Sol and Plaza de España, its large, well-decorated rooms are much in demand all year round. Additional facilities include a bar (popular with locals), a café, gift shop, sauna and babysitting service.

(40) Hotel Gaudí ** K10**
9 Gran Vía, t 91 531 22 22, f 91 531 54 69, e gaudi@hoteles-catalonia.es; metro Gran Vía; wheelchair accessible.
A good choice for business travellers, this small, bright modern hotel has excellent facilities, including jacuzzis in most rooms and a gym.

(85) Petit Palace Londres * I11**
2 C/ Galdo, t 91 531 41 05, f 91 531 41 01, w www.hthotels.com; metro Sol. Wheelchair accessible.
The Petit Palace company has taken over several Madrid hotels and resurrected them as glossy boutique hotels. Each room is different and sports an upbeat, corporate look with lots of shiny light wood, tasteful artwork and plenty of extras, including IDSL Internet connection, double-glazing and, for those super-serious business bods, a trouser press.

Moderate

(31) Hostal Barajas ** J9
17 C/ de Augusto Figueroa, 2º, t 91 532 40 78, e info@hostal-barajas.com; metro Chueca.
More upmarket than most of the hostales in the area, it is still quite relaxed, with the fashionable neighbourhood of Chueca right on the doorstep. All rooms have TV, minibar and air-con. There's a currency exchange.

(41) Hotel Atlántico I10
38 Gran Vía, t 91 522 64 80, f 91 531 02 10, e h-atlantico@mad .servicom.es, w hotel-atlantico .com; metro Callao.
Of the Gran Vía hotel lineup, this is one of the nicer options, although the rooms could be a little floral and fussy for some. Facilities include babysitting, currency exchange, air-con, satellite TV, café and safety-deposit boxes in all rooms.

(44) Hotel Mayorazgo ** H9**
3 C/ de la Flor Baja, t 91 547 26 00, f 91 541 24 85, e mayoraz@global net.es; metro Plaza de España; wheelchair accessible.

Offers traditional, international if anonymous – comfort. Faciliti include restaurant, piano-bar, h dresser, gift shop, currency exchange and car park.

(37) Hotel Monaco ** K10
5 C/ de Barbieri, t 91 522 46 30, f 9 521 16 01; metro Chueca or Gran V
One of Madrid's most beguili hotels, the Monaco was former brothel, frequented famously by King Alfonso XIII. The atmosphe persists in a leather and marble lobby, where a neon sign points the tiny bar, and in the more ela orate of the mirror-filled rooms, complete with canopies and raised baths. Discounts for stays a week or more.

(67) Hotel Regina* J11**
19 C/ de Alcalá, t 91 521 47 25, f 91 522 40 88; metro Sevilla.
Almost exactly halfway betwee Sol and Cibeles, this hotel has a going for it: the gay scene in Chueca is just to the north, and the Santa Ana/Huertas bar scen just to the south. The hotel itsel modern and unremarkable, son rooms decorated with truly awf green satin bedspreads, but the common areas are quaint and well tended. All rooms have air-con, satellite TV and safe. There' ISDN hookup, a café, a restaurar with buffet breakfast and a laundry service.

(4) Hotel Trafalgar * J6,**
off maps
35 C/ de Trafalgar, t 91 445 62 00 f 91 446 64 56; metro Iglesia.
Popular for not being on the beaten track, this hotel has sim furnished, pleasant rooms with air-con and Internet connectio

(24) HSR Santa Bárbara ** K8
4 Plaza de Santa Bárbara, t/f 91 446 23 45; metro Alonso Martíne
On one of central Madrid's mos pleasant squares. It's a nicely decorated, friendly place with ju 14 rooms.

(36) San Lorenzo * K10**
8 C/ de Clavel, t 91 521 30 57, f 91 79 78, w www.hotel-sanlorenzo. com; metro Gran Vía or Banco d España. Wheelchair accessible.

beige bedspreads and
den fixtures add a nice touch
his airy, sparkling-clean hostal
ween Chueca and Gran Vía,
steps away from a plethora of
, restaurants and clubs.
efully renovated, retaining the
inal stonework, this pleasant
el is just off the Gran Vía, so
l for shopoholics yet within
reach of the Prado and
oric centre. The rooms have a
Regency-style look and the
teria has an attractive court-
-style setting. All rooms have
, TV, telephone and air-con,
cold drinks are available in the
ption area. Facilities here
ude a travel agency and
king. No Amex.

expensive

2) **Hostal Besaya** H9
/ de San Bernardo, 8°, t 91 541
6, f 91 541 32 07, w www.
albesaya.com; e hrbesaya@
ine.es; metro Santo Domingo
ember of the European
ependent Hostel network, this
no-frills spot with the usual
non-and-beige décor in the
ns, all of which come with air-
TV and phone. Some rooms
out on to San Bernardo and
tiled rootops of the area to the
. Coffee machine, message
rd and luggage storage.

7) **Hostal Domínguez** * J9
de Santa Brígida, t/f 91 532 15
metro Tribunal.
his simple but spanking-clean
tal above an excellent and
pensive Galician restaurant,
get what you pay for: simple,
like rooms with lace shower
ains, plus satellite TV and air-
in the upstairs rooms. Ask for
om that looks out on to pictur-
ue C/ de Santa Brígida.

5) **Hostal Don Juan** * J10
za de Vázquez de Mella, 2°, t 91
31 01, f 91 522 77 46;
ro Chueca or Gran Vía.
e you'll find a funky, zebra-tiled
r, velvet couch and big old
oire filled with books, but
, airy rooms with shiny tile

bathrooms, safety-deposit boxes,
TV and air-con. Other services
include luggage storage and
washing and ironing. If you don't
get in here, try the other hostales
in the same building.

(30) **Hostal Prim** L9
15 C/ de Prim, 2°, t 91 521 54 95,
f 91 523 58 48; metro Chueca.
On a quiet street close to
Recoletos, the Prim is ideal for
budget lodgings in an upscale
shopping neighbourhood. The
rooms have recently been refurbished with all mod-cons,
including air-con, heating and
updated décor.

(34) **Hostal Rico** ** J9
22 C/ de Fuencarral, 1°dcha, t 91 531
95 87; metro Tribunal.
Simple but clean, run by an elderly
couple, the rooms are large with
high ceilings and some have
fridges. Ideally located for those
in search of nightlife in Chueca
and Malasaña.

(25) **Hostales Sil & Serranos** **
J8
95 C/ de Fuencarral 2°, t 91 448 89
72, f 91 447 48 29, w www.
silserranos.com.
These two hostals are now under
the same management and the
rooms have been upgraded –
along with the price. Facilities
include satellite TV, air-con and
telephones.

(33) **HSR América** ** J10
19 C/ de Hortaleza, 5°, t 91 522 64
48, f 91 522 64 47; metro Gran Vía.
This is one of the classier inexpensive places at the noisy, grubby
Gran Vía end of the district, high
enough up for you not to be
aware of the buses thundering by
below. It has a clean, lived-in
atmosphere and a jolly, efficient
landlady. There's a TV lounge
and a sunny balcony off the
entrance hall.

(32) **Hostal Prada** * J10
19 C/ de Hortaleza, 3°, t 91 521 20
04, f 91 531 60 88; metro Gran Vía.
This family-run hostal on
Hortaleza has decent-sized,
spotless rooms with bath, TV and
air-con, plus an immense chande-

lier in the hallway. Ideally located
if you can stand the traffic.

(43) **HSR Hispano América** H9
63 Gran Vía, t 91 559 54 06, f 91 559
55 39; metro Gran Vía.
On the main hotel strip in a
craggy but still stunning old
building, and with some incredibly
diaphanous rooms looking out on
to the grand avenue below.
There's a huge green salon
lovingly cared for by the Chilean
owners. All rooms with TV, telephone and air-con, and, if you're
one of the chosen few, a painting
of Baby Jesus above your bed.

Cheap

(88) **Apartamentos Odessa** * K9
38 C/ de Hortaleza, 3°izqda, t 91 521
03 38, f 91 532 08 28, e sonsodesa@
retemail.es; metro Gran Vía. **Cheap**
Occasionally bills itself as catering
to gay clientele. Has a gloomy
reception and studio apartments
with kitchenette, bathroom
and TV. The reception area of this
hostal is filled with rainbows,
postcards and maps of gay
Madrid. Ho-hum rooms (with
bath). Laundry service, safety-
deposit box and coke machine
available to guests.

(29) **Hostal Almirante** * L9
4 C/ del Almirante, 2°, t 91 532 48
71; metro Chueca.
Slightly 1970s-style rooms (minus
the TV sets, which appear to be
even older), but the place is cute,
the owner nice and the price
is a steal – especially with breakfast included.

(38) **Hostal Corona** * K10
4 C/ de la Libertad, t 91 521 67 67;
metro Banco de España.
Slightly run-down hostal on a
perfectly picture-postcard Chueca
street. Rooms are small but sweet,
and those that look out on to the
street heave at night with the
neighbourhood nocturnal scene.

(39) **Hostal Río Navia** * K10
13 C/ de las Infantas, 3°izqda, t 91
532 30 50; metro Gran Vía.
The inside isn't quite as grand as
the outside, though the swooping

glass chandelier, little knick-knacks and carved wooden mirrors do help. Luminous rooms, some of which look out on to the street, others on to a reasonably well-kept patio. Rooms have a bathroom and TV.

To the West

(3) **Gran Hotel Conde Duque** **★★★★** H7
5 Plaza del Conde del Valle Suchil, t 91 447 70 00, f 91 448 35 69, w www.hotelcondeduque.es; metro San Bernardo. Expensive.
Located in a residential square in the Chamberí area, and frequented by well-to-do families, the hotel is a good choice for the traveller who prefers to see how Madrid really lives. The professional and attentive staff and pleasant, refurbished rooms are the selling points. Facilities include Internet access, currency exchange, fax in rooms, café and garden. You can lop more than a quarter off the price for weekend stays.

(1) **Hotel Tirol ★★★** F7
4 C/ del Marqués de Urquijo, t 91 548 19 00, f 91 541 39 58, w www.t3tirol.com; metro Argüelles. Moderate.
Slightly off the beaten track, and for that reason better value than many hotels only marginally more central. Spacious, airy rooms, clean, and close to the lovely Parque del Oeste. There's a car park, currency exchange and café. All rooms have air-con and satellite TV.

Apartment Hotels

(26) **Aparthotel Tribunal** J8
1 C/ de San Vicente Ferrer, t 91 522 14 55, f 91 523 42 40, w www.apart hotel-tribunal.com; metro Tribunal. Moderate.

A slightly unattractive, modern building on the outside, with bright, modern studio apartments on the inside, reasonably priced for the amenities, which include bathroom, kitchenette, direct telephone, satellite TV and 24-hour reception. Children and well-behaved pets are welcome.

Youth Hostels

Madrid is not exactly a youth hostel town. Of the three official IYHF *albergues*, two are inconveniently located – a hefty metro or bus ride for one, and a spooky Casa de Campo location for the other – and the third tends to be crowded with school groups. The pricing is standard throughout: €7.80 for those under 26 and €11.55 for those over 26. The price includes a bed in a dormitory room and breakfast.

(2) **Albergue Juvenil** G7
28 C/ de Santa Cruz de Marcenado, t 91 547 45 32, f 91 548 11 96; metro San Bernardo or Argüelles.
Often has school groups.

(48) **Albergue Juvenil Richard Schirrmann** F10, off maps
Casa de Campo, t 91 463 56 99, f 91 464 46 85; metro Lago.

(49) **Albergue Juvenil San Fermín** F10, off maps
36 Avenida de los Fueros, t 91 792 08 97, f 91 792 47 24, e albergue@ san-fermin.org, w www.san-fermin .org; metro Legazpi; bus No.23 from Plaza Mayor or No.85, 86 or 59 from Estación de Atocha; wheelchair accessible.
With luggage storage, bike rental, washer, dryer, towel and sheet rental and Internet room.

Eating Out

No place in Spain, except perhaps the Costa del Sol, can offer such a wide choice. Besides the country's best gourmet restaurants, you can sample the cuisine of every region of Spain and a score of other lands without straying half a mile from the Puerta del Sol. Most of the old well-known establishments are in Old Madrid and the Santa Ana and Huertas area. Surprisingly, thanks to the sizeable Argentinian population in Madrid, you can get a good pizza in many places. Vegetarians are increasingly well catered for (see 'Vegetarian Restaurants', p.234).

Between restaurants and *tascas* (tapas bars; see below) are *comedores* (literally, dining rooms), often tacked on to the backs of bars, where the food and décor are usually drab but inexpensive, and *cafeterías*, usually those places that feature photographs of their offerings of *platos combinados* (combination plates) to eliminate any language problem – some are self-service, and most tend to be dreary bargains. *Asadores* specialize in roast meat or fish. *Marisqueras* serve only fish and shellfish; if you take a day trip (see pp.185–204), try to visit one in the country on a Sunday lunchtime, when all the Spanish families go out to eat and make merry.

Menu and restaurant vocabulary are included in the 'Language' chapter at the end of the book (see pp.273–6). Note that, unless it's explicitly written on the bill (*la cuenta*), service is not included in the total, so tip accordingly. Tips are not normally generous by US standards – up to 10% is plenty.

Spaniards are notoriously late diners: in the morning it's a coffee and roll grabbed at the bar, then a huge meal at around 2.30 or 3pm, then after work at 8pm a few tapas at the bar to hold them over until supper at 10 or 11pm, if they eat supper at all. After living in Spain for a few months this makes perfect sense, but it's exasperating for the average visitor.

Price Categories

Price categories are based on a three-course meal without wine:

expensive over €30
moderate €15–30
inexpensive up to €15

Specialities

Traditional *madrileño* cuisine is a reflection of the cooking of Castile: roast meats and stews. The pinnacle of the capital's culinary arts is *cocido* (see our recipe, p.233) – part soup, part meat and two veg. The meal, chickpeas and vegetables are cooked in broth, then removed and set aside. Added to the broth are *fideos* (long spaghetti), which is then served as the first course of a *cocido completo*. In winter, most restaurants offer a *cocido* on their Tuesday *menú del día* (Thursday is traditionally paella). Even the capital's most expensive restaurants offer their version of the dish.

Callos a la madrileña might just convince you to give tripe a go. Cooked in a rich spicy sauce based on *pimentón*, or sweet red pepper, the tripe is manageable, having been cut into bite-sized pieces.

Despite its land-locked location, Madrid ranks among the world's main consumers of seafood and fish. Oysters are readily available throughout the winter months, as are all other manner of crustacea, shipped down overnight from Galicia, along with *pulpo*, or octopus, a firm favourite in the capital's bars.

Tapas Bars

If you're travelling on a budget, you may want to eat one of your meals at a tapas bar or *tasca*. Tapas means 'lids'. They started out as little saucers of goodies served on top of a drink and have evolved over the years to form a main part of the world's greatest snack culture. Bars that specialize in them have platter after platter of delectable titbits, from shellfish to slices of

omelette, mushrooms baked in garlic, vegetables in vinaigrette, stews. All you have to do is pick what looks best and order a *tap* or *canapé* (an hors d'oeuvre), or *ración* (a big helping) if it looks really good. Occasionally, you w see the word *porción* on a men which means even bigger than *ración*. It's hard to generalize ab prices, but on average €6–9 of tapas and wine or beer really fi you up. You can always save mo in bars by standing up: sit at th charming table on the terrace a prices can jump considerably.

Simply Spain Tours
t 91 474 32 93, e simplyspaintou yahoo.es. Offers tapas tours of Madrid costing €25 each for six people maximum.

Old Madrid

Restaurants

Expensive

(41) **Botín** H12
17 C/ de los Cuchilleros, *t 91 366 17, t 91 366 30 26; metro Sol. Ope daily 1–4 and 8–midnight.* Hemingway called it 'the best restaurant in the world' no less According to the *Guinness Book Records*, it is the oldest restaura in the world, founded in 1725; 19 year-old Goya worked in the evening washing dishes here, a it even features, as the plaque says, in a scene in the classic 19th-century novel about Mad *Fortunata y Jacinta*, by Benito Pérez Galdós. Justly renowned its beautiful original interior ar roasts, it is one of the priciest in the area, but the quality–price ratio is unbeatable.

(47) **Casa Lucio** H13
35 C/ de la Cava Baja, *t 91 365 32 metro La Latina. Open Sun–Fri 1–3.45 and 9–midnight, Sat 9pm–midnight; closed Aug.* *Booking recommended for dinr* Historic *mesón* serving up hear traditional *madrileño* favourite from *cocidos* to roasts. It's apparently Penélope Cruz's favourite restaurant.

) **Casa Santa Cruz** I12
de la Bolsa, t 91 521 86 23,
21 61 60; metro Sol. Open
1–4 and 8.30–midnight.
rvations recommended.
nally the parish church of
 Cruz, this restaurant is an
 site throwback to another
rom its fabulously ornate
ining rooms to the menu
ssic Spanish cuisine, which
des items such as suckling
, steak in wine sauce,
nokes filled with shellfish and
 traditional dishes.
aily *prix fixe menús* cost
er person.

Ene H12
del Nuncio, t 91 366 25 91;
o La Latina. Open daily
–1am.
 it hurts. Decorated with
ar sculptures, columns and
rs with a black, white and
neme. A chunk of crumbly
esan accompanies your drink
aciones include such fusion
rites as *tempura with pesto.*
d choice of mains like grilled
 with ginger and honey
e, and there's a blow-out
ay brunch for just €18.

Mal de Amores H12
e Don Pedro, t 91 366 55 00;
o La Latina. Open Mon
m–midnight, Tues–Sun 1.30–5
.30–midnight. Reservations
gly recommended.
ned chrome bar, exposed
 and mood lighting. The food
des creative salads, carpaccio
ers and sushi. This is the
 where chic *madrileños* take
 loved one (or potential loved
for a special night. The
ce can be a little snooty, but
verall vibe is worth it.

La Nunciatura H12
del Nuncio, t 91 366 25 91;
o Sol or La Latina. Open
Sun 1–4 and 9–1, Fri and Sat
nd 9–1.30. Reservations
ted.
ive Mediterranean cuisine in
ish but relaxed atmosphere,
contemporary photography
 e walls and the easy-on-the-

eye waiting staff dressed totally
in black. Starters include fried
goat's cheese and crab *croquetas,*
and main dishes are meaty –
lamb with quince, venison with
onions, duck with mango jam –
though fish and grilled veggies
are available.

(43) **Posada de la Villa** H12
9 C/ de la Cava Baja, t 91 366 18 80;
metro La Latina. Open Mon–Sat
1–4 and 8–midnight, Sun 1–4pm;
closed Aug.
Muy auténtico, both in the décor
and in the kitchen, where a wood-
fired oven produces succulent
suckling pig. Although popular
with tourists, the food is excellent
and the building spectacular.

Moderate

(11) **Café Lion** H11
4 C/ de los Bordadores, t 91 365 30
05; metro Sol. Open Mon–Thurs
1–4 and 8–2.30, Fri and Sat 1–5 and
8–4, Sun 8pm–4am.
Book a table here on Friday or
Saturday and, aside from the
excellent seafood, much of it with
a Catalan feel, you'll get the bonus
of soothing piano music you dine
into the wee hours.

(9) **Casa Ciriaco** G12
84 C/ Mayor, t 91 548 06 20;
metro Opera; wheelchair acces-
sible. Open Thurs–Tues 1–4 and
8–midnight; closed Aug. Amex not
accepted.
Founded in 1917, with a beautiful
old tiled bar for tapas grazing and
tasty traditional food in the
restaurant. The king and queen are
said to dine here. Try the paella.

(40) **Casa Gallega** H12
8 Plaza San Miguel, t 91 547 30 55;
metro Sol. Open daily 1–4 and
8–midnight.
Just off the Plaza Mayor sits this
traditional Galician restaurant
(there's another branch at 11 C/
Bordadores), which has been
packing them in since 1940. The
seafood is brought from Galicia
and, although the terrace gets
crowded in summer, it's worth
booking a table. The tapas are
also excellent.

Couples' City

For a special evening out, when
money is less of an object (or
you'd like to pretend that it is), try
one of the following restaurants,
picked for their intimate atmosphere or stylish food and décor:
Casa Marta (metro Opera; *see*
p.223), **Come Prima** (metro Sevilla;
see p.225), **Le Divellec** (metro
Núñez de Balboa; *see* p.229), **La
Fonda** (metro Retiro; *see* p.229), **La
Galette** (metro Retiro; *see* p.229),
Mal de Amores (metro La Latina;
see p.219), **Nicolás** (metro Retiro;
see p.229), **Thai Gardens** (metro
Serrano; *see* p.229), **Viridiana**
(metro Banco de España or Retiro;
see p.225).

(10) **Comme-Bio** H11
30 C/ Mayor, t 91 354 63 00; metro
Sol. Open Mon–Fri 9.30am–
midnight, Sat and Sun noon–
midnight. Reservations accepted.
This airy vegetarian restaurant
with soothing wood-and-tile
décor has an ample menu of
pizzas, salads and seitan and tofu
dishes, as well as a shop selling
everything from organic veggies
to soy yoghurt, fast sandwiches
and fresh juices to take away.

(56) **El Estragón Vegetariano** G12
10 Plaza de la Paja, t 91 365 89 82;
metro La Latina. Open daily 1–4.30
and 8–midnight.
El Estragón is vegetarian, with
some 20-odd tables distributed
throughout different levels. The
clientele is young, often expat,
and the mood relaxed. In addition
to a wide range of salads, you also
find curry, soyburgers, crepes and
pasta on the menu.

(84) **Emma y Julia** H13
19 C/ de la Cava Baja, t. 91 366 10
23; metro La Latina. Open
Wed–Mon 2–4, 9–midnight.
Locals flock to this Italian restaurant for its imaginative cuisine,
including such dishes as *ravioli
trufa* (ravioli and truffles) and ten
different salads. Located on one of
the city's most evocative historic
streets, the atmosphere is friendly
and intimate. Reserve in advance.

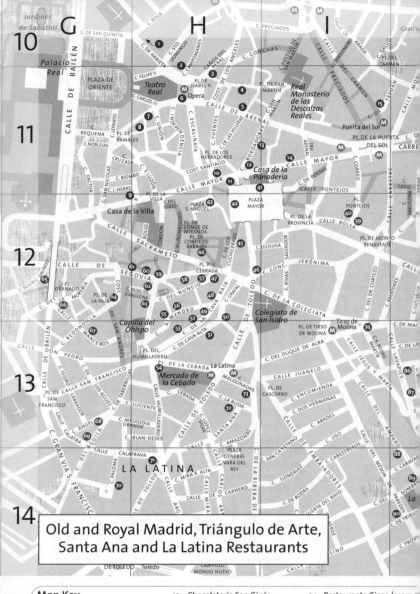

Old and Royal Madrid, Triángulo de Arte,
Santa Ana and La Latina Restaurants

Map Key

Map Key Continued

(85) La Musa G12

12 Costanilla de San Andrés 12, t 91 354 02 55; metro La Latina. Open daily 1.30–5 and 8.30–1.
A combo café restaurant and bar with free wedges of moist tortilla to accompany your apéritif while you muse over the menu. There's all kinds of healthy fare, such as fried green tomatoes with goat's cheese, four different salads, fried brie, croquettes and mini savoury-stuffed crepes.

(52) Palacio de Anglona H12

13 C/ de Segovia, t 91 366 37 53; metro La Latina. Open Sun–Thurs 1.30–4 and 8.30–1, Fri and Sat 1.30–4 and 8.30–2.
A popular, multi-level restaurant serving a wide choice of inter-national salads, pizzas and other dishes. There are also imaginative choices based on Spanish classics. It attracts a young, smart set. If you're looking for a quieter evening, ask for a table upstairs.

(58) Taquería del Alamillo G12

Plaza del Alamillo, t 91 364 20 88; metro La Latina. Open Tues 8pm–midnight, Wed–Sun 1.30–4 and 8–midnight. Reservations recommended.
This casual Mexican spot in a hidden corner of old Madrid is a favourite among *madrileños*. Specialities include *molcajetes*: stone gourds with sizzling strips of chicken or beef, which come with tortillas on the side. *Enchiladas en salsa verde* (green sauce), *quesadillas huitlacoche* (corn grain) and classic nachos with guacamole are available. If you're lucky, dinner is finished off with a shot of tequila on the house.

Inexpensive

(44) La Botillería de Maxi H12

4 C/ de la Cava Alta, t 91 365 12 49; metro La Latina. Open Mon–Sat 12.30–4 and 8.30pm–midnight, Sun 12.30–6pm. Cash only.
Quaint country-kitchen décor on a quiet stretch of one of Madrid's liveliest tapas neighbourhoods. Traditional *cocido* is served Friday and Saturday, and the *menú del día* of classic Spanish food is amazingly inspired and varied.

(45) Viuda de Vacas H13

23 C/ de la Cava Alta, t 91 366 58 47; metro La Latina. Open Mon–Wed, Fri and Sat 1.30–4.30 and 9–midnight, Sun 1.30–4.30pm.
This is the third generation of the Canovas family keeping Castilian cooking alive. Something of a mecca for the unpretentious foody – the restaurant has en-gendered many of the wine bars and restaurants which now popu-late this increasingly trendy area.

Cafés

(53) Café del Nuncio H12

9 C/ de Segovia, t 91 366 08 53; metro La Latina. Open daily 12.30pm–2.30am. Cash only.
A classic Madrid haunt, which spreads out on to the little pla outside in summertime. Their yummy milkshakes and sweet almond *horchata* (€3) are grea antedotes to the dehydrating effects of summer sightseeing

(13) El Riojano I11

10 C/ Mayor, t 91 366 44 82; metro Sol. Open daily 10–2 and 5–9, Oct–May; closed Sat–Sun June–September.
Just a few steps from Sol, this charming shrine to cream puff is nothing less than the purvey of fine traditional pastries to Spain's senators since 1885.

Tapas

(49) La Carpanta H12

22 C/ del Almendro, t 91 366 57 metro La Latina. Open Sun–Wed 11am–1.30am, Thurs 11am–2am, Fri and Sat 11am–2am.
Located at the epicentre of the weekend wine-and-*pinchos* scene, just off the Plaza de los Humilladeros, this young, lively bar offers a truly dizzying selec tion of wines (over 50, all excellent) and a wide variety of *pinchos* and tapas (beef carpac goat's cheese salad, wild mush rooms and pimientos, burgos cheese with anchovy garnish) pick at, either on the wooden tables and stools inside, or else outside, where the crowds spi out on summer weekends. Rea meals can be had in the restau ant in back, though space is tig

(14) Casa Labra I11

12 C/ de Tetuán, t 91 531 00 81; metro Sol; wheelchair accessibl Open Mon–Sat 11–3.30 and 5.30–11. MasterCard and Diners Club not accepted.
One of the oldest surviving ba tabernas in this area, founded 1860, Casa Labra gets a mentic Spanish history books as the s where the Spanish Socialist Pa was founded in 1879. Good tap especially salt cod *croquetas*, served on the original zinc counter, are another plus. However, if you are likely to bu

song after a couple of beers,
isn't the place for you – a
sque sign reads 'Prohibido
ar' (singing forbidden).

2) **Casa Paco** H12
*aza de Puerta Cerrada, t 91 366
5; metro Sol or La Latina. Open
–Sat 1.30–4 and 8.30–
night.*
of Madrid's classic *tabernas*,
nate and covered with
urful tiles, a good stop for just
pa or a dinner built around
ellent grilled meats. Around
–30 for the full whack.

---

urros y Chocolate

madrileño speciality is *churros*
ks of fried batter) dipped into
thick hot chocolate, generally
en for breakfast. Try one of the
wing places:

La Boutique del Churro, *67 C/
ndrés Mellado, t 91 544 57 27;
ro Argüelles; G6. Open daily
am–2.30pm.* Going for over
ears.

2) **Chocolatería San Ginés**,
*dizo San Ginés, 5 C/ del Arenal,
365 65 46; metro Sol; H–J11.
n Tues–Sun 6pm–7am.* At any
, but especially in the wee
ll hours, you can take
solation dipping a *churro* in
colate at this very famous
e.

3) **Muñiz**, *3 C/ de Calatrava, t
56 21 77; metro La Latina; H14.
n daily 6.30am–11pm.* A real
ghbourhood *churros* pitstop,
ect for pre-Rastro sustenance.

) **Valor**, *138 C/ de Fuencarral, t
48 44 24; metro Bilbao; I6.
n Sun and Tues–Thurs 8.30–1
4.30–11, Fri and Sat 8.30–1 and
–2.* This noted chocolate
nd from Villajoyosa finally
ned its doors in Madrid a few
rs back, and their thick,
ming hot chocolate, with or
hout cream, is best enjoyed
churros or their homemade
ond cookies.

---

(37) **La Casa de las Torrijas** I12
*4 C/ de la Paz, t 91 532 14 73;
metro Sol. Open Mon–Sat 10–4
and 6–10.30; closed Aug.*
An atmospheric blast from the
past with a colourful tiled and
mirrored bar. There's a fine
selection of wines and a rarity –
torrijas, sweet bread fritters, a bit
like French toast but soaked in
wine and spices and dipped in
sugar before they're fried.
Savoury tapas, too.

(95) **Entretapas y Vinos** H11
*31 C/Major, t 91 365 90 10; metro
Sol. Open daily 9.30-midnight.*
A smarter-than-most tapas bar
with cutting-edge décor of
exposed steel pipes coupled with
rustic wooden tables and chairs.
Plenty of tabla tapas choice so
ideal for large families or groups.
Smaller morsels include sauteed
shrimps with garlic mayonnaise
and watercress salad. Wine is
served in giant goblets and there's
an excellent choice.

(59) **El Postino** G13
*2 C/ de los Mancebos, t 91 366 58
40; metro La Latina. Open daily
noon–4 and 8–1.30. Amex not
accepted.*
An unassuming tapas bar in a
slightly less-trampled zone of old
Madrid. With things such as tasty
breaded mushrooms and shrimp
tortillas, the fare is a bit more
creative than your usual wine and
pinchos joint, though the old
standbys – *ensaladilla rusa, calamares*, chorizo – are also available.
On sunny weekends, arrive by 2pm
at the very latest if you want to
grab one of the outdoor tables
and bask in the shadow of
massive, ancient San Andrés
across the way. *Raciones* €5–9.

(39) **El Púlpito** H12
*10 Plaza Mayor, t 91 366 21 88;
metro Sol. Open daily 10.30am–
midnight.*
The least touristy bar on the plaza,
named not for its octopus
tapas but for the little 'pulpit'
tucked in over the Arco de
Cuchilleros, from where a friar
harangued the *madrileños* to rise

---

up on 2 May 1808. Try the
albóndigas (meatballs).

(54) **Taberna Chica** H12
*7 Costanilla de San Pedro; metro
La Latina. Open Mon–Thurs
9pm–1am, Fri–Sun 1.30pm–1.30am.
Cash only.*
A quirky, homespun bar with
cute twentysomethings behind
the counter. Modern chill-out
music and a relaxed, casual
atmosphere. There are free
Spanish classes on Mondays and
Tuesdays from 9–11pm; all you
have to do is buy a drink.

(50) **La Taberna del Zapatero** H12
*27 C/ del Almendro, t 91 364 07 21;
metro La Latina. Open Mon–Fri
1–4 and 8–midnight, Sat–Sun
1–midnight.*
One of the new breed of gourmet
tapas bars, with a delicious range
of inventive titbits including an
addictive *pisto manchego* and an
excellent wine list.

(38) **La Torre de Oro** H–I11
*26 Plaza Mayor, t 91 366 50 16;
metro Sol. Open daily 10am–1am.*
A noisy, hole in the wall tapas bar
lined with gory bullfighting pics
and (a rarity these days) a free
tapa with every drink with delicious *pescaditos fritos* (whitebait)
and other delights, served by
cheerful waiters.

(46) **Vinoteca Maestro Villa** H12
*8 C/ de la Cava Baja, t 91 364 20 36;
metro La Latina. Open daily
midday–4, 8pm–midnight.*
A wine bar in a handsome old
building, named after an old band
leader. There's a wide selection of
Spain's best vintages, by the glass
or bottle, with tapas and *raciones*.

Royal Madrid
Restaurants
Moderate

(8) **Casa Marta** H11
*10 C/ de Santa Clara, t 91 548 28 25;
metro Opera. Open Mon–Sat
1.30–4 and 9–midnight.*
Behind the Teatro Real, this intimate restaurant offers superb

service, a relaxed atmosphere and some beautifully prepared dishes, such as *el bacalao Marta* or *duelos y quebrantos* – a stew mentioned in *El Quijote*. Very reasonable prices.

(4) **Cornucopia** H11
1 C/ de la Flora, t 91 547 64 65; metro Opera. Open Tues–Sun 1.30–4.30 and 8.30–midnight.
Tucked away on the ground floor of a 19th-century palace can be found this gem of a restaurant. It's European cuisine with a slight American flavour, like an eight-leaf salad with raspberry-sherry vinaigrette with a colourful tiled and mirrored bar. The wines are affordable and good and there's a reasonable midday menu.

(3) **Entre Suspiro y Suspiro** H11
3 C/ de Caños del Peral, t 91 542 06 44; metro Opera. Open Mon–Fri 2–4.30 and 9.30–11.30, Sat 9.30–11.30pm. Reservations recommended.
One of Madrid's precious few restaurants serving *haute* Mexican cuisine, with truly authentic chicken in mole sauce, a variety of *ceviches* and rich, filling bean soup

---

Madrileño's City

If you want to watch the locals as you guzzle *cocido* and other *madrileño* specialities, or you fancy getting in with the in crowd, try one of the following '*muy castizo*' restaurants:

La Barraca (metro Gran Vía; *see* p.232), **La Bola** (metro Opera; *see* p.224), **Casa Ciriaco** (metro Opera; *see* p.219), **Casa Gallega** (metro Sol; *see* p.219), **Casa Hortensia** (metro Tirso de Molina; *see* p.227), **Casa Lucio** (metro La Latina; *see* p.218), **Gula Gula** (metro Gran Vía; *see* p.233), **Lhardy** (metro Sol or Sevilla; *see* p.225), **Lombok** (metro Chueca; *see* p.233), **Malacatín** (metro La Latina; *see* p.227), **Salvador** (metro Chueca; *see* p.234), **Azul Profundo** (metro Chueca; *see* p.235), **Tienda de Vinos** (metro Chueca; *see* p.234), **Viuda de Vacas** (metro La Latina; *see* p.222).

(*crema de frijoles*). Vegetarians will not be disappointed.

(57) **Terraza 'El Ventorillo'** G12
14 C/ de Bailén, t 91 366 35 70; metro Opera. Open Sun–Thurs 11am–2am, Fri and Sat 11am–2.30am.
One of the most traditional *terrazas*, with good food and tapas to go with the lovely views on to the cathedral and Parque de Atenas below.

Inexpensive

(1) **La Bola** H10
5 C/ de la Bola, t 91 547 69 30; metro Opera or Santo Domingo; wheel-chair accessible. Open daily 1.30–4 and 8.30–midnight. Cash only.
Known for its peculiar version of *cocido madrileño* – served in a clay urn – La Bola's old-world interior is very much the place for a hearty meal on a cold winter's evening.

(6) **Oh Pizza Mía!** H11
2 Plaza Isabel II, t 91 547 21 24; metro Opera. Open daily 1–4 and 8–1; bar-café upstairs open daily 9am–midnight for drinks and tapas.
Stills of Spanish movie stars cover the brick walls of this downstairs dining room, serving perfect thin-crust pizza and focaccia for pre- or post-theatre meals. The upstairs bar is a neighbourhood classic.

Cafés

(86) **Café del Real** H11
11 Plaza de Isabel, no phone; metro Ópera. Open daily 10–1am.
Attracts a gently bohemian crowd with its scruffily comfy atmosphere and great location smack bang on this pretty square. A great place for breakfast with all kind of fancy coffees, teas and delicious pastries to choose from.

(7) **Café Vergara** H11
1 C/ de Vergara, t 91 559 11 72; metro Opera. Open Mon–Fri 7.30am–midnight, Sat and Sun 7am–2am.
Welcoming, cushiony banquettes, mirrors and pretty portraits on the walls make this worthy of basking in the shadow of the Teatro Real across the street. Fine, standard

croissants for breakfast as well snacks such as tortillas and fille croissants (€4–4.75), and luscio cheesecakes and other sweets.

(2) **La Oriental** H10
5 C/ de Campomanes, t 91 541 83 metro Opera. Open daily 9.30–2 and 4–9. Amex not accepted.
A bright, happy, lemon-painted tearoom with an oddly Northe California flair. Stools and table front, and loungey couches in back. Homemade chocolate bonbons, marmalade and a wic selection of teas, from jasmine and English Breakfast to wild berry and minty green tea.

(5) **Viena Capellanes** H11
30 C/ del Arenal, t 91 559 53 97; metro Opera. Open daily 9am–9pm. Amex not accepted.
A branch of one of Madrid's mo venerable patisseries, it's busy a slightly impersonal, but perfect a pitstop when touring, and wit just enough sustenance – baby sandwiches (€0.75), croissants a other bits of *bollería* (€1–3), scrumptious cheesecakes and tarts (€2–5) – to keep you going

The Triángulo de Arte

Restaurants

Expensive

(71) **El Cenador del Prado** L12
4 Paseo del Prado, t 91 429 15 61; metro Antón Martín or Sevilla. Open Mon–Fri 1.30–4 and 9.30–midnight, Sat and Sun 9.30pm–midnight; closed Aug.
Delicious Mediterranean cuisin served in luxurious surroundin

(23) **Paradis Madrid** L11
14 C/ del Marqués de Cubas, t 91 429 73 03; metro Banco de Espa wheelchair accessible. Open Mon–Fri 1.30–4 and 9–midnigh Sat and Sun 9pm–midnight; clo Holy Week and 3 weeks in Aug.
Catalan dishes are served up in delightful old mosaic-tiled dini room. Good regional wines.

) Viridiana M11
*de Juan de Mena, t 91 523 44
netro Banco de España or
o. Open Mon–Sat 1.30–4 and
–midnight; closed Aug. Diners
not accepted.*
ough a symbol of the
omic boom of the late 1980s,
iana is no nouveau riche
gout. One of the best wine
rs in the capital, faultless but
eet service, and imaginative
:lassical dishes make for a
norable meal.

derate

) Restaurante Ginza K11
*za de las Cortes, t 91 429 76 19;
o Banco de España. Open
–Sun 1.30–4 and 8.30–
ight.*
e are more than 50 varieties
shi at this labyrinthine
nese restaurant. Downstairs
ushi bar with a conveyor belt
which you can grab the sushi
grabs you – once you're done,
empty plates are used to
ulate your bill. Upstairs is a
e, simple dining room with
y Japanese flower arrange-
ts, thanks to the owner's
ection with the local Floral
ssociation.

xpensive

) La Mazorca M14
*seo de Infanta Isabel, t 91 501
; metro Atocha. Open Tues–
.30–4 and 9–11.30, Sun
-4pm.*
mely vegetarian place
a chimney which offers
od respite from the hustle
bustle of the nearby Reina
a museum.

fés

) Ritz L11
*za de la Lealtad, t 91 521 28 57;
o Banco de España. Open for
kfast 7.30–11am, for tea
-7.30pm, for drinks and snacks
am–1am.*
per yourself at Madrid's
hest outdoor tearooms in the
ens of the Hotel Ritz.

Tapas

(87) El Brillante L14
*7 Calle del Doctor Drumén, no
phone; metro Atocha. Open
Mon–Sat 1pm–midnight.*
Handily situated just around the
corner from the Reina Sofía and
one of the best places to grab a
tasty and cheap *bocadillo* in
between the cultural cruising.

Santa Ana and Huertas

Restaurants

Expensive

(30) Come Prima J12
*27 C/ de Echegaray, t 91 420 30 42;
metro Sevilla. Open Tues–Sat
1.30–4 and 9–midnight, Mon
9pm–midnight. Reservations
recommended.*
A giant step up from Madrid's
often uninspiring Italian offerings,
Come Prima imported a chef from
London's famed San Lorenzo to
dream up a mouthwatering menu
from all over Italy: *vitello tonato*,
risotto selvatico (wild mushroom
risotto), prawn brochettes in mint
sauce, as well as pasta and meat
dishes. The elegant Italian-country
décor and fashionably dressed
fellow diners make it a great place
for a night out.

(20) Errota-zar K11
*3 C/ de los Jovellanos, t 91 531 25 64;
metro Banco de España. Open
Mon–Sat 1–4 and 9–midnight.*
A family-run restaurant located on
the second floor of the Casa Vasca
(Basque House), which feels like a
Basque version of the Rotary Club,
homey but elegant, decorated in
soothing tones of green. The
Olano clan serves dishes from the
region of Guipúzcoa such as
bacalao al pil-pil, white beans
from Tolosa, warm prawn salad
and, of course, *txacoli*, the light,
tart white wine native to
Guipúzcoa. Try the *trufas* (truffles)
in season.

(16) Lhardy J11
*8 Carrera de San Jerónimo, t 91 522
22 07; metro Sol or Sevilla. Open
Mon–Sat 1–3.30 and 8.30–11, Sun
1–3.30pm.*
A Madrid institution (see p.124),
founded in 1839 and nearly
unchanged. The dining rooms
upstairs feature French and *muy
castizo madrileño* cuisine.
Downstairs, clients help themselves and select sweet or savoury
delicacies, then pay at the door.

Moderate

(18) Al Natural K11
*11 C/ de Zorrilla, t 91 369 47 09;
metro Banco de España. Open Mon–
Sat 1–4 and 9–midnight, Sun 1–4pm.*
A macrobiotic and vegetarian
restaurant with a homey atmosphere serving tasty fresh dishes
like corn pancakes with savoury
fillings, mushroom stroganoff and
judías verdes con piñones (green
beans with pignoli nuts). There's a
yummy selection of sweet and
savoury fare to take away. The
weekday three-course *menú* is €10.

(17) La Ancha K11
*7 C/ de Zorrilla, t 91 429 81 86;
metro Banco de España. Open
Mon–Sat 1.30–4 and 8.30–11.30.*
Chances are you'll be rubbing
shoulders with an errant MP
taking it easy after a hard day at
the nearby Parliament. The
formula is simple: impeccable
service, the finest ingredients and
wines, and dishes that know their
limits, based on traditional cuisine.

(88) Asia Society K12
*37 C/ de Lope de Vega, t 91 429 92 92;
metro Antón Martin. Open
Tues–Sat, 1.30–4pm, 9.30–12.30am.
Booking recommended.*
Presided over by New York
chef/partner Jamie Downing, this
is genuine pan-Asian cuisine
(rather than fusion). The menu
offers a wide range of dishes from
across the eastern continent and
each dish has the distinctive style
and flavour of a single nation.
There are Thai-style rice cakes
with satay sauce, Mongolian
dumplings, Goan-style *masala*
and fabulous puddings, such as

banana fritter kebabs doused in chocolate sauce and ice cream.

(89) **Don Zoko** J11
3 C/ de Echegaray, t 91 429 57 20; metro Sevilla. Open Mon–Sat 1.30–4, 8.30–11.30.
There's oodles of noodle dishes to choose from here (14 to be exact), plus a vast range of sashimi and sushi. To avoid hours of dithering, order one of the *combinados* like the belt-loosening *makounouchi matsu* (which includes miso soup, tempura, sashimi, grilled salmon, grilled pork in ginger sauce, beef, vegetables and rice). The *yakitori* (chicken kebabs) are also superb.

(31) **El Caldero** J12
15 C/ de las Huertas, t 91 429 50 44; metro Antón Martín. Open Mon 8.30pm–midnight, Tues–Sat 1–4 and 8.30–midnight.
El Caldero offers rice and vegetable dishes from Murcia, and has been packing 'em in for 25 years. Bite the bullet and try the *picadillo de morcilla murciano con piñone* (black pudding and pine nuts).

(28) **El Tocororo** J12
3 C/ del Prado, t 91 369 40 00; metro Sevilla. Open Tues–Sun 1.30–4 and 8.30–midnight.
Here you can munch on tasty *tostones* (fried plantains), *ceviche*, *ropa vieja* (meat strips in seasoning) or chicken in mole sauce and other classic Cuban dishes. The surroundings are bright and friendly, with South American art on the walls. You can even finish your meal with a Cuban cigar. Try to book for a Saturday night when there is live music.

Inexpensive

(68) **Arrocería Gala** K13
22 C/ de Moratín, t 91 429 25 62; metro Antón Martín. Open daily 1.30–5 and 9–2. Cash only.
The splendidly luminous interior patio of Gala and their single-price menu of paellas and risottos has been drawing the crowds for over a decade now.

(15) **Artemisa** K11
4 C/ de Ventura de la Vega, t 91 429 50 92; metro Sevilla. Open daily 1.30–4 and 9–midnight.
One of the capital's oldest vegetarian places although there are a couple of non-veggie dishes on the menu. Too brightly lit for romance, but the food is reliably good. *Menú del día* €9.

(67) **La Biotika** K12
3 C/ del Amor de Dios, t 91 429 07 80; metro Antón Martín. Open daily 1.30–4.30 and 8–11.30; shop open Mon–Sat 10am–11pm, Sun and hols 1.30–4.30 and 8–11.30. Cash only.
Tucked away between Atocha and Huertas for over 20 years, this plant-filled wholefoods eatery has a tasty and filling *menú* for €7.50 (always with vegan options), plus a cute shop with things like veggie *croquetas* and scrumptious carrot cake for takeaway.

(90) **La Finca de Susana** J11
10 C/ Caballero de Gracia 10, t 91 523 44 07; metro Sevilla. Open daily 1–3.45.
Susana's continues to draw the crowds with excellent food, great prices and stylish dining space with its lofty palms and white walls. The menu will suit the fussiest of folk with its vast choice of rice dishes, fish, veggie specials and salads. The *pollo con pisto y arroz* (chicken with ratatouille and rice) and *tempura* come particularly recommended.

(29) **Pizzeria Cervantes** K12
8 C/ del León, t 91 420 18 98; metro Antón Martín. Open Wed–Mon 9.30–1am, Tues 7pm–1am.
Tucked away on a cobbled street not far from the Prado, this centuries-old *taberna* was converted into a lively neighbourhood creperie by a friendly bunch of Argentinian exiles. Excellent pastas and salads (loads of veggie options) plus an economical and filling *menú del día* for €8.

Cafés

(33) **La Suiza** J12
2 Plaza Santa Ana; metro Sevill▮ Open Sun–Thurs 7.30am–midn▮ Fri 7.30am–1am, Sat 7.30am–3▮
Has fantastic displays of pâtis▮ and pavement seating where ▮ can while away the morning w▮ your *café con leche*.

Tapas

(27) **Bacco** K12
17 C/ de Manuel Fernández y Gonzáles, t 91 420 21 75; metro Sevilla. Open daily 7pm–2am. Cash only.
With a slightly more *modernil▮* décor (kooky spiral lamps) tha▮ most of the other traditional tapas bars in Huertas, Bacco serves a variety of excellent, creative tapas similar to those ▮ the Basque country. Treats suc▮ fresh tuna with pimientos, cla▮ crab salad and mozzarella-and▮ tomato tapas come in canapé ▮ as *pinchos* (€2–3 a pop). *Racior▮* such as goat's cheese with zucchini and the classic tortill▮ also on offer for €7–10.

(35) **Las Bravas** J12
3 C/ de Alvarez Gato, t 91 532 2▮ metro Sol. Open daily 11–3.30 a▮ 7.30–2.
Nothing less than an institutio▮ with three branches. The nam▮ comes from the hot sauces poured liberally on their deep-fried potato chunks. The ideal stopping-off point to take on ▮ carbohydrates as you make yo▮ way through the many bars dotted around the Santa Ana a▮

(34) **La Casa del Abuelo** J11
12 C/ de Victoria, t 91 521 23 19; metro Sol. Open Sun–Thurs 11.30–3.30 and 6.30–11.30, Fri a▮ Sat 11.30–4 and 6.30–1.30.
A colourful bar, founded in 190▮ and still famous for Grandad's sizzling shrimp.

(19) **Casa Manolo** K11
7 C/ de los Jovellanos, t 91 521 4▮ metro Sevilla. Open Tues–Sat 1–4.30 and 8.30–midnight, Sun▮ and Mon 1–4.30pm.

s tapas and *churros* in a con-
, old-fashioned atmosphere.

) Cervecería Cervantes K12
ra de Jesús, **t** *91 429 60 93;*
o Banco de España or Antón
'n. Open Mon–Sat noon–1am,
oon–4pm. Amex not accepted.
steins lining the walls give
lace a vaguely German feel,
te the bar's eminently
ish name and the lineup of
legs behind the counter.
e are splendid tapas, which
de dainty *tostadas* of grilled
rooms, salmon or smoked
€2.25), the classic *pulpo*
go (€10.50), smooth, melty
platters (€7.50 including
boar) and much more.

) El Hecho K12
de Huertas, **t** *91 429 95 90;*
o Antón Martín. Open
Thurs 1pm–3am, Fri and Sat
3.30am. Amex not accepted.
able, never-empty corner bar
e less-trodden end of
tas. Popular for its exotic
ails, wines of the week and
pés with dainty *pimientos* or
ovy and goat's cheese,
ng others.

) El Jaraiz J11
'le de Echegaray, **t** *91 369 48*
etro Sol. Open Mon–Sat
dnight.
of the new breed of tapas
selling *nouvelle* tapas like
efort and dates accompanied
ant goblets of wine. The bar
ormer *bodega* and still has
of atmosphere despite its
bed pine spruce up.

) El Salón de Prado J12
e del Prado, **t** *91 429 33 61;*
o Antón Martín. Open daily
-midnight.
he place to write that epic
etter, this sumptuously
nt café has live chamber
c on Thursdays. Food is of the
and delicious variety, like
ted salmon canapés and a
e of sweet treats.

) La Moderna J12
de Santa Ana, **t** *91 420 15 82;*
o Sevilla. Open Sun–Thurs
–12.15am, Fri and Sat
–1.15am.

Probably the best of the half-a-
dozen or so tapas bars which line
the south side of the Plaza Santa
Ana. Hemingway did not drink
here, which means that the
proprietors make an effort to
provide a good range of wines and
imaginative tapas.

(69) **Taberna los Conspiradores**
K12
33 C/ de Moratín, **t** *91 369 47 41;*
metro Antón Martín. Open
Tues–Thurs 7.30pm–1am, Fri
7pm–2.30am, Sat and Sun 1–5
and 7–3.
A curious tiny neighbourhood bar
specializing in tapas from the
region of Extremadura – delicious
cured and soft cheeses and hams,
plus *migas* (fried breadcrumbs
with sausage). Fun and airy
despite its microscopic size.

(26) **Taberna Dolores** K12
4 Plaza de Jesús, **t** *91 429 22 43;*
metro Antón Martín. Open daily
11am–1am
Tucked away, this wood-panelled
relic from the 1930s owes its
fame to the sublime canapés it
serves, alongside a beautifully
pulled *caña*.

La Latina, Embajadores and Lavapiés

Restaurants

Moderate

(60) **La Burbuja Que Ríe** G13
16 C/ del Ángel, **t** *91 366 51 67;*
metro Puerta de Toledo. Open daily
8.30–4.30 and 8.30–midnight.
The 'laughing bubble' presumably
refers to the gargantuan quantities of cider – albeit still – poured
here. Excellent-value Asturian
food and often crowded.

(73) **Casa Hortensia** J13
6 C/ del Olivar, **t** *91 539 00 90;*
metro Tirso de Molina. Open
Tues–Sat 1–5 and 8.30–1.30, Sun
8.30pm–midnight.
The emphasis is very much on the
food, so don't be put off by the
lack of décor. Asturian cooking at
its best, with a *fabada* – bean stew

– famed throughout the city,
served with traditional cider
poured from shoulder height by
the waiters.

(94) **La Cueva de Gata** K13
19 C/ Moratín, **t** *91 360 09 43;*
metro Antón Martín. Open
Mon–Sat 12.30–4, 8.30–midnight.
Painted a sunny yellow with a
19th-century brick-vaulted ceiling,
this restaurant attracts a buzzy
young clientele with its nouvelle
twist on traditional Spanish fare.
Try the *crepes rellenos de setas y
puerros* (crepes filled with oyster
mushrooms and leeks) or
gazpacho with melon. Doubling
as a gallery for local artists, the
paintings are for sale.

(64) **Malacatín** H13
5 C/ de la Ruda, **t** *91 365 52 41;*
metro La Latina. Open Mon–Sat
1–3.30pm; closed 15 July–15 Aug.
Cash only.
For a genuine Madrid experience,
book their renowned *cocido*
(€15 including bread and wine)
for lunch and ask what time to
show up.

(66) **La Recoba** J12
27 C/ de la Magdalena, **t** *91 369 39
88; metro Antón Martín. Open*
daily 9.30pm–6am.
A legend in its time and mere
steps from the Filmoteca, this
smoky little spot is possibly the
only place in Madrid where you
can eat a filling pizza at 4am. You
can chomp on *empanadas* (try the
meat-filled Argentinian variety),
salads and crêpes to the strains of
bolero, tango or whatever live
music is on tap for the night.

Inexpensive

(81) **Alchuri** K14
21 C/ de Argumosa; metro Lavapiés.
Small and friendly, with some
vegetarian dishes.

(79) **Casa Asturias** J14
4 C/ de Argumosa, **t** *91 527 27 63;*
*metro Lavapiés. Open daily
9am–2am. Amex not accepted.*
This little corner restaurant has a
lively bar scene, television on, and
friendly waiters serving solid,
good Asturian food in the surprisingly quiet dining room in the

Outdoor City

Eating out in the open is an option in the Spanish capital right through the year. Try any of the places around the lake in the Casa de Campo (metro Lago) for lunch, or one of the following restaurants: **Boñar** (metro Noviciado; *see* p.232), **Casa de Vacas** (metro Serrano; *see* p.229), **Currito** (metro Argüelles; *see* p.235), **El Espejo** (metro Banco de España; *see* p.229), **Ritz** (metro Banco de España; *see* p.225), **La Plaza de Chamberí** (metro Bilbao; *see* p.233), **Taquería del Alamillo** (metro La Latina; *see* p.222), **Terraza 'El Ventorillo'** (metro Opera; *see* p.224), **El Viajero** (metro La Latina; *see* p.227), **Matilda** (metro Serrano; *see* p.229).

back: try the *merluza a la sidra* (hake in cider sauce) or *fabada*, the classic Asturian bean stew. Excellent value.

(78) **Doner Kebap Istanbul** J14
9 C/ de Valencia, **t** *91 467 59 09*; *metro* Lavapiés. **Open** *Tues–Thurs 1–5 and 7–1, Fri 1–5 and 7–3, Sat 1pm–3am, Sun 1pm–1am. Cash only.*
Turkish delights abound in this spic-and-span kebab house, and filling, tasty falafels can be had for €3. Plenty of vegetarian platters are available for €2–3, but beware: the *kebab vegetal* is especially addictive.

(61) **Fausto el Paladar** G13
1 C/ del Aguila, **t** *91 364 56 40*; *metro* La Latina. **Open** *Mon–Thurs 12.30–5 and 8.30–11, Fri and Sat 12.30–5 and 8.30–1, Sun 12.30–midnight. Amex not accepted.*
This casual, friendly Cuban enclave on the fringes of La Latina is a great place to sip a mojito and dig into a plate of *arroz a la cubana*. Weekend nights, the walls shake with live music.

(80) **El Granero del Lavapiés** K14
10 C/ de Argumosa, **t** *91 467 76 11*; *metro* Lavapiés. **Open** *daily 2–4.30pm; closed Aug.*
A popular vegetarian lunch choice, with a *menú* for €8.50 and lots

of tasty things to choose from. Try the *calabines rellenos* (stuffed marrow).

(93) **Elqui** K13
18 Calle de Buenavista 18, **t** *91 468 04 62*; *metro* Antón Martín. **Open** *Tue–Sun 1–4, Fri–Sat 1–4, 9–midnight.*
This light and bright vegetarian buffet offers great quality and value. The décor is delightfully quirky and you can pile up your plate with all sorts of goodies, including stir fries with tofu, mushrooms and asparagus, savoury crepes, soyburgers and a tantalising array of salady fare.

(76) **Peyma** J14
C/ del Sombrerete, **t** *91 467 13 69*; *metro* Lavapiés.
A modern and busy bar-restaurant with outdoor seating and a filling €12 lunch *menú*.

(48) **El Viajero** H13
11 Plaza de la Cebada, **t** *91 366 90 64*; *metro* La Latina. **Open** *Tues–Thurs 1pm–12.30am, Fri and Sat 1pm–1am, Sun 1–7pm.*
A rare three-storey bar-restaurant serving delicious Spanish fare and pasta dishes (the ravioli filled with pumpkin in a light cheesy sauce is exquisite). After dinner, scoot down to the chill-out bar on the second floor for a *copa*. In summer there's a rooftop terrace for drinks and snacks.

Cafés

(72) **Café Barbieri** J13
45 C/ del Ave María, **t** *91 527 36 58*; *metro* Lavapiés. **Open** *Sun–Thurs 3pm–2am, Fri–Sat 3pm–3am.*
A beautiful old café, yellowed with age, with huge, Baroque wall mirrors and a civilized atmosphere. Soothing by day (symphonies play in the background and there are speciality coffees and infusions to enjoy over a newspaper) and quietly sophisticated and sociable by night, this café also offers occasional film-screenings.

Tapas

(62) **Almacén de Vinos** G14
21 C/ de Calatrava, **t** *91 365 36 4*; *metro* La Latina. **Open** *daily 11– and 7–10.*
One of the most atmospheric fashioned bars in La Latina, dres in traditional tiles, with equall authentic tapas, serving excell seafood and crisp, chilled *verm*

(65) **Café Tirso de Molina** I13
9 Plaza Tirso de Molina, **t** *91 42; 56; metro* Tirso de Molina. **Ope** *Sun–Thurs 8.30pm–1.30am, Fri Sat 8.30pm–2am. Cash only.*
A cavernous, atmospheric neig bourhood bar – the best of the bunch in this slightly down-trodden area – with humungo brick arched windows, stained glass on the ceiling and yumm mini-portions of paella served along with your drinks. Lunch-time menu €6.90, dinner €8.4

(75) **Casa Montes** J13
40 C/ de Lavapiés, **t** *91 527 00 6 metro* Lavapiés. **Open** *Tues–Sat noon–4 and 8–midnight, Sun noon–4pm.*
Easily overlooked, but one of t longest-running bars in Lavapi Genial Don Cesar pours some excellent wines, and serves fin tapas such as *mojama* (cured fish), anchovy canapés and de cate cured ham.

(77) **Taberna de Antonio Sánchez** J14
13 C/ de Mesón de Paredes, **t** *91 78 26; metro* Tirso de Molina. **C** *Mon–Sat noon–4 and 8–midn Sun noon–4pm.*
One of the landmarks of Lavap a friendly *taberna* founded by bullfighter in 1830 and full of taurine memorabilia. Excellen tapas or full meals.

(74) **Taberna del Avapiés** J13
5 C/ de Lavapiés, **t** *91 539 26 55 metro* Antón Martín. **Open** *Mo Thurs 7.30pm–1am, Fri 7.30pm– 2am, Sat 1–3.30 and 7.30–2, Su 1–4.30pm. Cash only.*
Located in an old ecclesiastic g in Madrid's former Jewish neighbourhood. The staff are

ually helpful – if you're lucky
might let you do some
ng before you select your
rage of choice. Tapas are a cut
e the usual: well-selected
ses from all over Spain
⊃–3 per *tapa*), and lovingly
ared salads (€3–5) are tasty
resh.

w Madrid:
stellana and
lamanca

staurants

ensive

) **Le Divellec** M7
* Villa Magna, 22 Paseo
Castellana, *t* 91 587 12 34;
*o Núñez de Balboa. **Open**
-Sat 1–4 and 8–11.30.
vations essential.
s one of Madrid's top
met restaurants, with a
ch chef who really knows his
Excellent seafood. *Menú*
nd €35.

) **La Fonda** N9
de Lagasca, *t* 91 564 40 44;
*o Retiro. **Open** daily 1.30–4*
.30–midnight.
oscale, quietly sophisticated
an restaurant serving such
atory Catalan dishes as
eixada (salted cod with
to, red pepper, onion, white
s and olives) and *escalivada*
peppers and aubergines), as
as a variety of inspired dishes
contemporary twists such as
spinach with ham, raisins
bine nuts. Fish stews are also
ciality. Perfect for an elegant
out.

) **El Olivo** M6, off maps
e General Gallegos, *t* 91 359 15
*etro Cuzco. **Open** Tues–Sat 1–4
⊃–midnight.
ok a Frenchman, Jean Pierre
elle, to make Spaniards
eciate the finer points of olive
Mediterranean cuisine at its
with Jean Pierre always on
to advise. Aside from the

myriad oils, one of the best selections of sherry in the capital.

(60) **Thai Gardens** M9
5 C/ de Jorge Juan, *t* 91 577 88 84;
*metro Serrano. **Open** Sun–Thurs 2–4 and 9–midnight, Fri and Sat 2–4 and 9–1. Reservations recommended.*
Winner of the Spanish international gourmet award in 2003, fronds, waterfalls and exquisite East Asian décor make this one of the sexiest restaurants in Madrid. The food is as attractive and well-dressed as the beautiful-people crowd that eats here. Spring rolls and *sate* are standard staples, but the more exotic the dish the better: try the chicken with mint and shallots in lime sauce. Curries are delicate and flavourful. Weekday *menú* €22.

Moderate

(52) **L'Entrecote** N7
70 C/ de Claudio Coello, *t* 91 435 35 17; *metro Serrano. **Open** Mon–Sat 1–4 and 9–midnight.*
Don't waste your time looking at the menu. Start with a green salad, move on to the entrecote, with the best chips in town, then pop next door to the Chantilly Patisserie for a cake.

(49) **El Espejo** L9
31 Paseo de Recoletos, *t* 91 308 23 47; *metro Banco de España. **Open** daily 1–3 and 9–midnight; café open throughout the day.*
Despite its location, and the elaborate (but fake) 1920s décor, El Espejo offers excellent food at affordable prices. There's a beautiful outdoor terrace in the centre of the Paseo de Recoletos. The *menú* varies according to the time of year.

(63) **La Galette** N9
11 Conde de Aranda, *t* 91 576 06 41; *metro Retiro. **Open** Mon–Sat 2–4 and 9–midnight.*
Dimly lit, vaguely Victorian décor, with velvet trimmings and candles. Think English tearoom gone mad. An endless menu offers everything from French onion soup and *croquetas* to delicate,

ladylike salads, meat loaf, tuna in pastry puff and decadent, scrumptious desserts such as cherry and apple cobbler. Tons of vegetarian options. Come at night – the romantic décor works best after dark.

(48) **Gran Café Gijón** L9
21 Paseo de Recoletos, *t* 91 521 54 25; *metro Banco de España. **Open** Sun–Fri 9am–1.30am, Sat 9am–2am.*
A legendary haunt of Madrid's intellectuals, the Gijón has been in business since 1888, and is still good for breakfast, a set-price lunch or afternoon tea or coffee.

(65) **Nicolás** M10
4 C/ de Villalar, *t* 91 431 77 37; *metro Retiro; wheelchair accessible. **Open** Tues–Sat 1.30–4 and 9–midnight.*
Unpretentiously postmodern, Nicolás keeps the food imaginative but based on sound principles of home-cooking. Eating here is a leisurely affair, so take your time.

(57) **La Taberna de la Daniela** P8
21 C/ de General Pardiñas, *t* 91 575 23 29; *metro Goya. **Open** Mon–Thurs noon–4.30 and 8–11.30, Fri and Sat noon–4.30 and 8–1. Booking essential; Amex, Master-Card and Diners Club not accepted.*
Don't even think of just turning up. If you want to enjoy one of the best *cocido madrileños* in the capital (and this is all they offer, aside from sea bream in the evenings), then you'll have to book. If you can't get a table, pass by to try the tapas.

(51) **Teatríz** N8
15 C/ de Hermosilla, *t* 91 577 53 79; *metro Serrano; wheelchair accessible. **Open** daily 1.30–4 and 8.30–12.30.*
See and be seen at this fashionable bar-restaurant, designed in 1989 by the French master of nocturnal architecture, Philippe Starck, who converted the interior of the Teatro Beatriz into a suitably theatrical and trendy refuge for the *barrio*'s gilded youth. The loos, with their marble slabs and mirrors, take the Marqués de Salamanca's famous flush toilet on to another plane altogether.

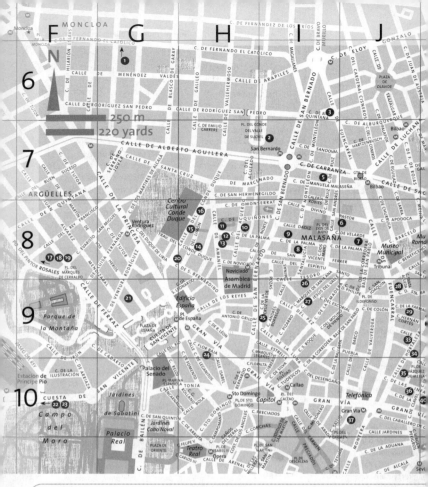

Glorieta Emilio Castelar

C. DE DIEGO DE LEÓN

New Madrid, Gran Vía, Malasaña, Chueca and West Restaurants

Separate tapas bar provides more down-to-earth eats.

Inexpensive

(58) Ketutín P9, off maps
47 C/ de Ricardo Ortiz, **t** *91 356 91 24;* **metro** *El Carmen.* **Open** *Tues–Sat 1.30–4 and 9–midnight, Sun 9pm–midnight.*
Just across the M30 ring road from the bullring at Ventas, Ketutín is very much a neighbourhood restaurant. Home cooking at its best, with the emphasis on roast meats, soups and other traditional Castilian dishes. The lunchtime menu, at €10, is unbeatable.

(68) Matilda N9
14 Callejón de Puigcerdá, **t** *91 435 89 37;* **metro** *Serrano.* **Open** *Mon–Fri 1–4 and 8.30–midnight, Sat 1–4.*

Interesting fusion-style menu including *langostinos al curry con coco y arroz* as well as more down-home US favourites like caesar salad and old fashioned apple pie. Regular wine tastings.

Cafés

(50) Embassy M8
12 Paseo de la Castellana, **t** *91 576 48 77;* **metro** *Serrano or Colón.* **Open** *Mon–Sat 9.30am–1am, Sun 9.30am–11pm.*
Since 1931 this has been the fashionable tearoom in this diplomatic corner of Madrid, with plenty of atmosphere to go with its little sandwiches or cocktails.

(64) Mallorca M10
6 C/ de Serrano, **t** *91 577 18 59;* **metro** *Retiro.* **Open** *daily 9.30am–10pm.*

Madrid's pastry shop and gourmet food store extraordinaire, with excellent coffee, fresh squeezed orange juice and adorable mini sandwiches (salmon and cream cheese, cured ham), quiches, vegetable tarts and croissants at the little bar. An excellent spot for checking out the local shopaholics taking a breather in between Armani and Adolfo Domínguez.

Tapas

(61) **La Biotza** M9
27 C/ de Claudio Coello, **t** 91 781 03 13; **metro** Serrano. **Open** Sun–Thurs 9am–midnight, Fri and Sat 9am–1am.
Long wooden tables with high stools, tiled walls and floors and exposed copper pipes give this place a hip-yet-earthy feel, and the tempting display of *pinchos* at the bar keeps it busy with a steady clientele of Spanish yuppies. Creative canapés include tuna with melted gouda, grilled mushrooms with shrimp and grilled pimientos with anchovies. *Raciones* cost around €4–9 and include the ubiquitous *croquetas* as well as more inspired offerings such as Vietnamese spring rolls.

(55) **El Cantábrico** O6
39 C/ de Padilla, **t** 91 402 50 42; **metro** Núñez de Balboa.
Excellent draught beer, with a variety of fresh seafood from, predictably, the northern coast of Cantabria. A great place to meet or to start the evening.

(59) **Casa Braulio** P9, off maps
43 Avenida de los Toreros, **t** 91 356 11 82; **metro** Ventas. **Open** Mon–Fri 8am–11pm, Sun noon–4pm.
A must if you fancy a quick *tapa* before or after attending the bullfights at Ventas, which is just round the corner. Braulio has been packing them in for 60 years, lured by the home cooking. They'll also prepare snacks to take into the ring.

(56) **La Tierruca** P7
55 C/ de General Diaz Porlier, **t** 91 402 87 69; **metro** Diego de León.

Open Mon–Fri 10–3 and 7–11, Sat and Sun 7–11pm.
Tucked away in the heart of Salamanca is this tiny bar with some of the best fried sardines and prawns in the capital. Every customer is treated as though a life-long regular. A great place to watch football, as the owners are Atlético de Madrid fans.

Gran Vía, Malasaña and Chueca

Restaurants

Expensive

(35) **Robata** K10
31 C/ de la Reina, **t** 91 521 85 28; **metro** Gran Vía. **Open** Wed–Sun 1.30–3.45 and 8–11.
Given that Madrid boasts the third largest fish market in the world (after Tokyo and San Francisco), little wonder that there should be so many good Japanese restaurants. Robata has a sushi bar, normal tables or a Japanese salon.

Moderate

(27) **Al Hoceima** J9
8 C/ de la Farmacia, **t** 91 531 94 11; **metro** Chueca. **Open** Wed–Sun 1.30–4 and 9–midnight, Mon and Tues 9pm–midnight; closed Aug.
One of the longest-established Moroccan restaurants in the capital, Al Hoceima offers well-priced dishes such as couscous and other North African specialities.

(36) **La Barraca** K10
29 C/ de la Reina, **t** 91 532 71 54; **w** www.interocio.es/labarraca; **metro** Gran Vía. **Open** daily 1–4 and 8.30–11.30. Reservations recommended.
An upscale *arrocería* which continues the high art of Spanish rice – paellas, 'black' rice and other delicacies are the speciality here, but regular meat and fish dishes are also available. The wine list is extensive and excellent. Menú del día €25.

(23) **Boñar** I9
14 C/ de Cruz Verde, **t** 91 521 260 **metro** Noviciado. **Open** daily 7am–3am.
A taste of León in the heart of Madrid. The portions are more than generous, with a good ran of quality meats and fish cooke simply but well. In the summer they put tables and chairs out the pavement.

(24) **Cantina Mexicana** I9
31 C/ del Tesoro, **t** 91 522 04 16; **metro** Noviciado. **Open** Mon–Sa 7–2am.
The first Mexican restaurant to open its doors here, back in 198 the *cantina* has built up a loyal following for its extensive rang of well-priced tacos and other Mexican delights. There's a sele tion of Mexican beers and tasty cocktails.

(47) **Ciao Madrid** K8
7 C/ de Argensola, **t** 91 308 25 19 **metro** Alonso Martínez. **Open** Mon–Thurs 1.30–3.45pm and 9.30–midnight, Fri–Sat 9.30–12.30pm.
An airy, relaxed Italian restaura with starters including delicate *grigliata de verduras* (grilled vegetables), ham and anchovy bruschetta and *mousse de parr sano*. The main dishes vary from classics such as *carpaccio de solomillo* and *saltimbocca* to inventive risottos – the *setas de bosque* (wild mushrooms) are especially good – and pastas.

(37) **La Cocina del Desierto** K
1 C/ de Barbieri, **t** 91 523 11 42; **m** Chueca or Gran Vía. **Open** daily 1.30–4 and 9–12. Reservations recommended at the weekend.
Exquisite Northern African déc complete with bronze chalices and handmade rugs and cushi and excellent North African dishes, from creamy hummous grilled pimiento salad, from me pies to *tajines*. The *menú de degustación* offers a little bit of everything, and is one way (for per person) to deal with the inevitable indecision.

Extremadura K9

de Libertad, t 91 531 89 58;
o Chueca. Open Tues–Sat
4 and 9–midnight, Sun
4pm.

ame says it all. If you want a
of this western, and still
ly remote, region, then this is
lace. *Migas* (breadcrumbs
bacon and grapes) and
er salads, backed up by roast
, and finished off with home-
orujo (schnapps) of varying
urs – with the addition of a
or a lizard in the bottle.

Gula Gula K10

n Vía, t 91 522 87 64; metro
Vía. Open Mon–Thurs 12.30–4
8–midnight, Fri and Sat
–4 and 8–2, Sun 8pm–
ight. Booking essential.
of Madrid's many gay
over successes. Drag queen
esses, loud, this is a place to
nd be seen. The food is good,
a set *menú*, or a salad bar.

El Inca K9

de Gravina, t 91 521 77 45;
o Chueca. Open daily 1.30–4
–midnight.

id is finally waking up to
ian food. Start things off
a fine pisco sour, and move
the house speciality, *cebiche*
seafood, marinated in lime
. There's a fine selection of
dishes such as *seco de*
ro – a lamb stew in a cilantro
– all at a reasonable price.

Lombok K10

de Augusto Figueroa, t 91 531
metro Chueca. Open Mon–Fri
nd 9–midnight, Sat 9pm–
ight.

sexy, minimalist restaurant's
to fame is its owner, Jesús
uez, the one-time host of the
ous trashy TV show *Gente*
hispa (People with Sparkle).
star-owned spot the food is
isingly excellent, the staff
dly and ambience downright
e, which explains how the
is still a huge success even
poor Jesús was rocked by
dal and lost his TV job in 2000.
ood is creative and eclectic –

Cocido (serves six)
Ingredients:
3 litres water
200g ham
500g stewing beef
1 marrow bone
100g salt pork
500g garbanzos, soaked
1 turnip, cut in quarters
1 small stewing hen
1 stalk celery, cut in sections
2 leeks, cut in sections
1 onion, spiked with 4 cloves
3 carrots, halved lengthwise
6 medium potatoes, peeled and
  halved
3 cloves garlic, chopped
salt and pepper
1 small cabbage, coarsely chopped
150g chorizo sausage
150g morcilla sausage
200g fine noodles or rice or bread
parsley or mint
a spicy tomato sauce
Method:
  Bring water to boil in a large pot
and add the ham, beef, bone and
salt pork. Skim off all the scum
that rises to the surface, then turn

down the heat, cover and simmer
for two hours. Then add the
garbanzos, turnip and hen and
simmer for another 40mins. Then
add the celery, leeks, onion,
carrots, potatoes, garlic, salt and
pepper, and cook until the vegetables are soft.
  While this is cooking, boil the
cabbage, chorizo and morcilla in a
separate pot, and drain. In a frying
pan, heat some oil and fry the
cooked cabbage.
  Strain the broth from the meat-
and-vegetables pan into another
pot and boil. Cook the noodles or
rice in it and serve as soup for the
first course, sprinkling a bit of
parsely or mint on the top. If you
use bread instead, cut into thin
strips, put in the bowls and ladle
the soup on top. For the second
course, cut the meat and sausages
into pieces and serve on a platter,
with the vegetables on a second
platter. Serve the tomato sauce
separately, to be added to the
meat or vegetables as each
diner chooses.

vegetable tempura, asparagus
quiche, black spaghetti with lobster
and garlic – and the desserts are
decadent and delicious.

(4) **La Plaza de Chamberí** K6
10 Plaza de Chamberí, t 91 446 06
97; metro Iglesia. Open Mon–Sat
1–4 and 8.30–midnight.
It's a delight eating outdoors here
on a summer's evening. They serve
traditional Spanish cooking with
an emphasis on fish.

(33) **Restaurant Zara** J10
5 C/ de las Infantas, t 91 532 20 74;
metro Gran Vía. Open Mon–Fri
1–4.30 and 8–11.30.
Great Cuban food, a friendly
neighbourhood atmosphere (if you
smile hard enough at the waitress)
and good frozen daiquiris.

(26) **Ribeira do Miño** J9
1 C/ de Santa Brígida, t 91 521 98 54;
metro Tribunal. Open Tues–Sun 1–4
and 8–midnight. Reservations
recommended at the weekend;
cash only.

A classic, bustling *marisquería*
with rushing waiters, and lobsters
and fish nets on the walls. Meat
and other dishes are available, but
the mind-boggling *mariscadas*, a
pile of every shellfish known to
the Galician coastline, is the must-
have meal here, served with bread
and cold white wine. Takeaways
are available.

(28) **El Rincón de Pelayo** K9
19 C/ de Pelayo, t 91 521 84 07;
metro Chueca. Open daily 2–4 and
8–midnight.
This intimate, delicately decorated
restaurant offers a variety of
carefully concocted Spanish dishes
(chicken in garlic sauce, vegetable
purées) as well as food for the more
adventurous (ostrich fillets, for
example). The daytime *menú* is €12.

(41) **Sarrasín** K9
8 C/ de la Libertad, t 91 532 73 48;
metro Chueca. Open Mon–Sat 1–4
and 9–midnight.
With its policy of a fixed-price
menu, (just €8 midday and €12 for

dinner) and a limited choice of dishes based on simple but tasty ingredients, this is one of the more enjoyable and affordable of the many (mainly) gay restaurants now flourishing in Chueca.

(22) **Vegetalia** H9
5 C/ de la Flor Baja, t 91 542 73 17; metro Santo Domingo.
A vegetarian restaurant with the emphasis on international cuisine. Try the wines made from organically grown grapes.

Inexpensive

(32) **Chez Pomme** J10
4 C/ de Pelayo, t 91 532 16 46; metro Chueca or Gran Vía. Open daily 1.30–5 and 8.30–12.30. Diners Club not accepted.
A mod vegetarian spot in the heart of Chueca, with appropriately green tiling and tables and Japanese-style lanterns. The *menú del día* is good value at €12 and includes a salad or purée of the day, plus an inventive main meal – spinach pie, rice-and-beans or vegetarian *empanada*.

(66) **Círculo de Bellas Artes** K11
2 C/ del Marqués de Casa Riera, t 91 521 69 42; metro Banco de España. Open daily 1.30–4pm.
Who would have guessed that in one of Madrid's grandest build-

---

Vegetarian Restaurants

Madrid used to be a veggie's nightmare, but things have changed and the capital now boasts a wide selection, many of them excellent value. Try one of the following:

Al Natural (metro Banco de España; *see* p.225), **Elqui** (metro Antón Martín; *see* p.228; Gran Vía, *see* p.232), **La Biotika** (metro Antón Martín; *see* p.226), **Chez Pomme** (metro Chueca; *see* p.234), **Comme-Bio** (metro Sol; *see* p.219), **El Estragón Vegetariano** (metro La Latina; *see* p.219), **El Granero del Lavapiés** (metro Lavapiés; *see* p.227), **La Mazorca** (metro Atocha; *see* p.225), **Vegetalía** (metro Santo Domingo; *see* p.233).

---

ings, in a giant chandeliered salon looking out on to the confluence of the great thoroughfares of the Gran Vía and Alcalá, you could eat a quite excellent midday meal for a set price of €10.50? A little-known secret, and the food isn't half bad: things such as *bacalao con pisto* (cod with mixed vegetables in tomato sauce), duck carpaccio and pork brochettes in sweet and sour sauce make it interesting. *À la carte* is pricier (€14–18 per person), but the site makes it worthwhile.

(69) **El Pepinillo de Barquillo** K10
42 C/ de Barquillo, t 91 310 25 46; metro Chueca. Open daily 1.30–5, 9–1am.
A gem of a restaurant hidden away on a fairly dull street. There's nothing dull about El Pepinillo, with its giant pickle hanging from the ceiling walls lined with wine bottles and dishes that range from snails and spaghetti to veggie dishes with panache.

(46) **La Mordida** K9
13 C/ de Belén, t 91 308 20 89; metro Chueca or Alonso Martínez. Open Mon–Thurs 1.30–5 and 8.30–1, Fri and Sat 8.30pm–2am. Amex not accepted.
A Mexican restaurant with brightly coloured walls, a huge mural *à la* Diego Rivera at one end, the Aztec calendar mounted on the ceiling, Mexican recipes painted on the tabletops, *ranchera* music and, of course, Mexican food. Specialities include *cochinita pil-bil* (spiced pork) and *guajolote mole* (chicken in mole sauce), but staples such as quesadillas, guacamole and tacos are also available. Festive, fun and reasonably priced.

(38) **Salvador** K10
12 C/ de Barbieri, t 91 521 45 24; metro Chueca. Open Mon–Sat 1.30–4 and 9–11.30.
A famous neighbourhood hangout that has remained true to its bullfighting roots since it opened in 1941. They serve stalwartly traditional, cheerful food including tasty *bacalao* and the omnipresent *croquetas*.

(39) **Tienda de Vinos** K9
Corner of C/ de Barbieri and C/ Augusto Figueroa; metro Chuec Open Mon–Sat 1–4.30 and 9.3 midnight, Sun 9.30pm–midnig
Not a wine store, but a renow scruffy restaurant, famous anc beloved for selling every dish a the same low price – hence its more popular name, La Comur

Cafés

(29) **Acuarela Café** K9
10 C/ de Gravina, t 91 522 21 43; metro Chueca. Open daily 3pm–3am.
Antique chic and a lively atmo phere at this trendy gay café. Wine, caipirinhas and aromati teas are on offer. It's especially convenient for shoe-shoppers is located right near the disco stores on Augusto Figueroa.

(67) **Café de Círculo de Bella Artes** K11
2 C/ del Marqués de Casa Riera, t 91 521 69 42; metro Banco de España. Open Sun–Thurs 9am–1pm, Fri and Sat 9am–3a
Madrid's celebrated fine-arts centre has a large café which looks rather like a ballroom bu one of the most relaxed places linger in the city centre. It has ostentatious *terraza* on the Ca de Alcalá which is open all yea

(44) **Café Comercial** K9
7 Glorieta de Bilbao, t 91 521 56 metro Bilbao. Open Sun–Thurs 7.30am–1am, Fri and Sat 7.30ar 2am.
North of the Museo Municipal and an institution among the locals and intelligentsia. It has cushy old leather seats for prolonged sitting and reading

(30) **Café Figueroa** J9
17 C/ de Augusto Figueroa, t 91 16 73; metro Chueca. Open Sun Thurs 2.30pm–midnight, Fri an Sat 2.30pm–2.30am.
Chueca's gay crowd favour this place, a chatty, relaxed late 19t century café.

Café Isadora J8
*de Divino Pastor, t 91 445 71
etro Bilbao. Open daily
-2am.*
é in homage of Isadora
an – her wannabes, along
art students, young hippies
ntellectuals, are the habitués.

Café Manuela I8
*de San Vicente Ferrer, t 91 521
metro Tribunal. Open daily
m–3am.*
Art Deco café holds story-
g nights and poetry recitals,
erves excellent drinks.

Café Ruiz I7
*de Ruiz, t 91 446 12 32; metro
ernardo or Bilbao. Open
Thurs 2pm–2am, Fri and Sat
3am. Cash only.*
end among *madrileños*. The
wood, mirrors and corduroy-
lstered banquettes are
stakeably Spanish, as are the
e fumes in the rooms further
Peaceful by day, crowded
oisy at night. All the typical
es, plus some intriguing ice
n delicacies such as the *tierra
ego*: chocolate and vanilla ice
n with whisky, hazelnuts and
nocolate (€5.50).

Mamá Inés Café J9
*de Hortaleza, t 91 523 23 33,
w.mamaines.com; metro
Vía or Chueca. Open daily
–2am.*
s the spot for those wishing
eck out Madrid's boy toy
p scene, right on the main
of the gay neighbourhood.
handy for sipping a coffee or
nd snacking on the baby
wiches and treats like white
late cake with raspberry
e. Good for bumper bacon
gg breakfasts as well. A fun,
dly relaxed atmosphere.

Zahara I10
*an Vía, t 91 521 84 24; metro
o. Open daily 9–1am.*
t, rambling and noisy café,
e you can surf through a
uccino while checking your
, bone up on the day's news
a pile of free papers or just
ck and people-watch.

Tapas

(25) La Copla I9
*1 C/ de Jesús del Valle, t 91 522 44
22; metro Noviciado. Open
Tues–Sat 1–4 and 8–2am, Sun 1–4.
Cash only.*
A homey but cavernous wine bar
in one of Madrid's older though
lesser-known neighbourhoods.
Aside from the usual tapas
(*croquetas*, etc), there is an excellent selection of tortillas with
varied fillings and a delicious
Andalusian-style *pisto pescaito*
(ratatouille with seafood).

(8) El Maño I8
*64 C/ de la Palma, t 91 521 50 57;
metro Noviciado. Open Thurs–Sun
noon–4 and 7.30–midnight.*
Known for its tasty homemade
tapas and very reasonable prices.

(43) Santander K9
*25 C/ de Augusto Figueroa, t 91 522
49 10; metro Chueca. Open
Mon–Sat 11–4 and 7.30–11.*
More than a hundred tapas, all
well priced. Among the highlights
are the *choux de langostinos* and
the cod chunks.

To the West

Restaurants

Expensive

(71) Azul Profundo K9
*8 Plaza de Chueca, t 91 532 25 64;
metro Chueca. Wheelchair
accessible. Open daily 1.30–3.15
and 9–11.30.*
Reservations recommended at
weekends. In the same hot spot as
the former Stéphane y Arturo
restaurant – so a lot to live up to.
Décor is similarly upbeat and
colourful and the set price €30
menu changes every 15 days and
includes a good variety of starters
– like hummous and almond and
mushrooms dip, followed by
primarily meat and fish mains and
predictably scrummy desserts.

(2) La Vendimia I7
*7 Plaza del Conde del Valle de
Suchil, t 91 445 73 77; metro San
Bernardo. Open Mon–Sat 1–4 and
9–midnight, Sun 1–4pm.*

Set in one of the capital's loveliest
and overlooked squares, this
Neoclassical celebration of all that
is best about modern Basque
cooking is an absolute treat. Try
the *txangurro*, a type of lobster, in
its many forms.

Moderate

(20) Casa Mingo F10
*2 Paseo de la Florida (by the Ermita
de San Antonio de la Florida),
Parque del Oeste, t 91 547 79 18;
metro Argüelles. Open daily
11am–midnight. Cash only.*
An authentic Asturian *sidrería* and
roast chicken emporium,
unchanged over the decades, with
plenty of outdoor tables.

(16) Casa de Valencia F8
*58 Paseo del Pintor Rosales, t 91 544
17 47; metro Argüelles or Ventura
Rodríguez. Open Mon–Sat 1–6 and
8.30–midnight, Sun 1–6; closed Aug.*
Rice rules here, with more than 14
different paellas, and a range of
fideuá (paella done with maca-
roni), all washed down with a
stunning range of cavas. The
lunchtime *menú* costs just €12.

(21) Currito F10
*Pabellón de Vizcaya, Casa de
Campo, t 91 464 57 04; metro Lago.
Open Mon–Sat 1.30–4 and 9–11.30,
Sun 1.30–4pm.*
In summer, this is quite simply the
best open-air place to eat in
Madrid. It's not bad inside either. It
might seem like a long trek from
the centre, but it's not that far to
savour excellent roast meats and
fish (or better still barbecued)
along with more modern dishes,
and all accompanied by
fine wines.

(72) Gumbo I9
*15 Calle Pez, t 91 532 63 61; metro
Noviciado. Open Tues–Thurs 2–4
and 9–midnight, Fri–Sat 2–4 and
9–12.30; Sun 9–midnight.*
Dedicated to New Orleans cuisine,
this restaurant has built up a
faithful clientele since it opened
in mid 2003. Owner, chef Matthew
Scot, is from New Orleans and
knows his stuff. Menu includes
gratin mussels, fried green

tomatoes, barbecued king prawns and pork chop stuffed with caramelized onions with peanut butter tart to finish. Simply decorated in mint-green and orange, there are daily specials and cocktails on offer.

(73) **Madrilia Restaurante** J10
6 Calle de Clavel, t 91 523 92 75; metro Gran Vía. Open daily 2–4pm and 9.30–midnight.
A classy new restaurant on a quiet street away from the Gran Vía bustle with minimalist décor and an imaginative menu. Dishes include a healthy choice of pasta, rice, poultry and fish dishes, some, like *magret de pato a la miel y al pomelo* (duck with honey and grapefruit), given the definite nouvelle treatment twist. Madrilia attracts lots of smart business folk at lunchtime. Get here early to ensure a table.

Inexpensive

(11) **Subiendo al Sur** H8
5 C/ de Ponciano, t 91 548 11 47; metro Noviciado or Plaza de España. Open Mon–Sat noon–5 and 7–midnight, Sun 8pm–midnight.
A little hippie haven, this place bills itself as 'more than a restaurant' as it is a co-operative whose profits are distributed among NGOs and worthy causes. The cosy, casual interior is littered with pamphlets, bulletin boards and magazines filled with alternative happenings. The weekday *menú* is an astounding €7 and offers things such as vegetarian lasagna, paprika chicken and dishes with an international tang. Desserts include homemade kefir and tropical fruit shakes.

Cafés

(17) **Café Bruin** F8
48 Paseo del Pintor Rosales, t 91 541 59 21; metro Argüelles.
Long established and excellent purveyor of ice cream and other refreshments, near the *teleférico*.

(15) **Café Conde Duque** H8
32 C/ del Conde Duque, t 91 541 01 49; metro Noviciado or San

Bernardo. *Open Mon–Fri 9am–midnight, Sat 3pm–2am. Cash only.*
A vaguely Hollywood-in-the-30s vibe with Charlie Chaplin posters and movie stills on the walls. Across the street from the mammoth Conde Duque arts complex, it serves everything from cappuccinos and other caffeinated delights (for example, Hawaiian coffee, a blend of iced coffee, ice cream and heavy cream) to daiquiris, screwdrivers and other cocktails, as well as canapés and snacks.

(10) **Café Moderno** H8
1 Plaza de Comendadores, t 91 531 62 77; metro Noviciado. Open Mon–Thurs 3pm–2am, Fri and Sat 3pm–3am.
One of the most pleasant places to watch the sun go down, on a traffic-free square with a playground in the middle. As the light fades and the children are bundled away to supper, locals mellow out over their *copas*.

(18) **Café Rosales** F8
36 Paseo del Pintor Rosales, t 91 547 71 66; metro Argüelles. Open Mon–Thurs 3.30pm–1am, Fri and Sat noon–2.30am, Sun noon–1.30am.
Elegant sandwiches and drinks, and outdoor tables.

(19) **El Jardín Secreto** G8
2 C/ del Conde Duque, t 91 541 80 23; metro Plaza de España. Open Mon–Sun 5.30–midnight.
An Asian paradise with rattan furniture from Indonesia, hanging lamps from the Philippines and teas from Ceylon, India and China. Plus homemade cakes and ice creams.

(13) **Mendocino Café** H8
11 C/ de Limón, t 91 542 91 30; metro Noviciado or Plaza de España. Open Mon–Thurs 9am–midnight, Fri 9am–2am, Sat noon–2am, Sun noon–midnight.
A San Francisco café magically transported to a cobbled Spanish lane: oil paintings on the walls (for purchase), weekly poetry readings, easygoing staff and even a Sunday brunch with pancakes and maple syrup or scrambled eggs (€10). Occasional exhibitions and other

Architectural City

For those who can't stop sig seeing even when they're eati the following restaurants are either set in lovely buildings o have remarkable décor, some cutting edge, some traditional
Botin (metro Sol; *see* p.218), (
Santa Cruz (metro Sol; *see* p.21
Círculo de Bellas Artes (metro Banco de España; *see* p.234),
Cornucopia (metro Opera; *see* p.224), **El Espejo** (metro Banco España; *see* p.229), **Paradis Ma**
(Banco de España; *see* p.224),
Posada de la Villa (metro La Latina; *see* p.219), **Teatríz** (metr Serrano; *see* p.229).

cultural activities make this a neighbourhood hangout for t local artsy types.

Tapas

(14) **El Café sin Nombre** H8
10 C/ del Conde Duque, t 91 54 72; metro Plaza de España. Op Mon–Fri 9.30am–2am, Sat 8am–3am.
In addition to pâtés, anchovy canapés and *empanadas*, you also find mango tea and baby quiches on the menu. Brick w display local photographers' v

(12) **El Cangrejero** H8
25 C/ de Amaniel, t 91 548 39 3 metro Noviciado. Open Mon, T and Thurs–Sat 11.30–4 and 7–1 11.30am–4pm.
A straightforward, unpretenti neighbourhood bar serving superb beer and mussels.

(9) **La Taberna de Corps** H8
1 Plaza de Corps, t 91 547 53 27; metro Noviciado or Plaza de España. Open daily 1.30pm–1a Cash only.
Though slightly grotty on the inside, this place has the grea fortune of possessing a quiet, relaxing outdoor patio with a great view on to the massive, gorgeous Centro Cultural Con Duque across the street. Plus has, arguably, the best *empanadas* (try the tuna with raisins) in town.

Nightlife

Madrileño Tipples

The *aperitivo* – a quick drink in a bar before lunch or dinner – forms an integral part of daily life in Spain, and the capital is no different. The traditional tipples of the capital are beer, sherry, wine and vermouth.

Beer should typically be served *al método antiguo*, which involves a fast initial pour, letting the *caña* settle, and then topping it up. The result is a creamy, refreshing glass. Unlike in Britain, beer is more expensive than wine. The most popular brand is Mahou (try Mahou Five Star if you see it), the local speciality, but San Miguel and Cruzcampo and Barcelona's Aguila can also be had – most bars sell it cold in bottles or on tap.

When a Spaniard invites you to have a *copa* (glass), it will nearly always be filled with **sherry**. *Fino* (dry, light and young – the most famous is Tío Pepe) and *manzanilla* (very dry) are the sherries of choice for the capital's inhabitants. Unlike the warm furniture polish which passes for sherry in Britain, *fino* is served ice cold, and typically accompanied by a couple of *gambas a la plancha*, or prawns. Other varieties are *amontillado* (a bit sweeter and rich) and *oloroso* (a very sweet dessert wine), which can be either brown, cream or *amoroso*.

Vermut is similar to Martini Rosso, and has been popular with the working classes in Madrid since the 19th century. It should be served *al grifo*, or on tap, in a small glass with soda and no ice, and can be found in the dwindling number of *tabernas* in the city.

Perhaps because of the poor quality of local grapes, *madrileños* have no problem in mixing red wine. The result in summer is the delicious and refreshing **tinto de verano**: red wine over ice and lemon, with a healthy measure of lemonade. Less expensive restaurants offer red wine and lemonade as standard with their *menú del día*.

Spanish **brandy** is extremely palatable; the two most popular brands are 103 (very light in colour) and Soberano, both drunk extensively by Spanish labourers and postmen as early as 10am. **Anís** (sweet or dry) is also quite popular. **Sangría** is the famous summertime punch of red wine, brandy, mineral water, orange and lemon with ice, but beware – it's rarely made very well, even when you can find it.

Each region has its wine and liqueur specialities and nearly every monastery in Spain seems to make some kind of herbal potion. The north of Spain, where apples grow better than vines, produces **cider**, or *sidra*, which can come as a shock to the tastebuds. Ground almonds whipped to create **horchata** are refreshing in the summer.

Spanish Wines

No matter how much other costs have risen in Spain, wine has remained refreshingly inexpensive by northern European or American standards. What's more, it's very good and there's enough variety from the various regions of the country for you to try something different every day. There are 30 areas in Spain under the control of the Instituto Nacional de Denominaciones de Origen (INDO), which acts as a guide to the consumer and keeps a strict eye on the quality of Spanish wine.

Catalunya is best known for its wines from Penedés and Priorato, the former producing excellent whites and some fine reds (try Gran Caus 87). One of the most typical Catalunyan whites is Blancs en Noirs, which, like the dry white wines of Tarragona, is excellent with fish or as an *aperitivo*. Some of the best sparkling wines (*cava*) come from Sant Sadurni d'Anoia, near Barcelona; Mestres Mas Vía can rival any standard champagne.

Navarra has some excellent reds. Navarra's neighbour, **La Rioja**, is the best-known and richest for wine in Spain, producing a great range from young white heavy, fruity reds; its *vino de gr reserva* spends five years ageir oak barrels and another in bot before release to the public.

In **La Mancha**, Valdepeñas is Spain's most prolific area; its young, inexpensive table wine are sold everywhere, and make even a potato tortilla somethi special. **Valencia** has some fres dry whites and a distinctive ro (Castillo de Liria). **Euskadi** is known for its very palatable 'green' wine, Txacoli, while **Galicia**'s excellent Ribeiro rese bles the delicate *vinho verde* o neighbouring Portugal. Other good wines from Galicia are Rí Baixas and Valseorros, pleasan light vintages that complemer the regional dishes, seafood in particular.

Bars

In Madrid there are more ba per square metre than any oth city in Europe, so there's alway somewhere to go, from belove ancient holes in the wall which haven't been decorated since time of Alfonso XII, to chic bou vard cafés, where the *madrileñ jeunesse dorée* discuss movies modern art.

First-time visitors to Madrid often surprised at just how lat the capital's inhabitants stay o In general, people go to *tascas* (tapas bars; *see* the 'Eating Ou chapter) or *tabernas* in the pos work hours for a beer and a *tap* or two, and then move on to *ba de copas* (bars that only serve drinks) as the night wears on. In the summertime, *terrazas* are especially popular, most notably those lining the Paseo de la Castellana north of the Plaza de Colón. Discos don't ev begin to get started until 1am at the earliest, which puts the 11pm dinnertime into a more logical perspective.

other feature of the capital's
tlife is the way certain areas
e developed a scene of their
, with dozens of bars within
king distance, all catering to a
icular social set or age group.
Spaniards are not as exclusive
he British: most bars still play
clectic mix of music, and few
y any sort of dress code –
pt for in the Salamanca area.
rule generally is to settle on
rea, and then wander from
to bar until the wee hours,
ng the revelries with a hot
colate before collapsing
bed.

r tapas bars (although many
e bars listed in this chapter
serve some tapas, too),
he 'Eating Out' chapter,
17–36. For gay bars see also
and Lesbian Madrid',
67–9.

erta del Sol,
aza Mayor
d Opera

ing the most touristy part of
rid, this area is somewhat
haracteristic of the city in the
ing, but there are some good
s. The Plaza de Oriente is a
utiful place to enjoy an
ant late-evening drink over-
ing the Palacio Real, and there
a number of discos within
reach.

rvecería La Plaza H12
za San Miguel, **t** 91 548 41 11;
ro Sol. **Open** daily
–12.30pm.
't be put off by the English
u, this is a lively local bar
looking the market with an
esting collection of historic
uit tins lining the bar and
ally) an even more interesting
ction of locals. The pisto con
vos (ratatouille with eggs) is
mmended if you get peckish
tween drinks.

Anciano G11
/ de Bailén; **metro** Opera. **Open**
s–Tues 11–4 and 6–midnight.
vermut on tap and, as

expected, a dizzying array of
wines. An old-world atmosphere
(if slightly overlit) on a shady
corner across the street from the
Palacio Real.

Café de las Descalzas K11
3 Plaza San Martín; **metro** Sol or
Callao. **Open** Mon–Thurs 4pm–
2am, Fri and Sat 4pm–3am.
Steps away from the convent of
the same name, this is a multi-
room lounge which was superhip
during the movida years and is
still something of a hangout for
the boho/artsy crowd.

Café de Oriente G11
2 Plaza de Oriente; **metro** Opera.
Open daily 1–4 and 9–midnight.
Located on top of the remains of
the San Gil convent, this is actually
quite a fancy restaurant, but the
bar scene outside is tremendous
on spring and summer evenings.
Perfect for whiling away the hours
before heading out to dance.

El Limbo G12
39 C/ de Bailén; **metro** Opera or La
Latina. **Open** Mon–Thurs 10pm–4am,
Fri and Sat 10pm–5am. Cash only.
A trip back in time to the 1970s,
with kitschy décor and an
eclectic, alternative scene offering
the occasional cabaret, art exhibition and anything else that takes
their fancy. Good trance music at
the weekend.

Palace H11
7 Plaza Isabel II; **metro** Opera.
Open daily 7pm–3.30am, cover
charge €5–12, including a drink.
In the bowels of the Cine Real, this
bar/dance hall offers dance sets
with a live orchestra as well as a
potpourri of oddball entertainment, including humour and
cruise-ship-style cabaret.

Palacio de Gaviria H11
9 C/ del Arenal; **metro** Sol or Opera.
Open daily 10.30–dawn, cover
charge €7–15.
A 19th-century palace turned into
a macro venue, its many salons
host a range of moods and music.
Attracts an international crowd.

Couples' City
For an evening à deux, these
bars have more relaxed atmos-
pheres and you can even hear
yourself think above the music:
Ambigu 16 (metro Plaza de
España; see p.244), **La Brocense**
(metro Antón Martín; see p.240),
Café Belén (metro Chueca or
Alonso Martínez; see p.243),
Café Madrid (metro Chueca or
Alonso Martínez; see p.243),
La Taberna de los Cien Vinos
(metro La Latina, see p.240).

Barrio de los
Austrias

Just west and south of the Plaza
Mayor, the neighbourhood radiating down the streets Cava Alta,
Cava Baja, Almendro and Segovia
are great for bar-hopping,
whether on a week night or on a
Saturday or Sunday afternoon. The
scene is mainly twenty- and thirtysomething, the prices slightly
dear, the tapas a bit more exquisite than usual. But lots of fun.

El Almendro H12–13
13 C/ del Almendro; **metro** La
Latina. **Open** Wed–Sun 1–4 and
7–midnight.
A neighbourhood legend, with
old-fashioned décor and castizo
atmosphere, although the crowd
is distinctly young and cute.

Bar Matritum H12
19 C/ del Nuncio; **metro** La Latina.
Open Wed–Mon 3.30pm–3am.
Cash only.
An airy, modern little bar with
gold-tinted walls and an upstairs
balcony looking out onto the
ancient church of San Isidro in
Madrid's oldest neighborhood. All
the usual drinks plus a good selection of world coffees.

El Bonanno H13
4 Plaza Humilladero; **metro** La
Latina. **Open** daily 1–4 and 8–1.
Despite bearing the same name
as one of New York's most famous
mafiosos, this is an oddly modern,

Movida

As novel as it seemed almost two decades ago, historians tell us that the *movida* was nothing new: in the time of Philip III, when Madrid was the capital of an empire, it was considered the second-best party city after Paris. If not sex, drugs and rock 'n' roll, there was plenty of sex, wine and boleros to draw in pleasure-seekers from across Europe. It was the start of a distinguished tradition. Sometime between then and now the *madrileños* acquired their nickname, *los gatos*, the 'cats', for their nocturnal habits.

Although you may well think Madrid still burns the candle at both ends, *madrileños* wax nostalgic about the boom years of the 1980s, when four decades of creativity and energy pent up under Franco suddenly exploded on the scene, and Madrid swung like a pendulum on speed and declared itself the capital of the world. The Socialists' hearty support of the arts and culture, the rise of a vibrant counter-culture, the general prosperity and good times, liberal drug laws, and the *madrileños'* own appetite for fun combined to make a heady decade of white nights. Their feet never seemed to touch the ground, as *la marcha* swept them from bar to bar in a frenetic cacophony of laughter, smoke and high spirits, recorded in the films of Pedro Almodóvar, the Pied Piper of the movida, and one of the very few figures to come out of the whirlwind with an international reputation.

The inevitable hangover began when the bills came due, even before Spain's great year of 1992 had ended. The Socialists were slowly washed away in a tide of scandal and corruption, the wilder clubs and bars were forced to close, and funding for the arts and festivals was slashed. The huge energy of the *movida* has split into various scenes, or *ambientes*, including a very lively gay scene that attracts trendy straights. The current right-wing administration, representing a Silent Majority who like to retire early, has been agitating furiously to squeeze Madrid into the mould of a respectable northern European-style capital, to the point of writing laws that would fine people for waiting for a bus outside a bus shelter, and closing down the bars at 3am. Fortunately no one pays much attention: the *gatos* are still prowling most nights until dawn, or well into the morning, only now they do it mostly at the weekend.

---

drinking and tapas spot. But in last few years there has been a veritable explosion of new bars opening in the little zone strad-dling Huertas and Atocha, farth away from the Plaza Santa Ana and moving towards the Paseo Prado. Tiny, atmospheric little b with oddball decorations and exotic cocktails mix in with exc lent neighbourhood wine-and-tapas bars which are far more authentic than their counterpa in and around Santa Ana.

Alhambra J11

9 C / Victoria, t 91 521 07 08; met Sol. Open Tues–Sun 10–2am, Mc 6pm-2am.

Easy to spot with its frontage o vivid Andalucían tiles, this is on of the oldest and most atmos-pheric taverns in Madrid dating from 1929. During the day, it's a fairly tranquil place serving dri and tapas. The flip-side is at nig when the bar livens up with *sevillana* music and dancing – despite the lack of elbow-room

Begin the Beguine K13

27 C / de Moratín; metro Antón Martín. Open Sun–Thurs 8pm–12.30am, Fri and Sat 8pm–3.30a Cash only.

With a mind-boggling array of old wine and liquor bottles, this is a curious spot and perfe if you don't have much to say t your companion. Just read the walls! Wine €1.50–2.50, mixed drinks €4–5.

La Boca del Lobo J12

11 C / de Echegaray; metro Sevill Open Mon–Sat 11pm–5am

This old-time cellar bar plays old-time music from the 30s up to the 60s, and attracts a cheerful, pleasantly mixed cro

La Brocense K12

30 C / de Lope de Vega; metro Antón Martín. Open Sun–Thurs 7pm–2.30am, Fri and Sat 7pm–4am. Cash only.

An eccentric little Victorian-inspired tearoom/*coctelería* wi lace curtains, wicker chairs, scented candles and frothy coc tails served in round tubs. A lo

---

unassuming bar which, for some reason, attracts huge crowds on weekday evenings and on week-ends that overflow on to the prime people-watching and hanging-out location smack in the middle of the Barrio de los Austrias action. An excellent starting point for neighbourhood bar-hopping.

La Taberna de los Cien Vinos H12

17 C / del Nuncio; metro La Latina. Open Tues–Sun 1–3.45 and 8–1. Cash only.

A great alternative to the equally legendary Taberna los Austrias (*see* p.223) next door, the Cien Vinos has plenty of wine and a carefully culled list of *raciones* and salads served in a quiet, calm,

more elegant atmosphere than its next-door neighbour.

El Tempranillo H13

38 C / de la Cava Baja; metro La Latina. Open daily noon–4 and 8–1.

A warm brick-and-stone locale with a mind-boggling array of wines – over 160 – from all over Spain, plus tasty egg *revueltos* and salads.

Santa Ana and Huertas

Huertas and Santa Ana attract the widest range of people, with bars to suit every taste. Plaza Santa Ana and the surrounding area is a famous and popular

xing spot where you can actu-
talk to your companion, with
sy music accompaniment.

afé Prado J12
*rado 4, t 91 429 33 61; metro
Open Mon–Thurs 2pm–2am,
Sat 2pm–2.30am, Sun
–1am.*
of the capital's best-known
with an evocative moody feel.
e are comfy, velvet seats,
ntive waiters and a pianist on
rsdays (at least) during the
er months.

rdamomo J12
*' de Echegaray; metro Sevilla.
n daily 9pm–4am.*
 jazz and modern flamenco
he music of choice in this
ular spot in the centre of the
ist hell of Echegaray. Yet
lamomo rises above the fray,
sionally attracting the odd
osito of the Spanish movie
music scene.

rvecería Alemana J12
*za Santa Ana; metro Sevilla.
n Sun, Mon, Wed and Thurs
am–12.30am, Fri and Sat
am–2am.*
rfect German-Spanish beer-
and one of Hemingway's
y old watering holes. It has a
nating display of photos and
r taurine memorabilia. Still a
favourite, despite being on
ourist trail.

Comedia J11
*' del Príncipe; metro Sevilla.
n Sun–Thurs 10pm–3am, Fri
Sat 10pm–5am.*
cation in the heart of the
a Ana district means it's
ys full, but a spacious interior
good-natured young crowd
es it a good starting-off point
he night.

Creazione K11
*Ventura de la Vega, t 91 429
'; metro Sevilla. Open daily
5pm, 8–1.30am.*
nt yet hip bar-restaurant
easy on the eye colourful
r set against original stone
. Livens up at night with an
rdly mobile young crowd.

Ducados Café J11
*3 Plaza de Canalejas; metro Sevilla.
Open daily 9am–dawn.*
A spacious, wicker-and-flowered-
upholstery venue that is oddly
relaxing in the late afternoon,
with good Cuban and other
strains of Caribbean music as the
night wears on. Its wide-open
windows out front are great for a
relaxing, watch-the-passersby
drink, while inside the music in
the downstairs bar gets louder
and more danceable.

Los Gabrieles J11
*17 C/ de Echegaray; metro Sevilla.
Open daily 2pm–2am.*
A handsome, cool, ancient (19th-
century) bar, lined with decorative
tiles and full of loud music and
lively company. Note that the
prices here double after 5pm.

Los Gatos K12
*2 C/ de Jesús; metro Antón Martín.
Open daily 11am–2am.*
A veteran bar with a relaxed local
ambience and a loyal following
among the *torero* crowd.

Naturbier J12
*9 Plaza Santa Ana; metro Sevilla.
Open Sun–Thurs noon–1am, Fri
and Sat noon–3am.*
Brews its own German-style beer
to traditional recipes. Popular with
tourists and students.

Taberna de la Elisa K12
*42 C/ de Santa María; metro Antón
Martín. **Open** Sun and Tues–Thurs
6.30pm–2.30am, Fri and Sat
6.30pm–3.30am.*
Lots of beers on tap and smoke in
the air in this odd combination of
Spanish corner bar and Irish
tavern that offers live Celtic music
on occasion, as well as other varieties of European folk music.
Friendly and fun.

La Venencia J12
*7 C/ de Echegaray; metro Sevilla.
Open daily 1–3.30 and 7.30–1.30.*
 An atmospheric historic bar
with peeling paint and cobwebs.
Attracts a macho crowd here to
indulge in the countless varieties
of sherry from rows of bottles
and vats.

La Vieja Estación M14
*Avenida Ciudad de Barcelona;
metro Atocha. **Open** May–Sept
daily till 6am.*
The city's largest and wildest
multi-*terraza* can be found in a big
chasm right next to Estación de
Atocha. With bars, dancefloors
and an Argentine restaurant
spread over several layers, this is
one of the best places in the city
for dancing out beneath the stars.

O'Neill's J11
*12 C/ Príncipe, t 91 521 20 30; metro
Sol. **Open** daily from 1pm.*
Cavernous vast and dark pub
decorated in the usual over-
themed Irish style. *The* place for
watching football in town,
especially if any blarney folk are
kicking the ball.

Villa Rosa J12
*17 Plaza de Santa Ana; metro
Sevilla. **Open** Mon–Sat 11pm–5am.*
A classic stop on any nocturnal
itinerary in Madrid, the Villa Rosa
has seen everyone from Federico
García Lorca to Pedro Almodóvar
pass through its doors, and was
featured in Almodóvar's *High
Heels*. With a varied mix of entertainment, it always has
something fun to offer – a bit
more interesting than the typical
tortilla-and-cerveza joints on
this plaza.

Viva Madrid J12
*7 C/ de Manuel Fernández y
González; metro Sevilla or Antón
Martín. **Open** daily 1pm–2am.*
One of Lorca's old haunts, which
retains its gorgeous tiled façade;
inside there are more coloured
tiles, carved wood and caryatids,
plus the obligatory free-flowing
beer taps.

La Latina, Lavapiés and Embajadores

Lavapiés and La Latina are the
working-class counterpart to the
more polished streets of the
Austrias neighbourhood, and have
recently been undergoing an inva-
sion of young hippies and theatre

people who mix in well with the multicultural crowd that lives here. Embajadores, the neighbourhood to the south of Lavapiés, has pretty tree-lined streets and more modern bars and buildings, though there is less to choose from than in Lavapiés.

La Botana H12

C/ Príncipe d'Anglona 1, t 91 366 91 13; metro La Latina. Open Mon–Sat 1pm–1am.
Funky Mexican tapas bar with all the favourites like nachos and *papas ranchero* (fried potatoes in a spicy tomato sauce), plus four types of tequila to add a little sizzle to your snack.

Café Barbieri J13

45 C/ del Ave María; metro Lavapiés. Open Sun–Thurs 3pm–2am, Fri and Sat 3pm–3am.
Virtually unchanged since it opened its doors in 1902, and as popular as ever with both elderly *castizos* and newer arrivals.

La Candela J13

2 C/ del Olmo; metro Antón Martín. Open daily 10.30pm–5.30am.
A bare-bones bar with *trompe l'oeil* designs on the wall, this is the place to enjoy a drink and check out Madrid's real *gitano* scene, complete with occasional impromptu flamenco performances if you're lucky. Things don't get going until 1am at the earliest.

Corgui H12

C/ Rollo 8, t 91 547 10 05; metro La Latina. Open Mon–Sat 1.30–4.30pm and 9–midnight.
Exposed stone walls, orange paintwork and plenty of metal equal an upbeat modern look at this popular bar with its tapas of *tostas* and extensive wine list. Outside *terraza* for summer sipping.

El Eucalipto J14

4 C/ de Argumosa; metro Lavapies.
A pretty blue-painted, narrow little bar, lined with bottles. It has very friendly staff and a deservedly high reputation for its wonderful mojitos.

La Peluquería J13

44 C/ del Ave María; metro Lavapiés. Open daily noon–3am. Cash only.
In a former beauty salon (hence the bar's name), this eclectic joint sells more than sexy herbal teas and mojitos: the rugs hanging behind the counter, the jewellery in the glass vitrine and the artwork on the walls. A hippie spot.

La Redicha J13

C/ Lavapiés 25, t 91 539 75 81; metro La Latina. Open Mon–Sat 9.30am–1.30am.
Don't be put off by the gloom, this is a super-friendly neighbourhood bar, crammed full of locals in for their brandy and coffee combo in the mornings, followed by the lunchtime brigade here for the famed *pimientos asados y setas* (fried peppers and oyster mushrooms) – and so it goes on.

Taberna San Isidro H12

C/ Toledo 24, t 91 365 02 44; metro La Latina. Open daily 8.30am–1.30pm.
An unpretentious old-fashioned bar, despite its location on the tourist trail. If you number more than two, indulge in a plateful *patatas bravas* with seven *salsas* (sauces) washed down with a flagon or more of scrumptious *sidra de barril*.

Tapasentao H13

Calle Almendro 27; metro La Latina. Open Mon–Fri 1.30–4 and 8–midnight, Sat 1–1, Sun 1–midnight.
This simple bar is an essential part of the *barrio* with its old-fashioned brocade wallpaper and healthy 20-plus tapas choice. Attracts the after-work crowd with its excellent choice of wines, including *rioja joven* when in season.

El Viajero H13

7 Plaza de la Cebada; metro La Latina. Open Tues–Thurs 1pm–12.30am, Fri and Sat 1pm–1am, Sun 1–7pm.
An ever popular bar-restaurant with a lovely rooftop bar in summertime. Three floors' worth of music and bar action.

Salamanca

The Salamanca neighbourho is distinctly upmarket, and ma for the over-30s. There are ofte dress codes – many of the bars don't accept trainers, for examp

Matilda N9

14 Callejón de Puigcerdá, t 91 43 89 37; metro Serrano. Open Mon–Fri 1–4 and 8.30–midnigh Sat 1–4.
Tucked down one of the classie side streets in the city, this bar-restaurant attracts a 30-something upwardly crowd especially during the summer when the outside terrace is buzzing. Regular wine tasting evenings get booked up fast.

Teatríz N8

15 C/ de Hermosilla; metro Serr Open daily 1.30–4 and 9–1.
Now something of an institutio Teatríz's 80s designer interior s packs the Salamanca smart set Restaurant, disco and bar, all in one former theatre.

Gran Vía and Chueca

Gran Vía itself has seen bette days, with its slightly decrepit movie houses and the shady scene on the streets to the nor but it remains a centre of nigh time activity, especially when i comes to discos. If you head up Fuencarral or Hortaleza towar Chueca and Alonso Martínez, further down towards the Ban de España, you'll find lots of fu little spots for a drink. Chueca overwhelmingly gay (*see also t 'Gay and Lesbian Madrid' chap but the bars listed here are popular with both straight an gay customers.

Bodega Ángel Sierra K9

11 C/ de Gravina; metro Chueca Open Thurs–Tues 10.30–4 and 7.30–11; closed Aug.
A classic place to drink – it's a traditional *vermut* bar, with th house version on tap.

'é Belén K9
*'e Belén; **metro** Chueca or*
*:o Martínez. **Open** daily*
m–2.30am.
y, intimate bar on a tranquil
t at the northern end
ueca. In the summer, the
ers are open and both the
: and mood are relaxing
velcoming.

'é Libertad K10
*'e la Libertad; **metro** Chueca*
*nco de España. **Open** daily*
–2am.
: are live singer-songwriter
rmances in this tiny,
ke bar with a vaguely
ish/Andalucían
'ative scheme.

'é Madrid K9
*'e Belén; **metro** Chueca or*
*o Martínez. **Open** daily 6pm–*
closed Sun in July and Aug.
ngly decorated Art Nouveau
'ith frescoes on the ceiling. A
heme, both in the music and
:tro drinks. Alcoholic coffees
speciality, like the Cosaco, a
y shake made with chocolate,
n and cognac. But the best
is the vibe – neither the
: nor the booze ever pound
ard.

np K10
'el Marqués de Valdeiglesias;
*› Banco de España. **Open***
·Sat 6pm–3.30am, Sun
·2.30am.
y, funky and vaguely gay, but
of an anything-goes atmos-
: in this bar *de copas* that also
s fashionable food to its irre-
'bly fashionable crowd.

vecería Santa Bárbara K8
*'a Santa Bárbara; **metro***
*o Martínez. **Open** daily*
'm–11.30pm.
'd with twenty-somethings
ekends. There's a good
›or scene.

seo Chicote K10
*'n Vía; **metro** Gran Vía. **Open***
·Thurs 8pm–2.30am, Fri and
›m–3.30am.
t Deco haven which never
d during the Civil War and, in
t years, has had its original
1940s furnishings immaculately restored. Chicote was famous for his cocktails, as well as his clientele – Ava Gardner, Grace Kelly and Hemingway were all regulars here.

Cock K10
*16 C/ de la Reina; **metro** Gran Vía. **Open** daily 7pm–3am.*
A hideously expensive cocktail bar, but unique in its 1920s fake country-house décor and popular among the beautiful people, including writers, actors and occasionally a princess or two.

Del Diego K10
*12 C/ de la Reina; **metro** Gran Vía.*
A stylish cocktail shake away from Chicote, and founded by one of Chicote's barmen, inventor of the 'Diego' (vodka, kirsch, lime and peach).

Star's Dance Café K10
*5 C/ del Marqués de Valdeiglesias; **metro** Banco de España. **Open** Mon–Fri 1pm–2, Sat 1pm–4am*
A loungey spot during the day, but this fun, funky, gay-friendly spot comes alive at night, with techno and house music blaring from the DJ station mounted on the wall. All sorts of entertainment is on offer all week long, from art exhibitions to fashion shows. Weekend nights are total dance fever in the downstairs disco den.

Malasaña and Chamberí

Malasaña is still distinctly grungy, although smartening up a bit – it would now be better described as 'artsy' or 'alternative'. It is filled with so many bars, and so many of them so similar, that it's hard to recommend any in particular. Head for the Plaza Dos de Mayo, and take in the atmosphere from any of the open-air tables. After that, a wander up Calle de la Palma, and round back up Calle de San Vicente Ferrer, gives as good a feel of the flavour of the place as you'll need.

Outdoor City

Late on summer evenings, *madrileños* move outside and cluster in various of the city's squares and streets, either at the outside tables of cafés or around makeshift outdoor bars (*see* 'Botellones', p.244). Streets and squares where there is generally a lively outdoor party going on are:

Calle de Argumosa (metro Lavapiés), **Calle de Lavapiés** (metro Lavapiés), **Calle de Manuel Fernández y González** (metro Sevilla or Antón Martín), **Jardines de las Vistillas** (C/ de Bailén; metro La Latina), **Paseo de la Castellana** (metro Colón), **Paseo del Pintor Rosales** (metro Argüelles), **Plaza del Dos de Mayo** (metro Bilbao), **Plaza Humilladero** (particularly on Sunday mornings after the Rastro market; metro La Latina), **Plaza de Oriente** (metro Opera), **Plaza de la Paja** (metro La Latina), **Plaza Santa Ana** (metro Sevilla), **Plaza Santa Bárbara** (metro Alonso Martínez), **La Vieja Estación** (*see* p.241; metro Atocha).

Bodegas la Ardosa K6
*70 C/ de Santa Engracia; **metro** Iglesia. **Open** daily 9–3 and 6–11.30. Cash only.*
A classic bar in the heart of residential Chamberí, it's brightly lit and offers a thirst-quenching *vermut al grifo* (vermouth on tap), as well as tasty tapas. You can also eavesdrop on the latest Chamberí gossip – it doesn't get more local than this.

Cafeína I9
*18 Calle del Pez; **metro** Noviciado. **Open** Mon–Sat 7pm–3am.*
Small dark bar with stone walls, plush red sofas and a hip young feel. A good place to start the evening before shifting into club-cruising mode.

Lola Loba I8
*38 C/ Palma, **t** 91 522 71 55; **metro** Noviciado. **Open** Mon–Sat 10–2am.*
A smoky late-night bar with occasional live music and a laid-back vibe.

Botellones

In April 2002, the Spanish Interior Ministry imposed stricter limits on drinking in public areas and increased the legal age for buying alcohol from 16 to 18 years. This measure was aimed primarily at eradicating Spain's *botellones* – when millions of teenagers throughout the country congregate and drink in the streets into the early hours of weekend mornings, leaving behind them piles of rubbish and the stench of urine and stale beer.

Youth and other groups argue that under-age drinking is not a new trend, that Spain's liberal attitude to alcohol and drug consumption is a model for other tightly controlled societies with more serious problems of abuse. Also that young revellers are forced into the streets because of price-hiking in bars and nightclubs, especially since the introduction of the euro. The reality is that the laws have done little to quell public drinking in Madrid and more recent measures are perhaps more realistic – the hiring of extra cleaning crews for the dawn shift.

Louie Louie I8
43 C/ de la Palma; metro Tribunal.
An under-30s crowd is drawn to this famous bar, where you'll have to knock to get in. The walls are covered with every imaginable bit of music paraphernalia, and the music played is classic 1970s rock. Lots of motorcycle helmets here.

Penta J8
4 C/ de la Palma; metro Tribunal. Open daily 9pm–4am.
A legendary bar from the movida years, when it was called Pentagrama. It has now toned down its name and its ambience, though it is still a shrine to pop and rock, indifferent to the many trends that have come and gone.

Pobre Gaspar I8
33 C/ Palma, t 91 522 38 42; metro Noviciado. Open daily 1.30–midnight.
Something of an institution for those in the know, this small bar with its much-coveted lounge-around cubicle, caters to the non-boozy brigade with a range of aromatic teas. Alternatively, there is a whole range of imported beers to wash down the tasty selection of tostas.

Sofa Club J9
26 C/ de Fuencarral; metro Tribunal. Open Thurs–Sat 10pm–2am.

Electronica and drum-and-bass in the cavernous Mercado Fuencarral, a shopping arcade extraordinaire. Not a bad way to start the evening, especially if you are planning a Malasaña bar crawl.

La Tabernilla H8
2 C/ Cristo, t 91 541 41 12; metro Noviciado. Open daily 1–1.
A delightful small family-owned bar lined with pics of local folk and family. Outside terrace on small pedestrian street and award-winning *croquetas* for the peckish.

Tetería Coctelería No.1 I9
1 C/ de las Minas; metro Noviciado. Open daily 6pm–1am. Cash only.
With funky clamshell lamps on the walls and glass windows on the floor from which blue light emanates from the basement, this alternative bar/tearoom is like a 1960s living room. Best when the sun goes down.

La Vía Lactea J8
18 C/ de Velarde; metro Bilbao or Tribunal. Open daily 7.30pm–3am.
Still stuck in an early-1980s time-warp, but none the worse for it.

To the West

The area around Plaza de España is quieter and less youth-oriented than the bar scenes to be found in Malasaña, Chueca,

Lavapiés and La Latina. The so[c] life at this end of the city tend[s] focus on the *terrazas* on Paseo Pintor Rosales, the after-movie bars on Martín de los Heros, a[nd] the wine spots on Calle de Fer[...]

Ambigu 16 G8
16 C/ de Martín de los Heros; metro Plaza de España. Open d[aily] 7pm–2.30am.
Cushioned couches, blue light[s] and excellent mojitos in this lounge. You can actually hear yourself talking over the musi[c.] For the still-in-leather-jeans thirtysomething crowd.

Bar El Oleo H8
1 C/ del Cristo; metro Plaza de España or Noviciado. Open dai[ly] 6pm–2am.
A tiny bar with a biker atmosp[here] on a lively little alleyway just o[ff] Conde Duque, with house mu[sic] and giant canvases on the wa[lls.] The mojitos and other mixed drinks cost about €4–5.

Bar El Plaza G9
3 C/ de Martín de los Heros; me[tro] Plaza de España. Open Wed–Su[n] 7.30pm–3.30am.
A stark, modern bar with shin[y] wood floors, undulating easy chairs and a prismatic tiled ba[r] full of young professionals enjoying their post-movie drin[ks,] and if you're lucky you might catch live music or a theatre p[iece] which occasionally materializ[es] (free of charge) on weekend nights. Drinks €4–6.

Café de las Estrellas G9
5 C/ de Martín de los Heros; me[tro] Plaza de España. Open Wed–M[on] 6pm–2am.
Movie stills and posters are o[n] brick walls in this cheerful, bu[sy] bar. For mixed drinks, spiked coffees and snacks while en-gaging in post-movie discussi[on.]

Colorado Express G9
4 C/ de Martín de los Heros; m[etro] Plaza de España. Open daily 6pm–2am. Cash only.
One of the few places in Mad[rid] where you can get Budweiser [in] the bottle (€2.50) and snarf d[own]

llent Mexican and South
rican bar snacks. Packed
good.

trevinos F8
/ de Ferraz; **metro** Ventura
íguez. **Open** Mon–Sat 12.30–4
–midnight.
dern, yuppie shrine to wine,
a selection of raciones to go
the booze.

sso Bar H8
del Conde Duque; **metro** Plaza
paña. **Open** Mon–Thurs
m–2am, Fri and Sat 8.30pm–
m. Amex not accepted.
machines and stuffed
als hanging behind the
ter make for strange bar-
ws, but the house music is
nt and the air-conditioning a
ome – and rare – respite in
ummertime.

ubs

ou're only here for a short
and plan to do culture by day
clubbing by night, you'll need
a siesta in – things don't
start happening here until
ast midnight. Many of the
listed above also play music
have dancefloors, and many
e venues listed under 'Music'
e 'Entertainment' chapter
double as clubs (see p.248).
ore gay clubs (some of the
wing have gay nights), see
the 'Gay and Lesbian Madrid'
ter, pp.267–9.

axim I15
da de Toledo, **t** 902 10 40 28,
ww.spaceofsound.net; **metro**
a de Toledo. **Open** Wed–
midnight–5am; **adm** €8–10.
e here for heavy dancing
heavy spending – drinks are
heap) after bar-hopping
igh Lavapiés. There are
al rooms and dance floors
different themed nights
ughout the week. Check the
ite for an update.

ena G8
de la Princesa, **t** 91 559 19 43;
o Plaza de España. **Open** daily
ight–5am.

A huge converted warehouse
welcomes all crowds to its endless
nights of techno and occasional
world music.

Black Jack J11
11 C/ del Príncipe, **t** 91 547 57 11;
metro Sevilla. **Open** daily 10.30pm–
dawn.
Large labyrinthine cellar-like
disco downstairs playing funky
disco music with more soulful
upstairs bar.

Pink Flamingo I10
13 C/ de Mesonero Romanos, **t** 91
531 48 27; **metro** Gran Vía. **Open**
Wed–Sun midnight–5am.
A predominantly gay crowd
generates a great atmosphere in
this small hip club with Kite Boy
just one of the top DJ's spinning
the sounds.

Joy Madrid H11
11 C/ del Arenal, **t** 91 366 37 33;
metro Opera or Sol. **Open** daily
from 10pm; **adm** €10–15
The capital's best-known and
best-loved disco is a classic, with
pounding music, lights and
scantily clad go-go dancers of
both sexes. It attracts a varied
fauna, from businessmen to
drag queens.

Kapital K13
125 C/ de Atocha, **t** 91 420 29 06;
metro Atocha. **Open** Thurs–Sat
midnight–6am; **adm** €12.
With seven floors of fun, including
cinema, karaoke bar and chill-out
areas, the idea is you don't need to
go anywhere else. At this price,
you'd better be sure. The rooftop
terrace bar has fantastic views.

Kathmandú H11
3 C/ de Señores de Luzón, **t** 91 634
42 01; **metro** Sol or Opera. **Open**
Thurs midnight–5am, Fri and Sat
midnight–6am; free admission.
Dance your bum off (drinks not
cheap) in this almost 20-year-old
disco with comfy places to sit and
a chilled-out atmosphere. Sounds
include groove, Latin, jazz, funk
and hip hop.

Lolita Lounge & Bar L4
3 Manuel de Falla, **t** 629 90 99 89,
w www.lolitalounge.net; **metro**
Cuzco.

This is a seriously cool new club
which has bring-your-own-film
nights (Tuesdays), as well as
sushi, DJs and theme nights,
including (at the time of writing)
Thursday's Lolita nights with
make-overs, tattoos, manicures
and the mildly worrying-sounding
'slave auctions'!

Long Play J10
2 Plaza Vázquez de Mella, **t** 91 531
20 66; **metro** Gran Vía or Chueca.
Open Thurs–Sun midnight–dawn.
Techno and house music on one of
Chueca's busiest little plazas.
Saturday nights are insane.

Midnight H9
13 C/ del Amaniel, **t** 91 354 63 45;
metro Plaza de España or
Noviciado. **Open** Thurs–Sun
midnight–5am.
Hosts various nights, the most
popular of which is 'Cocoon' on
Thursdays for techno and hard
techno. Lots of surprisingly international DJs have popped in. There's
another branch at 35 Gran Vía.

Ohm
4 Plaza de Callao, **t** 91 531 01 32;
metro Callao. **Open** Thurs–Sun
midnight–dawn.
Pop and house music. Sunday
night is 'Week-end' night, a bit
more subdued than the other
nights, but that isn't saying much.

Pachá J8
11 C/ de Barceló, **t** 91 447 01 28;
metro Tribunal. **Open** Thurs–Sat
midnight–dawn; **adm** €12 (one
drink included).
A multilevel disco, formerly the
Barceló theatre, which, since 1982,
has been the Studio 54 of Madrid.
A bit past its prime, it is nevertheless a city landmark and worth a
visit to say you've been there.

Palacio de Gaviria I11
9 C/ del Arenal, **t** 91 526 60 69;
metro Sol or Opera. **Open** daily
from 10pm–dawn; **adm** €8–15.
Located in a former palace,
Gaviria's labyrinthine and ornate
interior offers a range of ambi-
ences and attracts a mixed crowd.

Soho O9

50 C/ de Jorge Juan, t 91 577 89 73;
metro Príncipe de Vergara. Open
Mon–Sat 8pm–2.30am.
An attempt at creating a New York
atmosphere in the heart of
Madrid's snooty Salamanca neighbourhood. Good funk and soul
music on the second floor.

El Sol J10

3 C/ de los Jardines, t 91 532 64 90;
metro Gran Vía. Open Tues–Sat
11.30pm–6am.
Endearingly scruffy, Sol occasionally puts on live gigs, but most of
the time offers late-night funk,
70s and 80s to an eclectic crowd
more interested in having a good
time than in being seen.

Soma H9

25 C/ de Leganitos, t 91 521 07 08;
metro Plaza de España.
Over the years this former
flamenco *tablao* has taken on
many guises. Currently housing a
techno club, its tiled décor and
labyrinthine interior offers
a cool escape from steamy
summer nights.

Soul Kitchen K8

1 Travesia de San Mateo, t 630 859
274, w wwwsoulkitchenclub.com;
metro Tribunal.
There are two of these clubs in
town (the other one is at Plaza de
Recoletos 16) and since re-opening
in 2002 they are among the
hottest late night venues in town,
dishing up healthy doses of hip
hop, rap, Latin reggae and garage.

Stella J–K11

7 C/ de Arlabán; metro Sevilla.
Open Thurs–Sat midnight–dawn.
An old bowling alley turned club.
Thursday night is a techno-house
fest known as 'Mondo'. It's 'The
Room' on Friday and Saturday
nights, which belong to resident
DJ Angel García.

El Torero J11

26 C/ de la Cruz, t 91 523 11 29; metro
Sol. Open Tues–Sat 11pm–5.30am.
1970s Spanish music is their hilarious speciality on the top floor, but
after a few numbers you can retire
to the excellent dance and house
music on the lower floor. Ten years
going and as strong as ever.

La Ventura J13

3 C/ del Olmo, t 91 468 04 54;
metro Antón Martín. Open Tues–
Thurs 8.30pm–2am, Fri and Sat
8.30pm–3am.
An eclectic three-floor dancehall
Lavapiés style: photo exhibitions,
occasional foreign-language
tertulias and theme nights mixed
with the varied dance-music menu
of jungle, trip-hop and electronica.
Easy-listening lounge in the bar.

Y'asta J10

10 C/ de Valverde, t 91 521 88 23;
metro Gran Vía. Open Mon–Sat
midnight–6am.
The generous give-anything-a-go
music policy ensures a wide
variety of sounds, from jungle to
techno pop in this temple to
1980s clubgoing. Things don't
really start until at least 2am.

Entertainment

Music

Classical and Opera

The reopening of the Teatro Real in 1997 has done much to re-invigorate Madrid's classical music scene, by freeing up other venues and attracting top-level visiting orchestras and compa-nies. Check the listings section in the daily papers.

Auditorio Nacional de Música Off maps
146 C/ del Príncipe de Vergara, t 91 337 01 40, t 91 337 01 39, w www .auditorionacional.mcu.es; metro Cruz del Rayo or Prosperidad; bus No.1, 9, 16, 29 or 51; wheelchair accessible.
Home to the Orquesta Nacional de España, the *auditorio* also stages some jazz events. The concert season is October to June, with guest orchestras. Getting tickets can be difficult due to the season-ticket policy, but last-minute tickets can often be had.

Círculo de Bellas Artes K11
2 C/ del Marqués de Casa Riera, t 902 42 24 42; metro Banco de España or Sevilla.
Guitar recitals, European soloists and Sufi music are just a few examples of the wildly varied music schedule, usually in one of the upstairs halls.

Fundación Juan March O7
77 C/ de Castelló, t 91 435 42 40, w www.march.es; metro Núñez de Balboa.
Has a tiny concert hall which offers free admittance to its noon events on Saturdays and Mondays, and at 7.30pm on Wednesdays.

Teatro Calderón I12
18 C/ de Atocha, t 91 429 58 90; metro Sol or Tirso de Molina.
One of Madrid's classic dramatic theatres which often hosts revivals of flamenco and other traditional Spanish music genres.

Teatro Monumental J12
65 C/ de Atocha, t 91 429 81 19; metro Antón Martín.

La Zarzuela

Castizo wit and repartee inspired the composers of the zarzuela, Madrid's own contribu-tion to Spanish popular culture. The name derives from the oper-atic entertainments written by Calderón de la Barca and performed for Philip IV in the Palacio de la Zarzuela (now the main residence of King Juan Carlos; *see* p.172). Popularized in the 18th century, these entertain-ments developed into light, sentimental operatic comedies, a cross between Gilbert and Sullivan and soap opera. Many of the zarzuelas are set in Madrid's intimate 19th-century tenements, the *corralas*. The subjects are usually everyday comedies of manners or on topical themes—one of the biggest zarzuela hits of 1910 was about the opening of the

The venue for most of state radio and television company Radio Television Española's recorded con-certs. Tickets are reasonably priced and usually available, but pro-gramming tends to be traditional.

Teatro Real H11
Plaza de Oriente, t 91 516 06 60, w www.teatro-real.com; metro Opera.
There's a full schedule of first-run opera in this spectacularly refur-bished opera house, almost 150 years old. Bel canto, symphonic works and ballets are also part of its programming.

Teatro de la Zarzuela K11
See 'Zarzuela' below.

Zarzuela

Light opera fans will want to take in a zarzuela, Spain's answer to Gilbert and Sullivan. The season lasts from June to September, although the Teatro de la Zarzuela and the Auditorio Nacional (*see* 'Classical and Opera', above) some-times stage winter productions.

Centro Cultural de la Villa M8–9
Plaza de Colón, t 91 575 60 80; metro Colon or Serrano; wheelchair accessible.

Gran Vía. All are performed wit mix of witty dialogue, song and dance. The parents of Placido Domingo were singers in the zarzuela; Charlie Chaplin borrowed the story of one, *La Violetera*, for his *City Lights*.

Zarzuela hit its peak at the e of the 19th century, but was sti going strong until the advent the Civil War and the utterly humourless dictatorship that followed it. Since then, it has enjoyed something of a revival and, while not many new prod tions are hitting the boards, th are revivals of the classics ever summer. The zarzuela perform in situ, at La Corrala in Embajadores, is the best way t see one. The favourite is the classic *La Revoltosa* by Rupero Chapí, in which all the action takes place in a tenement hous just like La Corrala.

The theatre in the massive modern complex often offers a zarzuela line-up in the summer

La Corrala J14
12 C/ de Tribulete; metro Lavapié These are not the most polishe performances, but the tenemen setting and festive mood more than compensate. Performance start at 10pm and the box offic opens one hour before.

Teatro de la Zarzuela K11
4 C/ de los Jovellanos, t 91 524 5 00; metro Banco de España or Sevilla; wheelchair accessible.
A magnificent building recallin La Scala in Milan, the Zarzuela offers much more than its nam might suggest: from light oper to chamber music and recitals of all sorts.

Jazz and Blues

An enthusiastic jazz and blue following means big names co to Madrid, particularly in late summer, when the northern cit of San Sebastián, Bilbao and Vitoria all host jazz and blues festivals, allowing artists to fit couple of extra dates. The prob

at the venues concerned are
l, and with a guaranteed
ic, so advertising is minimal.

r Café Clamores J7
*de Alurquerque, t 91 445 79
www.salaclamores.com;
o Bilbao. Open Mon–Thur,
pm–3am, Fri–Sat 7pm–4am.*
out fail, you can get your
dose of jazz here, starting
ptly at 10pm. Smoky but fun,
with lots of twists – tango-
red jazz, Cuban jazz and
variants have all passed
ugh their doors.

fé Central J12
*aza del Ángel, t 91 369 41 43;
o Sol or Antón Martín. Open
–Thurs noon–1am, Fri and Sat
–3am; adm often €6–12.*
d among the world's best jazz
es by *Wire* magazine, Café
ral attracts world-class
es to a genuine café setting.

Coquette H11
*de las Hileras; metro Opera.
daily 8pm–2.30am;
d Aug.*
live blues at the weekends
a smokey, late-night feel.

lileo Galilei H5
*C/ de Galileo, t 91 534 75 57;
o Islas Filipinas.*
e heart of the student
hbourhood of Argüelles, this
um-disco specializes in
er-songwriters, which means
ever know quite what you're
, but it's always interesting.

ribaldi Café H11
*de San Felipe Neri, t 91 559 27
etro Sol or Opera.*
ely little cave with an almost
line-up of all strains of jazz
blues.

pulart J12
*de Huertas, t 91 429 84 07;
o Sol or Antón Martín. Open
7pm–2am; adm €2–6.*
cts local players, with the
hasis on a rowdy good time.
get a little too crowded
eekends.

gundo Jazz Off maps
*de Comandante Zorita, t 91
4 37; metro Cuatro Caminos.*

*Open daily Mon–Wed, live
performances from midnight.*
With a 1960s flavour, this place
on the northern edge of Madrid
has its loyal following. Blues and
R&B, too.

Vapor Blues Off maps
*52 C/ de Doctor Esquerdó, t 91 504
21 50; metro Sainz de Baranda.
Open daily 11pm–4am.*
Live music Thursday through
Saturday, for the over-25
blues/rock/soul set. An excellent
place for good beer (many
imported brands) and good music.

Pop, Rock, Latin and World

Madrid manages to attract its
share of super-acts, despite
lacking a decent indoor super-
venue; the climate allows for
summer open-air concerts in any
of the capital's large football
stadia. Forget the listing section of
the newspapers and buy the
pocket-sized, weekly listings
guide, the *Guía del Ocio*. Most
venues double up as bars or clubs.

Berlín Cabaret K5
*11 Costanilla de San Pedro, t 91 366
20 34, t 91 365 55 45; metro
La Latina. Open Sun–Thurs
11pm–5am, Fri and Sat 11pm–6am.*
Slightly decadent, slightly risqué,
always pounding and with occasional drag shows. A classic now
staged in the new venue of the
Nuevo Teatro Alcalá.

The Bourbon Café J11
*Carrera de San Jerónimo 5, t 91 522
0302; metro Sol. Open daily
1pm–6am.*
Kitschy American décor, big screen
music videos, cajun and creole
cooking and live country and
western and jazz music nightly
(Wednesday–Sunday).

Café del Mercado H14
*Puerta de Toledo, t 91 365 87 39;
metro Puerta de Toledo. Open daily
10pm–4am.*
Salsa took Madrid by storm in the
early 90s. The fever has cooled off
somewhat but, if you're looking to
dance the night away, try this

place. It's in the by now almost
abandoned market at the end of
Calle de Toledo, but continues to
attract top-class bands and plays
hot tracks.

Café la Palma I8
*62 C/ de la Palma, t 91 522 50 31;
metro Noviciado. Open Sun–Wed
4pm–3am, Fri and Sat 4pm–5am.*
Part bar, part chill-out zone, part
music venue, the Palma has
carved a niche for itself as a
relaxed club offering local talent a
showcase. Everything from
flamenco to blues, taking in
Cuban *trovadores*.

Finnigans L9
*Plaza de las Salesas 9, t 91 310 05 21;
metro Chueca. Open 11am–late.*
One of several Irish theme pubs
in the city which regularly feature
Celtic bands. Others include
Kitty O'Shea's, O'Neill's and the
Irish Rover.

Honky Tonk K7
*24 C/ de Covarrubias, t 91 445 68
86; metro Alonso Martínez. Open
daily 9.30pm–5.30am.*
Run by the ex-bassist of the
world-famous-in-Spain rock band
Mermelada, this place has been
around for at least two decades.
Good rock and blues, either via
DJ or *en directo*.

Oui I9
*C/ Marqués de Santa Ana 11, no
phone; metro Noviciado. Open
Thurs–Sat 10pm–3am.*
A loyal clientele have followed this
fabled bar to its new location –
disguised so heavily it's hard to
find. This is the spot for a serious
dose of electronica and some truly
entertaining staff.

Palace H11
*7 Plaza Isabel II; metro Opera. Open
daily 7pm–3.30am; cover charge
€5–12, including a drink.*
In the bowels of the Cine Real,
this bar/dance hall offers dance
sets with a live orchestra as well
as a potpourri of oddball
entertainment, including humour
and cruise-ship-style cabaret.

Palacio de Gaviria H11
9 C/ del Arenal; ***metro*** *Sol or Opera.*
Open *daily 10.30pm–dawn; cover charge €7–15.*
A 19th-century palace turned into a macro venue, its many salons host a range of moods and musics. Attracts an international crowd.

La Riviera E15
Paseo Bajo de la Virgen del Puerto, t 91 365 24 15; ***metro*** *Príncipe Pío.*
Open *Fri–Sun 11pm–5am.*
One of the best live-music joints in town, a bit of a trek from the centre but worth it for the quality alternative rock that is played here.

Sala Caracol J15
18 C/ de Bernardino Obregón, t 91 527 35 94; ***metro*** *Embajadores.*
Open *Wed–Sun 9pm–dawn.*
Everything from experimental dance and modern flamenco to heavy metal and hip-hop.

Sala Sol J10
3 C/ Jardines, t 91 361 1184; ***metro*** *Gran Vía.* ***Open*** *daily 9pm–4am.*
A stone's throw from Gran Vía, this is one of the city's hottest live rock and alternative venues. Very sweaty and very loud.

Siroco H8
3 C/ de San Dimas, t 91 593 30 70; ***metro*** *San Bernardo.* ***Open*** *Wed and Thurs 9.30pm–4am, Fri and Sat 11pm–5am.*
A small temple to live music: hip-hop, acid jazz and everything electronic.

Space of Sound, Off maps
Plaza Estación de Charmatín, w www.spaceofsound.net; ***metro*** *Charmatín.*
The mother of all late-night clubs, Space of Sound is fast building itself into a quasi Ministry of Sound empire. Sunday is the biggie when the enormous Sala Macumba is heaving to a mix of funky house, techno pop and disco.

La Taberna Encantada K13
2 C/ de Salitre, t 91 528 52 38; ***metro*** *Antón Martín.*
One of the nerve centres of the Latina-Lavapiés nocturnal bar scene, this is alternative heaven: live folk, rock and world music.

Taberna Triskel J8
3 C/ de San Vicente Ferrer, t 91 523 27 83; ***metro*** *Tribunal.* ***Open*** *daily noon–3am.*
Pulls in some excellent local players for its late-night jam sessions.

Zanzíbar K9
9 C/ de Regueros, t 91 319 90 64; ***metro*** *Alonso Martínez.*
Each week a donation is made to a different charitable organization. Prices are low, in keeping with the not-for-profit philosophy. The music ranges from African rock to salsa and other world music.

Cinema

Cinema-going remains popular in Madrid, perhaps because, at around €6–8, it's still so much cheaper than in other European capitals. Spanish cinema has had its ups and downs over the years, and the glory days of state funding ended with the arrival of a conservative government. In creative terms, the director of *Women on the Edge of a Nervous Breakdown*, Pedro Almodóvar, still casts his shadow large over the scene, and his style of postmodern *costumbrista* is much copied.

The Callao metro stop at Gran Vía is the mecca for big-screen Hollywood-import fans, with the occasional local big-budget production drawing in the crowds. Down the Gran Vía at Plaza de España are four multi-screen cinemas specializing in subtitled foreign language movies. Madrid has no film festival, preferring not to compete with San Sebastián's annual jamboree.

For listings information, there are several freebies, including the *Guía del Ocio* (in Spanish), *En Madrid What's On* (in Spanish and English) and *In Madrid* (in English). All three are generally available at the tourist office. The two main newspapers, *El País* and *El Mundo*, have complete daily listings. For foreign-language entries look under the '*versión original*', '*subtitulada*' or '*VOS*' heading.

Mainstream

Although usually showing dubbed Hollywood imports, these three cinemas are worth a visit, if only for their pre-war opulent décor and hilarious hand-painted movie posters.

Cinesa Capitol I10
41 Gran Vía, t 902 33 32 31; ***metro*** *Callao; wheelchair accessible.*

Cinesa Gran Vía I10
66 Gran Vía, t 902 33 32 31; ***metro*** *Callao.*

Palacio de la Música I10
35 Gran Vía, t 91 521 62 09; ***metro*** *Callao.*

Foreign Languag and Art House

The following may occasiona show films in English with Spanish subtitles.

Alphaville G8
14 C/ de Martín de los Heros, t 9 559 38 36; ***metro*** *Plaza de Españ wheelchair accessible.*
One of the capital's first art-ho cinemas, Alphaville boasts a ca and bookshop.

Filmoteca K13
Cine Doré, 3 C/ de Santa Isabel, t 369 11 25; ***metro*** *Antón Martín.*
Spain's national film theatre offers interesting seasons, a good bookshop, a café and in summer an open-air screen. And the price can't be beaten: a €1.35 a ticket (€10.22 for 10 film it's by far the best quality–price ratio for air-conditioned entertainment in Madrid.

Pequeño Cine Estudio I6
1 C/ de Magallanes, t 91 447 29 metro Quevedo.
A tiny, little-known art house specializing in movies from Hollywood's golden age – Humphrey Bogart, Bette Davis, Orson Welles et al.

Princesa G8
3 C/ de la Princesa, t 91 541 41 0 w www.cinentradas.com; ***metr*** *Plaza de España.*

six screens, Princesa is more
ʼortable than most *multicines*,
they let you take drinks in.

noir Plaza de España G8
de Martín de los Heros,
ʼ41 41 00; **metro** Plaza de
ña; wheelchair accessible.
Renoir is an old favourite,
cially on Sunday movie night.

lmo Cinepex Ideal I12
de Doctor Cortezo, **t** 902 22 09
ʼetro Sol or Antón Martín.
screens mix the best in
ʼrts with independent
ish efforts, plus you can go
ing in Huertas after the show.

en Air

adrid's summer festival, the
ʼos de la Villa, offers two
nings a night throughout
August and the first two
s of September at a giant
-air screen in the Parque
Bombilla, on the Avenida de
dolid, close to the church of
Antonio de la Florida. Not for
us cinema fans, but it allows
o mix with the locals.

eatre

drid has never been able to
ʼlish as confident a thespian
mage as its rival Barcelona.
no national theatre as such,
rs are very much on their
when it comes to getting
uctions mounted.
rtheless, even with drastic
cks in state and local govern-
funding, a wide range of
re remains on offer.

ssical and
ntemporary

ʼtro Albeniz I12
de la Paz, **t** 91 531 83 11; **metro**
ʼheelchair accessible.
lbeniz is the centrepiece of
utumn festival, and puts on a
range of dance and music,
casing visiting international
anies, as well as domestic
mporary productions.

Teatro de la Comedia J11–12
14 C/ del Príncipe, **t** 91 521 49 31,
w www.teatroentradas.com;
metro Sevilla or Sol.
The home of the Compañía
Nacional de Teatro Clásico (Spain's
equivalent of the Royal
Shakespeare Company), this
theatre was built in 1874, the work
of Agustín Ortiz de Villapalos, who
added a quasi-Arabian flourish to
the interior. You can almost always
count on seeing something by Tirso
de Molina, Calderón de la Barca or
Lope de Vega, plus some of the
lesser-known Golden Age playwrights, though the performances
can be slightly dumbed-down.

Teatro Español J12
25 C/ del Príncipe, **t** 91 360 14 80;
metro Sevilla or Sol; wheelchair
accessible.
Worth a visit if only for its
mid-18th-century interior,
although its productions of early
20th-century Spanish works have
won international acclaim.

Alternative

El Canto de la Cabra K9
8 C/ de San Gregorio, **t** 91 310 42 22;
metro Chueca.
One of the more experimental
theatre groups, featuring the work
of contemporary writers, both
Spanish and international. In
summer, they perform outdoors
on the adjoining square.

Ensayo 100 K6
20 C/ de Raimundo Lulio, **t** 91 447
94 86; **metro** Bilbao.
A small theatre dedicated to
showing the work of 'undiscov-
ered' theatrical talent. During the
Festival de Otoño, works in English
are occasionally performed.

El Montacargas C12
19 C/ de Antillón, **t** 91 526 11 73;
metro Puerta del Angel.
A lively cultural association which
runs a wide range of events,
including children's shows,
cabaret, workshops and very
creative theatre.

Sala Cuarta Pared J16
17 C/ de Ercilla, **t** 91 517 23 17; **metro**
Embajadores; wheelchair accessible.
A wide range of programming,
from kids' theatre to modern
dance and contemporary
Spanish drama.

Sala Triángulo K13
20 C/ de Zurita, **t** 91 530 69 91;
metro Antón Martín;
wheelchair accessible.
Perhaps the best-known and most
consistently creative fringe
theatre in Madrid.

Teatro Alfil I9
10 C/ del Pez, **t** 91 521 58 27; **metro**
Noviciado; wheelchair accessible.
Something of an institution on
Madrid's alternative scene, the
Alfil is a comfortable-sized theatre
with a cabaret feel lent by the in-
house bar and tables and chairs.
Recently rescued from closure by
internationally known comedy
group Yllana, the focus is increasingly on humour, and the theatre
is venue to one of Europe's best
comedy festivals in spring.

Dance

There are two main dance
companies in Spain, the Compañía
Nacional de Danza and the Ballet
Nacional de España. The capital
also boasts its own Ballet de la
Comunidad de Madrid, with the
emphasis on well-known Spanish
and French works. The capital
hosts several dance events and
festivals throughout the year,
many of them at the Teatro
Albeniz (see 'Theatre', above).
Keep an eye open for posters
and check the listings pages,
as well as the following venues.

Teatro de Madrid Off maps
Avenida de la Ilustracíon, **t** 91 730
17 50; **metro** Barrio del Pilar.
Out in the Barrio del Pilar
neighbourhood, near La Vaguada
shopping mall, this modern
exceptionally well-designed
theatre has an eclectic line-up
of Spanish and international
dance companies.

Teatro Real H11

*Plaza de Oriente, **t** 91 516 06 60; **metro** Opera; wheelchair accessible.*
The Teatro Real, also known as the Opera, is where you'll catch Nacho Duato's Compañía Nacional de Danza when they are in Madrid.

Teatro de la Zarzuela K11

*4 C/ de los Jovellanos, **t** 91 524 54 00; **metro** Banco de España or Sevilla; wheelchair accessible.*
A beautifully restored mid-19th-century miniature La Scala with a varied programme of dance and musical theatre.

Flamenco

A guitar and *corazón*-infused musical chronicle of the woes, heartbreak and nomadic melancholy of the Andalucían *gitanos*, flamenco is nonetheless often thought of as Spain's national dance, like the samba in Brazil or the tango in Argentina. This drama-filled spectacle is led by either a male singer (a *cantaor*) or a female singer (a *cantaora*), with the golden melody of a *tocaor* on the guitar. The two work together as a team, though the singer is the star, belting out a passionate tightwire of curving rhythms, laments, cries and professions of love, sadness, nostalgia and the like.

In Madrid, there are various places to see flamenco: professional ballet and dance companies occasionally incorporate flamenco into their programmes, but the most typical way to 'do' the flamenco thing is to go to a *tablao*, a dinner-theatre or cabaret experience that is often pricey and unavoidably filled with foreigners like you. But that's part of the deal and, anyway, even Pedro Almodóvar has been spotted at Casa Patas, supposedly the most touristy of the bunch.

Café de Chinitas H10

*7 C/ de Torrija, **t** 91 547 15 02; **metro** Santo Domingo. Performances Mon–Sat at 10.30pm.*
A *tablao*.

Candela J13

*2 C/ del Olmo, **t** 91 467 33 82; **metro** Antón Martín.*
If you want to mingle with players and other figures from the flamenco world – as well as their hangers-on – then a late-night drink here is a must. Performances usually start at 11pm.

Casa Patas J12

*10 C/ de Cañizares, **t** 91 369 04 96, **w** www.casapatas.com; **metro** Antón Martín. Performances 10.30pm Mon–Thur, 9pm and midnight Fri and Sat.*

Attracts some of the best performers, with dance a regu[lar] feature. The bar-restaurant is separate from the performing area, and famous faces from t[he] flamenco world are often seen there.

Corral de la Morería G12

*17 C/ de la Morería, **t** 91 365 84[ ] **w** www.corraldemoreria.com; **metro** Opera or La Latina. Performances daily at 10.45pm[.]*
A *tablao*.

Peña Chaquetón M16

*39 C/ de Canarias, **t** 91 671 27 7[ ] **metro** Delicias.*
Those looking for flamenco in[ ] purest form should head to or[ ] the capital's oldest, and last, *peñas*. This is a world away fro[m] the *tablaos*, with an almost so[ ] arly approach on the part of t[he] aficionados who turn up to he[ar] some of the finest singers and guitarists in the country.

La Soleá H12–13

*27 C/ de la Cava Baja, **t** 91 365 3[ ] 08; **metro** La Latina.*
Despite its touristy feel, it attr[acts] some good amateurs, and sing[ers] and guitarists make their way[ ] here to try their hand and see[if] they have that special someth[ing.] Also a favourite for neighbour[-] hood locals who just fancy the[ ] flamenco equivalent of a goo[d] singsong down the pub.

hopping

Shops in Madrid usually open Mon–Fri from 10am to 1 or 2pm, then reopen from 5 or 5.30 until 8 or 8.30pm. Most shops also open on Saturday mornings, while some, like book and record shops, may open on Sundays. More and more larger chain stores are open during the daytime siesta hours, and El Corte Inglés, for example, is open on the first Sunday of the month, while its record shop is open every Sunday.

Books and News

Foreign newspapers are sold at the larger stands around the Puerta del Sol, Gran Vía, Calle de Alcalá, Plaza de Cibeles and in the Salamanca district.

Booksellers K4
48 C/ de José Abascal; **metro** Ríos Rosas.
The capital's best shop for English titles.

La Casa del Libro I10
29 Gran Vía; **metro** Gran Vía.
Claims to be Spain's largest bookshop – there are several floors of it, including a so-so English-language section.

Crisol K11
2 C/ del Marqués de Casa Riera, **w** www.crisol.es; **metro** Banco de España.
Spain's biggest chain of bookshops. Most have a decent, small section of English-language books and some music, too. Reliable and open throughout the day.

El Corte Inglés (bookshop) I11
Puerta del Sol; **metro** Sol.
This corner branch of Spain's mega department store has an excellent selection of travel guidebooks and maps to just about everywhere in the world – including Madrid.

FNAC I10
28 C/ de Preciados, **t** 91 595 62 00; **metro** Callao or Sol.
With floor upon floor of CDs, videos, video games, books, magazines and newspapers, and a concert ticket agency.

Pasajes International Bookshop L8
3 C/ de Génova; **metro** Alonso Martínez.
A small, peaceful little bookshop in Chamberí with a good selection of English-language titles, both commercial fiction and more literary works.

Petra's International Bookshop H10
C/ Campomanes 13; **metro** Santo Domingo.
The name says it all; this is an excellent bookshop which has a range of good books in several languages – including English.

Clothes and Accessories

Madrid has not one fashion centre, but several, each with its own distinctive character. For designer labels, the streets to head for are those crisscrossing the self-confidently prosperous Salamanca district, north of the Retiro: Serrano, Goya, Claudio Coello, Velázquez and Ortega y Gasset (metro Serrano, Velázquez and Núñez de Balboa). Here are the international fashion celebrities, such as Chanel, Kenzo, Giorgio Armani and Versace (all on Calle de Ortega y Gasset).

For affordable mainstream fashion for men and women, the Calle de la Princesa between Argüelles and Moncloa metro stations is the best hunting ground, with particularly rich pickings at sale time. Other cheap-and-chic stomping grounds are the streets around Preciados and Sol, with lots of off-the-rack lycra and funky denim. For more upscale, creative clothes, the streets around the Plaza de las Salesas – Prim, Almirante, Conde de Xiquena, Argensola – have some good, non-chain stores, though original fashions don't come cheap in this neighbourhood. Chueca, though known for being a neighbourhood catering to gay men, has a surprising

number of funky shops selling offbeat and not terrifically ex[pen]sive women's clothing, and th[e] shoe outlets on Augusto Figue[roa] are not to be missed by anyon[e] with even the most minor foo[t] fetish. Hortaleza and Fuencar[ral] are the avenues for alternativ[e] fashion – club clothes, sporty-funky, vintage and purely outrageous can all be found o[n] these two drags radiating up the Gran Vía.

Expensive

Adolfo Domínguez M9
18 C/ de Serrano; **metro** Serran[o].
Minimalist and somewhat austere, he is a sacred cow of conservative women's fashion; think Giorgio Armani with a s[plash] of Spanish audacity. Their spo[rts] line, slightly cheaper, hovers somewhere between Polo Spo[rt] and Armani Jeans.

Agatha Ruiz de la Prada M[8]
8 C/ del Marqués de Riscal; **metro** Rubén Darío.
Fun, whimsical, Betty Boopish clothing for adults and adorab[le] creative togs for kids. Expensive, definitely original – outside Sp[ain] you are not likely to find many her cutesy appliqué designs.

Cortefiel I11
7 C/ Maestro Victoria; **metro** S[ol].
A Spanish chain that caters to well-groomed, mature, yet [fash]ionable women. A little pricey, worth it for the classy look, w[ith] an emphasis on separates.

Doble AA O8
22 C/ del Príncipe de Vergara; **metro** Velázquez.
Upscale urbanwear in a too-trendy shop (which has a less-fabulous branch on Fuencarral) that mixes cheap[er] lines such as G-Star, Evisu an[d] Quiksilver with Dolce & Gabb[ana,] Paul Smith, Toni Miró and oth[ers].

Javier Larraínzar O9
16 C/ de Castelló; **metro** Prínci[pe] de Vergara.
Modern, simple cuts and desi[gns] are made dazzling thanks to [...]

ner's keen eye for sumptuous
s and discreet colours. This is
osest you'll get to an atelier
drid. Made-to-order clothing
a possibility here.

ús del Pozo L9
*e Almirante; metro Colón or
o Martínez.*
quisite collection of filmy,
mery and romantic prêt-a-
r and bridal gowns, as well as
sories and jewellery.

we M9
de Serrano; metro Serrano.
e plus ultra of Spanish
er goods, from wallets and
to crocodile dresses.
geously expensive: only for
with good lines of credit
erious fashion victims.

ificación García M9
de Serrano; metro Serrano.
nish fashion icon, this
ner is Jackie O with a mini-
t Japanese look thrown in
ionally. Her delicate evening
s of gauze and chiffon
xquisite.

erto Verino N9
*de Claudio Coello;
Serrano.*
her Spanish designer you are
kely to find out of the country.
cut, sober and slightly conser-
though never boring, he is
ct if you're looking for classic
s with a bit of flair.

illa N9
*lejón de Jorge Juan;
Serrano.*
s the place to shop for the
nd famous crowd, with
-fashionable salespeople.
ollection is original and
e, but always with some
ern twist, and the lower-
d Jocomomola line has more
sical, amusing clothes for
t half the price. Even if you
afford it, worth a visit – the
es are inexpensive.

Less Expensive, More Fun

Cannibal J9
*Mercado de Fuencarral, shop No.45,
45 C/ de Fuencarral; metro Tribunal.*
Well-priced club clothes in the
Mercado de Fuencarral, which
some consider alternative-
clothing heaven.

La Compañía Multihispana J9
*30 C/ de Hortaleza; metro Gran Vía
or Chueca.*
An eclectic collection of lesser-
known Spanish designers, as well
as Sybilla's Jocomomola line. Lots
of easy separates with fun designs
and elegant fabrics.

The Deli Room J9
4 C/ Santa Bárbara; metro Tribunal.
Young Spanish designers equal
hip streetwise clothes.

Flip H11
19 C/ Mayor; metro Sol.
Up-to-the-minute casual clothes –
brands such as Miss Sixty, G-Star,
Gsus and Dickies – and a healthy
line-up of caps and aerodynamic-
looking bags and backpacks.

Glam J10
*35 C/ de Fuencarral; metro Tribunal
or Gran Vía.*
The king of designer-but-afford-
able fashions, with undulating
platform shoes and shiny lycra
and rubber dresses, as well as a
stylish line by the owner,
Fernando Cuevas.

No Comment J9
39 C/ Fuencarral; metro Tribunal.
Another hip boutique for cool
clubwear and urban designs.

Supreme F8
*24 C/ de Martín de los Heros;
metro Ventura Rodríguez or Plaza
de España.*
The coolest of Madrid's less
expensive cool-kid clothing shops.
Diesel, Carhartt, Homeboy and,
oddly, even Birkenstocks.

Chain Stores

Blanco
*14 C/ Mayor (metro Sol; H11–I12);
59 C/ de Goya (metro Velázquez).*
A Zara-like emporium, only sexier
and (if you can believe it) cheaper,
with everything from lingerie to
provocative stretch-denim
dresses, accessories and strappy
leather sandals and shoes.

Don Algodón N6
78 C/ de Serrano; metro Serrano.
Once all the rage, this cutie-pie
chain of Benetton-like clothes has
dipped a bit in the Mango-hungry
eyes of Spanish fashion victims.
However, the clothes are still as
adorable as ever, and it's still a
great place for classic-but-hip
clothes in natural fabrics.

Mango
*83 C/ de Goya (metro Velázquez;
P9); 75 C/ de la Princesa (metro
Argüelles; F6).*
Slightly provocative work clothes,
and tons of lycra, fake leather and
metallic fabrics, as well as a small
but decent selection of up-to-the-
minute sporty pieces. Good prices.

Zara
*20 C/ de Preciados (metro Sol; I11);
32 Gran Vía (metro Gran Vía or
Callao; I10); 126–8 C/ de Fuencarral
(metro Tribunal; I6); and many
many more.*
Zara could easily be considered
Spain's official women's clothier.
Great for last-minute, inexpensive
going-out clothes. Accessories and
shoes, too.

Vintage and Used Clothing

Marmota H14
*13 C/ de Mira el Río Baja; metro
Puerta de Toledo.*
Marmota has carved its own niche
in the funky, unused vintage
clothing market, with pieces
starting at the unbelievably low
price of €3.

Pepita is Dead K14
10 C/ de Doctor Fourquet;
metro Atocha.
A well-curated collection of vintage clothing from the 40s through to the 80s, and some great shoes in surprisingly good condition. The owner, Cristina Guisante, also sells her own line of crocheted bags, hats and clothes.

Ropero J9
45 C/ Fuencarral, 1st floor;
metro Tribunal.
An excellent selection of vintage second-hand clothing ranging from the 60s to 80s, so expect a heady mix of minis, geometric designs and flares.

Underground Moda H14
14 C/ de Mira el Río Baja; metro
Puerta de Toledo.
Very Saturday Night Fever – loads of retro 60s and 70s fashions, much of which is vintage and unused.

Shoes and Accessories

Caligae K9
27 C/ de Augusto Figueroa;
metro Chueca.
The hippest of the many discount shoe stores lining Augusto Figueroa and its cross streets in the heart of Chueca. Lots of Italian and British shoes at dirt-cheap prices, and even a few off-season Farrutxs.

Camper I10
3 C/ de Preciados; metro Callao.
This youth-oriented shoe company still makes its shoes in Mallorca, where the owner/head designer lives and dreams up his crazy but unbelievably comfortable rubber-soled shoes. With branches on Gran Vía, Hermosilla and Princesa.

Cristina Castañer N8
51 C/ de Claudio Coello; metro
Serrano.
The sexiest of Madrid's shoe stores, with strappy high heels aplenty. Not inexpensive.

Farrutx M10
7 C/ de Serrano; metro Serrano.
One of Spain's hallmark shoe

labels, Farrutx strikes the balance between sexy, classic, daring and elegant.

House of Flies K9
7 C/ Belén; metro Chueca.
A vast selection of groovy-looking shades imported from all over the world.

Joaquín Berau L9
13 C/ del Conde de Xiquena;
metro Colón.
This jewellery store has art-gallery airs, and for good reason: the delicate pieces of titanium, bronze, gold and silver are like mini-sculptures, exquisite and original.

Lurueña M8
54 C/ de Serrano; metro Serrano.
Has its own line of luxe leather shoes (day and night styles) as well as a small collection of other brands to attract the younger set, including Camper. Bags and accessories, too.

Maddox J9
45 C/ Fuencarral, 1st floor;
metro Tribunal.
The place to come for Birkenstocks, Campers and Clarks.

Piamonte K9
16 C/ de Piamonte; metro Chueca.
Piamonte has perfected the art of creating the cool, user-friendly, outrageously expensive bag.

Superga N8
23 C/ de Ayala; metro Serrano.
The latest in hyper-trendy Italian sporty shoes. Mostly sneakers, many of which look like what you wore in the late 70s, but they're back, and they raise more eyebrows with this trendy label on them.

Yanko
52 C/ de Lagasca (metro Serrano;
N8); 40 Gran Vía (metro Callao; I10).
Yanko is strictly leather, strictly traditional and strictly expensive. But as they are hand-tooled and extremely well crafted, they fall into the last-a-lifetime category and are worth the splurge.

Lingerie

Intimissimo I11
24 C/ Preciados; metro Sol.

Sexy women's lingerie with ple of lace and pure cotton, as wel a silky selection of stockings.

Meye Maier N9
14 Callejón de Jorge Juan;
metro Serrano.
One of Madrid's most exclusiv lingerie shops. Lots of white la and white cotton, of the pure-b sexy variety.

Department Stores and Mall

ABC Serrano N6
61 C/ de Serrano; metro Rubén D
The old headquarters of the ri wing newspaper *ABC*, in a fanc Neo-Mudéjar building. A some what incongruous mixture of fast-food, photo shops and clothing stores.

AZCA Off maps
Paseo de la Castellana and C/ d
Orense; metro Santiago Bernab
or Cuzco.
The famous Torre Picasso rises 157m above this immense, mul level shopping arcade. Everyth from garden equipment to lac lingerie, but it's a far from inspiring atmosphere in which drop your euros.

El Corte Inglés
3 C/ de Preciados (metro Sol; I11)
Plaza Callao (metro Callao; I10);
85–7 C/ de Goya (metro Goya; Q
79 C/ de Raimundo Fernández
Villaverde (metro Nuevos
Ministerios; K2); 56 C/ de la Prin
(metro Argüelles; F7). All branch
open Mon–Sat 10am–10pm, an
first Sun of every month.
Everything you could possibly want under one roof: super-market, department store, hai stylist, cafeteria, currency exchange, hardware store, trav agency, CDs and books.

Madrid 2 (La Vaguada) Off m
36 Avenida Monforte de Lemos
metro Barrio del Pilar.
A gigantic shopping mall in th very north of the city, with all chain stores that are otherwis littered about the streets of th city: Mango, Zara, Massimo Du Bershka, Cortefiel.

od and Drink

eite de Oliva Virgen K8
er of C/ de Mejía Lequerica
C/ de Hortaleza; metro
o Martínez.
e place to pick up excellent
oil, although it is notorious
s haughty staff.

ramelos Paco H13
de Toledo; metro La Latina.
enerations, its windows –
the multicoloured display
dless candies – have beck-
pint-sized Spaniards.
pecialities are the sickly
t alcohol-filled chocolates
almond nougat.

Casa del Bacalao F7
el Marqués de Urquijo;
o Argüelles.
e who have acquired a taste
alt cod can stock up at this
traditional, marble-floored
orium of the stuff.

sa Mira J11
rrera de San Jerónimo;
o Sol.
urrón, the almond nougat
was once made by Toledo's
ous communities, you can do
etter than this ancient shop
h also sells all sorts of other
ous goodies.

enllas G9
de Ferraz; metro Ventura
guez.
endary market filled with oil,
gar, anchovies, salmon
sse and other canned and
d items. There is also a devil-
tempting display of
dillos, making it a handy rest
as well.

bassy M8
seo de la Castellana;
o Colón.
urmet emporium (also an
nsive restaurant) best for its
out roast chicken, grilled
entos and adorable chocolate
cream puff creations. A wide
ty of salmons, pâtés,
ards, oils and cheeses.

Hespen & Suarez K8
15 C/ Barceló; metro Tribunal.
A superb upmarket deli with a
gourmet selection of food to
savour on the go; the sushi is
recommended.

Mantequerías González K12
12 C/ de León; metro Antón Martín.
First opened in 1931, this quaint
old *mantequería* has now become
a true *tienda del gourmet*, with an
excellent selection of wines from
all over Spain, cured and fresh
cheeses, pâtés, *foies* and a good
variety of Spanish sausages. The
freshly made *empanada gallega*
(tuna with raisins) is scrumptious.

**Mariano Aguado Vinos y
Licores** J12
*19 Calle Echegaray, t 91 429 6088;
metro Sevilla.*
A superb selection of wines and
liquors from all over España. If you
ask nicely, you may be able to
taste first...

Naturasi G6
*28 Calle Guzmán El Bueno, t 91 544
56 63; metro Aquëllas.*
This second branch of the
immensely popular health food
supermarket opened in 2003 with
more than 3,000 organic products
on sale, including organic meat,
cheese, fruit and veg, a herbal
shop and natural cosmetics.

La Oleoteca Off maps
*37 C/ de Juan Ramón Jiménez;
metro Cuzco.*
Arguably the best place in Madrid
to buy olive oil, as well as a dazzling
array of vinegars and olives.

La Pajarita M9
14 C/ de Villanueva; metro Colón.
Homemade chocolates and the
namesake caramel and
chocolate *pajarita*, a 'little bird' of
a bonbon for which the shop
became famous.

El Palacio de los Quesos H11–12
53 C/ Mayor; metro Sol or Opera.
An atmospheric old shop which, in
addition to its exhaustive range of
cheeses, also sells fine wines and
other Spanish delicacies.

El Riojano I11
10 C/ Mayor; metro Sol or Opera.
Has a deservedly high reputation
for sumptuous pâtisserie.

La Vianda Asturiana J9
*47 C/ de Fuencarral; metro
Tribunal.*
The specialities are clearly the
fabes (white beans), cheeses,
sausages and sweets from this
northern Spanish province. Loads
of mustards as well.

Viena Capellanes L8
*4 C/ de Génova; metro Alonso
Martínez; with branches
throughout the city.*
Deliciously rich cakes, decent
wines and coffees.

Sweet Nuns

The cloistered nuns in Madrid
still earn their way in the world by
baking and selling their goods on
revolving drums that preserve
their privacy.

Convento de las Carboneras H12
*C/ del Codo (off Plaza de la Villa);
metro La Latina or Sol.*
They make a choice of 11 different
sweets, including almond pastries,
tasty dry biscuits called the 'bones
of Fray Escobas', *mantecados*
(butter cakes) and *tocinitos de
cielo* ('heavenly bacon') – a rich
caramel custard.

Monasterio de la Visitación I8
*72 C/ de San Bernardo; metro San
Bernardo.*
The nuns here make delicious
pastas de Santa Eulalia, a pastry
invented by one of the nuns, as
well as plum cake, tea biscuits
and *mantecados*.

Samovar N5
*5 C/ de Diego de León;
metro Núñez de Balboa.*
For pastry delicacies, as well as
marmalade, honey and candies
made in convents across Spain.

Markets

Market shoppers should be aware that the mêlée round a busy stall is actually the *madrileño* version of an organized queue. The convention is that each new arrival calls out '*¿Quién es el último?*' ('Who's last?') in order to find out their place in the serving order – often the cue for a great deal of good-natured argy-bargy and verbal jostling for position. Nobody would dream of standing in line.

Mercado de Antón Martín K13
*5 C/ de Santa Isabel; **metro** Antón Martín. **Open** daily 9–2 and 5.30–8.30.*
One of the most central of Madrid's bustling *castizo* food markets, with two floors of permanent stalls selling all manner of fresh produce.

Mercado de las Maravillas Off maps
*122 C/ de Bravo Murillo; **metro** Cuatro Caminos.*
A beautiful ('marvellous') building in a bustling neighbourhood, great for a taste of real Madrid.

Mercado La Paz M–N8
*28 C/ de Ayala; **metro** Serrano.*
All the standard stalls – fruit, vegetables, cheese, meat, in an incongruously downmarket arcade in Salamanca.

Mercado de San Miguel H12
*Plaza de San Miguel; **metro** Sol.*
Fairly small but worth visiting for a glimpse of its ornate ironwork exterior. It's the Spanish market you imagined before coming to Spain.

El Rastro H13–I14
*Plaza de Cascorro, C/ de Ribera de Curtidores and around; **metro** La Latina. **Held** Sun morning.*
Madrid's most celebrated flea-market. The best time to visit is early in the morning, from autumn to spring: in summer the crowds are thicker and the spread of stalls thinner, and by mid-morning it's already hot. Once devoted solely to antiques and curios (this is the speciality of many of the permanent shops in this district), there are now stalls selling all sorts of junk – cheap shoes, jewellery, belts and bags; second-hand, ethnic and new-age fashions; plants; household goods; pirate tapes; and rack after rack of sunglasses. If it's antiques and curios you're after, head for the Calle de Mira el Río Baja and its neighbours. There are good bric-a-brac stalls in the Plaza del General Vara de Rey, and a few more upmarket shops in the sadly characterless Mercado Puerta de Toledo. The Plaza del Campillo del Mundo Nuevo is the place for plants and old books. Now that the Rastro has become as popular with tourists as with *madrileños*, the bargains are harder to come by, but if you've the time, and room in your suitcase, the shops and stalls are worth a look. Remember to keep an eye on your belongings.

Second-hand Book Market L–M14
*Cuesta de Claudio Moyano; **metro** Atocha.*
A street where, on fine days (and especially on Sundays), second-hand bookstalls offer their tempting and sometimes bizarre wares, maybe even the one title you've been searching for all these years.

Music

Escridiscos I10
*8 C/ del Postigo de San Martín; **metro** Callao.*
Though on first glance it looks like just another of the many music shops in and around Callao, this place is an emporium of mythic proportions, with indie rock, American and British imports, and Spanish pop, all used.

El Flamenco Vive H11
*7 C/ del Conde de Lemos; **metro** Opera.*
For the widest selection of flamenco recordings, as well as books on the subject, and even those dancing shoes you now need.

FNAC I10
*28 C/ de Preciados, **t** 91 595 62 0*
metro Callao or Sol.
With floor upon floor of CDs, videos, video games, books, magazines and newspapers, and a concert ticket agency.

The Level J8
*3 C/ de Divino Pastor; **metro** Bil* or Tribunal.
A DJ's fantasy, with rock, pop, techno, extended dance mixes and lots of imported tunes, too

Madrid Rock J10
*25 Gran Vía; **metro** Gran Vía.*
A large record store.

Museek Shop J8
*15 C/ de San Pablo; **metro** Tribur*
A wide selection, specializing in imported and national house, hard house, techno, hard techn hard dance, progressive and vo

Up-Beat Discos J8
*7 C/ Espíritu Santo; **metro** Tribu*
The flip-side of the store across street (above), this is the place t come for second-hand vinyl, including 60s soul, reggae and j

Specialities and Rarities

Antigua Casa Talavera H9
*2 C/ de Isabel la Católica; **metro** Santo Domingo.*
For great ceramics and tiles.

Ayllu J14
*1 C/ de Sombrerete; **metro** Lava*
For textiles and jewellery from Latin America.

El Arco Artesanía H12
*Plaza Mayor 9; **metro** Sol.*
Despite its situation right on t famous plaza, this crafts shop some excellent jewellery made local craftsmen.

El Caballo Cojo H12
*7 C/ de Segovia; **metro** Sol or Op*
Has an attractive 19th-century shop-front, behind which you find an astonishing range of exquisite ceramics, handicrafts and furniture.

a Seseña J12
de Cruz; metro Sol.
lace to go for traditional
ileño velvet-lined capes,
illas and beautifully embroi-
Manila shawls.

ámica El Alfar N7
de Claudio Coello;
Núñez de Balboa.
oth traditional and modern
nics and tiles from some of
's best craftspeople.

ería Ortega H13
de Toledo; metro La Latina.
ver 100 years, the Ortega
y has been churning out
es of all shapes and sizes in
ost impossibly tiny shop
between the Plaza Mayor
a Latina metro stop.

uadernación Luna H10
de Campomanes;
Opera.
ttle shop has been binding
s for over 90 years.
erbound volumes and book
rations are a speciality.

Gil J11
2 C/ San Jerónimo; metro Sol.
Dating from 1880 with a magnificent selection of shawls,
mantones and *mantillas*.

Guitarras Artesanles H11
80 C/ Mayor; metro Sol.
A superb shop if you are looking
for a finely crafted Spanish guitar,
with an excellent selection and
helpful staff who will invite you to
twang (if you've got the nerve).

Maty I11
*2 C/ de Maestro Victoria (near
church of San Gínes); metro Opera.*
Everything for the serious
flamenco dancer, from castanets
in different woods and sizes and
low wide-brimmed black hats to
mantillas and haircombs.

Menkes I10
*14 C/ de Mesonero Romanos;
metro Gran Vía or Callao.*
Caters for all the basic needs of
performing classic Spanish dance,
as well as great Halloween/drag
queen outfits.

Museo de América E4
*6 Avenida de los Reyes Católicos;
metro Moncloa.*
The shop here has a small but
beautifully chosen selection of
gifts on Latin American themes.

Narciso Martínez J11
18 C/ de Espoz y Mina; metro Sol.
One of the world's top specialists
in moustache combs.

Sargadelos L7
46 C/ de Zurbano; metro Colón.
For something genuinely Spanish,
original and tasteful, the porcelain
produced by this Galician co-
operative is among the most
distinctive anywhere, and notable
for its lovely deep blues and
translucent whites. Its modern
designs are based on traditional
themes.

La Violeta J11
Plaza de Canalejas; metro Sol.
A Madrid classic selling only
sweets scented or decorated
with violets.

Sports and Green Spaces

:ctator Sports

tball (*fútbol*)

n their great sense of occa-
paniards flock to large
ng events, and the capital's
ain football stadia,
ging to Real Madrid and
o Madrid, regularly play
50,000-plus fans. Given
ccess of Spanish teams in
e, there are games on televi-
very night of the week
Friday.

dio Santiago
nabéu Off maps
Concha Espina (corner of
de la Castellana), *t* 91 457 06
tro *Santiago Bernabéu.*
1adrid is the wealthier
ore successful of the
's two teams – still more
:e David Beckham joined
am in mid 2003 – attracting
fashionable fan to its
stadium.

dio Vicente
lerón Off maps
eo de la Virgen del Puerto,
5 82 09; *metro* Pirámides;
chair accessible.
o de Madrid's ground, down
river. It may not be as smart
Santiago Bernabéu, but the
fans pride themselves on
vorking-class credentials.

lfighting

fighting continues to pack
crowds, and is worth an
ated billion pounds a year.
ring San Isidro festivities
e biggest names at the
s bullring, while August and
mber's holidays – many in
lages around the capital –
arge crowds to impromptu
is. If you really must take in
the Madrid columnist
so Umbral has called a
al shame, head for:

a de Toros de las
tas Off maps
de Alcalá, *t* 91 726 35 79,
w.las-ventas.com; *metro*
s; wheelchair accessible.

Bullfights

In the newspapers, don't look
for accounts of the bullfights
(*corridas*) on the sports pages:
look in the 'arts and culture'
section, for that is how Spain has
always thought of this singular
spectacle. Bullfighting combines
elements of ballet with the primal
finality of Greek tragedy. To
Spaniards it is a ritual sacrifice
without a religion, and it divides
the nation irreconcilably between
those who find it brutal and
demeaning, an echo of the old
Spain best forgotten, and those
who couldn't live without it. Its
origins are obscure. Some claim it
comes ultimately from the bull
games of Minoan Crete, or from
Roman circus games; others say it
started with the Moors, or in the
Middle Ages, when the bull faced
a mounted knight with a lance, a
practice called *rejoneo*. The first
recorded one in Madrid took place
in 1474.

Modern bullfighting, like that
other ultra-Spanish art form,
flamenco, is quintessentially
Andalucian. The present form had
its beginnings around the year
1800 in Ronda, when Francisco
Romero developed the basic
pattern of the modern *corrida*;
some of his moves and passes,

Between March and October
there are *corridas* here every
Sunday afternoon. Note that
tickets (no credit cards) are sold
only two days in advance at the
ring and range from €3.50 for a
cheap seat in the full sun (*sol*) to
€72 or more for the best seat in
the shade (*sombra*); buy directly
from the office at Las Ventas to
avoid the hefty commission
charges. No matter where you sit,
rent a cushion, and buy a sandwich wrapped in foil from one of
the nearby bars, where, not
surprisingly, the speciality on the
menu is *rabo de toro* – stewed
bull's tail.

and those of his celebrated
successor, Pedro Romero, are still
in use today. The first royal
aficionado was Ferdinand VII, who
promoted the spectacle across the
land as a circus for the discon-
tented populace.

In keeping with its ritualistic
aura, the *corrida* is one of the few
things in Spain that begins strictly
on time. The show commences
with the colourful entry of the
cuadrillas (teams of bullfighters,
or *toreros*) and the *alguaciles*, officials dressed in 17th-century
costume, who salute the 'president' of the fight. Usually three
teams fight two bulls each, the
whole show taking only about
two hours. Each of the six fights,
however, is a self-contained
drama performed in four acts.
First, upon the entry of the bull,
the members of the *cuadrilla*
tease him a bit, and the *matador*,
the team leader, plays him with
the cape to test his qualities. Next
comes the turn of the *picadores*,
on padded horses, whose task is
slightly to wound the bull in the
neck with a short lance or *pica*,
and the *banderilleros*, who agilely
plant sharp darts in the bull's back
while avoiding the sweep of its
horns. The effect of these wounds
is to weaken the bull physically

Basketball

It's a popular spectator sport,
and the capital boasts two top
teams: Estudiantes and Real
Madrid. The main basketball
stadium – the Palacio de Deportes
– is currently being re-built after
suffering serious damage due to
fire. Temporary alternative venues
include the Palacio Vistalegre, C/
Utebo 1 (off maps), *t* 91 422 07 81.

Activities

Skiing

Skiing is not a sport that is
instantly associated with Madrid,
although there are good slopes

without diminishing any of its fighting spirit, and to force it to keep its head lower for the third and most artistic stage of the fight, when the lone *matador* conducts his *pas de deux* with the deadly, if doomed, animal. Ideally, this is the transcendent moment, the *matador* leading the bull in deft passes and finally crushing its spirit with a tiny cape called a *muleta*. Now the defeated bull is ready for 'the moment of truth' and dedicated to a member of the audience. Silence falls. The kill must be clean and quick, a sword thrust to the heart; ideally the bull dies in seconds. The corpse is dragged out to the waiting butchers.

More often than not the job is botched, and the always vociferous crowd is merciless in its criticism. Most bullfights, in fact, are a disappointment, especially if the *matadores* are beginners, or *novios*, but to the aficionado the chance to see one or all of the stages performed to perfection makes it all worthwhile. When a *matador* is good, the band plays and the hats and handkerchiefs fly to the shouts of '*Olé, olé!*' (from the Moorish 'Allah! Allah!'). A truly excellent, spine-tingling performance earns as a reward from the president one, or both, of the

bull's ears; or rarely, for an exceptionally brilliant performance, both ears and the tail. A spirited bull who puts on a good show can get the thumbs up from the crowd, and get a return ticket to the ranch.

Since the Civil War, bullfighting has gone through a period of troubles similar to those of boxing in the USA. Scandals of weak bulls, doped-up bulls and bulls with the points of their horns shaved have been frequent. Attempts at reform have been made, and while it was commonly thought it would all lead to a decline in bullfighting's popularity, the opposite has occurred. More people than ever, from all walks of society, flock to the bulls, and some of the young star *toreros* have attained the celebrity status that pop singers have elsewhere: José Tomás, the heart-throb Jesulín de Ubrique, Enrique Ponce, El de Galapagar and Cristina Sánchez, the best of the few women who have taken up the cape. Major fights are nationally televised.

There are bullrings all over Spain, and as far afield as Arles in France and Guadalajara, Mexico, but Madrid's striking Neo-Mudéjar arena, Las Ventas, is the high shrine of the art, the Carnegie Hall for *toreros*.

Offers a pool, seven tennis cou a 'multisport' room, a paddleb court and a football field.

Piscinas Casa de Campo B1 *Casa de Campo, t 91 463 00 50 metro Lago or Puerta del Ange bus No.31, 33, 36 or 39. Open m May to mid September daily 10.30am–8pm.*
In addition to the outdoor poo there is also a weight room ar freestyle gymnasium.

Polideportivo Barrio del Pilar Off maps *C/ de Monforte de Lemos, t 91 79 43; metro Barrio del Pilar or Begoña; bus No.49, 67, 83 or 12 Open Mon–Fri 9am–8pm.*
With space reserved for nude sunbathing, this place gets a cross-section of Madrid flockii to its three open-air pools in t summer. You can also have a football, handball, mini-baske tennis, hockey and judo. Weig room and indoor pool, too.

Polideportivo de la Elipa Off maps *Acceso Parque de la Elipa, t 91 35 11, t 91 430 39 39; metro La Estrella; bus No.71 or 113.*
Five swimming pools, plus badminton, football, baseball, tennis and softball. There is a solarium for nude sunbathing

Jogging

Joggers are not advised to t the city centre, but the Parqu Retiro is good for a short turn you can organize the transpo get out to the Casa de Campo got acres and acres of largely unvisited woodland. Some are frequented by prostitutes they tend to keep themselves themselves, and incidents ar but unknown. Besides which, police patrol the area heavily. There is a gay cruising area u the *teleférico* cable car. Parque la Dehesa de la Villa (*see* 'Gree Spaces', p.263) is nice and has established running circuit.

around 50km north at Puerto de Navacerrada. Closer still is the following site, which can be combined with a meal out for those not too saavy when it comes to slippery slopes.

Xanadú Snow Park Off maps *Arroyomolino (22km from centre), t 902 361 309; bus no. 496, 524, 528 from Principe Pio. Open Mon–Thurs 10am–midnight, Fri 10am–2am, Sat 9am–2am, Sun 9am–midnight; adm per hour adults €10, children €8.*
This themed park opened in mid 2003 and has a ski area of 18,000 square metres that perfectly reproduces a winter ski resort (including those après ski bars and restaurants). Classes are available as well as equipment hire (around €8).

Swimming and Sports Facilities

For the visitor, a day out at a municipal open-air pool in summer offers a fascinating slice of Spanish life. Madrid has a surprisingly wide network of public swimming pools, some of which are located within larger athletic complexes which also offer things like tennis courts, paddleball courts, football fields, etc. The best (and most accessible by public transport) of the bunch are:

Canal de Isabel II Off maps *54 Avenida Islas Filipinas, t 91 554 51 53; metro Ríos Rosas. Open daily 11am–8pm. Wheelchair accessible.*

If

re are a number of golf
es in the metropolitan area,
of them cheap, the best
ped being:

**b de Campo Villa
Madrid** Off maps
tera de Castilla, 2 km,
50 08 40; **bus** *No.84.*
daily 8.30am–dusk.
-six holes. Not cheap, but
e of the few places where
on't need to be a member
t in.

livar de la Hinojosa Off maps
da de Dublín, **t** *91 721 18 89;*
Campo de las Naciones.
Mon–Fri 8.30am–11pm, Sat,
nd hols 8am–11pm.
ine-hole course and one
een-hole course, plus a
g range.

een Spaces

mpo del Moro E10–F11
de la Virgen del Puerto;
Príncipe Pío. **Open** *winter*
-Sat 10am–6pm, Sun and hols
-6pm; summer Mon–Sat
–8pm, Sun and hols 9am–8pm.
nal garden directly behind
alacio Real and accessible
the entrance on the Paseo de
gen del Puerto or the Cuesta
n Vicente. A tremendous,
enclave with 20 hectares of
space, it was opened to the
c by King Juan Carlos I in a
sh of monarchic generosity
8.

Casa de Campo A7–D11
See p.170.

Jardines de Sabatini G10
C/ de Bailén; metro Plaza de España.
Splendid, meticulously manicured
gardens that some might say
are a poor man's version of
those at Versailles. Topiary and a
quaint pool make a perfect post-
touring picnic spot on spring or
summer afternoons.

Parque El Capricho Off maps
Avenida de la Alameda de Osuna;
metro Canillejas; bus No.101. **Open**
Sat, Sun and hols 9am–6.30pm, till
9pm April–Sept.
One of the prettiest gardens in
Madrid. A residence was founded
here in 1783 by the Duchess of
Osuna, the most cultured woman
of her age, who hired Pierre Mulot,
architect of the gardens of the
Petit Trianon, to design her
gardens. The Duchess, a friend of
Goya's and rival to the Queen
Maria Luisa and the Duchess of
Alba, was famous for her parties.
After the death of the dissipated
last Duke of Osuna in 1882, the
house was demolished and the
gardens abandoned and
neglected until they were
purchased by the Comunidad de
Madrid in 1974. Now beautifully
restored, they are an oasis of
romantic coolness in the brash
new developments.

Parque de la Dehesa de la Villa
Off maps
*Metro Francos Rodríguez or
Valdezarza.*

One of the lesser-known but
oldest and most striking green
zones in all of Madrid, Dehesa de
la Villa dates back to the 15th
century and the reign of Charles
IV, when it was part of the royal
residence of El Pardo (*see p.172*).
It was officially turned into a park
in 1970, and has a running circuit
and kilometres' worth of green
space. Bring refreshments,
though: there isn't much here.

**Parque Enrique Tierno
Galván** Off maps
Metro Méndez Alvaro.
Located just behind Las Delicias
train station, this park has a
whopping 54 hectares to its credit,
plus Madrid's planetarium and a
conference centre.

Parque Juan Carlos I Off maps
Glorieta de Don Juan de Borbón;
metro Campo de las Naciones;
bus No.122. **Open** *winter daily*
8am–10pm, summer daily
7am–midnight.
Built around an olive grove, it has
an artificial river, fountains and
canals, 'cybernetic water displays'
on summer evenings in front of
the amphitheatre, sculptures, and
lots of young trees that will
make it a shady refuge in about
20 years.

Parque del Oeste C5–E7
See p.168.

Parque del Retiro M10–O14
See p.106.

Real Jardín Botánico L–M13
See p.108.

Children's and Teenagers' Madric

ildren

ain has the lowest birthrate
rope, but children are
present in Madrid. This is not
uch to do with some demo-
hic quirk as the fact that
ren aren't regarded as a race
t: if the *madrileños* are cats,
are kittens, and you'll find
up until the wee hours in
and restaurants, having a
time as their parents blithely
d chat away into the night
a group of friends.
general, children can visit
id's museums either for free
lf-price, and transport on the
o and buses is free for those
r 8. Train fares are 60 per cent
e adult fare. For kids under 12,
id has several *centros de ocio*
by-the-hour play centres);
k the *Guía del Ocio* listings
azine under 'Niños'. Nappies,
ulas, etc, are widely available
adrid in supermarkets
pharmacies.

bysitting

st of the more expensive
ls will arrange for babysitting.
natively, English-language
azines and papers, such as *In*
id, will often have listings for
sh-speaking babysitters.

ting Out

general, children's various
ns and flights of fancy are
ectfully accommodated in
urants – it is never difficult to
up something simple to suit
by, toddler or picky child. At
urants, the rule of thumb is
mon sense: the cheaper and
casual you go, the easier it is.
perchic or fancy ethnic
urants it is inevitably harder
pease snooty waiters or find
e-pleasing treats for tots.

Museums and Attractions

Casa de Campo A7–D11
See p.170.
Kids might enjoy getting there
via the *teleférico* from Paseo
del Pintor Rosales. Madrid's
zoo-aquarium (*see* below),
amusement park and largest
outdoor swimming pools are all
there. The Parque de Atracciones
has some of Europe's scariest
rides and noisiest music.

Faro de Moncloa F5
See p.171.
An inland lighthouse with a lift to
whizz you up to the observation
platform for kid-friendly views of
the city.

Museo de América E4
See p.171.
With its ancient mummies and
pre-Columbian artefacts, it's an
interesting spot for vaguely
culturally minded kids over the
age of 10. However, if your basic
archaeological museum is likely to
bore your child, so will this.

Museo de Cera L9
See p.142.
Totally tacky waxworks, complete
with a terror train and Virtual
Reality Stimulator.

Museo de Ciencias Naturales (Natural History) M3–4
See p.148.
In the Jardín de las Piedras ('stone
garden') children can frolic around
the giant rocks and fossilized tree
trunks sitting out in the open air.
In the Real Gabinete ('royal
cabinet'), an array of molluscs,
insects, fish, reptiles, birds and
mammals are on display. In
general, the museum offers an
educational approach to its collections, making it especially
accessible to kids.

Museo Nacional Ferroviario L17
See p.118.
In the old Delicias train station,
this museum offers not only a
great example of 19th-century
ironwork in the building's exterior,
but also all the charm of the
old train cars, locomotives
and engines.

Museo Naval L11
See p.106.
With model ships, coats-of-arms,
weapons and maps, it's a museum
that teaches and entertains.
Entire rooms are dedicated to
specific battles, such as Lepanto
and Trafalgar.

Museo Real Madrid Off maps
*Estadio Santiago Bernabéu, Puerta
3; metro Santiago Bernabéu.
Open Tues–Sun 10.30am–7.30pm;
adm €3.50.*
All you ever wanted to know
about the city's best-loved football team, Real Madrid, whose
goals, victories and champion-
ships are lovingly chronicled in
this museum's glass cases.

Parque de Bomberos Off maps
*4 C/ de Boada, Puente de Vallecas,
t 91 478 65 72; metro Puente de
Vallecas. Open Mon–Sat 10am–
1.30pm; adm free.*
A fun trip down fireman's lane,
with stories and anecdotes
relating to the history of firemen
in Spain. The firemen themselves
guide us through this romp, and
children can admire the old horse-
drawn carriages as well as the
newer state-of-the-art trucks.

Planetario Off maps
See p.118.
What could be more fun than
peering up at the stars via the
telescopes and cosmically
connected computers in this
state-of-the-art planetarium?
There is also a theatre and
audiovisual centre with a rotating
calendar of events and shows.
A kids' favourite.

Zoo-Acuario de Madrid Off maps
See p.170.
The combo zoo-aquarium has over
2,000 humanely kept animals.
There are kid-pleasing shows at
the dolphin pool and a children's
zoo. Bloodthirsty kids may
particularly enjoy the snake den
or the aquarium, filled with

hammerheads and other sharks. There are also train- and boat-ride possibilities.

Outside Madrid

Aquasur

Aranjuez, t 91 891 60 34; cercanía C3 from Atocha. Open daily 10am–8pm; adm €5 Mon–Fri and €11 Sat and Sun.

A water park that includes minigolf, a wild-west fort, mini-zoo and even karaoke as well as pools and slides, and makes a good trade-off after visiting Aranjuez's royal palace (*see* p.196). Aquasur's big claim to fame, however, is the largest Jacuzzi in Spain – it holds up to 80 sweaty sunbathers at once.

Aquópolis

Villanueva de la Cañada, t 91 815 69 11; free bus leaves from Plaza de España (corner Cuesta San Vicente) at 11am and noon on weekdays, and 11am, noon, and 1pm at the weekend. Open 14–30 June daily noon–7pm, 1 July–2 Sept daily 11am–8pm; adm €12.50.

Billed as the largest aquapark in Europe, Aquópolis boasts zigzag toboggans, a 26m 'Super Slide', and the 'Black Hol' (sic). There is also a surfing pool, 'adventure' lake and landlubbing leisure activities.

Cosmocaixa

C/ Pinto Velázquez s/n, Alcobendas, t 91 484 52 00. Take bus nos.151/152/153/154/156/157 from Plaza Castillo. Open Tues–Sun 10–8; adm adults €3, children under 7 years free.

Great for kids, this is an entertaining hands-on interactive science museum with the added plus of small animals to touch for tots.

Safari Madrid Off maps

Aldea del Fresno. By car South–West to Navalcarnero (N–V) then follow signs. Open daily 10.30am–sunset; adm adults €10, children €6.

A good-value wild animal park including big cats, elephants and monks, plus pedalo lake, go karts and shows.

Warnerbros Park

San Martín de la Vega, t 91 821 12 34. Open April–June, Sept Mon–Thurs 10am–8pm, Fri–Sat 10am–midnight, July–Aug daily 10am–midnight, Oct–mid Nov Fri–Sun 10am–8pm; adm adults €32, children €24.

Opened in April 2002 with five themed areas with rides, including Cartoon Village, Hollywood Boulevard, Old West Territory and Super Heroes. One drawback is that you can't take your own food or drink into the park which hikes the (already expensive) price still further.

Entertainment

Teatro de Titeres del Retiro M10

Close to Puerta de Alcalá entrance, Parque del Retiro, t 91 813 25 33; metro Retiro.

Open-air puppet shows Sat and Sun at 1.30pm. During August, an international puppet festival attracts companies from around the world (performances daily at 7.30pm, 9pm and 10.30pm).

IMAX Off maps

Parque Tierno Galván, C/ de Meneses, t 91 467 48 00; metro Méndez Alvaro; wheelchair accessible.

For kids aged six and up, the cinema puts on big wildlife do[cu]mentaries in which language won't pose much of a problem.

Teenagers

The eternal number-one act[ivity] among peer-conscious teeny-boppers is shopping, and there['s] never a short supply of shops [in] Madrid to keep them happy. Te[ens] might particularly enjoy some [of] the markets, especially El Rastr[o] (*See* 'Shopping', pp.253–9.)

Some of Madrid's more piqu[ant] neighbourhoods have fun atm[os]pheres to soak up, particularly Chueca, with little shops sellin[g] candles and knick-knacks; Noviciado, squished between Calles Princesa and San Berna[rdo] with great shops, cafés and a general art-school ambience; Ba[rrio] de los Austrias, especially arou[nd] the Calle Mayor, with the Plaza [de la] Miguel and its covered market[,] and La Latina and Lavapiés, wh[ich] can be fun for discovering odd little shops, bars and galleries.

Madrid is filled with museu[ms] that would be interesting to teenagers. For example, the Re[ina] Sofía (*see* p.113) has excellent u[p]-to-the-minute art exhibitions, many are short enough not to exhaust the shortest of attenti[on] spans. The Reina Sofía's two ex[hi]bition spaces in the Parque del Retiro, the Palacio de Velázque[z] and the Palacio de Cristal, are a[lso] nice jaunts for teenagers, as the[y're] usually very edgy and contem[po]rary. The Palacio Real's entirely over-the-top decoration may w[ow] even the most jaded teen.

Gay and Lesbian Madrid

The gay scene is out there in every way, shape and form, centring on the neighbourhood of Chueca, a formerly drug-infested area now happily festooned with rainbow flags, hip clothing stores, art galleries and the occasional leather bar. The traditional denizens of the area seem to co-exist quite happily with their new gay neighbours, and the rest of the city is coming around as well, though you are not likely to see too much same-sex smooching outside Chueca. Politically, things are very PC, but some *madrileños* might not be so open-minded. Chueca comes even more alive than usual during the last week in June, when Gay Pride is celebrated with a parade that stretches from the Puerta de Alcalá to the Puerta del Sol – 150,000 people attended in 2001 – and an all-weekend party complete with live bands and open-air bars in the streets of Chueca.

Organizations

Colectivo de Lesbianas, Gays, Transexuales y Bisexuales de Madrid (COGAM) and Federación Estatal de Lesbianas y Gays (FELG), 37 C/ de Fuencarral, general **t** 91 522 45 17, helpline **t** 91 523 00 70, **f** 91 524 02 00, **w** www.cogam.org; **metro** Gran Via. **Open** daily 5–11pm.
Madrid's largest and most vocal gay organization, which publishes a monthly politically oriented magazine, *Entiendes?*, available in kiosks in Chueca. Offers all sorts of facilities and services.

Fundación Triángulo, 25 C/ de Eloy Gonzalo, 1º, general **t** 91 593 05 40, helpline **t** 91 446 63 94, **w** www.fundaciontriangulo.es; **metro** Quevedo. Resources for the gay community in Madrid.

Magazines

There is a plethora of gay-oriented magazines available in Madrid, some free and others not.

The best known of the bunch is *Shangay*, a hilariously hip freebie that is omnipresent in Chueca's bars, shops and cafés, and offers great music and club information as well as fluffy star-oriented articles. There's also the *Shanguide*, which is almost exclusively bar and club listings. *Zero* covers more current events, while *Gesto* is the latest magazine and tries to offer the most challenging, provocative content – lots of culture news. Other magazines readily available include *Mensual* and *Spartacus*, the international gay guide.

Shops

A Different Life K9
30 C/ de Pelayo, **w** www.lifegay.com; **metro** Chueca.
Books, CDs, videos and cute gift items. Down the street at No.3 is a sister store selling perfume, cosmetics, lingerie and accessories.

Berkana K9
11 C/ de Gravina; **metro** Chueca.
A gay bookstore and café, with magazines and journals.

Librería Alazraki K9
12 C/ de Gravina; **metro** Chueca.
A more esoteric, New Agey bookstore offering tarot and astral chart consultations in addition to spiritual, erotic and other alternative types of reading material.

Eating Out

El Armario K10
7 C/ de San Bartolomé, **t** 91 532 83 77; **metro** Chueca. Closed Aug.
Expensive.
Many people consider this to be one of Madrid's most gourmet gay restaurants, with exotic dishes such as the Chinese noodle nest with stir-fried vegetables.

Café Acuarela K9
10 C/ de Gravina, **t** 91 522 21 43; **metro** Chueca. **Open** Sun–Thurs 3pm–3am, Fri and Sat 3pm–4am.
Antique chic and a lively atmosphere at this trendy gay café. Has a comfy mixture of candelabra,

angelic cherubs and velvet cus-ions. It crams in a mixed client and is very relaxed, but can ge pretty packed.

Café Figueroa K9
17 C/ de Augusto Figueroa, **t** 91 16 73; **metro** Chueca. **Open** Mor Thurs 2.30pm–1am, Fri and Sat 2.30pm–2.30am, Sun 4pm–1am
Chatty, relaxed 19th-century ca

Divina K10
13 C/ de Colmenares, **t** 91 531 37 **metro** Chueca. **Open** Tues–Sat.
Moderate.
Ultramodern Spanish cuisine, including ostrich steaks and e orately concocted fruit desser

Gula Gula K10
1 Gran Via, **t** 91 522 87 64; **metro** Gran Via. **Open** Mon–Thurs 12.3 and 8–midnight, Fri and Sat 12.30–4 and 8–2, Sun 8pm–midnight. Booking essen **Moderate**.
One of Madrid's gay crossover successes. Drag queen waitres loud, this is a place to see and seen. The food is good, with a s menu or a salad bar.

Madrilia J10
6 C/ de Clavel, **t** 91 523 92 75; **m** Chueca. **Open** daily 2–4 and 9.30–midnight; closed Sun in A **Inexpensive**.
Serves creative Mediterranean cuisine in a modern and smoo designed restaurant.

Momo K9
41 C/ de Augusto Figueroa, **t** 91 71 62; **metro** Chueca. **Open** dail 1–4 and 9–midnight. **Moderate**
Creative cuisine and adorable waiters to entertain you.

Sarrasín K9
8 C/ de la Libertad, **t** 91 532 73 4 **metro** Chueca. **Open** Mon–Sat and 9–midnight. **Moderate**.
With its policy of a fixed-price menu, and a limited choice of dishes based on simple but ta ingredients, this is one of the more enjoyable and affordable the many gay restaurants now flourishing in Chueca.

s and Clubs

k and White K9
de la Libertad, t 91 531 11 41;
Chueca. Open Sun–Thurs
4am, Fri and Sat 9pm–5am.
ts older men and younger
like to its disco.

ising J9
e Pérez Galdós, t 91 521 51 43;
Chueca or Gran Vía. Open
hurs 8pm–3am, Fri and Sat
4am.
en but allows women in
rs. Fairly heavy scene – porn
as the night wears on.

o Refugio I12
Doctor Cortezo; metro
Martín or Tirso de Molina.
Wed–Sun midnight–dawn.
esdays are hot and heavy
massages and XXX room.

ape K9
e Gravina; metro Chueca.
10pm–dawn.
nly lesbian bar with
egum pop music. Fridays
aturdays offer live shows.

n's Dance Club I10
a del Callao; metro Calloa.
Us here spin a diverse
section of music in a
g-edge atmosphere.
d place to start the night.

upe J13
e Torricella del Leal; metro
. Open daily 9pm–3am.
ts gay men and women to
fee bar by day. In the
ng it's relaxed, with good
and regular drag acts.

dea J13
e la Cabeza; metro Lavapiés.
Tues–Sun 11pm–5am.
s men at weekends, and is
ps the capital's best-known
n disco.

Leather K9
42 C/ de Pelayo, t 91 308 14 62;
metro Chueca. Open Sun–Thurs
9pm–3am, Fri and Sat 9pm–4am.
As its name suggests, tending
towards the heavier side.
There are shows every night,
and it is very much part of the
circuit. Men only.

No Se Lo Digas A Nadie K11
7 C/ de Ventura de la Vega, t 91 369
17 27; metro Sevilla.
A multi-purpose venue with a
café/disco/bar which was once
almost exclusively women-only,
but now welcomes lesbians and
gays. It hosts private parties, drag
shows and other entertainments,
and it doubles as an occasional
meeting place for militant
action groups.

Ohm I10
4 Plaza de Callao; metro Callao.
Open Fri and Sat midnight–6am.
For people of all stripes – gay,
lesbian, straight. A fun, crazy
dance scene.

The Rainbow Party Zone K10
34 C/ Libertad; metro Chueca.
A firm fixture on the gay scene
with plenty of chill-out space and
dance floors where you can strut
your stuff.

Rick's J10
6 C/ de Clavel; metro Gran Vía.
Open daily 11.30pm–dawn.
Not Humphrey Bogart's hangout
exactly, this Rick's Café is an institution among Madrid's gay and
lesbian dance crowd. Pumped-up
bodies and flimsy clothing is the
name of the game here.

Shangay Tea Dance I10
37 Gran Vía, t 91 531 48 27; metro
Gran Vía. Open Sun 9pm–2am.
Without a doubt the best tea
dance in Madrid. Also plays great
disco music and has shows.

Soho K9
6 Plaza de Chueca; metro Chueca.
Open Tues–Sun 9pm–dawn.
The nerve-centre of Madrid's gay
neighbourhood, and in the
summertime the outside tables
are excellent for people-watching.

Strong Center H10
7 C/ de Trujillos, t 91 531 48 27;
metro Opera or Sol. Open daily
midnight–dawn.
If you're looking to lose yourself,
then head for the legendary
darkroom. It's very, very large...

Tábata H11
12 C/ de Vergara, t 91 547 97 35;
metro Opera. Open Wed–Sat
11.30pm–dawn.
Recently all the rage among the
gay dance crowd, despite its inconveniently un-Chueca location.

Truck K9
10 C/ de Gravina, t 91 532 89 21;
metro Chueca. Open daily
from 8pm.
A lesbian place that's open to
everyone, offering a terrace bar.

Why Not? K10
6 C/ de San Bartolomé; metro
Chueca. Open daily 11.30pm–dawn.
Mainly a gay scene, but heteros
are generally welcomed – a fun
atmosphere.

XXX Café J10
12 C/ Clavel, t 91 532 84 15; metro
Gran Vía. Open Sun–Thurs 1pm–
1.30am, Fri and Sat 1pm–2.30am.
Frequented more by men than
women, it is an obligatory stop on
the gay bar circuit.

Festivals

a city that embraces the old
he new with gusto, Madrid
on some excellent fiestas,
ng from new artsy events to
host traditional. Among the
fun are the old-fashioned
neighbourhood *verbenas*, or street
als, the occasion for women
ul out their long flouncy
es and put a carnation in
hair, while men don their flat
and jackets.

e tourist office has a Web site
www.munimadrid.es, which
events on a monthly basis, as
their bi-monthly *En Madrid*
's On leaflet. The best thing
is head for the tourist office
in town and look in the *Guía
cio*, which always offers
nsive coverage of festivals.

uary

che Vieja
c–1 Jan
munal gathering in the
ta del Sol to see the old year
ry the Latin custom of eating
pe with each of the 12 chimes
rings good luck.

s Reyes (Epiphany)
an
end of the holiday season is
ed on the 5th by a big parade
feast celebrating the arrival of
Magi in Bethlehem. Children
their presents on the 6th.

ruary

CO
Feb
e international contemporary-
air, at the Feria de Madrid.

rnaval
late Feb
week leading up to Lent is
sion for a parade, a certain
unt of dressing up, gigs in the
and parties. Uniquely
rileño, however, is the wacky
al of the Sardine (*Entierro de la
na*), an old tradition in which
pier mâché sardine in a coffin
raded around the city with a
band on Ash Wednesday and
to rest in the Paseo de la
da near the entrance to the
de Campo.

March

Día de la Mujer
8 Mar
International Woman's Day, celebrated with a march down Calle
de Atocha and festivities in the
evening across town, especially in
the various bars.

Semana Santa (Holy Week)
There are enough citizens with
Andalucían roots in Madrid to
make sure Semana Santa doesn't
pass by unnoticed. Processions of
various weighty religious floats
showing scenes of the Passion by
brotherhoods of Penitentes in
their hoods (copied by the Ku Klux
Klan) take place in most of
Madrid's old neighbourhoods.

May

Fiesta del Trabajo
1 May
Still the occasion for a
Communist-Socialist-Anarchist
march through the city centre,
and a party in the Casa de Campo,
with music, beer and food from all
the regions of Spain.

Dos de Mayo
2 May
An official holiday celebrating
Madrid's rising against Napoleon's
forces in 1808, so memorably
depicted by Goya. The main events
take place around the Plaza Dos
de Mayo in Malasaña, including
live bands. The Comunidad de
Madrid stages other events, especially in the Jardines de las Vistillas
by the Palacio Real.

Festimad
Early May
A festival of alternative music and
film by the new and young in
Spain. Musical events take place in
the Círculo de Bellas Artes.

Madrid en Danza
Early May–early June
International dance festival in
various venues across the city.

San Isidro
15 May
Madrid's patron saint has his feast
day on the 15th, but merits a
whole week of festivities leading
up to the big day. The bullfights at

Las Ventas last an entire month,
and with typical *madrileño*
modesty are claimed to be the
most important in the world.
Everything from traditional events
to flamenco shows takes place in
the Plaza Mayor, Casa de Campo,
Las Vistillas, etc.

Feria del Libro
Late May–early June
The biggest book fair in the
Spanish-speaking world in the
Parque del Retiro.

June

San Antonio de la Florida
13 June
A *verbena* honouring Madrid's
celestial match-maker. According
to tradition, those young women
hoping to get hitched should
deposit 13 pins in the baptismal
font of the church of San Antonio
de la Florida and pray for San
Antonio to do his work.

PhotoEspaña
Mid-June–mid-July
A very popular expo featuring
photographers from around the
world in venues across the city.

July

World Music Getafe and the Fiesta Africana
Both in the industrial suburb of
Getafe and a short walk from one
another. The first concentrates on
music and the second on culture,
crafts, food and more music.

Veranos de la Villa (Summers in the City)
July–mid-Sept
Features a wide range of music
and dance, in the Centro Cultural
Conde-Duque, Las Ventas arena
and elsewhere.

August

Verbena de San Cayetano and Lorenzo
10 Aug
Neighbourhood festival of
Lavapiés with open-air concerts,
streetside bars and decorations.

Verbena de la Paloma
14–15 Aug
The biggest of the lot, celebrating
the Assumption of the Virgin.

It takes place in the Barrio de los Austrias, from Calle de Bailén to the Plaza Mayor. *Madrileños* dress up in their traditional clothes, and dance the *chotis* along the colourful, lantern-decorated streets of old Madrid.

September

Semana Internacional de Moda (International Fashion Week)
Mid-Sept
Many designers from Spain's extremely active fashion scene participate in fashion shows and cocktail parties for those in the know.

Fiestas del Partido Comunista
Mid-Sept
A three-day (Fri–Sun) fun-fest of music, food and theatre in the Casa de Campo.

October

Festival de Otoño
Late Oct–Dec
The autumn festival has grown to become one of the biggest music and theatre events in Madrid, with a huge variety for all tastes.

Language

Castellano, as Spanish is properly called, was the first modern language to have a grammar written for it. When a copy was presented to Queen Isabel in 1492, she understandably asked what it was for. 'Your Majesty,' replied a perceptive bishop, 'language is the perfect instrument of empire.' In the centuries to come, this concise, flexible and expressive language would prove just that: an instrument that would contribute more to Spanish unity than any laws or institutions, while spreading itself effortlessly over much of the New World.

Among other European languages, Spanish is closest to Portuguese, French and Italian – and, of course, Catalan and Gallego. Spanish, however, may have the simplest grammar of any Romance language, and if you know a little of any one of these, you will find much of the vocabulary looks familiar. It's quite easy to pick up a working knowledge of Spanish; but Spaniards speak colloquially and fast. Expressing yourself may prove a little easier than understanding the replies. Spaniards will appreciate your efforts, and when they correct you, they aren't being snooty: they simply feel it's their duty to help you learn. If you already speak Spanish, note that the Spaniards increasingly use the familiar *tú* instead of *usted* when addressing even complete strangers.

Pronunciation

Pronunciation is phonetic, but somewhat difficult for English-speakers.

Vowels

a short *a* as in 'car'
e short *e* as in 'set'
i as *e* in 'be'
o as *o* in 'lost'
u silent after *q* and in gue- and gui-; otherwise long *u* as in 'flute'
ü *w* sound, as in 'dwell'
y at end of word or meaning 'and', as *i*

Dipthongs

ai, **ay** as *i* in 'side'
au as *ou* in 'sound'
ei, **ey** as *ey* in 'they'
oi, **oy** as *oy* in 'boy'

Consonants

c before the vowels *i* and *e*, it's a *castellano* tradition to pronounce it as *th*; many Spaniards and all Latin Americans pronounce it in this case as an *s*
ch like *ch* in 'church'
d often becomes a slight *th*, or is almost silent, at end of word
g before i or e, pronounced as *j* (*see* below)
h silent
j as *ch* in 'loch' – a guttural, throat-clearing *h*
ll *y* or *ly* as in 'million'
ñ *ny* as in 'canyon' (the ~ is called a *tilde*)
q *k*
r usually rolled, which takes practice
v often pronounced as *b*
z *th*, but *s* in parts of Andalucía

Stress

Stress is on the penultimate syllable if the word ends in a vowel, an n or an s, and on the last syllable if the word ends in any other consonant; exceptions are marked with an accent.

If all this seems difficult, consider that English pronunciation is even worse for Spaniards.

Practise on some of the place names:

Madrid ma-DREED
Trujillo troo-HEE-oh
León lay-OHN
Jerez her-ETH
Sevilla se-BEE-ah
Badajóz ba-da-HOTH
Cáceres CAH-ther-es
Málaga MAHL-ah-gah
Cuenca KWAYN-ka
Alcázar ahl-CATH-ar
Jaén ha-AIN
Valladolid ba-yah-dol-EED
Sigüenza sig-WAYN-thah
Arévalo ahr-EB-bah-lo

Basic Vocabulary

Greetings

Hello *Hola*
Good morning *Buenos días*
Good afternoon *Buenas tarde*
Good night *Buenas noches*
Thank you *Gracias*
You're welcome *De nada*
I'm sorry *Lo siento*
Please *Por favor*
Excuse me *Perdón*
Goodbye *Adiós*
Sir *Señor*
Madam *Señora*

Driving

rent *alquiler*
car *coche*
motorbike/moped *moto/ciclomotor*
bicycle *bicicleta*
petrol *gasolina*
driving licence *carnet de cond*
exit *salida*
entrance *entrada*
danger *peligro*
no parking *estacionamento prohibido*
give way/yield *ceda el paso*
roadworks *obras*
Note: Most road signs will be international pictographs

Transport and Directio

aeroplane *avión*
airport *aeropuerto*
bus/coach *autobús/autocar*
bus/railway station *estación*
bus stop *parada*
customs *aduana*
platform *andén*
seat *asiento*
ship *buque/barco/embarcade*
ticket *billete*
train *tren*
I want to go to... *Deseo ir a...*
How can I get to...?
  ¿Cómo puedo llegar a...?
Where is...? *¿Dónde está...?*
When is the next...?
  ¿Cuándo sale el próximo...?
What time does it leave (arriv
  ¿Sale (llega) a qué hora?
From where does it leave?
  ¿De dónde sale?
Do you stop at...? *¿Para en...?*
How long does the trip take?
  ¿Cuánto tiempo dura el viaje

t a (return) ticket to...
*ero un billete (de ida y
lta) a...
 much is the fare?
 ánto cuesta el billete?
 aquí
 allí
 cerca
 jos
 zquierda
 derecha
 ght on *todo recto*
 r esquina
 e plaza
 t calle

 e
: time is it? *¿Qué hora es?*
 o'clock *Son las dos*
 f past 2 *...las dos y media*
 uarter past 2 *...las dos y cuarto*
 uarter to 3
 s tres menos cuarto
 ch mes
 semana
 día
 ing *mañana*
 noon *tarde*
 ing *noche*
 hoy
 rday *ayer*
 pronto
 rrow *mañana*
 temprano
 tarde

 s
 day *lunes*
 day *martes*
 nesday *miércoles*
 sday *jueves*
 y *viernes*
 rday *sábado*
 ay *domingo*

 pping and
 ghtseeing
 uld like... *Quisiera...*
 re is/are...?
 ónde está/están...?
 much is it? *¿Cuánto vale eso?*
 abierto
 d *cerrado*
 p/expensive *barato/caro*
 banco
 ing/box office *taquilla*
 ch *iglesia*
 eum *museo*
 tre *teatro*

pharmacy *farmacia*
post office *correos*
postage stamp *sello*
shop *tienda*
Do you have any change?
 ¿Tiene cambio?
telephone *teléfono*
toilets *servicios/aseos*
men *señores/hombres/caballeros*
women *señoras/damas*

Accommodation
Where is the hotel?
 ¿Dónde está el hotel?
Do you have a room?
 ¿Tiene usted una habitación?
Can I look at the room?
 ¿Podría ver la habitación?
How much is the room per
 day/week?
 *¿Cuánto cuesta la habitación
 por día/semana?*
...with 2 beds *...con dos camas*
...with double bed
 ...con una cama matrimonial
...with a shower/bath
 ...con ducha/baño
...for one night/one week
 ...para una noche/una semana
elevator *ascensor*
bathroom *servicio/cuarto de baño*

Eating Out

Restaurant Vocabulary
menu *carta/menú*
bill/check *la cuenta/la nota*
change *cambio*
set meal *menú del día*
waiter/waitress *camarero/a*
Do you have a table? *¿Hay mesa?*
...for one/two? *¿...para uno/dos?*
Can I see the menu, please?
 ¿Podría ver el menú, por favor?
Do you have a wine list?
 ¿Hay carta de vinos?
Can I have the bill (check), please?
 La cuenta, por favor?
Can I pay by credit card?
 *¿Puedo pagar con tarjeta de
 crédito?*
Where are the toilets/restrooms?
 ¿Dónde está el servicio?

Fish (*Pescadoes*)
acedías *small plaice*
adobo
 fish marinated in white wine
almejas **clams**

anchoas **anchovies**
anguilas **eels**
arenque **herring**
ástaco **crayfish**
atún **tuna**
bacalao **codfish (usually dried)**
berberechos **cockles**
bogavante **lobster**
boquerones **fresh anchovies**
calamares **squid**
cangrejo **crab**
caracoles **snails**
centollo **spider crab**
chanquetes **whitebait**
chipirones...en su tinta
 cuttlefish...in its own ink
dorado/lubina **sea bass**
escabeche
 pickled or marinated fish
gambas **prawns**
langosta **lobster**
langostinos **giant prawns**
lenguado **sole**
mariscos **shellfish**
mejillones **mussels**
merluza **hake**
mero **grouper**
mojama **cured tuna**
navajas **razor-shell clams**
ostras **oysters**
percebes **barnacles**
pescadilla **whiting**
pez espada/emperador **swordfish**
platija **plaice**
pulpo **octopus**
rape **anglerfish**
rodaballo **turbot**
salmón **salmon**
trucha **trout**
veneras **scallops**
zarzuela **fish stew**

Meat and Fowl
  (*Carnes y Aves*)
albóndigas **meatballs**
asado **roast**
buey **ox**
callos **tripe**
cerdo **pork**
chorizo **spiced sausage**
chuletas **chops**
cochinillo **suckling pig**
conejo **rabbit**
corazón **heart**
cordero **lamb**
entrecot **sirloin**
faisán **pheasant**
fiambres **cold meats**

hígado **liver**
jabalí **wild boar**
jamón de York **raw cured ham**
jamón serrano **baked ham**
lomo **pork loin**
morcilla **blood sausage**
pato **duck**
pavo **turkey**
perdiz **partridge**
pinchos morunos
  spicy mini kebabs
pollo **chicken**
rabo/cola de toro
  **bull's tail with onions and
  tomatoes**
salchicha **sausage**
salchichón **salami**
sesos **brains**
solomillo **sirloin steak**
ternera **veal**
  Note: *potajes, cocidos, guisados,
  estofados, fabadas* and *cazuelas*
  are various kinds of stew.

Vegetables (*Verduras y Legumbres*)

alcachofas **artichokes**
apio **celery**
arroz **rice**
arroz marinera
  rice with saffron and seafood
berenjena **aubergine (eggplant)**
cebolla **onion**
champiñones **mushrooms**
col/repollo **cabbage**
coliflor **cauliflower**
endivias **endives**
espárragos **asparagus**
espinacas **spinach**
garbanzos **chickpeas**
judías blancas **white beans**
judías pintas **kidney beans**
judías verdes **green beans**
lechuga **lettuce**
lentejas **lentils**
maíz **corn**
patatas (fritas/salteadas/al horno)
  potatoes (fried/sautéed/baked)
pepino **cucumber**
pimiento **red pepper**
puerros **leeks**
remolacha **beetroot (beet)**
setas **Spanish mushrooms**
zanahorias **carrots**

Desserts (*Postres*)

arroz con leche **rice pudding**
bizcocho/pastel/torta **cake**

blanco y negro
  ice cream and coffee float
budín **pudding**
flan **crème caramel**
galletas **biscuits (cookies)**
helados **ice creams**
natillas **vanilla pudding**
pasteles **pastries**
queso **cheese**
tarta de frutas **fruit pie**
tarta de queso **cheesecake**
turrón **nougat**
yogur **yogurt**

Fruits (*Frutas*)

albaricoque **apricot**
arándano **blueberry**
cereza **cherry**
ciruela **plum**
dátil **date**
durazno **nectarine**
frambuesa **raspberry**
fresa **strawberry**
manzana **apple**
melocotón **peach**
naranja **orange**
nectarina **nectarine**
pera **pear**
piña **pineapple**
plátano **banana**
pomelo **grapefruit**
uva *grape*
zarzamora **blackberry**

Condiments

ali-oli **garlic mayonnaise**
mantequilla **butter**
mayonesa **mayonnaise**
mermelada **jam**
mostaza **mustard**
pimienta **pepper**
sal **salt**

Breakfast (*Desayuno*)

churros **fried batter sticks**
cruasán **croissant**
cruasán a la plancha
  **toasted croissant, served with
  butter and jam**
porras
  fried dough, light and greasy
tostada
  **thick slice of toast, served with
  butter and jam**

Typical Dishes

bocadillo **sandwich on bague**
cocido
  **stew pot with ham hock,
  chicken, beef, garbanzos, ca
  rots, onions and other vege
  bles; broth is served as the
  first course.**
croquetas
  **croquettes with béchamel
  sauce and ham bits**
empanada
  **pasty-like pie crust with tu
  and pimiento filling**
fabada
  **Asturian stew with white
  beans, chorizo, peas
  and sausage**
gazpacho
  Andalucían tomato soup
huevos estrellados
  **fried eggs, 'broken' atop a b
  of potatoes**
huevos revueltos (or, more ofte
  'revuelto') **scrambled eggs**
patatas bravas
  **fried potatos in spicy
  orange sauce**
pisto **ratatouille-style
  vegetable dish**
tortilla
  omelette with egg and pota

Drinks

agua **water**
agua con gas **bubbly water**
batido **milkshake**
café con leche **espresso with**
café cortado
  espresso with a splash of m
café sólo **espresso**
caña **small glass of draught b**
cava **champagne-like drink**
cerveza **beer**
champán **champagne**
ginebra **gin**
infusiones **herbal teas**
jerez **sherry**
manzanilla
  pre-dinner sweet white win
ron **rum**
rosado **rosé wine**
sangria **fruit punch with red w**
sidra **fermented cider**
vermut **vermouth**
vino blanco **white wine**
vino tinto **red wine**
zumo **fruit juice**

...dex

Madrid Street Maps

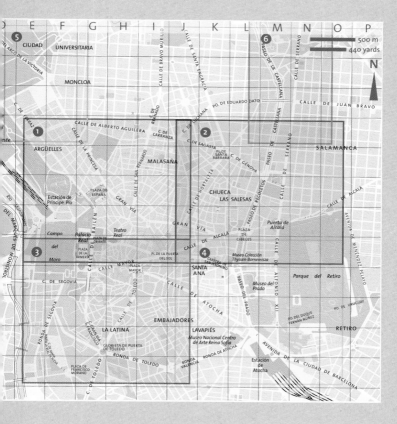

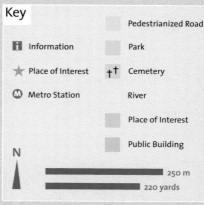

Key

Information

★ **Place of Interest**

M **Metro Station**

Pedestrianized Road

Park

† **Cemetery**

River

Place of Interest

Public Building

N

250 m
220 yards

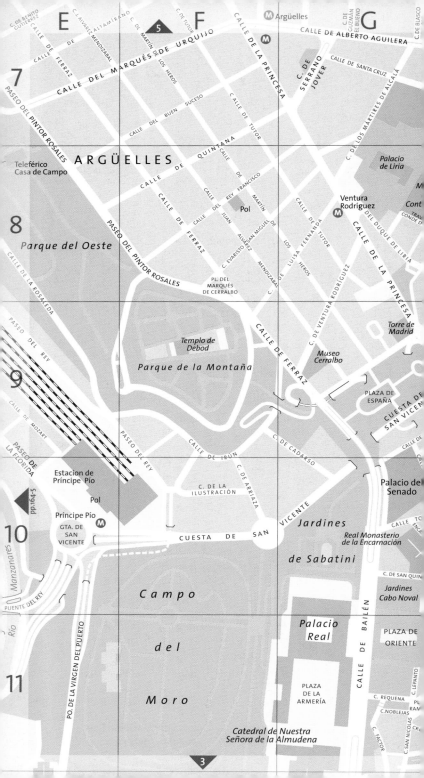

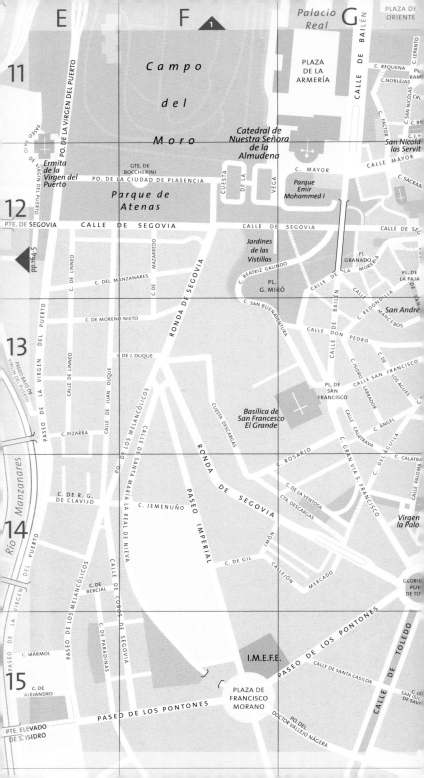

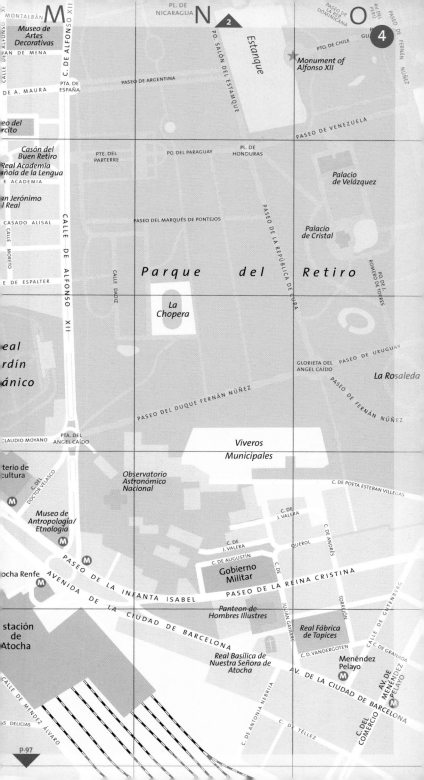

D Facultad de Medicina **E** **F** **G**

5
OLROA

3

CALLE DE ISAAC PERAL

CALLE DE JULIAN ROMEA

CALLE DE DOMÉNICO SCARLATTI

E.T.S.I. Aeronáuticos

Hospital Clínico San Carlos

PASEO DE SAN FRANCISCO DE SA

C. DE MANUEL BARTOLOMÉ COSSIO

C. DE PROFESOR MARTIN

4
E.T.S.I. Navales

C I U D A D

C. DOCTOR JIMÉNEZ DIAZ

Clínica la Concepción

PL. DE CRISTO REY

CALLE DE CEA BERMÚDE

C. tou-rid

Museo de América

Centro Américano Cooperacion

AV. DE LOS REYES CATÓLICOS

U N I V E R S I T A R I A

CALLE DE JOAQUÍN MARIA LÓPEZ

AV. DEL ARCO DE LA VICTORIA

AV. DE LOS REYES CATÓLICOS

Hospital Militar Generalisimo Franco

C. MINISTRO IBAÑEZ MARTIN

CALLE DE ISAAC PERAL

CALLE DE GAZTAMBIDE

CORTÉS

AVENIDA DE SÉNECA

Pabellón de Gobierno U.C.M.

CALLE DE DONOSO

C. DE HILARIÓN ESLAVS

C. DE CORTÉS

5
pp.1645

Arco de la Victoria

CALLE DE FERNÁNDEZ DE LOS RÍOS

M

Moncloa M

★ Faro de Moncloa

M O N C L O A

PASEO DE RUBERTO CHAPI

PL. DE LA MONCLOA

CALLE DE FERNANDO EL CATÓLIC

PASEO DE MORET

Ministerio del Aire

CALLE DE LA PRINCESA

C. A. DE HITA

HILARIÓN ESLAVS

CALLE DE MENÉNDEZ VAL

MELLADO

6
C. LISBOA

CALLE DE F. LOZANO

CALLE DE MARTIN DE LOS ROBLEDO

CALLE ROMERO DE LOS HEROS

CALLE DE GAZTAMBIDE

CALLE DE ANDRÉS

CALLE DE RODRÍGUEZ SAN PED

CALLE DE FERRAZ

C. J. ALVAREZ BENITO

GUTIÉRREZ

CALLE DE TUTOR

M

Argüelles M

C. DE ALBERTO AGUI

PASEO DEL PINTOR ROSALES

C. J. ALVAREZ MENDIZABAL

ALTAMIRANO

M

CALLE DE LA PRINCESA

7
C. DE FRANCISCO Y JACINTO ALCÁNTARA

C. DE FERRAZ

CALLE DEL MARQUÉS DE URQUIJO

CALLE JUAN ALVAREZ MENDIZABAL

C. DE MARTIN DE LOS HEROS

CALLE DEL BUEN SUCESO

CALLE DE TUTOR

C. DE SERRANO JOVE

FRANCISCO Y JACINTO ALCÁNTARA

A R G Ü E L L E S

C. DE QUINTANA

1

C. DEL MAESTRO RIPOLL

CALLE DE VITRUVIO

C. DE J. DE LA CIERVA   Rep.
Argentina

6

3

C. DE FRANCISCO SILVELA

C. DE PABLO ARANDA

Ministerio
de Medio
Ambiente

PASEO DE LA CASTELLANA

MTO. A LA
CONSTITUCIÓN

C. DE JOSÉ

CALLE DE SERRANO

CALLE

C. DE CASTELLÓN DE LA PLANA

C. DE OQUENDO

CALLE DE VELÁZQUEZ

Museo de
Ciencias
Naturales

GUTIERREZ-ABASCAL

C. DE PEDRO DE VALDIVIA

C. DE PEDRO DE VALDIVIA

CALLE DE HOYOS

4

C. DE PEDRO
DE VALDIVIA

E BRETO DE
HERREROS

PASEO DE LA CASTELLANA

C. DE PINAR

CALLE DEL PINAR

CALLE DE LÓPEZ DE HOYOS

CALLE DE MARÍA DE MOLINA

DE JOSEE
BASCAL

PL. DEL
DOCTOR
MARAÑÓN

Gregorio
Marañón

Museo
Lázaro
Galdiano

CALLE DE NÚÑEZ DE

p.139

C. DE LÓPEZ DE HOYOS

C. DE H. BÉCQUER

C. DEL GENERAL ORÁA

LAGASCA

C. DEL GENERAL ORÁA

C. DE

C. DEL   GENERAL   ORÁA

5

p.139

C. DEL
GENERAL ORÁA

CALLE DE SERRANO

C. DEL

Museo
orolla

CALLE DE MIGUEL ANGEL

GLORIETA
EMILIO
CASTELAR

COELLO

CALLE DE   DIEGO   DE   LEÓN

CALLE DE VELÁZQUEZ

DEL GENERAL MARTÍNEZ CAMPOS

C. DE FORTUNY

US
Embassy

CLAUDIO

CALLE

DE

DE BALBOA

Pol

C. DE RAFAEL CALVO

DE

C. DE MALDONADO

LAGASCA

C. DE MALDONADO

CALLE

C. DE NÚÑEZ

SALAMANCA

PUENTE DE ENRIQUE DE LA

GTA. DE
RUBÉN DARÍO

SEO DE
UARDO
DATO

MATA GOROSTIZAGA

CALLE   DE   JUAN   BRAVO

6

Rubén
Darío

CALLE DE ALMAGRA

La Unión y
el Fénix

C. DEL FORTUNY

Museo de
Escultura
al Aire Libre

ABC
Building

CLAUDIO COELLO

LAGASCA

Núñez de Balboa

CALLE DE VELÁZQUEZ

DE BALBOA

CALLE DE JENNER

CALLE DE PADILLA

CALLE DE PADILLA

C. DE NÚÑEZ DE BALBOA

CALLE DE ALMAGRA

CALLE DE MONTE ESQUINZA

Bankinter

CALLE DE MARQUÉS DEL RISCAL

PASEO DE CASTELLANA

CALLE DE SERRANO

Banco
Santander

CALLE

DE JOSÉ ORTEGA Y GASSET

CLAUDIO COELLO

LAGASCA

CALLE DE VELÁZQUEZ

DE NÚÑEZ DE BALBOA

7

CALLE   DEL   FORTUNY

CALLE DE ZURBARÁN

C. DEL MARQUÉS
DE VILLAMAGNA

CALLE   DE   DON   RAMÓN   DE   LA   CRUZ

CALLE
DE
NCA
ARRA

CALLE DE LAGASCA

C. DE NÚÑEZ

2

Attractions Finder

BARCELONA

Dana Facaros & Michael Pauls

PARIS

Dana Facaros & Michael Pauls

VENICE

Dana Facaros & Michael Pauls

CADOGANguides

Cadogan City Guides...
the life and soul
of the city

CADOGANguides
well travelled well read

No more excuses – *just go!*

flying visits
ITALY
great getaways by budget airline

CADOGANguides

flying visits
FRANCE
great getaways by budget airline, train & ferry

CADOGANguides

flying visits
SPAIN
great getaways by budget airline & ferry

CADOGANguides

Flying Visits make travel simple

CADOGANguides
well travelled well read

CADOGAN**guides**
well travelled well read

coming in 2004:
Buying a property: ABROAD
Buying a property: IRELAND
Buying a property: CYPRUS
Buying a property: GREECE
BUYING ABROAD

THE SUNDAY TIMES
Buying a property
SPAIN
Nick Elder, Harvey Holtom & John Howell

THE SUNDAY TIMES
Buying a property
ITALY
Monica Larner & John Howell

SUNDAY TIMES
ing a property
FRANCE
...e & John Howell

THE SUNDAY TIMES
Buying a property
PORTUGAL
Harvey Holtom & John Howell

THE SUNDAY TIMES
Buying a property
FLORIDA
Christian Moen, John Howell & Marcell Felipe

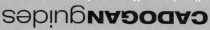

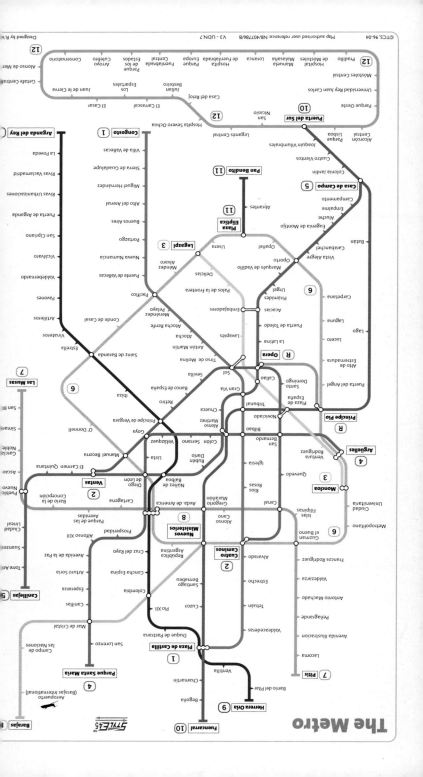

The Metro